Mid-Atlantic

SKI & SNOWBOARD AMERICA™

Contact

Dear Readers:

Every effort was made to make this the most accurate, informative, and easy-to-use guidebook on the planet. Any comments, suggestions, and corrections regarding this guide are welcome and should be sent to:

Outside America™
c/o Editorial Dept.
300 West Main St., Ste. A
Charlottesville, VA 22903
editorial@outside-america.com
www.outside-america.com

We'd love to hear from you so we can make future editions and future guides even better.

Thanks and happy trails!

SKI & SNOWBOARD AMERICA™ GUIDES

Mid-Atlantic

SKI & SNOWBOARD AMERICA™

Second Edition

The Complete Guide to Downhill Skiing, Snowboarding, Cross-country Skiing, Snow Tubing, and More Throughout the Mid-Atlantic Region

by John Phillips

FALCON®

Guilford, Connecticut
An imprint of The Globe Pequot Press

Produced by
Beachway Press Publishing, Inc.
300 West Main St., Ste A
Charlottesville, VA 22903
www.beachway.com

Cover Design by Beachway Press

Maps designed and produced by Beachway Press

Find Outside America™ at **www.outside-america.com**

Library of Congress Cataloging-in-Publication Data is available.

ISBN 0-7627-0845-X

Manufactured in the United States of America
Second Edition/First Printing

Acknowledgments

Special thanks to the following: Chris Dennis for his editorial help, Dan Hartinger and Brian Moran for their photography and assistance, Keith Murlless for his insight into North Carolina skiing, Ned West for his expertise on Pennsylvania's Laurel Highlands region, Jeff Wright for his knowledge of the Pocono Mountain region, Alex Torres, Carl Ohlke, Vay McNeil, Marco DiPaul, Rich Lucera, Simon Webb, Scott Adams, Chuck Samuels, Chip Chase at White Grass, Gil Willis at Elk River, Joe Stevens at Snowshoe, Steve McKnight, Gina Bertucci at Camelback, Jerry Geisler at Wisp, Dave Zunker at Wintergreen, Bob McKinney at Mount Rogers, Terry Seyden at Pisgah National Forest, John Sharp at Mount Mitchell State Park, the Malinowski family for their computer support, my family, and my wife, Mary, for her patience.

Table of

Contents

A note from the folks behind this endeavor…

We at Outside America look at guidebook publishing a little differently. There's just no reason that a guidebook has to look like it was published out of your Uncle Ernie's woodshed. We feel that guidebooks need to be both easy to use and nice to look at, and that takes an innovative approach to design. You see, we want you to spend less time fumbling through your guidebook and more time enjoying the adventure at hand. At any rate, we hope you like what you see and enjoy the places we lead you. And most of all, we'd like to thank you for taking an adventure with us.

Happy Trails!

Introduction

First, a Disclaimer...

Relative to western and northeastern mountains, remaining ski regions just can't compare. The topography and natural conditions of the Rockies, Sierras, Cascades, and Vermont's Green Mountains offer unparalleled skiing and snowboarding.

Although sporadic snowfall, washout rains, and severe fluctuations in temperatures and conditions riddle many mountains here in the "Banana Belt," numerous other Mid-Atlantic ski areas lie in higher-elevation, major snow-belt regions. West Virginia, for example, has an arctic micro-climate within its expansive Monongahela National Forest that allows four ski areas to operate with a primarily natural snow base. Snowfall here averages 150 to 180 inches per year. The same Great Lakes snow belt runs through Pennsylvania's Blue Knob, Seven Springs, and Hidden Valley, as well as Maryland's Wisp Resort. Little-known Ski Denton in northcentral Pennsylvania also averages over 100 inches of yearly snowfall. Even North Carolina gets its share. Neighboring Beech and Sugar Mountain both average 70 to 80 inches per year at their 5,000-foot elevations (though snow stashes tend to be short-lived because of the warm Gulf Coast effect). *(See U.S. snowfall map on page 4)*.

But, more realistically, you never know what you're going to get from a Mid-Atlantic winter. It's a roll of the dice. Some winters provide plenty of snow and/or cold temperatures. Other winters are lame and tame. Temps can ascend into the sixties just like that, and a ski area's season can last all but a couple of months without ever getting their full terrain open. Worse yet, precipitation can come in the form of rain, freezing rain, sleet, or ice, while high winds and thunderstorms can kick a resort right in the behind as well. Then there's the ice effect, thanks to the freeze-thaw rotations which soften snow at times during the day and re-freeze during the colder nighttime temps. Relentless snowmaking and grooming combat the freeze-thaw, but there's only so much that can be done.

Also take into consideration that Mid-Atlantic ski areas attract throngs of people but hold a lot less skiable terrain than resorts up north and out west. That means skiable acreage gets chewed up pretty quickly. A Mid-Atlantic resort is considered big if it has over 100 available acres. That total might make up one or two runs out west!

Inside the Mid-Atlantic

Most Mid-Atlantic ski areas rely on advanced snowmaking systems in order to keep their lift tickets moving. Because weather patterns are so unpredictable, skiers and snowboarders are wise to bring goggles, hats, and scarves along for the trip. Snow guns may be firing just at the moment you hit the slopes, and it's often hard to predict when a sudden cold snap will hit a mountain or lingering winds will affect normal comfort zones.

Granted, the majority of these ski areas have vertical drops (the distance in altitude between the base of the ski area and its highest point) that are less than half of the New England giants—and an even further cry from Rocky Mountain, Sierra, and Cascade resorts. The one factor the region has in its favor is numbers. With so many resorts in easy reach of numerous urban centers, Mid-Atlantic skiers can pick and choose as they wish.

Though most "mountains" here are technically considered plateaus, plenty of steep trails exist for upper intermediate and advanced skiers, albeit mostly short-lived. Pennsylvania's Blue Knob, in the heart of the state's Laurel Highlands region, offers a spate of steeps that wind through glades, drop over headwalls, and skirt rocky, mountainous obstacles. West Virginia's Timberline is also expertly designed with numerous steep, tree-lined trails in the high country of Canaan Valley. And Pennsylvania's Elk and Montage Mountains host plenty of heavily pitched black diamond trails on their networks.

Experts who ski the Mid-Atlantic also know that the region is home to formidable mogul areas, which provide difficult bumpy track that's left ungroomed for advanced skiers to negotiate. The region's mogul terrain is further complicated by notorious "eastern ice," which tends to develop when the sun goes down and freezing temperatures set in.

It's the voluminous beginner terrain, though, for which the Mid-Atlantic is widely regarded. Advanced skiers may find a half-day is more than enough to satisfy them at many local resorts, but novices and intermediates have plenty of smoothly groomed terrain available for learning and developing. Over 40 percent of skiers and snowboarders in the Mid-Atlantic rank their skills as beginner to intermediate, and the region serves as ideal training grounds for this crowd.

According to the National Ski Areas Association, over 700 ski areas existed in the U.S. during the mid-1980s. That number shrunk to just over 500 by the early 1990s. While other ski areas have faded over the years, over 50 Mid-Atlantic facilities have battled the barriers to make homes here, including one of the country's most recent major ski resort to open up shop. Southern Pennsylvania's Whitetail Resort began selling lift tickets just 10 years ago, attracting strong visitor bases in both Baltimore and Washington, DC, while western PA's Laurel Mountain recently re-opened its trails commercially after a long hiatus.

Making Snow in the Mid-Atlantic

Ever wonder just how snow is made? Well, no one makes snow any better than our very own Mid-Atlantic resorts. And it's more out of necessity than anything else. Fact is, Mid-Atlantic ski areas are exquisitely adept at making snow, considering the temperature fluctuations and inconsistent natural snow our winters present. Many resorts, including Pennsylvania's Camelback and Seven Springs and West Virginia's

Snowshoe, routinely get high marks for snowmaking from national publications.

First thing to note is that there's no such thing as "artificial" snow. Natural and machine-made snow are identical in composition, both made from water and air. While natural snow is formed high above in the atmosphere, manmade powder is made at or near ground level by mixing the right amounts of compressed air and water in a snowgun.

Machine-made snow can be made in different consistencies and qualities. For example, early-season snow is often produced with a higher water content in order to create a base layer of snow and to cover variations in terrain. Later in the season you'll often find dryer snow is produced to form the soft, powdery snow surface favored by most snow riders. Air temperature and humidity, combined with water and airflow to the snowgun, determine the type of snow produced. There's also an industry threshold and general rule of thumb known as the "100 Rule." That is, temperature and humidity together cannot exceed 100 to make snow. The lower the number, the better. The colder and less humid the air, the more snow that can be produced. While snowmaking can occur at 30–32 degrees, it's far less efficient than pumping out snow in the teens and low-twenties.

Many Mid-Atlantic ski areas use state-of-the-art snowmaking systems that employ miles of pipe to transport water and air, massive air compressors, and huge numbers of snowguns to blast powder throughout the mountain. And while different resorts employ varying strategies to keep their mountains white, you can nearly always count on them doing all they can under the conditions presented to them. Remember, there'd be nothing to ride on most of the time without this mixture of compressed air matter. And that brings us to...

Natural Snowfall in the Mid-Atlantic?

We're not known for our consistent snowfall, but you might be surprised to learn there is some good snow out there. We get most of our snow from the "lake effect," in which cold northwesterly winds drop out of Canada and meet moisture from the Great Lakes—primarily Lake Erie. The snow belt runs parallel to Pennsylvania's I-79, affecting higher elevations and ski areas like Pennsylvania's Seven Springs, Laurel Mountain, Blue Knob, and Hidden Valley; Western Maryland's Wisp Resort; and the eastern high mountains of West Virginia: Snowshoe, Timberline, and Canaan Valley. These resorts all average over 100 inches of natural stuff per year, including a whopping 180 inches at Snowshoe's 4,800-foot elevation.

Southern storms are more rare but pack a punch when they do come around. Snow from the south tends to be in the form of a big blast and of the wetter, heavier variety. Back during the blizzard of 1993, North Carolina's high-elevation ski areas got over 50 inches dumped between two storms!

That Nasty Ice—The Scourge of the Mid-Atlantic

Sure, ice is a vile, nasty cancer that spreads across our Mid-Atlantic mountains and plateaus. Nevertheless, Mid-Atlantic areas work their tails off making conditions as good as possible. And, if you can ride Mid-Atlantic ice, you can slide on just about anything, anywhere. Keep a look out for the ice patches, but if you hit them, stay cool and ride straight through. You'll be out before you know it and on your way. Just don't panic and try to turn too hard. While you may do some damage to your ski/snowboard tips, it's better than getting banged up.

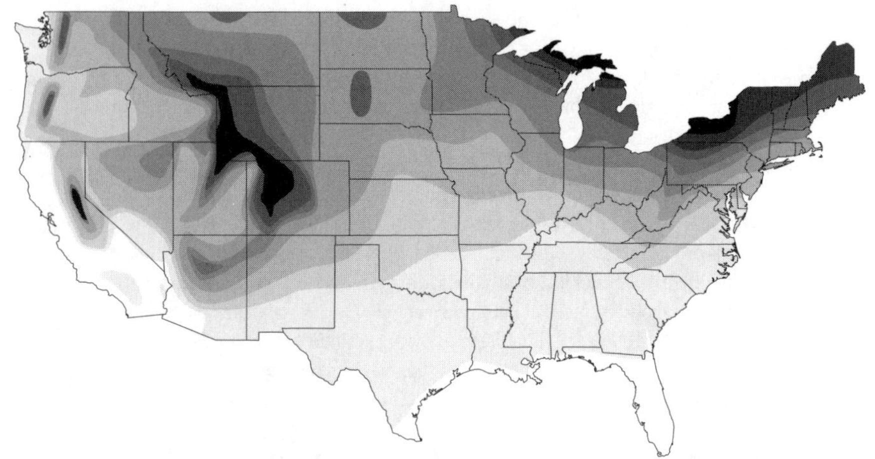

Average annual regional snowfall for the continental U.S.
(darker areas indicate heavier coverages)

It's also important to remember that our Mid-Atlantic mountains don't have the kind of skiable acreage as up north and out west. And because we have so many snow riders here, snow tends to get cut up much quicker. Plus, there's the freeze-thaw snow rotation that afflicts our mountains. Most of the time, your best bet for prime conditions are early mornings runs. You may encounter ice by early afternoon if conditions aren't peak.

Know Your Snow

It's always a good idea to check ahead of time before heading out to the mountains. Calling the area's ski report and checking its Web site will give you a pretty good indication of what kind of snow to expect. There is some differential among ski areas when it comes to ski reporting, but for the most part you can look for accurate snow conditions information.

Primary Surface: The type of surface in which conditions represent at least 70% of the terrain open to skiers.

Secondary Surface: The next most prevalent type of snow on the slopes.

Variable Conditions: Used when no single term describes surface conditions on at least 70% of the terrain.

Fresh Powder: Loose, fluffy, flaky snow crystals (both natural and machine-made) that have not been compacted.

New Snow: Natural or machine-made snow within the past 24 hours.

Wet Snow: Snow that is moist and sticky as it falls...it becomes heavy when it's compacted, making turns a bit more difficult.

Packed Powder: Loose powder (machine-made or natural) that is compacted either by a machine or by skier traffic. Most snow riders prefer this type of snow.

Loose Granular: Loose, sand-like grains of snow. Formed when powder thaws, refreezed, and crystalizes. May be a fast surface.

Wet Granular: Loose or frozen granular snow that has become wet and soft from a thaw or rainfall. Skiable, but turns are more difficult on this surface.

Frozen Granular: Wet or grainy snow that has frozen, forming a solid or crusty textured surface. This type of snow causes very fast, vibrating rides and requires caution in controlling speed.

Ice: Created by rain, followed by a freeze or by ground water seeping onto the base and freezing. It is the fastest surface and poses the most difficulty in turning and controlling speed.

Corn: Large granules, sometimes the size of corn kernels, formed by freeze-thaw cycles typical of spring. When the surface is loose and the temperatures are above freezing, corn skiing can be great, with more controllable speed and easier turns.

The Price We Pay to Ski & Board...Is It Too Much?

Think the cost of skiing and snowboarding in the Mid-Atlantic is outrageous? Think you're being raked over the coals every time you gruffly pull out your wallet at the ticket counter?

Understand this. While Mid-Atlantic ski area prices have naturally gone up over the years, the rate at which lift tickets and rental rates have increased is much less than our nation's inflation rate. Ski areas compete to keep their prices down, trying to make their margins in other ways, like equipment rental income and food and lounge sales. Remember, these guys have to invest serious coin for snowmaking/water, grooming, and other vital maintenance measures. And, given the uncertainty of Mid-Atlantic winter weather, many—if not most—ski areas struggle just to stay financially afloat.

Ski areas nationwide are feeling the same effects and threats of consolidation, resort mergers, and buyouts that all businesses today are. The independently owned-and-operated ski area isn't a dinosaur yet, but it gets harder and harder to stay competitive in an ever-changing industry. The bigger ski industry development corporations want the biggest chunk of the skier market.

Still feeling bilked and hustled by ski resorts? We're not the Rockies or the Cascades, and it's hard to even make a comparison to the Green Mountains up north. But it's all we've got within a short haul in your ride. Support your Mid-Atlantic ski areas!

Snow Tubing Emerges from the Pack

How important has snow tubing been to the Mid-Atlantic ski industry? For some ski areas, it's been the difference between operating in the red and black. Tubing can turn a tidy revenue stream with easier maintenance and upkeep and fewer devoted resources than a resort's ski trails. Just sling up a simple tow lift, crank out the snow on the chutes and lanes, groom them with a Snowcat, and let the tubers rip.

Tubing has been around in Canada for last 12 years or so. One Quebec ski area decided to crunch its numbers and do a cost-benefit analysis on lift tickets vs. tubing tickets. It didn't take long before the resort converted all its ski hills into tubing chutes.

Bigger Mid-Atlantic areas like Pennsylvania's Seven Springs can turn out more than 40,000 tubing tickets in a season. And, tubing can also help offset losses during lean, warm winters since it doesn't take a lot of manmade snow to get a tubing lane going. Here on the east coast, one of the first places snow tubing caught on was at tiny Blue Marsh, near Reading, PA. Today, there aren't many places in the Mid-Atlantic you won't find snow tubing. It's a great winter alternative for the family as well as for non-skiers.

Tips for Planning Your Mid-Atlantic Trip

- Always call ahead to the resort's ski report AND check its Web site to check for weather, trail conditions and openings, and operating lifts. But don't rely solely on the resort's conditions reports. Also check out weather.com and plug in the name of the town or nearest town for the resort to which you're headed. You can also take a peek at state government DOT Web sites to get updated travel and road conditions for your drive. For example, check out www.dot.state.pa.us for Pennsylvania's current highway and road conditions.
- Renting equipment on-site at the resort? Expect long weekend lines. It's not always the case at every resort, but a long wait can cut into the time on your lift ticket. Arrive early or later, or consider renting off-mountain. Off-site equipment rentals are cheaper and often newer, and you can save yourself some time if the shop is on the way. On the flip side, there are advantages to renting at the ski area. You can pick the type of equipment, and even upgrade to something better, usually for a minimal fee. And, if anything malfunctions, it's a short trip to the shop to get it replaced free. Plus, you don't have to lug your equipment to and from the slopes.
- If you're planning on taking a lesson, always call in advance to reserve a spot and time. Also, take advantage of learn-to-ski and snowboard packages, which usually include ticket, rental, and group lesson. Bear in mind, though, that beginner tickets often are limited to bunny and/or beginner lifts/slopes. Learning packages can often be the equivalent of temporary child care and the chance for parents to hit the trails if the resort doesn't have a nursery/day care center. Unless you're sure, always reserve services in advance of your trip.
- Plan your day's trail strategy in advance. Consider riding lesser-known trails that might serve up the best snow, avoiding heavily traveled trails with chewed-up snow (unless you're an early bird), and steering clear of peak lift times that can eat away at your slope time.
- Looking to save some money on your trips? Bring a cooler with your own food and

drinks and store it in a resort locker or inside your car. Food and drinks account for sizable margins at ski areas, but if you want to support the Mid-Atlantic ski industry economy, consider your lunch or dinner a donation! If so, save yourself some time by chowing down at off-peak hours like 11 A.M. or after 1 P.M.

- Scouting out an overnight or weekend trip? Be sure to do some homework. There are some good deals to be found out there, but only if you look. Use the web to find resort listings and call local Chambers of Commerce for more listings. You might just find a great house or condo while saving a good chunk of money if you look around. For example, West Virginia's Canaan Valley has plenty of beautiful rental houses with incredible mountain views at affordable rates. And, there's a good bet there's still good snow in March, when rates drop 20–30 percent. True, it's hard to predict weather and conditions, but you can take an educated guess when it comes to planning your vacation.

Getting Your Bang for this Book's Buck

This guide is intended to provide every piece of information you'll need to get the most out of your Mid-Atlantic winter trips. Select a resort and skim through the subcategories to find what you want quickly. Take a look at **Mountain Statistics** and **Did You Know?** for valuable quick-hitting information. You can also refer to the **web sites** offered for up-the-minute information, and find reviews of the trail systems, broken down by advanced, intermediate, and beginner. A separate section explores the snowboarding scene at each resort, including first-hand looks into the terrain parks, halfpipes, quality of terrain, instruction, rentals, and more.

Alpine Resorts

The major portion of this book comprises alpine (or downhill) ski areas. Each of the following Mid-Atlantic ski area listings adopt the same format, with resorts in Pennsylvania, Maryland, West Virginia, Virginia, and North Carolina listed in alphabetical order. Because of the relatively large number of ski areas in Pennsylvania, the state is broken down into two categories: Major Alpine Resorts and Other Alpine Ski Areas. North Carolina is classified similarly.

First, the ski area's address and all relevant phone numbers are listed, including any toll-free and direct ski reports, and numbers for information, lodging, or reservations. Credit cards accepted at the ski area are also identified, typically used for lift tickets, rentals, instruction, dining, and ski shop items. Next, Internet and E-mail addresses are provided by participating resorts. Skiers may use a resort's Internet address to find up-to-the-hour trail conditions, number of operating slopes and lifts, and other basic information about the ski area. E-mail is generally used to offer suggestions, complaints, or ask questions, and can be accessed via a separate address or inside the resort's Internet site.

The guide then provides the resort's daily operating hours, excluding holiday times, and the normal open and close dates during its ski seasons. Since weather patterns vary dramatically, open and close dates are based on the resort's average season.

Quick-reference mountain and resort statistics are also listed for each ski area; their definitions appear in the Glossary of Terms appendix. Readers can use these statistics to get a glimpse of the mountain's offerings, including elevation, vertical drop, breakdown of slopes and trails, longest run, average annual snowfall, percentage of snowmaking on the trail system, percentage of trails equipped for night skiing, number and type of lifts, and uphill capacity.

Information Sections

- **Getting There** displays full directions from regional metropolitan centers to the ski area.
- **Lift Tickets** provides the times and rates of daily lift passes, and indicates any reduced rates for children, seniors, group rates, midweek specials, and any other discount packages. Lift rates are generally priced relative to the size of the ski area's trail network and proximity to metropolitan areas. Though many Mid-Atlantic resorts seem pricey, there are some good ways to save money on lift tickets. Be sure to inquire about any discounts, special days, and group-skier discounts; and watch for ski coupons at supermarkets, ski shops, and in local newspapers. You can also cash in on reduced rates by joining a large group with a local ski club. Consult your local ski shop for a list of ski clubs in your area. Those who are trying skiing for the first time may wish to choose a smaller ski area, where lift tickets are more affordable, slopes are less crowded, and instruction may be more personalized.
- **Ski School** shows the number of full- or part-time instructors employed by the ski area. Most Mid-Atlantic instructors are PSIA certified (Professional Ski Instructors of America) and use the American Teaching System (ATS), which is among the most respected teaching systems in the world. The section goes on to display private and group instruction rates, and lists all adult and childrens' programs offered, with times and rates included. Many resorts offer learn-to-ski packages that include rental, lesson, and lift ticket, while others offer complementary group instruction for first-time skiers who rent skis or snowboards. Offered at selected resorts, SKIwee and MINIrider are SKI magazine-sponsored national programs aimed at introducing young children, generally aged four to 11, to skiing and snowboarding, and include instruction and supervision, optional lunch, and play time.
- **Adaptive Skier Program** indicates any available programs for physically disabled skiers.
- **Racing** lists any junior or adult programs offered for slalom racing. NASTAR (National Association of Standardized Racing) is a national racing program employed by many ski areas, which provides a designated trail with slalom gates for time-trial runs. Racing programs are displayed by the trail on which they are typically held, and include rates and times (often weekends only).
- **Base/Summit Lodge Facilities** is a list of amenities offered at a ski area's lodge(s), typically including ski and rental shops, cafeterias/restaurants/lounges, specialty shops, lockers, and any other lodge features.
- **Day Care** lists operating child supervision hours and rates, if offered. This is an important consideration for parents whose children are too small for the slopes, or just don't care to ski. Day care is usually offered on weekends, with weekday hours at many larger resorts.
- **Other Winter Sports** lists any other recreation offered either at the resort or nearby, (excluding snowboarding, which warrants its own section). The list includes snow tubing, cross-country skiing, Telemark skiing, snowshoeing, snow skating, snowmobiling, ice fishing, ice skating, horse-drawn sleigh rides, and sledding.

For resorts with snow tubing parks, the book identifies the length of the tubing area, number of lanes, vertical drop (when available), type of uphill transport, ticket rates, and hours. For cross-country skiing, any on-site or nearby destinations are listed and cross-referenced to the second half of the book where readers will find full information on touring centers, state parks and forests, and national recreation areas. Telemark skiing, snowshoeing, and snow skating are listed if they are permitted on the resort's trail network, with rental and instruction rates provided when available. Snowmobiling, ice fishing, ice skating, horse-drawn sleigh rides, and sledding are featured with location and rental and instruction rates.

- **Lodging** displays all on-site and numerous nearby overnight accommodations, with locations and phone numbers provided. Lodging usually includes houses, townhouses, condominiums, chalets, inns, cabins, hotels/motels, and bed & breakfasts. Most on-site and nearby accommodations offer affordable ski-and-stay packages, some of which include meals and/or free lodging for children.
- **Dining/Aprés-ski** is a list of on-site and nearby eateries, lounges, and nightspots with locations and phone numbers listed.

The text throughout each alpine skiing section offers a broad dissection of each ski area, including an analysis of slopes and trails relative to different skier abilities, average natural conditions, mountain topography, snowmaking capability, and typical resort crowds. It also offers historical tidbits, recommendations, and other pertinent information. Within most alpine-resort sections is a separate snowboarding segment, which examines the scope and details of available snowboarding terrain, including parks, terrain gardens, and halfpipes. It also features information on events, races, instructional programs, and equipment rentals.

Cross-Country Skiing Destinations

Immediately following the book's Alpine Resorts section is a second section on cross-country (Nordic) skiing. When natural snowfall is sufficient, cross-country skiing is available at designated touring centers, national and state parks and forests, and national recreation areas. Addresses and all relevant phone numbers are provided, as well as any Internet or E-mail addresses. Additionally, average annual snowfall and elevation are detailed for each area. Where applicable, cross-country ski touring centers are listed first, followed by state parks and forests; with states listed in the same order as in the alpine resorts section. Cross-country ski touring centers provide marked, groomed (track-set) trail systems for skiers, and generally offer rental equipment and/or instruction. Trails are groomed by tracking snowfall with snowmobiles, machines, or skis. Pennsylvania and West Virginia are the only states herein that offer touring centers.

State and national parks, forests, and recreation areas make up the remaining cross-country trail systems provided in the book. Multi-use hiking and skiing trails are available here, and often there is a park office on-site wherein guests can check in, obtain trail maps, and get necessary information. Office hours are generally from 8:30 A.M. to 4:00 P.M. Readers should remember that the addresses listed often identify the location of park headquarters, and not necessarily the site of the ski trails. While many headquarters are in the same general area as the trail systems, others are miles away, sometimes in more urban settings.

Pennsylvania's Laurel Ridge and several other state parks in West Virginia are equipped with their own cross-country touring centers, and as a result is listed under that section. A limited number of other state parks and forests in Pennsylvania, West Virginia and Maryland offer on-site concessions with rentals and/or instruction, as well as year-round cabin lodging, either fully equipped or primitive (without running water/bathrooms). The book also mentions, when available, nearby lodging options and phone numbers, including bed and breakfasts, resorts, inns, and hotels/motels. To a limited degree, restaurants and eateries are provided, with phone numbers.

Be sure to call touring center and park offices before departing to learn current snow conditions on the trail networks and on the roads leading to them. Their employees should also provide important trail information, such as any obstacles or barriers. Likewise, phone ahead to alpine ski areas for current conditions—or just to make sure they're open.

Happy trails!

Skiing: Past to Present

Origins

The original form of skiing is known as cross-country, or Nordic, which was crafted thousands of years ago in Scandinavia. Several 3,000-year-old models with leather bindings were uncovered here, and skis dating as far back to 2500 B.C. have been discovered in Siberia.

Over 1,500 years ago, inhabitants of Scandinavia, northern Russia, and Central Asia required an efficient means of transport during their long, snow-filled winters. Further evolution of the ski occurred as militaries in winter combat used them during the thirteenth and seventeenth centuries in Scandinavian regions, giving them a more efficient means of movement. In Norway, the first ski troopers began operating in 1747, using long, wooden ski boards and a pole for basic transportation through snow-covered mountains. From centuries of practical applications, skiing as sport was born.

Skiing as a Sport

Skiing was brought to America by Scandinavians in the early 1800s. It is believed to have taken hold when gold miners in California's Sierra Nevada mountains strapped on 12-foot skis made of solid oak—one long ski and one short—with a heavy pole used for push-off. Farther north in the Rockies, Idaho's Sun Valley holds the distinction as being the country's first ski area, opening in 1936 and having been inspired by Union Pacific Railroad president W. Averell Harriman.

The Mid-Atlantic was not without its own pioneers, as Pennsylvania's Big Boulder, the now-defunct Laurel Mountain, and Ski Roundtop did something few other resorts could offer. Each opened its mountain to skiing within reasonable drives of major metropolitan areas. And it's only fitting that a region plagued by fickle winter conditions is credited with helping to develop and refine an innovative artificial snowmaking system that would be used by ski areas throughout the country. Big Boulder was the first resort to commercially apply the system, devised by local inventor John Garish, who used a garden hose and varying water pressures to create one of the country's first snow guns.

Cross-Country Skiing

With the emergence of alpine skiing as a popular sport, Nordic skiing had become nearly a forgotten pastime from its humble Scandinavian origins. But lately its re-emergence is growing beyond its faithful coterie of followers. The physical benefits that cross-country offers far outweigh those of alpine skiing, requiring considerable stamina and strength over longer distances. The sport combines a full cardiovascular workout with a discovery of the great outdoors. When a strong natural snow base develops in their areas, Nordic skiers traverse woodland trails at designated touring centers, state parks and forests, and national recreation areas. Here they can encounter rugged topography, varied wildlife, and scenic vistas. But perhaps the most appealing aspect of Nordic skiing is that one can roam on just about any open surface with enough of a powder base. In fact, many skiers simply use parking lots, campgrounds, road shoulders, golf courses, or open fields.

This variation of skiing has generated substantial interest and become a major facet of the U.S. ski industry. Ski Fest—an annual celebration of cross-country skiing to be held at selected sites throughout the U.S. and Canada—will be featured at two Mid-Atlantic locations during the 1997–1998 season: Pennsylvania's Hidden Valley and West Virginia's White Grass Ski Touring Center. Ski Fest offers free lessons for first-time cross-country skiers, ski equipment and product demonstrations, and numerous events. You can find dates and further information on the World Wide Web at: http://www.cross-countryski.org/skifest.html.

As far as equipment is concerned, the difference between an alpine and Nordic ski is size, width and binding. Nordic skis are thinner and usually longer than alpine skis; and Nordic boots are attached to the skis only at the toe, allowing the heel to lift off, similar to a person's walking motion. A sticky wax coats the Nordic ski's base so that skiers can push off the ski and turn.

Telemark Skiing

While alpine skis have themselves undergone serious changes in design ("shaped" skis, also known as hourglass or parabolic skis, are designed to ease novice skiers into carving turns —a skill that most agree is more difficult to learn on standard skis), Nordic skis also have some interesting variations. Over a decade ago, ski skating was developed—a faster technique that involves using steps similar to ice-skating. In addition, Telemark skiing—its name derived from the Telemark district of Norway—is a variation of downhill skiing, but on Nordic skis. The "tele" turn is its distinguishing component: The outside ski is advanced ahead of the other, then turned inward at a continually widening angle through the carve. To facilitate this propulsive motion, Telemarkers use specially designed skis that are usually lighter and thinner than alpine skis. The sport's hybrid nature allows Telemark skiers to hit both backcountry trails and commercial downhill slopes. This versatility has brought a wider range of skiers out to test their mettle on the slopes of Mid-Atlantic resorts, many of which permit Telemarking (though you're not likely to spot an abundance of Tele skiers on any alpine mountain).

Snowboarding

Snowboarding has not only taken the ski industry by storm—it's practically taken over as the number-one pastime among the ranks of young snow-sport enthusiasts.

The American-bred sport was created in the 1960s by inventor Sherman Poppen, whose "Snurfer" was a popular toy-store item that sold over one million sets. Snurfers were made of wood, and steered by a rope attached to the front tip. The modern snowboard would be pioneered in the late 1970s when surfer Jake Burton teamed with champion skateboarders Tom Sims and Chuck Barfoot to design a single, metal-edged board that would run faster than skis and be able to carve mountains with ease. Burton picked up the idea when he jokingly participated in a ski resort Snurfer event, and later realized that a foot-retention device would allow more stability on the wooden board. He took his concept to Vermont's Stratton Mountain, incorporating into his designs steel edges and high-back foot bindings more familiar to skiers.

It took awhile for the U.S. ski industry to accept the alternative snowboard into its tradition-laced sport. As recently as 1985, only seven percent of ski areas in the country permitted snowboards on their trail networks. Today just a small number of resorts still restrict boarding, and they're hard-pressed to ignore its economic potential. Like skis, modern snowboards come in varying sizes and weights, but differ depending on the style of rider, offering varying shapes and flex patterns. Boards are generally broken down into four types: race, alpine, free-riding, and freestyle, and nearly all are made of a wood core, fiberglass, and p-tex. Not surprisingly, the world's largest manufacturer and seller of snowboards is Jake Burton.

Amazingly, snowboarding's growth shows no visible sign of slowing. It's estimated that more than 12 percent of the country's lift tickets sold during the 1996–97 season were to snowboarders, and the rate is growing each year. Boarders can either shred downhill slopes cutting giant-slalom turns, or roam "freestyle" in designated snowboard parks filled with obstacles made of hard-packed snow—or just about any "hits" the ski area will allow. Since ski areas generally prohibit dangerous jumping on their trails, snowboard parks allow freestylers the opportunity to catch air on obstacles such as gap jumps, spines, tabletops, slides, quarterpipes, ramps, and wales. While snowboard parks are more prevalent and easier to maintain, some resorts construct cylindrical trenches of hard-packed snow known as halfpipes—an idea taken from skateboard parks and ramps. Halfpipes are difficult to maintain, requiring an expensive grooming apparatus or the constant work of employees to keep them operating. A fair number of Mid-Atlantic ski areas offer halfpipes, though natural conditions often limit their availability.

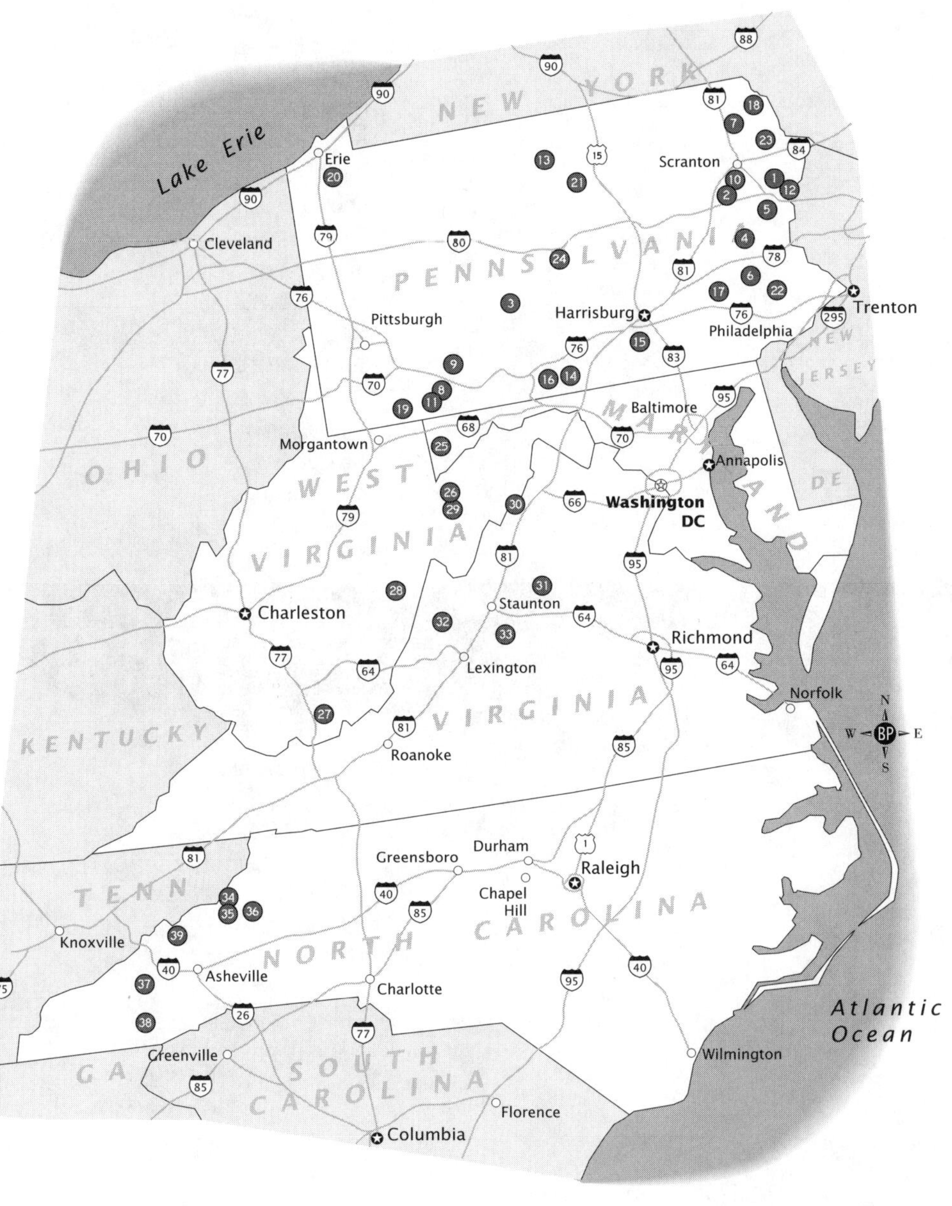
Lake Erie
NEW YORK
PENNSYLVANIA
OHIO
WEST VIRGINIA
MARYLAND
NEW JERSEY
DE
VIRGINIA
KENTUCKY
TENN
NORTH CAROLINA
SOUTH CAROLINA
GA
Atlantic Ocean
Erie
Cleveland
Scranton
Pittsburgh
Harrisburg
Philadelphia
Trenton
Baltimore
Annapolis
Morgantown
Washington DC
Charleston
Staunton
Lexington
Richmond
Norfolk
Roanoke
Greensboro
Durham
Chapel Hill
Raleigh
Knoxville
Asheville
Charlotte
Wilmington
Greenville
Florence
Columbia
N
S
E
W
BP

Major Alpine Resorts

1. Alpine Mountain
2. Big Boulder/Jack Frost
3. Blue Knob
4. Blue Mountain
5. Camelback
6. Doe Mountain
7. Elk Mountain
8. Hidden Valley Resort
9. Laurel Mountain
10. Montage Mountain
11. Seven Springs
12. Shawnee Mountain
13. Ski Denton
14. Ski Liberty
15. Ski Roundtop
16. Whitetail

ALPINE RESORTS: PENNSYLVANIA

Other Alpine Ski Areas

17. Blue Marsh
18. Mount Tone
19. Mystic Mountain
20. Mountain View at Edinboro
21. Ski Sawmill
22. Spring Mountain
23. Tanglewood
24. Tussey Mountain

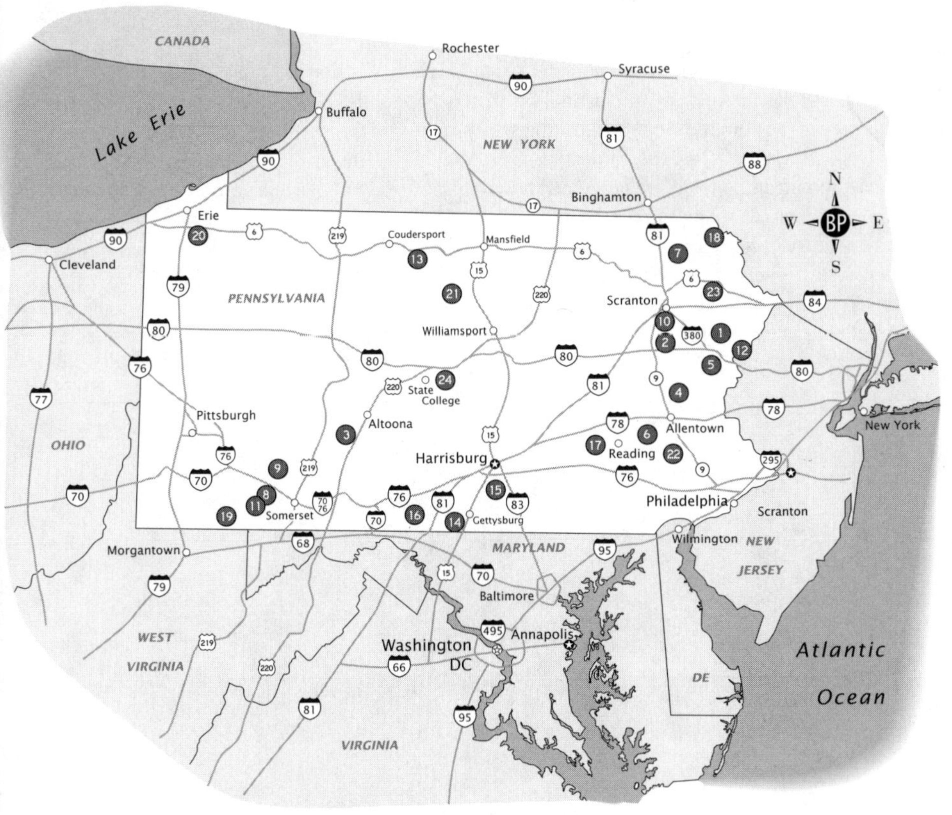

With over 30 ski areas, Pennsylvania currently ranks third among all states in total alpine ski facilities, behind New York (59) and Michigan (43). (Downhill giant Colorado has 28 big-mountain resorts.) Most of Pennsylvania's ski areas are clustered inside or near the tourist-laden Pocono Mountain range, while a batch of resorts lie in the bountiful snow region of the Laurel Highlands, located one hour southeast of Pittsburgh. The newest addition in the Highlands is actually an old one favorite. Laurel Mountain resurfaced after a 15-year layoff and is now making big strides. A handful of other ski areas are scattered throughout the state, including southern Pennsylvania's Liberty, Roundtop, and Whitetail, which lure a big skier base from nearby Washington, DC and Baltimore.

After the state's first private slopes and chair lift opened in what would later become mega-resort Seven Springs, the first commercial ski areas began to surface in the 1950s. Though its mountains and plateaus were but small bumps compared to what was being offered in New England, several eastern Pennsylvania ski areas got off the ground and running. Skeptics scoffed at the notion of skiing in the "Banana Belt"—a reference to terrain suited more to agriculture than skiing. Big Boulder brought several metropolitan areas to the forefront of alpine skiing, relying on a pioneering snowmaking system that was first developed on its mountain. As the Seventies rolled around, an onslaught of ski areas opened to demanding Mid-Atlantic skiers with the strength of powerful new snowmaking systems.

Today the state is highly regarded for its beginner to intermediate mountains, with abundant bunny terrain and smooth, well-groomed novice track. Nearly all of its ski areas offer solid instruction that caters to young and old alike. What many Mid-Atlantic skiers don't realize is that upper intermediate to advanced skiing does exist in Pennsylvania—albeit in somewhat limited quantities. Trail networks filled with diverse terrain can be found at Blue Knob, Elk, Laurel, Montage, Seven Springs and Blue Mountain. And strong intermediate trails surround some surprisingly fun terrain at numerous other areas such as Ski Denton, Jack Frost, and Camelback.

Alpine Mountain

1

Alpine Mountain Ski Resort
P.O. Box 309, Route 447
Analomink, PA 18320

Information/Ski Report: (570) 595–2150
Internet: *www.alpinemountain.com*

Email: alpinemt@ptd.net
Credit Cards: VISA, MC, Discover

Operating Hours: 8 A.M.–9:30 P.M. daily
Season: December to March

Backdrop

Alpine Mountain can pretty much guarantee two things. You won't lose sight of anyone in your group on the small, single-face mountain, and you'll be able to ski the trails five times over with no lift lines. It's one of Pennsylvania's oldest ski areas, having opened up shop here in the southern Poconos during the late 1950s under the name Timber Hill Ski Area. Ownership changed hands in 1983, taking on Alpine Mountain as its moniker.

Alpine falls into the beginner category, with 21 straight, wide trails on an easy 500 feet of vertical drop. Its gentle terrain caters mostly to families and groups. Those new to the sport or still learning will find their confidence rising as they ski most of the trails. One of the resort's strengths is its varied winter activities, both on-site and just off the mountain. In conjunction with Wilderness Recreations, the resort maintains a snowmobiling center and rental shop on its own course served by 100 percent snowmaking. Snowtubing is now available, snowboarders have a park and halfpipe, and snow skaters are welcome on the trails, with skate rentals available. Nearby at Evergreen Park, a cross-country skiing center operates when a five-inch snow base covers its nine-hole golf course. Penn Hills Resort offers ice skating with rentals and lessons in its indoor rink as well.

Trail Profiles

Alpine is a beginner's mountain, so it's no shock that few options exist for advanced snow riders. Six black diamond trails are more-or-less nice cruising runs. The exception is *The Bumps*—an extension of black diamond *Rocket* that serves up modestly sized moguls. *Power Line* and intermediate *Outer Edge* have a few steep dips and partial turns built into the terrain.

Beginners and first-timers won't be let down with the trail network's wide and nicely groomed track. *Alpine Way* is a 3,500-foot novice cruising run that offers a panoramic view of the Pocono Mountains from its summit and a running creek at its base. It uses all 500 feet of Alpine's vertical drop on gentle, rolling terrain nearly 100 feet wide. Carving the intermediates on the mountain's right side won't be too difficult either. They're pitched only slightly steeper than the green runs, and wide enough to negotiate any gradual turns.

Two areas in front of the base lodge are reserved for learning skiers but situated inappropriately at the runout of four upper trails. Solid instructional programs serve two different age groups. Alpine also offers free winter start specials leading up to the Christmas holidays, including complementary beginner lessons and rentals on selected days.

Mountain Stats

Base Elevation: 600 feet
Summit Elevation: 1,150 feet
Vertical Drop: 550 feet
Longest Run: 3,500 feet
Primary Slope Direction: North to northeast
Slopes and Trails: 3 beginner, 12 intermediate, 6 advanced
Skiable Terrain: 60 acres
Lifts: 2 quad, 1 double
Uphill Capacity: 5,800 skiers per hour
Average Annual Snowfall: 55 inches
Snowmaking: 100% of area
Night Skiing: Nightly to 9:30 P.M.

Getting There

- **From southern NJ:** Take the Garden State Parkway north to 287 north to I-80 west to PA Exit 52. Take Exit 52 off I-80 west, then left onto Route 447 north. Follow Route 447 10 miles to Alpine Mountain.
- **From metro NY and northern NJ:** Take George Washington Bridge or Lincoln Tunnel to I-80 west to Delaware Water Gap Bridge. From here take PA Exit 52 off I-80 west. Follow directions above.
- **From Philadelphia area:** Take the N.E. Extension of the PA Turnpike to Exit 33. Follow Route 22 east past Allentown to Route 33 north to Route 209 north, then pick up I-80 east and PA Exit 52. Follow directions above.
- **From Baltimore and Washington:** From I-695 in Baltimore, take I-83 north to I-81 north to I-80 east to PA Exit 52, then follow directions above.

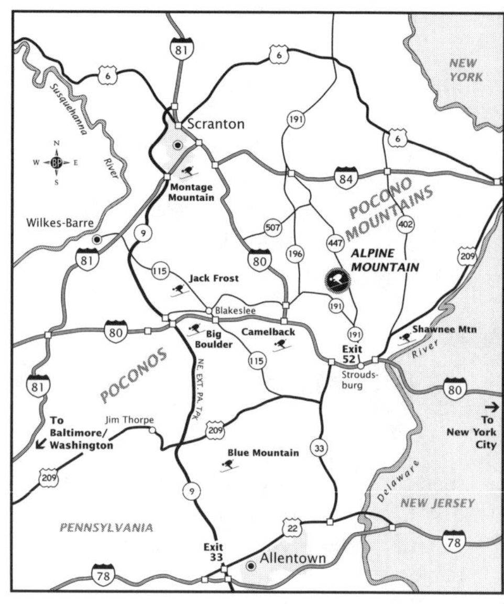

Snowboarding Highlights

Alpine did away with its Original Sin Snowboard Park on the far-side *Rockaway* trail and converted it into an all-rider terrain park on *Swivel*, just above the resort's halfpipe. Look for changing obstacles like jumps, gaps, spines, and wales in the terrain park, which has a decent grade but no immediate lift access. The Alpine Quad lift does the trick in the meantime. Just slide back down on *Roller Coaster* or *Thunder Lane* to get back to the park and pipe.

The resort is otherwise snowboarder-friendly, holding races and events from December through February, including the 11-year-running Ski and Snowboard Bump Contest in January.

Snowboard Rentals: $27/day • **Snowboard School:** Learn-to-snowboard package: weekday $59, weekend $69 (includes all-area lift ticket, rental, lesson); Beginner snowboard package: weekday $54, weekend $64 (beginner area only).

More Fun in the Flakes

On-site

Six-lane **snowtubing** area with surface lift: $16/session; group rates: $12/person (minimum 10 people) • **Snowmobiling** course with snowmaking, operating daily: (half-hour ride: single $27, double $40) • **Sled Dog** snow skate rentals: $20/day; snow skating instruction offered.

Nearby

Indoor ice skating at Penn Hills Resort, daily from 10 A.M.–9 P.M. (rentals and instruction available; (570) 421–7721) • **Pony and carriage rides** at Colony Village, Analomink; (570) 595–3150.

Skier Services

It doesn't matter much that Alpine has just three lifts (two quad chairs and a bunny slope double chair). That's because the longest lift lines here run a mere three minutes. And tickets and other rates are bargain-basement compared to its Pocono competitors. You'll have to sort through the resort's myriad of changing specials and programs, but chances are there's a deal somewhere in there for you.

$ Lift Tickets

8 A.M.–5 p.m *or* 1 P.M.–9:30 P.M.: weekday $26, weekend $35 •.8 A.M.–12:30 P.M. OR 1 P.M.–5:30 P.M.: weekday $22, weekend $29 • 8 A.M.–9:30 P.M.: $34, $42 • 4:30 P.M.–9:30 P.M.: $21, $23 • Early/late-season (up to December 22 and after March 5): $18, $21 • Ages 15 & under: $21–$26 per ticket • Children 6 and under and seniors ski free • Group rates for 15 or more skiers • Season passes $315.

Ski Rentals

Rossignol, Dynastar • Weekday $20, Weekend/Holiday $22

Services

Ski School: PSIA certified; Private $42; Group $21 (10 A.M., noon, and 2 P.M. starting times); Learn-to-ski package: midweek $53, weekend $63 (includes ticket, lesson, rental); Beginner-ski package: midweek $47, weekend $57 (includes beginner-area ticket, lesson, rental) • **Special Programs:** Racing Clinics for ages 7–18 • **Adaptive Ski Programs** for the hearing and visually impaired • **Base Lodge Facilities:** Indoor/outdoor cafeteria, pizza shop, lounge, ski/rental/gift shops, lockers, game room • **Day Care** offered 9 A.M.–4 P.M. daily at the base lodge.

Room & Board

Located six miles north of East and West Stroudsburg, Alpine sits just about an hour or so from New York City and under two from Philadelphia. It's mostly a day-ski area, though guests can plan an affordable slopeside stay at the resort's **Alpine Village** on the mountain's summit, or at several resorts, villages, and inns nearby. All the trappings of urban life can be found in the Stroudsburgs, while nearby tourist attraction **Colony Village** offers year-round horseback and carriage rides, museum tours, restaurants, and pubs.

Lodging

On-site

Alpine Village slopeside chalets w/indoor pools, whirlpools, fully furnished/fireplace; 1–800–233–8240.

Nearby

Penn Hills Resort, Analomink, three miles from resort, w/saunas, whirlpools, fireplace • **Penn Estates Resort**, Analomink, six miles from resort, villas/homes, fully furnished, indoor pools, whirlpools, fireplace • **Penn Skiers Motel**, three miles from resort, Resort packages include midweek lift ticket, weekend discounts. Call 1–800–233–8240, (570) 421–6464 for info.

Other

Brookview Manor B&B Inn, Canadensis, 10 minutes from resort; 1–800–585–7974, (570) 595–2451 • **Hillside Lodge**, Canadensis, restaurant, fireplace, Jacuzzi, Murder Mystery Weekends; 1–800–666–4455, (570) 595–7551 • **Martinville Streamside Cottages**, Canadensis; (570) 595–2489 • **Village Court Motel & Cottages**, Canadensis; (570) 595–7888 • **Laurel Grove Inn & Resort**, Canadensis; 1–800–842–0497, (570) 595–7262 • **Pine Knob Inn**, Canadensis, circa 1847 country inn, restaurant/pub; 1–800–426–1460 • **Budget Motel**, East Stroudsburg; 1–800–233–8144, (570) 424–5451 • **Howard Johnsons Plaza Hotel**, Stroudsburg; 1–800–777–5453, (570) 424–1930 • **Paramount Motel**, East Stroudsburg; (570) 421–2141.

Dining/Aprés Ski

On-site

Cafeteria, pizza shop, lounge w/entertainment on weekend afternoons.

Nearby

Wayside Colony Saloon, Analomink, tavern/restaurant; (570) 595–3368 • **Reflections Night Club**, at Penn Hills Resort; (570) 421–6464 • **Barley Creek Brewery/Restaurant**, Tannersville; (570) 629–9399 • **Taylor's Pub at Colony Village**, Canadensis, sports bar/restaurant; (570) 595–7710 • **China Buffet**, East Stroudsburg; (570) 476–7658 • **Classy Sassy's**, Cresco; (570) 595–2680 • **Cappuccinos Ristorante**, Cresco; (570) 595–2833.

Big Boulder/ Jack Frost Mtns

Big Boulder/Jack Frost
P.O. Box 702
Blakeslee, PA 18610

Ski Report: 1–800–475–SNOW
Big Two InfoLine/Lodging: 1–800–468–2442
Jack Frost Information: (570) 443–8425
Big Boulder Information: (570) 722–0100
Internet: *www.big2resorts.com*
Credit Cards: AE, MC, VISA, Discover

Operating Hours:
Jack Frost: 8:30 A.M.–4 P.M. weekdays
8:00 A.M.–4 P.M. weekends
Big Boulder: 9 A.M.–10 P.M. weekdays
8 A.M.–11 P.M. Saturday
8 A.M.–10 P.M. Sunday

Season: December to late March

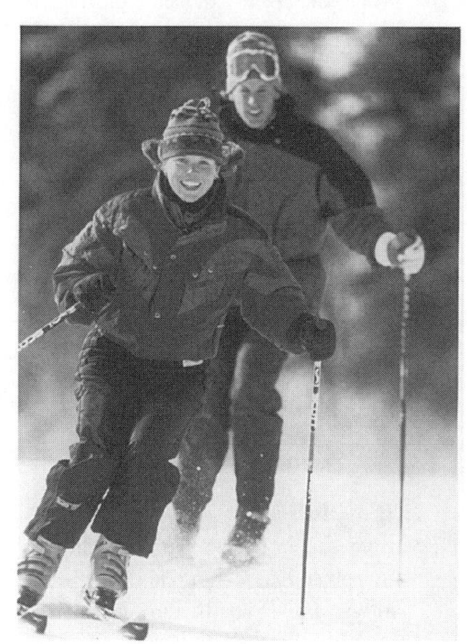

Backdrop

With modest plateaus and sporadic snowfall, Pennsylvania's Pocono region hardly seemed the right place to follow on the heels of the emerging western and New England ski resorts of the 1940s. Nonetheless, Big Boulder established itself on a wing and a prayer. A new snowmaking system would combat the region's common winter thaws to bring thousands of ready-minded skiers from three different major metropolitan areas.

As Pennsylvania's first commercial ski area, Big Boulder's rise prompted the creation of nearby Jack Frost Ski Area in 1972. Though blessed with only 600 feet vertical drop, Jack Frost complements Big Boulder's beginner and family reputation with steeper, upper-intermediate terrain. Frost and Boulder are separated by six miles, offer a reciprocal lift ticket, and are renowned for their impeccable snowmaking/grooming and posh vacation lodging. In fact, their snowmaking system was recently voted among the country's best in a *Ski* Magazine poll.

Getting There

Jack Frost

- **From the N.E. Extension of the PA Turnpike:** Take Exit 35 to Route 940 east. Follow signs four miles to Jack Frost on the left.
- **From New York/New Jersey:** Take Exit 43, then right onto Route 115 north, left on Route 940 west, follow signs four miles to Jack Frost on right.
- **From Baltimore/Washington, D.C.:** Take I-695 to I-83 north to Harrisburg, then pick up I-81 north/northeast to I-80 east. Bear right on access road for Exit 42 PA 940/PA-9 N.E. Extension Turnpike to Lake Harmony. Turn right on Route 940 to Jack Frost.

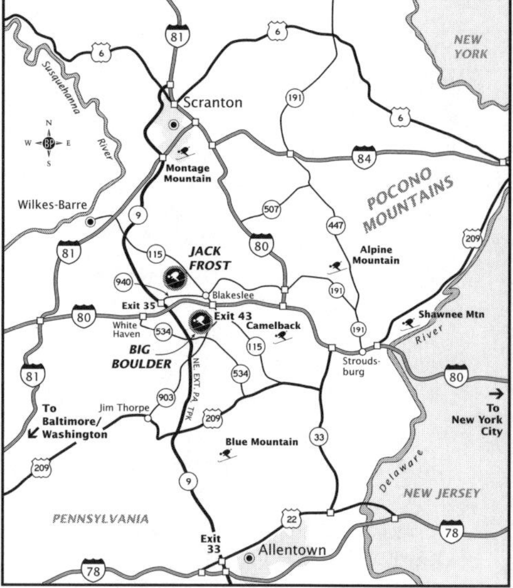

Big Boulder

- **From the N.E. Extension of the PA Turnpike:** Take Exit 35, following signs to I-80. Take I-80 east to PA Exit 43 and turn right onto Route 115 south. Turn right onto Route 903 south and follow signs to Big Boulder.
- **From New York/New Jersey:** Take I-80 west to Exit 43, then left onto Route 115 south. Turn right onto Route 903 south and follow signs to Big Boulder.
- **From Baltimore/Washington:** Take I-695 to I-83 north to Harrisburg, then pick up I-81 north/northeast to I-80 east. Then take Exit 43 PA-115 to Blakeslee, continue on 115 and turn right on 903, then right on 1003/Big Boulder Road to Big Boulder.

Mountain Stats

Base Elevation: Jack Frost: 1,400 feet; Big Boulder: 1,700 feet
Summit Elevation: Jack Frost: 2,000 feet; Big Boulder: 2,175 feet
Vertical Drop: Jack Frost: 600 feet; Big Boulder: 475 feet
Longest Run: Jack Frost: 3,200 feet; Big Boulder: 2,900 feet
Primary Slope Direction: North (both mountains)
Slopes and Trails: Jack Frost: 4 beginner; 8 intermediate; 8 advanced; Big Boulder: 4 beginner; 5 intermediate; 5 advanced
Skiable Terrain: Jack Frost: 75 acres; Big Boulder 55 acres
Lifts: Jack Frost: 1 quad, 2 triples, 4 doubles; Big Boulder: 2 triples, 5 doubles
Uphill Capacity: Jack Frost: 11,000 skiers per hour; Big Boulder: 9,600 skiers per hour
Average Annual Snowfall: Jack Frost: 55 inches; Big Boulder: 60 inches
Snowmaking: 100% of both areas
Night Skiing: Jack Frost: Trails close at 4 P.M. daily; Big Boulder: 100% of slopes, Sunday–Friday until 10 P.M., 11 P.M. Saturday (beginning late December)

Trail Profiles

Jack Frost

The trail system at Jack Frost manages to squeeze a lot of pitch out of its small 600-foot vertical drop, with suit-up-and-ski access off the resort's "upside-down" summit lodge. Check out the recently expanded East Mountain for advanced snow riding. Here, you can lay tracks on steep grades and ride the glades through the trees. When there's enough snow, look out for some tall cliffs on the East Face, or take some turns in the out-of-bounds glades. The terrain on this side is a fun but short trip down any way you ride it, and prepare to spend some time on the resort's archaic lifts. Look out for jumps on *Exhibition* and *Dematte's Demise*, and in the ever-improving terrain park.

The rest of Frost's terrain is solidly intermediate to advanced beginner, aside from the learning zones. Runs are narrow and curvy with a consistent pitch. Beginners have three bunny hills with an 11 percent grade off the summit lodge area, and two of the slopes are served by chairs. After knocking out the three bunny slopes, still-developing skiers may have a tough time transitioning to the resort's more steeply pitched green runs. Big Boulder is probably the better move for snow riders still learning the sport, though Frost's instructional programs are equally strong.

Big Boulder

Six miles away at Big Boulder, steeps are not as easy to find on this 475-foot-vertical mountain. Break off for a run down *Draufganger* and its winding downhill. One of the other two black diamonds—*Upper Sitzmark* or *Big Boulder*—gets bumped out with some sizable moguls. Compensating for lack of pitch, several trails offer jumps, dips, and bends, including *Merry Widow* and *Midway* slopes.

At Big Boulder, wide and well-groomed trails are designed for neophyte and developing skiers. The resort's reputable ski school uses two small parcels that are sheltered from other trails to teach beginners the basics. The next step for learning skiers may be the wide, easy tracks of *Little Boulder* and *Edelweiss*, each served by its own lifts. *Bunny's Elbow* is aptly named—it's an easy, straight run leading to a 160-degree switchback that's just right for skiers looking to work on their turning.

Snowboarding Highlights

Big Boulder sports a 400-foot halfpipe and the accompanying Bonk Yard, where boarders can find boxes, barrels, rail slides, and other changing features. A Pipe Dragon does a good job of carving and maintaining the halfpipe. Early-season openings are questionable, though, so call ahead first to find out if the park and pipe are running. The Bonk Yard is open nightly under lights, but without a dedicated lift to serve it.

At Jack Frost, snowboarding has gotten a lot more attention of late. The Badlands is a sweet terrain park that leads into a new 400-foot halfpipe, also carved by a Pipe Dragon. Beyond that, the terrain at Frost is much more conducive to snowboarders, offering jumps and twists throughout the mountain. On another note, prepare to take the long chair ride to the summit to revisit the Badlands and the pipe, and keep in mind that Jack Frost closes shop at 4 P.M. Both resorts routinely run competitions, events, and snowboard demo days, at which time boarders can sample tasty rides from major manufacturers.

Snowboard Instruction: Private $50, group $20 • **Rentals:** $32/day, $25/night

More Fun in the Flakes

With the abundance of alpine and four-seasons resorts in the Pocono region, the number of nearby tourist trappings and attractions is no surprise. For a nice getaway, try the **Water Gap Trolley** that winds through the Delaware Water Gap National Recreation Area. Within this national recreation area are natural and historic points of interest along the Kittatinny Ridge and a 25-mile stretch of the Appalachian Trail. Some of the other activities on which you'll be sure to find literature during a trip here include pony, carriage, and sleigh rides; outdoor tours; museums; and shopping at Pocono factory outlets and country craft stores. The two resorts are also well known for their numerous festivals held from spring through early fall. **Jack Frost's Irish Festival** runs each Memorial Day Weekend, and the treasured **Pocono Blues Festival** is held each July at Big Boulder. For information and a free Poconos Travel Guide covering all lodging, restaurants, indoor/outdoor attractions, and events, call 1–800–762–6667.

There's a lot more than downhilling for guests here. **Snowtubing** is offered at both resorts, along with groomed cross-country ski trails when there's enough of a natural snow base. A nearby groomed

snowmobiling course features rollers, tabletops, and other jumps, and is equipped with snowmaking. Bring your own mobile or rent one here.

Big Boulder

Snowtubing (on-site): 12 chutes, four lifts, exclusive kids' area, and family area with four- to six-person group tubes available. Rates: adult, open-close: $20/anytime, ages 15 and under: $16; tubing combo, with lift ticket: additional $10/anytime • **Two-mile cross-country skiing course,** contingent on deep natural snow base, off Edelweiss chair lift summit area, with trail access to Hickory Run State Park. Rentals/lessons available; trail fee $10, rental/trail fee $20.

Did You Know?

Commercial snowmaking in the U.S. was all but pioneered here at Big Boulder. In the early 1940s, local inventor John Garish was able to produce manmade snow by tinkering with a garden hose, sprinkler, and varying water pressures. His work enabled the resort to operate on a limited basis and helped pave the way for the snowmaking industry boom.

Jack Frost

Snowtubing (on-site): five chutes, new Launch Pad expert chute, two lifts, group rates available, Big Boulder rates apply • **Nine-mile cross-country ski course** (weather dependent) near the tennis court area, with rentals and lessons available at the cross-country ski center. Trail fee $10; group lesson, trail guide fee $15; rental and trail fee $20; group lesson, rental, and fee $35 • **Sno-Cross snowmobiling course,** located at Traxx Motorsports Park, with snowmaking, grooming, and rentals. Trail rates: $27/single, $40/double (rates per half-hour) • **Splatter paintball** (on-site): 2,500 wooded acres, available year-round, with full rental equipment.

Skier Services

Lift tickets are on par with other Mid-Atlantic ski areas. Buy your lift ticket in advance (before November's end), and get good discounts. Remember when doing this, though, that slope availability can't be predicted. Both Jack Frost and Big Boulder have also set up an affordable program for juniors. Skiers and snowboarders ages 6–15 can ride any session for $25, while ages 16–21 can ski for $30 anytime, any day. Use the same lift ticket for both mountains—just find your own way there.

Families might take note that Jack Frost's lodge is much more spacious than Boulder's. Additionally, crowds can form quickly on either mountain on any given weekend and holiday, and both resorts suffer from slow chair lifts. Call ahead first to find out how many lifts are running. As for night skiing, Boulder does a lot of business, especially for snowboarders. Night hours don't often begin until late December, weather permitting. You can also save lots of time if you're renting by getting your gear off-mountain. A number of rental shops can be found along the way to Boulder and Frost.

$ Lift Tickets

Jack Frost & Big Boulder

Open–close: weekday $36, weekend $42 • 4 P.M.–close: $25/anytime • Advance tickets (order by November 26): midweek $22, weekend $32; youth $22 • Ages 6–15 $25/anytime, ages 16–21 $30/anytime • Seniors ages 62–69: $25/anytime; ages 70+: $10/anytime • Midweek rates apply from opening to December 22 and after March 4.

Ski Rentals

$25/adult, $20/ages 15 and under • Snowblades: $25.

Services

Ski School: Jack Frost/Big Boulder: Private (reservations suggested): $50/hour; Group $20/hour; Group lesson/lift/rental package: $65; Discover package (lesson/lift/rental): $50; Kids' C'n Ski (ages 3–8): $50 w/rental, $35 without (includes lift ticket, three hours supervision); Kids' C'n Ride (ages 6–8) snowboarding, same rates apply; Adaptive Ski School: Solid program offered at Jack Frost • **On-Site Services: Day Care (Big Boulder):** Available with nominal charge from open to 5 P.M. (including lunch); half-day sessions; and 5 P.M. to close; **(Jack Frost):** Same as Big Boulder, but no night session.

Room & Board

Guests can base themselves on both mountains in the resorts' fully equipped houses, condominiums, and townhomes. There's just one full-service restaurant on the mountain, but plenty of other places to eat on-site and numerous establishments nearby along Route 940. The surrounding area is packed with family and couples' resorts, country inns, and lakeside communities that offer stately lodging and winter recreation such as cross-country skiing, snowmobiling, sledding, tobogganing, and ice skating. Over 30 bed and breakfasts/country inns, seven couples' resorts, numerous cabins/chalets/rental homes, and 60 hotels/motels are within 20 miles of both Jack Frost and Big Boulder. Call 1–800–762–6667 for free travel information/reservations or (570) 424–6050 for immediate tourist information. **Midweek packages** (minimum two nights) include lift tickets & meals; ages 8 and under stay, ski, & eat free.

Lodging

On-site

Jack Frost

Snow Ridge Village townhomes (up to eight people/unit), w/kitchen, fireplace, dining room, all appliances, some units w/hot tubs. Call for rates.

Big Boulder

The Villages lakeside townhomes and condos (up to eight people/unit), two–three bedroom units, same amenities as Snow Ridge Village, without hot tubs. Call for rates.

Dining

Jack Frost

E-2000 Bar/Lounge, with live weekend entertainment • **Cantina Bar/Lounge** • **Cafeteria**, pizzeria, outdoor barbecue.

Big Boulder

On-site

Blue Heron Grille overlooking Big Boulder Lake (on Lake Shore Drive), with casual dining, weekend buffet • **Cafeteria** • **Pizzeria** in Double Decker building • **The Cellar Nightclub**, w/live weekend entertainment • **Glass House Bar/Lounge** • **On Lake Shore Drive in Lake Harmony (just outside resort)** • **Lake Harmony Lodge Sports Bar Cafe**, (570) 722–8368 • **Shenanigan's of Lake Harmony**, (570) 722–1100 • **Close Quarters Restaurant**, (570) 722–8127 • Numerous restaurants/lounges nearby along Route 940.

Blue Knob

Blue Knob
P.O. Box 247
Claysburg, PA 16625

Ski Report: 1–800–458–3403
Info: 1–800–458–3403, (814) 239–5111

Internet: *www.blueknob.com*
E-mail: blueknob@nb.net
Credit Cards: MC, VISA, Discover

Operating Hours: 9 A.M.–10 P.M. daily
Season: December to late March

Backdrop

"Ski Good or Eat Woods—Blue Knob, PA" is the resort's official unofficial slogan. The Knob is not your typical Mid-Atlantic plateau. It is the Mad River Glen of the south—a classic skier's mountain with terrain that's diverse, lengthy, and downright gnarly on the black diamonds. If you consider yourself an advanced skier or boarder and think there's nothing good to ride in the Mid-Atlantic, you're in for a sweet awakening when you hit Blue Knob on a powder day. It is, without question, the most challenging area south of New York, and it rivals even some of its best areas. The mountain's 34 runs and 1,072 vertical feet boast a variety of terrain and pitches for all levels, extreme and intermediate gladed runs, open bowls, fast narrow chutes and gulleys, and nasty moguls. And, of course, there's long, smooth beginner and intermediate track for the leisurely skier.

The resort's summit area once served as the site of a World War II Air Force radar station and barracks. It was here that the first home-grown trails were cut and skied among the trees. Years later, a plane flying over the mountain on a clear May afternoon revealed to its passengers thick snow still holding strong. The same group on this plane opened the mountain for business in 1963. Today the top quarter of the mountain's land is state-park owned, while the remainder of the ski area is privately leased. The Knob is Pennsylvania's highest skiable mountain, just 41 feet shy of the state's tallest point on Mt. Davis in southwestern Somerset County.

Mountain Stats

Base Elevation: 2,100 feet
Summit Elevation: 3,172 feet
Vertical Drop: 1,072 feet
Longest Run: 9,200 feet
Primary Slope Direction: North
Slopes and Trails: 6 beginner, 14 intermediate, 14 advanced
Skiable Terrain: 100-plus acres
Lifts: 2 triples, 2 doubles, 3 surface tows
Uphill Capacity: 5,200 skiers per hour
Average Annual Snowfall: 120 inches
Snowmaking: 80% of area
Night Skiing: 40% of area, nightly until 10 P.M.

Getting There

- **From Philadelphia and Harrisburg:** Take the Pennsylvania Turnpike to I-99 (Route 220) north to Osterburg, then Route 869 west to Pavia. Follow signs to Blue Knob.
- **From northern Pennsylvania points:** Take I-80 south or Route 22 east to I-99 (Route 220), heading south to East Freedom. From East Freedom, take Route 164 west and follow signs to Blue Knob.
- **From Washington/Baltimore:** Take I-95 north to I-695 west to I-70 north. Then take the Pennsylvania Turnpike west to I-99 (Route 220) north to King/Claysburg exit–Business 220 north, and follow signs to Blue Knob. Alternatively, take I-99/220 north to Osterburg, then Route 869 west to Pavia, and follow signs to Blue Knob.

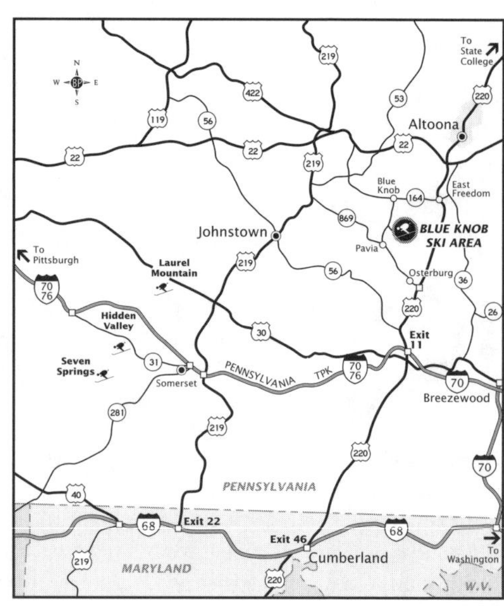

Trail Profiles

Steep, narrow trails contoured with shifting pitches and bends still define Blue Knob. But it's the advanced glades and bowls—true rarities in the region—that are the hallmarks of the Knob's advanced turf. Traversing the steep, tree-lined powder stashes of *East Wall Glades*, *Ditch Glades*, *Bone Yard Glades*, and *Mine Shaft Glades* will conjure up images of northeastern skiing. A mid-peak station off the Route 66 double chair lift gives you the chance to drop off early and access the lower mountain's challenging 14 runs. Be warned, though. This stuff is positively for advanced snow riders only. The gladed trails and *Upper Stembogan Bowl* show no deviation from their natural topographical state. Don't be surprised to encounter rocky outcroppings, chutes, cliffs, changing snow conditions, trees, and numerous natural obstacles in the trail paths. There's nothing remotely comparable to this hardcore terrain in the Mid-Atlantic, so exercise some caution. Snowmaking and grooming could still stand to improve here and all over the mountain. It's a pretty ambitious feat, though, considering the diversity of terrain, especially the difficult-to-maintain narrow runs.

No, this is not a mountain for the neophyte skier, but the resort does have some terrain just for beginners. Right in front on the lodge, an easy beginner area is wide open and has its own triple chair. Novices can graduate to nearby *Mambo Alley* and its long, twisting

Did You Know?

The Knob permits backcountry skiing and boarding outside its trail boundaries with sufficient snowfall. When it's good, it's great. Look for awesome powder stashes in the Knob's backcountry network off both boundary sides. Traveling up the triple chair, look out to the right and see if you can spot the big bowl and some open sections. This bowl-shaped side retains snow beautifully and is shielded from high winds. Access it above Jack Rabbit *trail, beyond its boundary, by heading out below the snowmaking pond, where you'll see ski tracks. Hop on and ride all the way down to the triple lift. There's nothing too steep over here, but it's superb snow riding. Just don't go to the top of the next ridge and drop off the back side, or you'll wind up on the access road instead of the triple chair.*

The other boundary side (off Stembogan*) has some more sweet terrain on a steep ridge. You might find skiers out there when there's lots of snow. But for the most part, this side tends to get buffeted with forceful winds that blow snow away. If you want to check it out, there's an easement off the top far side of* Stembogan Bowl *known locally as* Cliffhanger*. Go straight out past the rope atop* Stembogan Bowl*, pass the diesel compressor, circle back uphill a bit, then meet with the access condo road. Here you'll drop straight onto* Cliffhanger *and its vintage wide-open drops, finishing with a short trek back to the double lift.*

A word to the wise: If you find someone riding out-of-bounds, he or she is probably a local. And your best bet is to hook up and kindly tap him for some insight into these rare Mid-Atlantic gems. Just make sure to ride with a friend or group. You might get verbal warning from Ski Patrol, but there's little chance of getting your ticket cut and you're much safer this way. Best of all, most of the terrain winds up at or near one of the lifts. Just follow the open powder lines!

beginner track. They can also experience the full length of the mountain by taking nicely graded Runout trail all the way to the base double lifts. A devoted ski school offers personalized instruction and several good learning programs.

Advanced

Extrovert: extra-steep and crosses under both double lifts, packed high with beastly moguls the size of cars. Witness one of the Mid-Atlantic's steepest top-to-bottom runs, offering three pitches at 39 degrees • *Shortway*: narrow, gladed, and a solid grade • *Lower High Hopes*: continuous drop and fall-line descents along a narrow ridge line • *Lower Route* 66: fast with bumps • *East Wall Glades*: some seriously steep points, a boulder smack in the middle, and rocks or other natural obstacles to jump or avoid • *Ditch Glades*: Soft-powder riding in a nicely graded, narrow gulley. It's lined with trees on the right side, and be sure to keep an eye out for a stray rock here and there • *Mine Shaft Glades*: Not for the faint of heart! Major steepness, and a wide cut through tightly spaced trees. Converges with *Bone Yard Glades*, which also serves up some hair-raising, tree-lined descents.

Intermediate

Stembogan Bowl: steep hops in the upper bowl, freeform carving, a hairpin left turn onto *Stembogan* trail, and more good turns along the way. Just follow the flat *East Wall* traverse along the eastern ridge and hop in the bowl. You can jump in on any part of the bowl along the traverse, with the steepest part at its beginning. It's a little easier to jump into further down the traverse. Great trail for intermediates and above • *Expressway*: solid, long cruiser to tuck for speed and make turns • *Triple Glades* and *Forever Glades*: good challenge for intermediates. Not real steep, with time to negotiate around the trees, and a few drops to gain speed. The intermediate glades tend to shield wind and hold snow longer.

Beginner

Upper/Lower Mambo to *Runout* and *Jack Rabbit/Runout*: long beginner/intermediate cruisers over two-plus miles, some good pitches, and the mountain's full 1,072 vertical feet • Tame beginner area right off the lodge, with its own triple chair.

More Fun in the Flakes

The Knob has felt the impact of **Telemark** skiing's reemergence. Tele-skiing is allowed on all slopes (no rentals), and the neighboring golf course and surrounding backcountry trails are Nordic nirvana for cross-country skiers of all levels. Winter activities don't end after you leave the mountain. **Cross-country skiing**, **snowmobiling**, and **winter hiking** abound in the Laurel Highlands, while nearby streams and lakes hold some of Pennsylvania's best **ice fishing**. When the snow finally clears, the four seasons resort offers miles of mountain biking/hiking trails, a nine-hole golf course, tennis courts, indoor/outdoor pools, and a Jacuzzi, sauna, and steam room.

Snowtubing: open 4 P.M.–10 P.M. Monday–Friday, 9 A.M.–10 P.M. weekends; $12 per two-hour session; $17/4 hours • **Cross-country skiing** on Blue Knob's golf course and a large network of surrounding trails *(see page 234)* • **Sleigh rides** and ice skating at the condominium area • **Skis of all types** welcome on the trail network.

Snowboarding Highlights

A small terrain park with a few relatively tame jumps can be found on the beginner Condo trail. The same area formerly held a modest halfpipe, but grooming difficulty and constantly drifting snow accounted for its demise. Only time will tell if current plans for a bigger park come to fruition. In the meantime, boarders won't even think about a park or pipe when they witness the mountain's diverse and challenging terrain, especially the expert track on the lower half. Be sure to check out the Stembogan Bowl, shred the narrow track on *Shortway* and *Lower High Hopes*, and carve all of the glades if they're open. The whole mountain is filled with bumps, dips, curves, berms, and jumps. Experts won't want to miss out on out-of-bounds riding when there's plenty of snowpack. Look around for a local who can guide you, and be sure to travel in groups.

Snowboard Rentals: Day $27, half-day $18, twilight $27, night $18 • **Snowboard School:** Private $40/hour, group $25/hour

Skier Services

Lift tickets are moderately priced and long lift lines aren't all that common, despite slow and outdated lifts. Even if guests finish the entire mountain in a day, they may wish to get a second helping, which is why slopeside condominiums were built. The ski lodge is basic and somewhat tight quartered, but skiers will find everything they need without venturing far. The pub is a great place to kick back with a drink in front of the fireplace. A good house band provides the pulse on weekend afternoons.

Lift Tickets

9 A.M.–5 P.M.: weekday $28, weekend $40 • 1 P.M.–5 P.M.: weekday $23, weekend $34 • 1 P.M.–10 P.M.: weekday $28, weekend $40 • 6 P.M.–10 P.M.: weekday $18, weekend $20 • 9 A.M.–10 P.M.: weekday $35, weekend $43 • 15%–25% discounts for ages 12 and under and 65+ • Special rates for ladies (Monday/Wednesday), men (Tuesday), students (Tuesday/Thursday) • Group rates, multi-day packages available.

Ski Rentals

9 A.M.–5 P.M.: $21, half-day $15, twilight $21, night $15, 9 A.M.–10 P.M. $25.

New at the Knob

The resort plans to slightly re-contour Stembogan Bowl, but promises not to touch any of the double fall lines or change its unique character. Most likely, they'll just make it a little more user-friendly and allow for easier grooming. The resort will continue to improve overall snowmaking and grooming, upgrade its lighting for night skiing, and begin planting spruce trees to act as a snow buffer for the glade trails.

Services

Ski School: Private: $40/hour (begins on the hour and half-hour), Group: $25/hour (10 A.M., noon, and 2 P.M.); Kinderski Program (ages 4–10), offered daily, includes lesson, lunch, rental. Reservations recommended. Full day $65, morning $40, afternoon $40; Mountain Mashers (ages 9–16), includes ticket, instruction, and NASTAR racing; $65/skier/snowboarder; Learn to Ski package • **Racing:** NASTAR offered on High Hopes trail, with surface lift, weekends from 11 A.M.–2 P.M.; USSA Junior Ski Racing/Training Team for ages 8 and up, offered on weekends. Call resort for info • **Summit Lodge Facilities:** Ski and rental shops, ski school, cafeteria, lounge, lockers, ski school • **Day Care:** Available in the Alpine Village from 9 A.M.–5 P.M., for ages 2 years and older; $3/hour per child. Reservations required on weekdays only (814) 239–5111.

Room & Board

The resort has affordable condos, each with a kitchen and fireplace, in its **Alpine Village Center**, just down the road from the ski lodge. Take your last run of the day right back to your room on beginner *Condo* trail. Look for weekday and weekend specials at **Blue's condos**. An even better ski-and-stay option is in one of 10 privately owned, slopeside homes. The only other lodging is roughly 20 minutes away. Altoona and Bedford have numerous bed and breakfasts and hotels/motels. Tourist attractions include the working colonial village of **Old Bedford, Raystown Lake**, and several antique shops and stores in Blue Knob's surrounding villages.

Lodging

On-site

Blue Knob slopeside condominiums: (one–two bedrooms, studios, and lofts) with kitchen, fireplace, balcony, pool, Jacuzzi, sauna; call for rates • Privately owned slopeside and nearby chalets, condos, studios, and lofts, with pool, Jacuzzi; rates $135–$390/two days (Call 1–800–458–3403).

Nearby

Beford's Covered Bridge Inn B&B: Schellsburg, 18 miles from Blue Knob, six rooms, cottage, private bath, country decor; rates $65–$95/night, (814) 733–4093 • **Hickory Hollow Farm B&B**: Schellsburg; (814) 733–4639 • **Station Inn B&B**, Cresson: five suites with private baths, 1–800–555–4757 • **Holiday Inn-Altoona**: restaurant/lounge; (814) 944–4581 • **Ramada Inn**-Breezewood: restaurant, pool/Jacuzzi/sauna; 1–800–535–4025 • **Bedford, Pennsylvania** (25 miles from Blue Knob) • **Quality Inn**: Arena Restaurant/Lounge; (814) 623–5188 • **Best Western**: with hot tub, exercise room/sauna, restaurant/lounge; 1–800–752–8592 • **Judy's Motel**: 12 rooms, ski lift packages; (814) 623–9118.

Dining

On-site

Ski lodge cafeteria • **Mueller's Pub**, with live bands on weekend afternoons, open until 10:30 P.M • **The Clubhouse**, restaurant/bar, located at the condo area, with live bands on weekends.

Nearby (Claysburg)

Ranch House Family Restaurant, along Route 220, (814) 695–8825 • **Village Inn Restaurant**, RD 1; (814) 239–5191 • **Peggy's Diner**, RD 2; (814) 239–2196 • **Dane Anthony's Restaurant**, RD 1; (814) 239–8382.

(More) Things To Know

At how many other ski areas in the Mid-Atlantic can you look out over the summit and NOT see the bottom of the mountain? It speaks to Blue Knob's size that you can't. It is one bad mountain that rides bigger than its 1,072 vertical feet.

When two to three feet of powder come around, don't wait another minute. Cancel your plans, call in sick, find the babysitter, and generally avoid all other responsibilities...your mission on a day like this is to ride the Knob and relish its exquisitely diverse terrain.

Keep a close lookout for what's happening in the sky if you're looking to ride the good stuff. Between the resort's ski report, www.blueknob.com, *and* www.weather.com *(plug in Claysburg, PA), you should get a pretty good idea of what to expect.*

Travel alert: the drive to the summit can be hairy during or after a snow blast. It's the same access road Air Force personnel used back in the 1940s to reach the summit's radar station and barracks. If you're careful, you can get up the mountain in a car, but 4-wheel drive is recommended always. The weather here can change for the worse just like that. Look for some steep ascents and tight angled turns. And don't get caught behind a bus on a snowy day!

The Knob sits at an elevation of over 3,000 feet on a blustery ridge that sometimes gets hammered with prevailing winds. Prepare for this by bringing extra gear, especially for the long, slow lifts. Conditions aren't always difficult, though. It's not uncommon to ski a clear, beautiful bluebird day here. Be sure to break at the Mid-way Barbecue on days like these. You can get a bite to eat and your drink of choice on the outside snow deck while classic rock jams from overhead speakers.

Considering the mountain's unusual weather, sometimes the best-case scenario is to pick up six inches of sleet. This creates a hard pack and a stronger base, and is just what the glade trails can use to stay open. Another six inches of powder wouldn't hurt either.

When there's a winter thaw in effect, Blue struggles to keep its trails open. But unless things are really bad, you can expect at least 22 of 34 runs available, including Stembogan, Extrovert, High Hopes *and a few other lower-mountain expert trails. Even when the resort's not at full strength, there's often enough upper-mountain terrain open to present a good range of skiing challenges.*

A seemingly ramshackle summit lodge is actually full of rustic, homespun charm. You can get almost anything you need under these roofs, and there's a fireplace pub serving great drinks with live rock and blues acts on weekend afternoons.

Blue Mountain

Blue Mountain
Box 216
Palmerton, PA 18071

Ski Report: 1–877–SKI BLUE
Information: (610) 826–7700
Internet: *www.skibluemt.com*

Credit Cards: AE, MC, VISA, Discover

Operating Hours
8:30 A.M.–10 P.M. weekdays
7:30 A.M.–10 P.M. weekends/holidays
Season: Early December to mid-March

Backdrop

Local developer Ray Tuthill opened a small mom-and-pop ski area in the mid-1970s that he dubbed Little Gap, later changing the name to Blue Mountain. Over the years, Blue has made significant upgrades, invested some big bucks, and made great strides in capturing a chunk of the Pocono Mountain ski market. And, it has mastered the art of making and keeping good snow in an area that gets very little help from nature. Blue has three urban markets within its grasp (Allentown, Philadelphia, and Wilmington) and a varied trail network that fits most ability levels. Of Blue's 27 slopes and trails, three are over one mile long. There's also a good terrain park, halfpipe, and tubing park.

27 runs often a frozen granular base; a sure thing the good riding was going to be early rather than later. By 2 P.M., the good snow was getting skied out, with ice setting in on the middle of many trails All things considered, Blue Mountain should prove to be a worthwhile alternative for Washington, DC and Baltimore snow riders seeking a new taste in the Mid-Atlantic. The mountain compares favorably to DC's closest areas, and although there are no overnight accommodations at Blue, it's likely not too far for a day trip.

Mountain Stats

Base Elevation: 592 feet
Summit Elevation: 1,645 feet
Vertical Drop: 1,082 feet
Longest Run: 5,200 feet
Primary Slope Direction: South
Slopes and Trails: 11 beginner, 7 intermediate, 9 advanced
Skiable Terrain: 75 acres
Lifts: 1 high-speed quad, 4 doubles, 1 T-bar, 1 rope tow
Uphill Capacity: 8,600 skiers per hour
Average Annual Snowfall: 28 inches
Snowmaking: 100% of area
Night Skiing: 100% of area, nightly to 10 P.M.

Trail Profiles

Seven black diamonds have strong grades, but don't expect any super steeps. Try the upper half of *Main Street* for bumps and wide-open carving. The lower section of *Main Street* is groomed and a little less steep, but a long fun speed ride nonetheless. *Challenge* trail is the steepest continuous run—straight, wide, and groomed smooth down the fall line. It eventually slows to a brief shelf before a steep, short-lived headwall and runout called *The Falls*. Parallel to *Challenge* is black diamond *Razor's Edge*, which is partially open and nearing completion of its full length. Other advanced runs like *Chute* and *Midway* are fast, short jaunts down to *Main Street's* lower half. Beyond the terrain park, just a few jumps can be found on the mountain. On the other hand, look for narrow, off-trail connector paths that skirt through the trees on some of the mid-mountain trails.

The best intermediate run is a scenic cut through the trees called *Sidewinder*. It has a slew of sharp S turns and contours, is pitched enough for good speed, has varying widths, and usually has some of the mountain's best snow. The only other good, long blues are *Upper Switchback* and *Lazy Mile*. Better skiers may discover a half-day or night session is more than enough to satisfy them, but the trail network does have some good variety to it.

Novices have bunny slopes at both the summit and valley, along with two outstanding and lengthy beginner trails. 6,400-foot *Paradise* is a picturesque cruising run off the east summit that snakes on wide terrain with a decent grade for a green run. The other long green run is *Burma Road*, where you'll

Did You Know?

Blue Mountain has Pennsylvania's biggest vertical drop, with 1,082 feet. The resort purchased some additional land at the summit (Challenge trail) years ago that allowed for an increase in vertical.

Look out for speed traps if driving through Palmerton. And when you get to Blue, take your pick of parking: the valley/base lodge or the summit/main lodge. Tubing lanes, bunny slopes/ski school, snowboard halfpipe, and terrain park can all be found at the valley lodge. You can also get tickets, rentals, and lessons here, and take the double chair to the summit. The main/summit lodge is another five minutes' drive up-mountain (not unmanageable, but 4-wheel is recommended in snow). Here you'll find everything under one large roof. To enter the trails from the summit lodge, you need to have your lift ticket scanned your first time down.

find more good turning opportunities and well-groomed terrain. This is a good one for both novices and intermediates. The valley bunny hill holds good ski school programs that are sheltered from the trail network.

Getting There

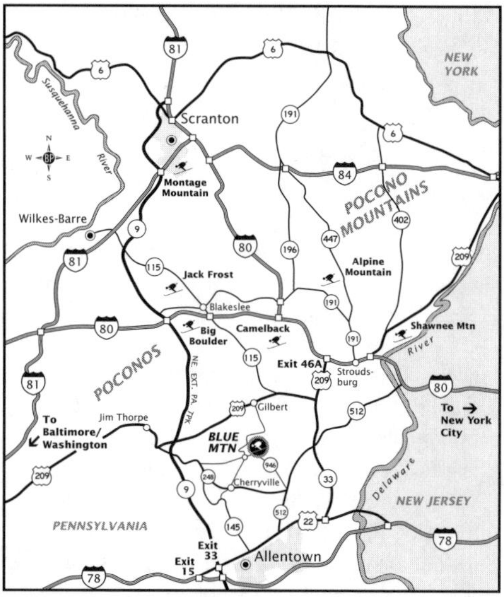

- **From Allentown**: Take Route 145 north (MacArthur Road), approximately nine miles to traffic light at far end of long bridge. Turn right onto Blue Mountain Drive for three miles to traffic light in Cherryville. Go through Cherryville approximately three miles straight through Danielsville to entrance just past the top of the mountain.
- **From Philadelphia**: N.E. extension of the PA Turnpike (Route 476) north to Lehigh Valley, Exit 33. After toll booths, bear right onto Route 22. Go approximately five miles to Route 145 north (MacArthur Road). Follow signs above from here.
- **From Harrisburg, Baltimore and points south**: Take I-83 north to Harrisburg, then take I-81 north to I-78 east. Take Exit 15 (Route 22 east) to Whitehall. Take Route 145 north (MacArthur Road), approximately nine miles to traffic light at far end of long bridge. Turn right onto Blue Mountain Drive for three miles to traffic light in Cherryville. Go through Cherryville approx. Three miles straight through Danielsville to the entrance just past the top of the mountain.
- **From I-80 (NY/NJ and central PA):** Follow I-80 to Exit 46A and Route 209 south. Follow 209 south 14 miles (follow 209 closely from four-lane highway) to the village of Gilbert. (After about six miles, be alert to where Route 209 leaves the four-lane highway.) At Gilbert, turn left off 209 at the stoplight next to the bank. Follow signs over country roads to Blue Mountain.

More Fun in the Flakes

Snow tubers will enjoy 1,000-foot runs on 125 feet of vertical drop. Ride in a group on Quadzilla tubes, or solo on single tubes. The tubing area is located at the valley/base lodge with convenient parking. Or, if you're a skier or snowboarder and thinking of bringing the kids along, Blue has you covered. Try one of the childrens' skiing/boarding programs, hit the snowtubing park, or use Blue's free midweek baby-sitting service for kids six months to five years of age ($2/hour on weekends).

Snowboarding Highlights

It was just a few years back that snowboarders weren't allowed on the mountain. Today it's a different story. The brass must've realized that snowboarders weren't so much of a threat after all, or maybe the revenue window just couldn't be ignored. If you talk to a local skier, they might tell you the place was better off in its pre-snowboard days. In any case, Blue now welcomes boarders with a 300-foot halfpipe and a terrain park for both riders and skiers. There's decent vertical in the halfpipe, especially in the middle where you can catch a lip. The end of the pipe is where you can really hop some air. It's also maintained pretty well by a Pipe Dragon groomer. Look for the pipe in front of the valley lodge, right next to the terrain park.

The terrain park holds about 1,000 feet of tabletops, ollies, quarterpipes, and other jumps, all maintained by a new Piston Bully groomer. Hop into the park and stick the first gap jump, then jump the tabletop. Get some speed and hit the quarterpipe, a couple of berms and rollers, and finish on the rail slide and a closing gap jump. The hits aren't tremendously huge and there's not a ton of vertical in the park, so pick up your speed if air is what you need. Also, plan on hoofing it back up or taking the double chair to the summit; the park and pipe don't have their own lifts just yet. As for the terrain, Blue has enough variety for all level boarders. Shred some steeps on the black diamonds or carve big S turns on intermediate *Switchback* and beginner *Burma Road*. Black diamond *Main Street* is fun, but if you want to continue riding beyond the lifts, make sure you have enough speed to get you through...or strap off and walk it!

Snowboard Instruction: Private $48/hour, $40 student/youth (private by appointment); group: $20, offered at 10 A.M., 2 P.M., and 6 P.M. First-time snowboarder package: $30, includes board, lesson, beginner slope access; all-mountain package: $75 • **Snowboard Rentals:** Day/twilight $30, night $22; ages 15 and under: $26, $20

Events, races, and sponsored festivities are staples each weekend, both day and night. Blue is also one of the stops on the **Subaru Master the Mountain tour**—a program stressing racing, new trends in equipment, and skier/snowboarder safety.

Other Winter Sports

Snowtubing with five lanes, each 800–1,000 feet long, with two tow lifts. Monday–Thursday, 4 P.M.–10 P.M.: $15; Friday 10 A.M.–10 P.M. $15; weekend sessions starting at 7:30 A.M. to 10 P.M.: $16–$20. Group tubing rates available for 15 or more people (reservations required). Call (610) 826–6633 • **Snow Blading**, with Salomon rentals • **Telemark skiing** allowed on all trails; no on-site rentals.

Skier Services

Blue's summit/main lodge is spacious and well-marked if not plush, and doesn't miss a beat on any skier service. Upstairs is an open, wrap-around cafeteria setting that overlooks the slopes, with lots of seating and a pub on the far end.

Lift Tickets

8:30 A.M.–12:30 P.M.: weekday $28, weekend (7:30 A.M.) $36 • 8:30 A.M.–5 P.M.: weekday $36, weekend (7:30 A.M.) $42 • 12:30 P.M.–5 P.M.: weekday $28, weekend $36 • 12:30 P.M.–10 P.M.: weekday $36, weekend $42 • 4 P.M.–10 P.M.: weekday $25, weekend $27 • Student rates (ages 16–21): weekday day or twilight: $30, weekend day or twilight: $32 • Reduced rates for ages 7–15 & senior citizens • "$10 Off" Tickets: Monday Mens Day, Tuesday Business Card Day, Wednesday Ladies Day • Group Rates for 15 or more skiers.

(More) Things To Know

Take advantage of midweek "$10 off" deals, like Men's Day Mondays, Business Card Day Tuesdays, and Ladies' Day Wednesdays. Students ages 16–21 can ride for $30 weekdays and $32 on weekends.

The two double chair lifts are a bit on the slow side, but the high-speed quad moves lines quickly and gets you up top in five minutes. Make early plans on Saturdays and holidays—it can get crowded at times. And, while Blue's snowmakers and groomers do all they can, some trails can get icy by early afternoon. If so, get your runs in early and fast, or ride the trail perimeters and look for good snow.

Ski Rentals

Saloman Step-in System: Day/twilight: $23, Night $18 • Ages 15 and under: $17, $20 • Shaped skis and Salomon Snow Blades available.

Services

Ski School: Private $48/hour, by appointment; Group $20 (10 A.M., 2 P.M., 6 P.M.); First-time Package: $25 (includes rental, lesson, and beginner lift ticket); $65 for all-mountain package; Explorers Program, for beginner to expert: $62/full day, $42/morning or afternoon two-hour session • **Main/Summit Lodge Facilities:** Two cafeterias, pub, ski school, day care, ticket windows, skier store, rental shop, lockers, babysitting service • **Valley/Base Lodge Facilities:** Ticket and rental shops, snowtubing, snowboard shop, vending area, lockers • **Day Care:** Free midweek service for kids six weeks to 5 years; 8:30 A.M.–9 P.M.; weekends: $2/hour from 7:30 A.M. to 9 P.M.

Skier Services

You won't be able to shack up for the night anywhere on the mountain, which is why Blue serves mostly locals and those within two hours' drive. There are a few B&Bs, cabins, and motels just off-mountain in Palmerton. Otherwise, hook up with a hotel in Fogelsville or Allentown, or try the historic town of Jim Thorpe. It's a popular ski-and-stay vacation, 25 minutes from Blue, with an old, working railroad station, a bevy of specialty and craft shops, and ongoing light displays during the winter holiday months.

Room & Board

Lodging

Nearby

The Roth House, quaint B&B, one mile from Blue Mtn; (610) 824–5341 • **Grassy Hill B&B**, overlooking Blue Ridge Country Club; (610) 826–2290 • **Lakeview Lodge B&B**, log cabin-style lodging; private bath, balcony, fireplace; (610) 377–8344 • **The Inn at Jim Thorpe B&B**, downtown, 22 rooms w/private bath; 1–800–329–2599 • **Sheraton Inn Jetport**, Allentown, indoor pool/sauna/Jacuzzi, restaurant; 1–800–383–1100 • **Days Inn**, Allentown, children stay free; (610) 395–3731 • **Hampton Inn,** Fogelsville, fitness room/sauna; (610) 391–1500 • **Comfort Inn**, Fogelsville, Fogey's Cafe & Lounge, fitness room; 1–800–951–7800 • **Allentown Hilton**, restaurant/sports bar, pool/sauna/fitness room; 1–800–445–8667 • **Barn House Village**, Bath, PA, 12 country suites, lounge; (610) 837–1234 • **Allentown Comfort Suites**, restaurant/pub, fitness room; (610) 437–9100 • **Mahoning Court Motel**, Leighton, restaurant; (610) 377–1600.

Dining/Aprés-Ski

On-site

Cafeteria, summit lodge pub w/live music/D.J. Thursdays, karaoke Saturdays.

Nearby (Palmerton)

Blue Mountain Pub • **Bert's Steakhouse & Restaurant**; (610) 826–9921 • **Covered Bridge Inn**; (610) 826–5400 • **Fireline Inn**; (610) 852–3400 • **Tony's Pizzeria**; (610) 826–6161 • **Hunan House Chinese Restaurant**; (610) 826–4567.

Camelback

Camelback
P.O. Box 168
Tannersville, PA 18372

Ski Report: 1–800–233–8100
Information: (570) 629–1661

Internet: *www.skicamelback.com*
E-mail: sales@skicamelback.com
Credit Cards: AE, VISA, MC, Discover

Operating Hours: 8 A.M.–10 P.M. daily
Season: Mid-December to late March

Backdrop

Big Pocono Ski Area opened way back in 1950–51, running sporadically for four years before hurricanes Connie and Diane shut things down. Millions of gallons of water were dumped on the mountain, causing massive runoff and destruction and taking the lives of more than 50 local residents. Skiing was restored a few years later when several Pennsylvania businessmen teamed with expert skier and Austrian Davis Cup tennis player Walter Foeger to design a new trail system here on this Pocono plateau southern ridge. A new name for the resort was declared after old geological maps revealed the mountain as "Camelback," attributed to its double-hump profile from the south. The resort skirted bankruptcy twice in the early going, but an aggressive new snowmaking system helped it survive here in the Mid-Atlantic's "Banana Belt."

Camelback is now a major Pocono player, having laid out considerable expense in upgrades over the years. Here's some of what $25 million over 10 years brings to the mountain: new terrain; increased uphill lift capacity and lighting; improved main lodge and expanded facilities; two impressive terrain parks and a halfpipe; and a separate snowtubing park to top it all off.

Camelback is not the steepest of Mid-Atlantic mountains. It is, however, a well-oiled resort with a good variety of beginner and intermediate terrain throughout 33 runs and 800 vertical feet. There's lots of elbow room on the mountain's impressive 150-plus skiable acres, and its 13 lifts (including two high-speed quads) work hard to keep you on the trails and not in line.

Mountain Stats

Base Elevation: 1,250 feet
Summit Elevation: 2,050 feet
Vertical Drop: 800 feet
Primary Slope Direction: South-southwest
Average Annual Snowfall: 50 inches
Skiable Terrain: 156 acres
Slopes and Trails: 19 beginner, 8 intermediate, 6 advanced
Longest Run: 1 mile
Lifts: 2 high-speed quads, 3 triples, 7 doubles, 1 surface tow
Uphill Capacity: 18,600 skiers per hour
Night Skiing: 95% of area, nightly until 10 P.M.
Snowmaking: 100% of area

Getting There

- **From Philadelphia:** Take the N.E. Extension of the PA Turnpike to Lehigh Valley Exit 33. Follow Route 22 east to Route 33 north to I-80 west and PA Exit 45 at Tannersville. Follow signs to Camelback Resort.
- **From Delaware:** Follow I-96 north to I-476 east, and follow signs above from Philadelphia.
- **From metro NY/NJ:** Take I-80 west to PA Exit 45 at Tannersville. Follow signs to Camelback Resort.
- **From Scranton:** Take Route 380 east to I-80 east to PA Exit 45 at Tannersville. Follow signs to Camelback Resort.
- **From Washington/Baltimore:** Take I-95 north to 695 north toward Towson, then I-83 north, I-81 north, and I-80 east to PA Exit 45 at Tannersville. Follow signs to Camelback Resort.

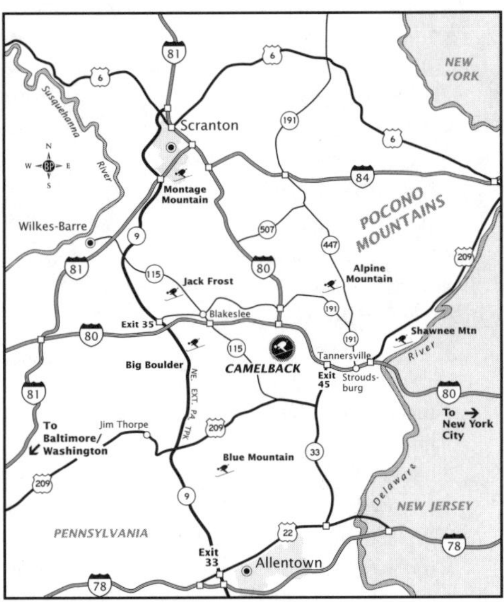

Trail Profiles

Don't look for too many big steeps here, and there aren't any tree runs to speak of. But an advanced snow rider can still manage a good time. Jump to your heart's content in one of the resort's two terrain parks. Test your time on Raceway's slalom race course, served by its own lift. Or lay tracks on the western side's four black diamonds. Sure, the stronger pitches turn tame somewhat quickly and the runs are short-lived, but you can really open it up on these wide-open, lesser-skied trails. Two trails here to note are The Asp and Marjie's

Did You Know?

Now you can squeeze more runs on your ticket by ordering it online at skicamelback.com. Your ticket will be waiting for you when you arrive. Plus, ski or ride six times and the seventh is on Camelback (ask for details).

Camelback does one remarkable job making and grooming snow for a mountain that faces south. In fact, a recent SKI *Magazine reader poll ranked Camelback #4 in the East for snow quality. New water and air pipelines help boost capacity of the snowmaking system, and new snowguns are in the works. Trail grooming will get an assist with the purchase of an additional Bombardier B-2000 vehicle. Altogether, there's 40 miles of pipe that transports water and air, 40,000 cfm compressor capacity, five groomers, and more than 1,400 snow guns. One way or another, the resort finds a way to keep its trails open and clean...all this in the face of several* El Niño *thaw-out winters!*

The resort also has an established adaptive skiing program that accommodates skiers with a wide range of physical disabilities by employing specialized equipment and teaching techniques. Call (570) 629–1661 for more information.

Delight. Extra wide and plenty fast, be sure to ride these out early in the morning before the good snow gets chewed up. On the eastern side is the reasonably pitched, seldom-skied, and longer Cliffhanger trail, which sometimes holds bumps.

Good blue-level runs include Pharoah and King Tut, both long cruisers on moderate steeps. Dromedary is an often-overlooked intermediate run you might be lucky enough to get all to yourself. Keep an eye out for it off the Marc Anthony lift and down Big Pocono Run. Scenic Nile Mile trail is Camelback's newest addition. It's extra wide at nearly 100 feet and contoured over an 18- to 22-percent pitch that's suitable for novices and intermediates. Located next to Cliffhanger, Nile Mile is also an effective means of alleviating some of the congestion of the central blue and green trails.

Green trails are wide, well groomed, and host varying pitches to help gain confidence. First-time skiers and snowboarders can use two broad areas of little gradient, each with two double chair lifts for easy access. Next, try Marc Anthony or Julius Caesar for long leisurely runs. Then hop on the Nile Mile and get a feel for upper-beginner snow riding with some good turning moments. Or, get on the Glen Lift and look for Oak Grove, Upper Moore's Ramble, and Turkey Trot. They're all located mid-mountain and isolated from more popular green trails. If you're taking a lesson, many programs are available and you'll find Camelback's instructors to be competent and friendly. Novices will enjoy Camelback's focused learning environment and variety of easier terrain.

More Fun in the Flakes

Snowtubing: Seven lanes, three tow lifts, and a new family tube lift; lights for night tubing; and its own ticket and parking areas at the base of the mountain. Look for the new underground walkway from the parking lot to the tubing area. Weekend: 8:30 A.M.–noon: $16; 8:30 A.M.–5 P.M. $19. Weekday: noon–5 P.M.: $16; noon–9 P.M.: $19; 5 P.M.–9 P.M.: $16 • **Snow blades**: day $29, night $20.

Snowboarding Highlights

Camelback didn't fool around when it created its freestyle snowboard haven. A 25,000-square foot snowboard/terrain park and halfpipe can be found on the western side's Laurel Glade trail. The 400-foot pipe gets full groom treatment from the resort's Pipe Dragon, and it operates under strong lights nightly. Look for the big gap jump at the pipe's finish.

An adjacent snowboard park is slightly less ambitious but mixes in changing hits like gaps, fun boxes, log slide, and a quarterpipe. The 800-foot park is nice and wide for big-arcing turns. What it doesn't have is a strong grade, but you can still manage good air time with enough speed. The Meadows triple lift conveniently serves the pipe, park, and a neighboring beginner run. For more jumps and hits, find your way to the new ultracross terrain park on Rhododendron Glen trail.

Snowboard Rentals: Rossignol, K2, Kemper, Avalanche; Day $29; night $20 • **Snowboard School:** Private: $55/hour; Snowboard Package (ticket, rental, and group lesson): midweek $66, weekend/holiday $74. Offered at 10:30 A.M., 2 P.M., and 6:15 P.M.

Skier Services

The sprawling resort's home base is by the gigantic clock tower. Guests will find four lodges with efficient services, numerous food venues, and comfortable aprés-ski lounges. If you need equipment, two separate rental shops just replaced their fleet with brand-new equipment. Lift ticket prices are on par with other Pocono ski areas. Look out for student rates, discount days, and incentive packages.

$ Lift Tickets

8 A.M.–5 P.M.: weekday $37, weekend $43 • 8 A.M.–12:30 P.M.: weekday $29, weekend $37 • 12:30 P.M.–5 P.M.: weekday $29, weekend $37 • 12:30 P.M.–10 P.M.: weekday $37, weekend $43 • Open–close: weekday $43, weekend $50 • 4 P.M.–10 P.M.: Monday–Thursday $24, Friday–Sunday $26 • Ages 18 and under: 12:30–10 P.M. midweek $25, weekend $29 • College Students: 12:30–10 P.M.: $30 midweek, 4 to 10 P.M.: $20 all week • kids under 46" tall in boots ski free, discounts for senior citizens • Group rates for 15 or more skiers.

New at Camelback

The mountain's entire east side now has full lighting, bring the total night trail count to 32. There's also a new Guest Welcome Center and ticket sales building that will get you on the mountain quicker than ever. Also look for a new Children's Learning Center, snowboard rental shop, and redesigned base area.

Camelback's new Business Center lets you hit the slopes and get some work done on the same day. The center sits in the main lodge and offers a workspace with full hook-up and connectivity, computer with high-speed Internet access, and fax and copy machines. Single-day access is $10, or $50 per season.

Ski Rentals

Day $23; Night $15.

Services

Ski School: 200 instructors; Private $55/hour; Advance Program Coaching Workshops: Snow Cats: $40/day, Adult Masters: $45/day; Ski School Package Lessons offered at 10:30 A.M., 2 P.M., and 6:15 P.M. and include ticket, rental, and group lesson. Midweek: $60, weekend/holiday $68; Sugar Bears program (ages 4–6): midweek: full day $70, half-day $55; weekend: full day $75, half-day $60; Ski/Boarding Bears (ages 7–12): midweek: full day $75, half-day $60; weekend: full day $80, half-day $70 • **Day Care:** Children 12 months to 4 years, offered 8 A.M.–5 P.M. on weekends only: $3/hour or $24/day • **Base Lodge Facilities/Summit Lodge area:** Ski school, rental shop, restaurants, lounges, cafeterias, pizza bar, childrens' learning center, day care, lockers • **Racing:** Weekends on Raceway trail • **Recreational Racing Class:** Adult $40/day; junior $35/day.

Room & Board

Guests can shack up in fully equipped slopeside and adjacent rental homes. The Village at Camelback has slopeside townhomes with a recreation center offering indoor tennis and swimming. Townhomes and chalets at **Northridge Station** are adjacent to Camelback, each with a fireplace. Overnighters can also choose from B&Bs and over 25 motels within 10 minutes' drive, all of which offer ski-and-stay packages.

The energy doesn't end when the sun goes down. Sip on a drink in one of Camelback's lounges and deck grills, or catch a live band on weekend afternoons and some weekdays. Or get a locally brewed beer just off mountain at **Barley Creek Brewing Company**, with live music Thursday through Sunday.

Lodging

On-site

Chalets and townhomes at Northridge Station and Village at Camelback; 1–888–345–1187, (570) 629–1661, or *camelbackrentals.com*.

Nearby Bed and Breakfasts

Brittania Country Inn, Swiftwater; (570) 839–7243 • **Holiday Glen**, Swiftwater; (570)

839–7015 • **Farmhouse B&B**, Mt. Pocono; (570) 839–0796 • **Memorytown B&B**, Mt. Pocono; (570) 839–1680 • **Mountain Manor Inn**, Marshalls Creek; 1–800–MANOR47, (570) 223–8098.

Other Nearby Lodging

Hojo Inn, Tannersville; 1–800–441–2193, (570) 629–4100 • **Hill Motor Lodge**, Tannersville; (570) 629–1667 • **Holiday Inn**, Bartonsville; 1–800–231–3321, 1–800–828–6879 (PA) • **Comfort Inn**, Bartonsville; 1–800–822–3275, (570) 476–1500 • **Countryside Cottages**, Bartonsville; (570) 629–2131 • **Knights Inn**, Bartonsville; 1–800–KNIGHTS, (570) 629–8000 • **Caesars Paradise Stream**, Mt. Pocono; 1–800–233–4141, (570) 839–8881.

Dining/Aprés-Ski

On-site

Base lodge: Two cafeterias, Deck Grill, Fireside Lounge, main lounge, pizza bar, deck grill • **Glen Lodge**: cafeteria, deck grill, lounge • **Sunbowl Complex**: cafeteria • **Cameltop**: cafeteria • **Main lodge lounge** open until 10 P.M. nightly, live music Friday–Sunday 2 P.M.–6 P.M., Saturday 3 P.M.–7 P.M.

Nearby

Barley Creek Brewing Co./Restaurant, Tannersville, one mile from mountain, six home-brews, live music Thursday–Sunday; (570) 629–9399 • **The Inn at Tannersville**, (570) 629–7056 • **Romano's Pizzeria**, at Crossings Factory Stores, Tannersville; (570) 620–2600 • **Smuggler's Cove**, Tannersville; (570) 629–2277 • **Shannon Inn & Pub**, East Stroudsburg, live Irish music; (570) 424–1951 • **Bailey's Steakhouse**, Mt. Pocono; (570) 839–9678 • **Fanucci's**, Swiftwater; (570) 839–7097 • **Ribs & More**, Bartonsville; (570) 421–7444 • **Lee's Japanese Restaurant**, Bartonsville; (570) 421–1212 • **Marco Polo's Restaurant & Lounge**, Reeders; (570) 629–6151.

(More) Things To Know

Want to get in lots of runs and not wait in line? With most of the traffic centering on the high-speed quad chairs, try the lesser-used Bailey Lift to ski the entire mountain's western side, or the Glen Lift to ski out the green and blue mid-mountain trails on the east side. You can also get a quick lunch in the tucked-away Glen Lodge and be back out on the trails in no time.

Are you a frequent Camelback skier or boarder? If so, save some money for the long term by shelling out $69 by November's end for a Camelcard. This gets you in seven nights a week at 50% off regular ticket price, 50% off day/twilight tickets Sunday through Friday, and 25% off day/twilight tickets on select Saturdays.

Bear Creek

Bear Creek Ski Area
101 Doe Mountain Lane
Macungie, PA 18062

Ski Report: 1–800–682–7107
Information: (610) 682–7100
Internet: *www.skibearcreek.com*
E-mail: skibearcreek@skibearcreek.com

Credit Cards: AE, VISA, MC, Discover

Operating Hours
9 A.M.–10 P.M. weekdays
8 A.M.–10 P.M. weekends

Season: Mid-December to late March

Backdrop

Skiing began here in the mid-1960s after several parcels of land were purchased on the low-lying plateau between Allentown and Reading. With just two slopes and a T-bar, the area would eventually grow to 15 runs and seven lifts. Ownership of Doe Mountain switched hands a few years back after years of struggle, and today the revamped ski area is known as Bear Creek. Improved snowmaking, an overhauled base lodge, and a new deck have helped turn the place around. An eight-lane snowtubing area with its own lift is based in front of the lodge. Tubing ticket sales are limited, so reserve in advance.

Bear Creek is one of the closest ski areas to Philadelphia, with its other primary markets serving Allentown, Reading, and Wilmington. While mostly a local day area, Bear does a good bit of night business as well.

Trail Profiles

An initial glimpse of the mountain and its modest 500-foot vertical won't strike a chord of fear in too many skiers. Doe sports just three short advanced trails, most notably the *Extreme*—a small but challenging mogul run with a decent pitch throughout its 2,000 feet. Otherwise, you can find some jumps on a new terrain park on Lower Grizzly.

Novices will have a hard time getting in over their heads almost anywhere on the mountain. There's a 7,400-foot, winding trail called Timberland, where you can ride at your own pace and practice turning. And there's a nice mix of wide and more-narrow beginner and

Mountain Stats

Base Elevation: 600 feet
Summit Elevation: 1,100 feet
Vertical Drop: 500 feet
Longest Run: 7,400 feet
Primary Slope Direction: North-northeast
Average Annual Snowfall: 40 inches
Slopes and Trails: 6 beginner, 6 intermediate, 3 advanced
Skiable Terrain: 90 acres
Lifts: 1 triple, 3 doubles, 2 rope tows, 1 T-bar
Uphill Capacity: 7,000 skiers per hour
Snowmaking: 100% of area
Night Skiing: 93% of area, nightly until 10 P.M.

Getting There

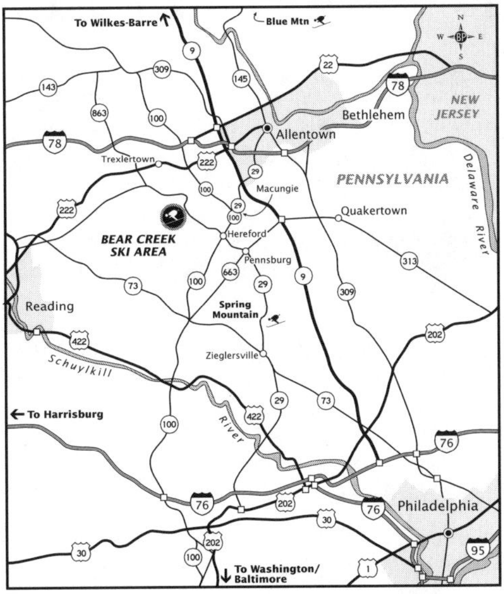

- **From Philadelphia area:** Take the N.E. Extension of the Pennsylvania Turnpike to the Quakertown exit and head right on Route 663 south to Pennsburg. At Pennsburg turn right on Route 29 north to the junction with Route 100 at Hereford. Cross Route 100, following it four miles to Doe Mountain.
- **From NY/NJ and points north:** Take I-78 west or Route 22 west to the Trexlertown exit. Follow Route 100 south to Macungie, and turn right on Church Street. Follow Church Street five miles to Doe Mountain.
- **From Baltimore, Washington, and points south:** Take I-95 to Route 202 north (Pennsylvania) to 100 north to Hereford. Turn left at the junction with Route 29 (at Turkey Hill Mini Market), and follow Route 29 for four miles to Doe Mountain.

blue runs that make for an easy transition from the bunny hills. First-time skiers have two expansive learning areas served by their own handle tow and double chair. Bear Creek's ski school is first-rate. Those just getting into skiing and snowboarding can take advantage of the resort's small class sizes and personal instruction.

Snowboarding Highlights

Riders have an exclusive snowboard park and 300-foot halfpipe on the Black Bear intermediate trail. The park hosts rail slides, fun boxes, barrels, and other hits. There's no dedicated lift here, so plan on riding the long chair or hoofing it back uphill. Snowboard competitions are centered mainly on the halfpipe, with new events held each season. For more jumps, hit the new terrain park on the other side of the mountain, served by the triple lift.

Snowboard Rentals: Weekday $24, weekend $28 • **Snowboard School:** Lessons available evenings and weekends only: $40/hour. Reservations recommended; Learn-to-Snowboard package: $55 weekend, $45 evenings (includes beginner-areas lift ticket, 1.5-hour group lesson, and rental)

More Fun in the Flakes

Snowtubing, in front of the main lodge: eoght lanes, with lift service; two-hour session $8, half-day $15, night $13. Sessions run from 9 A.M. to 5 P.M • **Snow skating**, with rentals available • **Telemark** and **cross-country skiing** permitted on slopes, no rentals.

Skier Services

Bear Creek is not a big mountain, and accordingly, you won't get gouged on prices. And while lift lines are slow, you'll get a lot of runs for your money. It's also a good place to take the kids, even if they don't ski. Look for free weekday childcare with the purchase of an adult lift ticket, or $4 an hour on weekends and holidays. Reservations are required.

Lift Tickets

Four-hour ticket: $23 weekday, $30 weekend • 8-hour ticket: $28 weekday, $37 weekend • 5 P.M.–10 P.M. $21 all week • Students ages 13–20: four hours: $20 weekday, $28 weekend; eight hours: $25 weekday, $34 weekend; night: $19 all week • Ages 6–12 and 62–69: four hours: $16 weekday, $25 weekends eight hours: $20 weekday, $27 weekend • Group rates for 15 or more skiers; daily specials, season passes available.

Ski Rentals

Four hours: $18 weekday, $20 weekend; eight hours: $21 weekday, $24 weekend; night: $17 all week • Ages 6–12: four hours: $15 weekday, $18 weekend; eight hours: $19 weekday, $22 weekend; night: $16 all week • Reduced rates for students ages 13–20.

Services

Ski School: Private $39/hour; Group $18/hour; Three-week childrens', teen, and adult programs; Learn-to-Ski package: $39 weekday, $49 weekend (includes beginner-areas lift ticket, 1.5-hour group lesson, and rental) • **Racing:** NASTAR held on Doe Run trail, Saturday and Sunday 11 A.M • **Day Care:** Offered 9 A.M.–9 P.M. in base lodge, free on weekdays.

Room & Board

There's no lodging at Bear Creek, primarily because few guests drive more than 45 minutes to get here. Skiers can base themselves in nearby Allentown and Reading in a pinch, while a handful of restaurants are located within miles of the mountain.

Lodging

Nearby

Landis Store Bed & Breakfast, Landis Store; (610) 367–0598 • **Cab Frye's Motel**, Palm; (610) 679–5955 • **Sheraton Inn Jetport**, Allentown; (610) 266–1000 • **Cloverleaf Motel**, Allentown; (610) 395–3367 • **Comfort Inn**, Allentown; (610) 391–0344 • **Comfort Suites**, Allentown; (610) 391–0344 • **Hampton Inn**, Allentown; (610) 391–1500 • **Holiday Inn**, Allentown; (610) 391–1000 • **Globe Inn**, East Greenville; (610) 679–5948.

Dining/Aprés-Ski

On-site

Cafeteria, bar & grill, with live music on some weekends.

Nearby

Buckeye Tavern, Macungie; (610) 966–4411 • **Red Lion Inn**, Macungie; (610) 845–2900 • **Italiano Delite**, Macungie; (610) 366–7166 • **Salvatore's Pizzeria**, Macungie; (610) 966–2844 • **Bally Hotel**, Bally; (610) 845–2440 • **Inn at Maple Grove**, Alburtis; (610) 682–4346 • **Olde Millside Inn**, Palm; (610) 679–9558 • **Topton House** Restaurant, Topton; (610) 682–4536.

Elk Mountain

Elk Mountain
RR3, Box 3328
Union Dale, PA 18470

Ski Report: 1–800–233–4131
Information: (570) 679–4400
Internet: *www.elkskier.com*
Email: elkskier@nep.net
Credit Cards: MC, VISA, Discover

Operating Hours: 8:30 A.M.–10 P.M. daily
Season: Early December to April

Backdrop

If you're jonesing for a dose of vertical and long runs, waste no time getting over to Elk. Its 150-plus skiable acres crushes that of most Mid-Atlantic areas, and a strong 1,000 vertical feet rides a lot bigger than the trail map indicates. There are more true black diamonds here (11) than anywhere around, and the nine blue runs are nearly as fun. By far, this is the most challenging and diverse terrain in eastern Pennsylvania. (Only western PA's Blue Knob has bigger steeps and tougher track.) Look for long, narrow runs with changing grades, awesome turns, and bountiful moguls. And because the resort is somewhat further out than other Pocono areas, you can bank on limited congestion and smaller lift lines. Don't expect fast chair rides, but do expect to lay plenty of tracks and get a lot of bang for your dollar.

If there's a drawback at Elk, it's getting from your car to the lodge. Guests have to hop on the back of a shuttle truck from the parking lot—gear in tow—and take a ride uphill to the base lodge. To get around this, make arrangements for an advance ticket or get yourself a season pass. When you arrive, just park your ride in the lot and hop on the adjacent nNorth quad or double chair to reach the summit.

Can't get out to the mountains because of your kids? No worries! Strap your gear up and bring the crew out to Elk. There are some great children's programs available, or you can use Elk's babysitting service. Child care availability is limited, so make your reservation at least 24 hours in advance. The service is offered on an hourly basis for kids at least two years of age.

You wouldn't just come here for the food, or would you? Make sure to stop for a bite at Elk's Wintergarden Restaurant. After all, Elk's food was voted #3 in the East by *SKI* Magazine.

Mountain Stats

Base Elevation: 1,693 feet
Summit Elevation: 2,693 feet
Vertical Drop: 1,000 feet
Primary Slope Direction: North
Average Annual Snowfall: 60 inches
Skiable Terrain: 150+ acres
Slopes and Trails: 6 beginner, 9 intermediate, 11 advanced
Longest Run: 1.75 miles
Lifts: 1 quad, 5 doubles
Uphill Capacity: 5,400 skiers per hour
Snowmaking: 98% of area
Night Skiing: 30% of area, nightly until 10 P.M.

Getting There

- **From Binghamton and northern New York points:** Take I-81 south to Exit 64 and follow signs for Elk Mountain.
- **From Philadelphia,** western Pennsylvania, southern New Jersey, or Delaware: Take the N.E. Extension of the PA Turnpike (Route 9) to Exit 39, then follow I-81 north. Take Exit 63 to Route 374 east toward Elk Mountain.
- **From Washington/Baltimore:** Take I-695 to I-83 north to Harrisburg. Then follow I-78 northeast for 20 miles to I-81 north. Take Exit 63 to Route 374 east toward Elk Mountain.
- **From NY City or northern NJ:** Take I-80 west to I-380 west. Follow I-380 west to I-81 north. Take Exit 63 to Route 374 east, following signs for Elk Mountain.

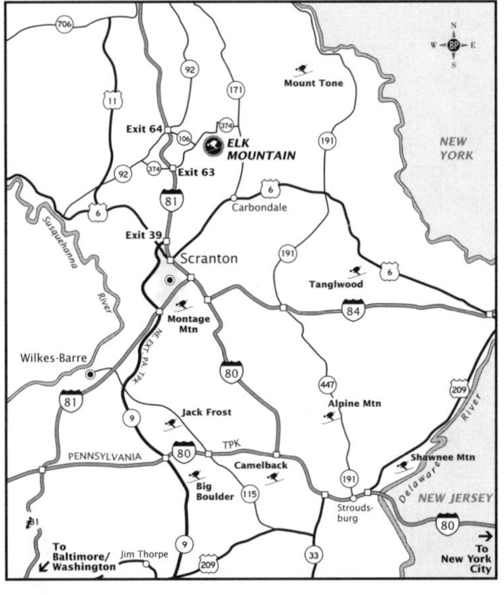

New at Elk

Already blessed with great terrain and a smart layout, Elk has focused its recent attention on improving snowmaking and grooming. A completely rebuilt snowmaking system includes on-mountain piping, a pump house and compressor building, 100-plus snowmaking guns, and a new snowmaking center. You can thank Elk personally for pumping $4 million in the right place by coming out and experiencing its exquisite terrain.

Trail Profiles

True, there's no comparison to be made with Western resorts or even New England's better ones. But where else within driving distance can you find consistent steeps, long top-to-bottom runs with no annoying intersections, and such rich diverse terrain? Advanced snow riders will love Elk's headwall drops, tight trails, bump masses, and overall tantalizing terrain on over 1,000 feet of verts.

The skier's right side holds the steepest terrain, where eight black diamonds of varying widths are lined up across the summit. Hit the steeps on *Slalom*, *Tuscarora*, and *Mohawk*. Then bang out the bumps on *Tunkhannock*. It embarks on a headwall to get you moving, levels off a bit into a nice mogul stretch, then drops off again into bigger bumps. Pick out your next line as you ride the quad lift back up *Tunkhannock*. Then make your way over to *Tecumseh* for more steep descents. And if you're lucky enough to catch Elk when it's ripe with freshies, be sure to tear up the bumps on *Seneca* and *Lackawanna*. Whatever the conditions, get to Elk as early as you can for the good snow.

Lots of blues to choose from here. Challenge yourself to the contours of *Delaware* and *Delaware Chute*. Or cruise away on *Mahican* and *Lenape* for continuous riding, and make big turns on the switchbacks on *Kickapoo*.

Though not a true beginner mountain, Elk does well in this department. Look for wide bunny slopes, solid instruction and programs, and sweet green runs with gradually increasing grades. First-timers have their own lift service on one bunny slope and another wide-open area right off the base lodge. The best novice trail for developing snow riders is *Lehigh*—a scenic 1.75-mile run with views over the mountain's western face.

Snowboarding Highlights

Traditionally a mountain committed to the definitive alpine ski experience, Elk now features a small snowboard park off beginner *West Slope* trail. There's not enough room for an array of hits here, but at least two big airs are guaranteed. On any given day, you might find moderate gaps and tabletops or a small quarterpipe. The park operates under lights until 10 P.M. nightly, with access off the Middle Chair lift.

But never mind the park. Carving-minded boarders will gladly feast on the trail network's diverse selection of runs. The mountain's east-face trails have the right sustained pitch and plenty of switchbacks for speed and big slalom turns.

Snowboard Rentals: Burton, $30/day or twilight session; $20/night; Boots only: $11 • **Snowboard School:** Ski school rates apply.

More Fun in the Flakes

Cross-country skiing at nearby Starlight Lodge *(see page 224)*, Ararat Lodge *(see Lodging)*, and two miles away on a new course behind Chet's Restaurant/Lounge • **Ice skating** two miles away at Carousel Bed & Breakfast *(see Lodging)*.

Skier Services

Day trippers make up the majority of Elk's skier base, mostly because there's no lodging on the mountain and just a scattering of night trails available (*Delaware/Delaware Chute*, black diamonds *Slalom* and *Susquehanna*, novice run *Tioga*, and a few lower-mountain beginner slopes). On the other hand, Elk is always one of the last Mid-Atlantic mountains to close each year. Season ticket holders are guaranteed at least 100 skiable days per year, and they have the luxury of instant lift access near the parking area. Expect rates to be on par with Pocono resorts, and be sure to ask for discount specials. Seniors and college students have $10 lift tickets on designated weekdays.

Lift Tickets

8:30 A.M.–4:30 P.M.: weekday $36, weekend $42 • 8:30 A.M.–12:30 P.M. or 12:30–4:30 P.M.: weekday $26, weekend $33 • 12:30 P.M.–10 P.M.: weekday $36, weekend $42 • 4:30 P.M.–10 P.M.: weekday $20, weekend $22 • 8:30 A.M.–10 P.M.: weekday $40, weekend $48 • Reduced rates for ages 6–12 and 65+ (ages 5 and under ski free).

Ski Rentals

Adult: weekend/holiday $20,Weekday $18, Night $15; children/seniors: Weekend/holiday $14, Weekday $14, Night $12 • Shaped skis: Adult: weekend/holiday $25, weekday $23, night $20; children/seniors: $20, $18, $16.

Services

Ski School: Call for current private and group rates; First-time skiers' package; SCOUTS programs for kids ages 3–5 and 4–7; Elk Mountain Rangers program for ages 7–12; Elk Mountain Cruisers program for ages 6–12, offered weekends and holidays • **Base Lodge Facilities:** Ski/rental shops, restaurants/cafeteria/lounges, day care, downstairs lockers • **Day Care:** Offered daily, reservations required • **Racing:** Junior slalom racing program for ages 8–19, offered weekends and holidays.

More Fun in the Flakes

There's no lodging directly on the mountain—a real bummer for such a great mountain that's a bit of a hike for many Mid-Atlantic skiers and boarders. There are, however, 25 motels and bed & breakfasts within 20 miles. Three quaint bed and breakfast houses lie within five miles—the Victorian-style **Carousel B&B**, **Whiffy Bog B&B**, and **The Ski Habit B&B**. Numerous country inn restaurants and taverns are also a short drive away. And antique enthusiasts can visit **Carriage Barn Antiques** in Clarks Summit (570–587–5405), or call the Top of the Endless Mountains Antique Dealers Association of Susquehanna County to find the dozen or so other antique shops surrounding Elk Mountain (1–800–769–8999).

Elk's base is clean and well organized but a bit on the small side, while the staff is down-to-earth and helpful. You'll find good home-cooked food at reasonable prices in the lodge, which sports several establishments including the highly rated **Wintergarden Restaurant**. There's not a ton of energy after hours, but the lounge is a fun place to wind down. Check out **Chet's Place** a few miles from Elk—home of the "ultimate buzz." Or make reservations at the **Crystal Lake Hotel** for a world-class meal and live piano tunes.

Lodging

Contact Elk for complete listing of nearby bed and breakfasts and motels.

Nearby

Carousel B&B, Union Dale, nine rooms w/private bath, ski discounts, on-site ice skating, rates $65–$85/night; (570) 679–2600 • **Stone Bridge Inn/Restaurant**, Union Dale, 12 rooms w/fireplace, indoor pool/hot tub, tavern overlooking Elk Mountain; (570) 679–9200 • **Oliveri's Crystal Lake Hotel**, Carbondale, restaurant/piano bar, rooms w/Jacuzzi; (570) 222–3181 • **Ramada Inn**, Clarks Summit, steak house/bar/cafe; (570) 586–2730 • **Orazzi's Blue Ridge Inn**, Carbondale, restaurant/lounge, rooms w/Jacuzzi; (570) 282–7224 • **Lodge at Newton Lake**, Carbondale, country lodging; (570) 222–3622 • **Ararat Lodge**, Thompson, restaurant/lounge, cross-country ski trails, hot tubs; (570) 727–3174 • **Holiday Inn**, 1–800–HOLIDAY • **Motel 81**, Dalton; (570) 563–1157 • **Mountain View Motel**, Clifford; (570) 222–5000.

Dining/Aprés-Ski

On-site

Two restaurants (fine dining and casual), cafeteria • **Wintergarden Lounge**, with live music Wednesdays 3 P.M.–7 P.M., weekends 3 P.M.–6 P.M., open until 11 P.M.

Nearby

Stone Bridge Inn/Restaurant, Union Dale, elegant dining, bands on some weekends, quiet atmosphere; (570) 679–9500 • **Chet's**, two miles from Elk, bar food, bands on Saturdays • **Mother Tucker's**, Union Dale; (570) 679–2980 • **Oliveri's** *(see Lodging listing)* • **The Windsor Inn**, Jermyn, reasonably priced menu and late-night tavern; (570) 876–4600 • **Mountain View Restaurant/Lounge**, Clifford, home-style cooking; (570) 222–5000.

Hidden Valley Resort

Hidden Valley Resort
4 Craighead Drive
Hidden Valley, PA 15502

Ski Report: 1–800–443–SKII
Information: (814) 443–8000
Lodging Information: 1–800–458–0175

Internet: *www.hiddenvalleyresort.com*
Credit Cards: VISA, MC, Discover

Operating Hours: 9 A.M.–10 P.M. daily
Season: December to late March

Backdrop

What began as a mom and pop restaurant and country inn back in 1949 soon became the base location for a new ski area known as Hidden Valley. A rope tow and two slopes would accommodate a growing number of skiers from Pittsburgh and surrounding areas. Washington, DC developer Kettler Brothers bought out the property in 1983, adding terrain, lifts, and the other goods to compete in the still-growing Mid-Atlantic ski market. Primarily a family and learning ski area, the resort's terrain is solidly beginner to lower intermediate, punctuated by wide, gentle cruising slopes and meticulous snowmaking and grooming.

The resort has had its problems of late, such as understaffed resources, questionable service, and the migration of some of its regulars to re-opened Laurel Mountain. But the resort is working to fix these issues and get back on track.

Trail Profiles

Not much to speak of here. The north summit has some new runs constructed from previously open terrain to serve as the resort's more advanced grounds. No steeps or variety around here, so find your way to the bumps on *Straight Shot* if you need some action. Other slightly challenging runs include *Thunderbird* and *Chabe*. If you're an advanced skier looking for a cardiovascular workout, this just might be your place. You'll have the north side practically all to yourself. If you want steeps and diverse terrain, look somewhere else.

> **Did You Know?**
>
> *One thing about Hidden Valley is certain. They know how to make snow. The resort can blanket the trails in no time at all, in the best and worst of conditions. And, without cluttered trails and big crowds, you can usually find some good snow to lay your tracks.*

The double-face mountain is manageable for novice skiers, and the trail and lift system both play out well. This is a nice place to teach kids on its wide-open, lightly pitched terrain. In fact, most of the green and some of the blue trails have an easy grade, which makes for a good transition from bunny hill to the slopes. Intermediate, extra-wide *Continental* and curvy, beginner *Mile-long* trails are the resort's most traveled runs. Count on competent instruction on two separate beginner hills, while a child care center is available for kids ages 3–5.

Getting There

- **From Pittsburgh**: Take the Pennsylvania Turnpike (I-76). At Donegal take Exit 9 onto Route 31 east for eight miles, following signs to Hidden Valley.
- **From Cleveland**: Take I-80 to the Pennsylvania Turnpike (I-76). Follow directions from Pittsburgh.
- **From Columbus**: Take I-70 east into Pennsylvania. At I-70/76 east (PA Turnpike), follow directions from Pittsburgh.
- **From points east**: Take the Pennsylvania Turnpike west to Exit 10 (Somerset). Follow Route 31 west for 10 miles to Hidden Valley.
- **From Washington/Baltimore**: Take I-695 to I-70 west (or I-270 to I-70 from Washington) into Pennsylvania. Then take the Pennsylvania Turnpike west, following directions from points east.

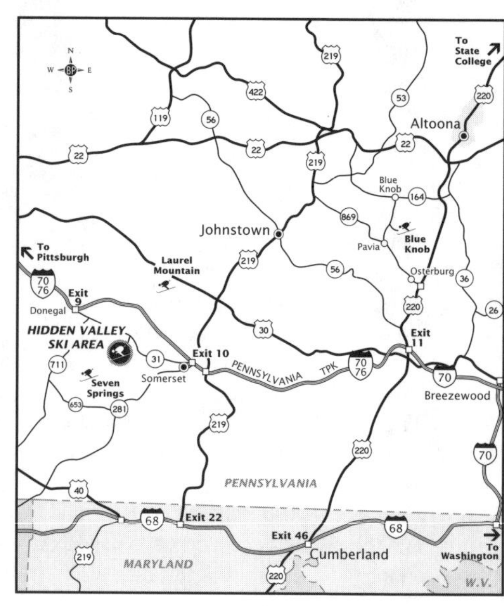

Mountain Stats

Base Elevation: 2,390 feet
Summit Elevation: 3,000 feet
Vertical Drop: 610 feet
Primary Slope Direction: North
Average Annual Snowfall: 150 inches
Skiable Terrain: 85 acres
Slopes and Trails: 10 beginner, 8 intermediate, 7 advanced
Longest Run: 1 mile
Lifts: 1 quad, 2 triples, 3 doubles, 2 handle tows
Uphill Capacity: 12,000 skiers per hour
Snowmaking: 98% of area
Night Skiing: 80% of area, nightly until 10 P.M.

More Fun in the Flakes

While snowtubing is a pretty big draw, the real gem is a 50-mile backcountry trail system atop Laurel Mountain for **cross country skiers**. The network features over 25 miles of marked, groomed trails and over 25 miles of mostly ungroomed trails through adjacent state parks. The resort also hosts **SkiFest**—a national celebration of cross-country skiing held at selected touring centers throughout the U.S.

Snowtubing, with surface tow, at the North Summit Center; call for rates; night tubing available under lights starting at 6 P.M • **Cross-country skiing**: on-site backcountry network, rentals $20/day. Nearby trails include Laurel Ridge State Park *(page 222)* and Kooser State Park *(page 236)* • **Snow Blades**: $20/session • **Snowshoeing** allowed on all trails; rentals ($20/person) offered at the North Summit Center.

Snowboarding Highlights

At the bottom of the *Jaguar* trail is a 400-foot halfpipe with 10-foot sidewalls and full snowmaking, grooming, and lights. Next door is the resort's new 600-foot snowboard park, serving up tabletops, rails, mounts and a few other variations. What snowboarders really need here is for the resort to string up a J-bar lift here. Otherwise, look for plenty of competitions, events, and racing.

Snowboard Instruction: Private $45/hour (by appointment), group $18 (11 A.M. and 2 P.M.) • **Snowboard Rentals:** $20/session.

Skier Services

Lift Tickets

9 A.M.–6 P.M.: weekday $30, weekend $40 • Noon–10 P.M.: weekday $30, weekend $40 • 4 P.M.–10 P.M.: weekday $25, weekend $30 • 9 A.M.–10 P.M.: weekday $40, weekend $55 • Ages 6–16 and 65–69: weekday $20–$24, weekend $25–$32 • Reduced rates for ages 6–12 and 65–69; under age 5: $10 • Group rates for 15 or more skiers.

Ski Rentals

$20/session, $10 ages 5 and under.

Services

Ski School: Private $45/hour, reservations required; Group $18 (10:30 A.M. and 2 P.M.); First-time skiers' package $30–$40; Mountain Munchkins childrens' program (ages 3–5), with ski instruction, play time, lunch; half day $40, full day $60; Junior Ski Program (ages 6–12) 10 A.M.–3 P.M. weekends, $50/child, rentals extra; Youth Racing Clinics (ages 6–16): $258/five consecutive days, ski/snowboard camps (ages 6–16): $195/three days, $360/six days • **Base Lodge Facilities:** Food court, restaurants, lounges, ski/rental shops, basket check, gift shop • **Day Care:** For children 18 months to 3 years of age, available 9 A.M.–6 P.M.; $5/child, additional $5 for lunch • **Adaptive Skier Program:** By appointment only • **Racing:** Sunday afternoon ski and snowboard competitions; During January, the resort hosts a special adaptive skier program and a Pennsylvania Special Olympics day.

Room & Board

On-site lodging includes town homes, single-family houses, and an inn. If you're planning a Hidden Valley vacation and don't want to stay on the mountain, the town of Somerset is 12 miles away. Numerous Victorian bed and breakfasts, chain motels, and restaurants can be found there.

Lodging

On-site (call 1–800–458–0175)

Studios and suites at **The Inn**; rates from $52–$105/person per night • One- to three-bedroom fully equipped **condos**, **town homes**, and **single-family homes** • **The Lake House**, with cheaper lodging for couples and groups.

Nearby (town of Somerset)

Bed and Breakfasts

Glades Pike Inn B&B, Route 30, six miles from resort, five rooms w/antique setting, $70–$85/night; 1–800–762–5942, (814) 443–4978 • **Bayberry Inn B&B**, 11 rooms, lounge, $40–$55/night; (814) 445–8471 • **The Inn at Georgian Place,** 11 rooms, posh setting, $95–$180/night; (814) 443–1043 • **Somerset Country Inn**, six rooms; (814) 443–1005.

Motels

Budget Inn, (814) 443–6441 • **Hampton Inn**, 1–800–HAMPTON • **Ramada Inn,** 1–800–272–6232 • **Days Inn-Somerset**, 1–800–325–2525 • Call Somerset County Chamber of Commerce for complete listing of lodging/restaurants; (814) 445–6431.

Dining/Aprés-Ski

On-site

Clock Tower Restaurant, with adjoining bar • **Slopeside Lounge** and the new slopeside **Glaciers Pub**, with live weekend entertainment • **Hearthside Restaurant** at the conference center, open year-round • **Snowshoe Lounge** and **Escapades Club**, with live entertainment • **Mountain Deli** (conference center).

Nearby

Laurel Mountain Inn, three miles from the resort, steakhouse/pub; (814) 443–2741 • **Myron's Restaurant** at Ramada Inn, Somerset, Exit 10 Pennsylvania Turnpike; (814) 443–4646 • **Cafe Fratelli,** Somerset; (814) 445–4477.

Laurel Mountain

Laurel Mountain Ski Area
P.O. Box 657
Ligonier, PA 15658

Ski Report: (877) 754–5287
Internet: *www.skilaurelmountain.com*

Operating Hours: 9 A.M.–10 P.M. daily
Season: December to late March

Backdrop

Long one of Pennsylvania's best-kept secrets, Laurel was first owned and run by the Mellon family as a private resort for the Rolling Rock Club. Laurel later opened its slopes to the public and became western Pennsylvania's first major ski area. Its heyday was during the fifties and sixties, when Pittsburgh and local-area skiers took advantage of the Laurel Highland's bountiful powder winters. Years of tough times eventually closed Laurel down in the mid-1980s, followed by a failed re-opening and numerous efforts to buy out and revitalize the ski area.

Finally, with more than 15 years gone by, the resurrected resort is back in business, and it's a sweet breath of fresh air for western Pennsylvania and Mid-Atlantic skiing. Laurel Mountain Land Company and Laurel Mountain Ski Company together made it all legal while a devoted new team of old, familiar faces put all the right pieces together. The mountain suffered through the thaws of El Niño its first season, but rebounded last year with the blessing of consistent snow and more enthusiastic skier reviews. The resort now enters the third full season of its new operation, and it looks like downhilling on this beautiful mountain is here for the long haul.

There's an impressive new summit lodge framed with glass on the back side to reveal incredible views overlooking Ligonier Valley and the ski slopes. And the resort's well-oiled operation features good snowmaking and grooming, as well as a hospitable staff and efficient services. Historic Midway Cabin (Laurel's original Rolling Rock Club ski lodge) has been renovated, serving up food and drinks on weekends. The old double chair was also restored, and a refurbished quad was trucked in practically new from another resort. Everything else has been replaced from the old resort, aside from the old warming hut at the mountain's base, where you can warm up before a roaring fireplace. There's a feeling on this mountain that lifts your spirit, and you can see it on the faces of those who ride it.

Mountain Stats

Base Elevation: 1,900 feet
Summit Elevation: 2,800 feet
Vertical Drop: 900 feet
Longest Run: 1.5 miles
Primary Slope Direction: Northwest
Slopes and Trails: 10 beginner, 6 intermediate, 3 advanced
Skiable Terrain: 64 acres
Lifts: 1 quad, 1 double, 2 handle tows
Uphill Capacity: 4,000+ skiers per hour
Average Annual Snowfall: 120 inches
Snowmaking: 80%
Night Skiing: 80% of area, nightly to 10 P.M.

Getting There

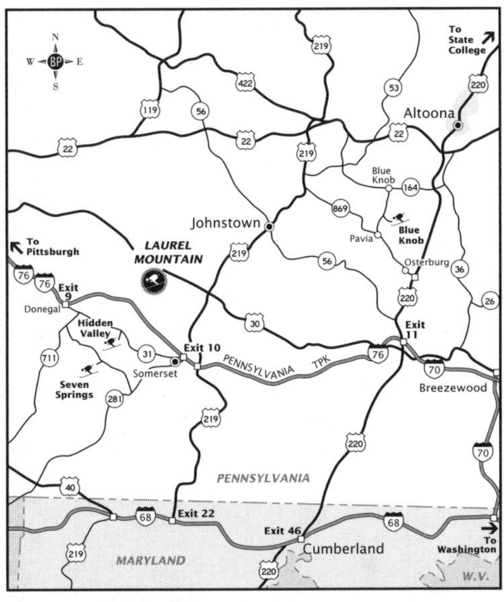

- **From Pittsburgh:** Take the PA Turnpike east to Exit 9/Donegal. Take 711 north to the Route 30 intersection in Ligonier. Turn left at the light onto Route 30 east. Follow for approximately seven miles to the top of Laurel Mountain and turn right on Summit Road, following for two miles to the ski area. **Optional Pittsburgh route:** Take the PA Turnpike to Exit 7, following Route 30 east through Greensburg, Latrobe, and Ligonier. Ski area is located just off Fort Ligonier via Route 30 east.
- **From Harrisburg and eastern PA:** Take the PA Turnpike heading west, take Exit 10/Somerset and turn left at light on Route 601 north. This turns into Route 985 north; follow to Route 30 west in Jennerstown and turn left at light on Route 30 west. Follow approximately five miles to top of Laurel Mountain and turn left at the ski resort sign onto Summit Road. Follow for two miles to the ski area.
- **From Baltimore and Washington, DC** (Coming from I-695 in Baltimore or I-270 near Washington, DC): Take I-70 west all the way to the PA Turnpike and head west on the Turnpike. Follow signs above from there.
- **From Route 30 Heading East:** Follow Route 30 east through Greensburg, Latrobe, and Ligonier. The ski area is located just off Fort Ligonier via Route 30 east.

New at Laurel

Look for new lighting on Deer Path *and* Bobcat *trails, a groomer for the halfpipe, an upgraded snowtubing park, new kids' instructional programs, and restaurant seating in the Laurel Lodge. Laurel hopes to be making snow on* Innsbrook*—an outstanding beginner trail—this season, and Midway Cabin will stay open for food, drink, and respites on weekends.*

Trail Profiles

Laurel isn't all just about green and blue runs complemented by one well-known killer black diamond. Laurel is about free-domain, freeform skiing and riding. Look around for bumps, jumps, and off-trail tracks all over the mountain. It's a good bet you'll be pleasantly surprised with the variety of terrain. The well laid-out network skies much bigger than what you'd judge from the trail map.

Double black diamond *Wildcat* holds all 900 feet of Laurel's vertical in one long, steep, continuous run peppered with bumps. You won't find many sustained steeps like this one in the Mid-Atlantic. Fly down its sharp initial descent and watch as you quickly approach the bumps. BIG bumps, that is. Test yourself here, or hug the right side for more groomed track. The moguls end as you come to an abrupt headwall that ledges out onto *Lower Wildcat*. Here you will encounter some of Pennsylvania's steepest stuff. New snowmaking and grooming provide good coverage on *Wildcat*, and it often stays clean without a lot of ice. The lone other black diamond is *Laurel Run* and its a short, steep cut parallel to *Wildcat*.

Mid-level skiers and boarders have some excellent terrain. Get your first morning tracks on *Dream Highway*—it feels like you're in a tunnel of hardwoods. It's a natural snow trail that twists and snakes on narrow terrain, with several options to cut through the trees or exit onto beginner *Snow Bowl*. Laurel's staple intermediate is Broadway—a long cruiser that serves as a great warmup run or practice trail. *Broadway* flows down to historic Midway Cabin, where you can take an energy break on weekends.

Take advantage of Laurel's excellent teaching and programs, not to mention slopes that aren't log jammed. *Tamecat* and *Ski Top* are good hills for initiates. Try *Bobcat* or *Snow Bowl* for a longer run at your own pace. Then give *Innsbrook* a shot. This is Laurel's signature beginner run, with a nice novice grade and plenty of turning over its 1.5 miles. It's natural-snow only, but holds hardpack well on this more-sheltered side of the mountain. The resort does intend to make snow on the trail soon.

Snowboarding Highlights

Find Laurel's halfpipe and terrain park by running *Tamecat* (the wide-open downhill right in front of the lodge) straight to its end. The halfpipe is pretty good if not terribly long, and it's kept in shape by a new Pipe Dragon groomer and Bombardier attachment to cut the pipe. You can also look forward to easy transport via the handle tow. Jump out of the pipe and meet the terrain park and its tabletops, a rail or two, and a few other hits. From here you have choices. You can hoof it back uphill to the handle tow, ride *Lynx* trail to access awesome steeps on *Lower Wildcat*, or carve sweet corduroy on *Lower Broadway* down to the quad lift. And if the mountain has powder, don't miss shredding down the undulating tree-lined narrows of *Dream Highway* and *Innsbruck*, each on opposite ends of the trail network's perimeter.

Snowboard Instruction: Private $35/hour (reservations suggested), 10 A.M. and 2 P.M. daily • **Rentals:** $25 daily

(More) Things To Know

Be sure to check ahead for winter conditions. The area gets 120 inches of snow per year on average, and there's always a chance of something falling from the sky. If you're coming from the east, you can take either the Pennsylvania Turnpike or hop on Route 30 west. The turnpike may or may not get you there quicker, but it does get plowed right away under snowfall. Route 30 is the more direct route to Laurel and you can save yourself the toll fee and possibly some time, but understand this drive can be perilous in bad weather. It's winding and steep as it rises in elevation, so be sure to log on to www.weather.com for Ligonier, PA. And if you do take Route 30, pray that you don't get stuck behind a big, slow rig as the route turns to one lane.

Bargain City! Lift tickets are damn cheap, and the resort is a good value any way you slice it. Team up with someone and get a private lesson from a pro for just $45 total, or grab at least one more and get a group lesson for $15 each. The resort also offers major early- and late-season price cuts (to the tune of half-price), and affordable five-week program packages during prime season.

The ski area sits within state park land, so there will never be any lodging on the slopes. But then that would just take away from Laurel's charm. Just a mile away, though, are some deals right now on lots at Laurel Mountain Village, with incredible vistas overlooking Ligonier Valley. Lots are in the mid-twenties and come sewered and watered, plus taxes are dirt low. Plans are in the works here for a full clubhouse with swimming pool, restaurant, and pub. Also up for sale are newer homes as well as some A-frames built 30 years ago when the ski area was in high gear. No rental homes are available, but in the meantime Laurel has partnered with local inns, B&Bs, and hotels with reasonable ski-and-stay packages, many of them close by in historic Ligonier.

More Fun in the Flakes

Snowtubing lanes next to the summit lodge: weekday: $9/two-hour session (4 P.M., 6 P.M., 8 P.M.); weekend/holiday: $12/two-hour session (11 A.M., 1 P.M., 3 P.M., 6 P.M., 8 P.M.). Group rates: $7/person midweek, minimum 20 persons (reservations required). Five-week group tubing pass (Monday–Friday): $30/person • **Cross country skiing** at Laurel Ridge State Park *(see page 222)* and Forbes State Forest *(see page 235)*.

Skier Services

You can also ski cheap and often by taking advantage of Laurel's discounted five-week packages, or get 20 friends together for discounted group rates.

Lift Tickets

9 A.M.–4:30 P.M.: Monday, Tuesday & Thursday: $22; Wednesday & Friday $16; weekend $32 • 1 P.M.–10 P.M.: weekday $22, weekend $32 • 4 P.M.–10 P.M.: Monday–Thursday $18, Fri.–Sat. $23, Sunday $20 • 25% discounts for ages 6–12 and 65–69.

Ski Rentals

Adult $20, ages 6–12 $15, ages 5 and under $10 • Snowblades $20.

Services

Ski School: Private $35/hour (reservations suggested), 10 A.M. and 2 P.M. daily; Mountain Kids Program ($55/skier, ages 6–12), weekends from 10 A.M.–3:30 P.M. (includes all-day instruction and games, lift ticket, lunch, unlimited drinks) • **Summit Lodge**: ticket windows, rental shop, cafeteria, downstairs pub, kids' game room, ski shop • **Aprés-ski:** Look for the Wildcat Lounge in the lodge's lower level. It's comfortable and warm with a big fireplace, and the lounge keeps a strong pulse with bands every weekend.

Room & Board

Lodging

Nearby

Bed & Breakfasts

Campbell House B&B, Ligonier: (724) 238–9812, *www.soupkid.com* • **Champion Lakes B&B**, Ligonier: (724) 238–5440, *www.pagolf.com* • **Colonial House On Main**, Ligonier: (724) 238–6804 • **Thee Olde Stagecoach B&B**, Jennerstown: (814) 629–7440, *www.oldstagecoachbandb.com* • **Quill Haven Country Inn**, Somerset: (814): 443–4514, *www.quillhaven.com*.

Inns

Ligonier Country Inn, Laughlintown: (724) 238–3651, *www.ligoniercountryinn.com* • **Lesley's Mountain View Country Inn**, Donegal: 1–800–392–7773, *www.shol.com/mtviewbb*.

Hotels

Ramada Inn, Ligonier: (724) 238–9545, *www.ramada.com* • **Hampton Inn**, Somerset: (814) 445–9161, *www.hampton-inn.com* • **Laurel Manor Motel**, Jennerstown: (814) 629–9058 • **Knights Inn**, Somerset, (814) 445–8933.

Did You Know?

Black diamond Wildcat *is one of the longest, steepest runs around. And the resort's snowmaking and grooming crew do one heck of a job keeping it clean, considering the gnarly terrain. A testament to* Wildcat's *steepness was the impossible installation of the snowmaking lines and lights. To bail the crew out, a bulldozer had to be called on to anchor a track hoe so ditches could be dug for the snow pipelines. Permanent, fixed tower guns were able to be installed, and the booms just have to be adjusted for wind conditions. Groomers take care of ultra-steep* Lower Wildcat *with Bombardier snowcats, but it's not an easy task. Snowcats need to move just a fraction of an inch before the long slide begins.*

The resort sits within nearly 500 acres of Laurel Mountain State Park, and works in harmony with the Pennsylvania Departments of Conservation and Natural Resources to keep an environmentally healthy eye on the mountain. Keeping its fingers crossed for more cold winters, Laurel expects to stay on solid ground and gradually add to its current 64 skiable acres. There are big chunks of terrain out there on the mountain, with capacity for 193 total skiable acres.

Montage Mountain

Montage Mountain
1000 Montage Mountain Road
Scranton, PA 18505

Ski Report: 1–800–GOT–SNOW
Information: (570) 969–SNOW
Internet: *www.skimontage.com*

Credit Cards: AE, MC, Discover

Operating Hours
9 A.M.–10 P.M. weekdays
8:30 A.M.–10 P.M. weekends

Season: Mid-November to late March

Backdrop

Montage opened its slopes in 1984 as a private, nonprofit corporation, run by a volunteer board of directors with hopes of building tourism in the region. Years of overwhelming maintenance costs forced the resort to switch hands in 1991 over to Lackawanna County, the securer of the ski area's debt. It made more sense at the time for the county to own and operate the resort since it serves as the broker of the region's tourism trade. The county also owns Lackawanna Stadium and its AAA affiliate Red Barons baseball team.

Not much has changed in the last decade at Montage. Aside from the addition of snowtubing, the resort still offers 21 varied runs on a smart trail layout. And while it doesn't boast the amenities of nearby Pocono areas, it doesn't get the same crowds either. That's probably because the resort sits just north of the Pocono Mountain range and is a little more of a haul for those coming from the big cities. Access to the mountain is relatively quick and easy off of Interstate 81.

Did You Know?

Montage doesn't get tons of snow but it knows just how to pump out Pocono powder. Capital investments continually go toward improving the snowmaking system. After all, that's what guests come back to ride on. Recently, the resort bolstered some of its terrain by installing 30 additional Water Sticks. The guns on the advanced North face are perpetually firing, fed by the large reservoir below it, so come prepared with the right face and head gear.

The North Face's White Lightning is Montage's signature black diamond—only 1,800 feet long but nicely steeped. It's got big nasty moguls, and the resort will often keep it bumped out so skiers and boarders don't fly at breakneck speeds. A winch cat groomer tames the bumps only when they form out of control.

Getting There

- **From NY and points north**: Take I-80 west into PA, get on I-380, and follow it to I-81 south. Take Exit 51 (Montage Mountain Road) and follow signs to Montage.
- **From eastern PA and Philadelphia area**: Take northeast extension of PA Turnpike to Exit 37 (I-81 north). Follow I-81 north to Exit 51 and follow signs to Montage.
- **From Washington/Baltimore, and points south**: Take I-695 in Baltimore to I-83 north. Follow to I-81 north to Exit 51. Follow signs to Montage.

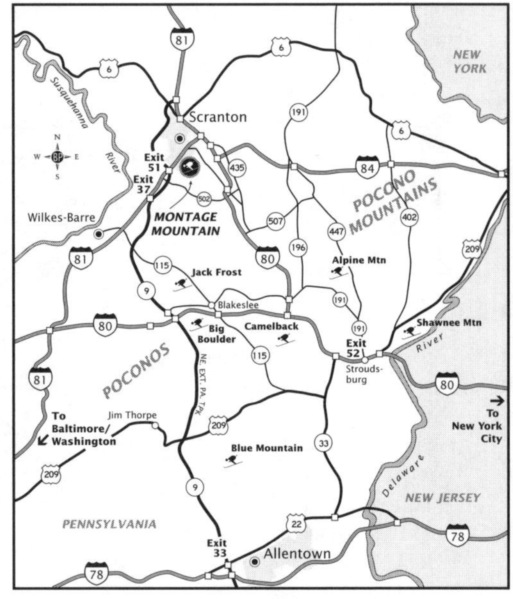

Trail Profiles

There's a good balance of terrain at Montage, with the greens, blues, and black diamonds separated for the most part to restrict intersecting traffic. The advanced North Face is usually pretty open and uncluttered, and several summit runs provide the full 1,000 feet of the mountain's vertical drop.

Get your practice run out of the way and move out to the North Face early to catch first tracks. Hit *White Lightning's* short-lived but steep double fall line and big uneven bumps, then finish strong on the lower steeps. The left side is steeper and a little more groomed but turns icy quickly, while the right side holds good snow stashes on the bumps. Hop a lift on

Mountain Stats

Base Elevation: 960 feet
Summit Elevation: 1,960 feet
Vertical Drop: 1,000 feet
Longest Run: 1.2 miles
Slopes and Trails: 8 beginner, 6 intermediate, 7 advanced
Primary Slope Direction: North to northeast
Average Annual Snowfall: 45 inches
Skiable Terrain: 140 acres
Slopes and Trails: 8 beginner, 6 intermediate, 7 advanced
Lifts: 1 quad, 3 triples, 1 double, 1 tow bars
Uphill Capacity: 8,000 skiers per hour
Night Skiing: 100% of area, nightly until 10 P.M.
Snowmaking: 100% of area

the Phoebe Snow quad and test neighboring *Boomer*. It's a little longer and a little less bumped out than *White Lightning*. Then try *Smoke*. Hop the headwall and a few bumps before closing out on the switchback. Next, move over to *Cannonball* for some jumps. You've just completed the North Face. But if there's a lean snow base, keep a lookout for debris such as loose rocks. And if the mountain gets a big dump of natural snow, make your way to the summit and *Upper Fast Track*. Here you'll find some off-trail action in the tall spruce stands by cutting right before the first headwall. Just be careful not to get your ticket stamped.

Montage's single continuous cruising run is the 1.25 miles of groomed track on *Upper/Lower Fast Track*. It's a fun trail that gets a little wider and steeper on the lower part. Other noteworthy intermediates are *Switch* and *Spike*, accessed off the Iron Horse triple chair.

Montage gets a lot of young skiers and riders, and they have a bunny area and several gentle green slopes that are completely isolated and lift-accessed. A good next step from the bunny trail is *Easy Street*. It skis on a small grade with some smooth turns through the woods. Novices can ride this to avoid the two brief, steeper drops on green circle *Highball*. A well-staffed ski school offers sound instructional programs right by the lodge.

Snowboarding Highlights

Boarders can air it out at Montage in one of the Mid-Atlantic's biggest terrain parks. The park sits in the intermediate *Upper Runway* trail and uses just about all of it for hits like gaps, spines, quarterpipes, and rail slides. The park is long and wide, with ample space between hits and plenty of runout. There's no dedicated lift serving the park, but you can use the nearby Iron Horse triple lift back up top to *Upper Runway*. Years ago, boarders had a halfpipe and park under this lift, but the grade was a little flat and the park was moved to its current location. A pipe has yet to be added to the mix.

Snowboard Rentals: Midweek $28, weekend $30, night $28 • **Snowboard School:** Five instructors: Private $35/hour; Group $15 per 1.25 hours; Learn-to-snowboard package: $60/weekend, $45/midweek (ages 7 and older, includes beginner lift ticket, rental, group lesson).

More Fun in the Flakes

Snowtubing: located near the base lodge: five lanes over 600 feet, with handle tow, and a new children's snowtubing area with three–four easy lanes. Both areas are equipped for night tubing. Available Monday–Friday 5 P.M.–10 P.M. and weekend three-hour sessions beginning at 8:30 A.M.: $12/person, $30/family • **Cross-country skiing**, conditions permitting, 30 miles away at Promise Land State Park. XC clinics are held on a nearby one-mile course, and annual five- and 10-kilometer cross-country ski races are held in February at nearby Wilkes-Barre Municipal Golf Course • **Ice skating** nearby at Lackawanna Stadium: $4 adult, $3/under age 18.

Skier Services

Rates are in line with Pocono areas, with some good discounts for kids under 15. The lodge feels the effects of old age and could stand some layout improvements, while the lift chairs are antiquated and slow. Thankfully, lift lines tend to be manageable so you can usually bank on a good day's number of runs. Look for the free ski check when its lines aren't too long.

Lift Tickets

Open.–5 P.M.: weekday $32, weekend $40 • Open–12:30 P.M.: weekday $26, weekend $31 • 12:30 P.M.–10 P.M.: weekday $32, weekend $40 • 5 P.M.–10 P.M.: weekday $21, weekend $23 • 20–25% discounts for children ages 5–15; kids under 5 ski free.

Ski Rentals

Midweek $20, weekend $22, night $17 • under age 15: $14/all times.

Services

Ski School: Private $45/hour; Group $22/1 1/4 hours (ages 11 and older) • Learn-to-ski program (ages 11 and older): $40/all times; Superkids (ages 5–10): daily at 10:30 A.M., 2 P.M., 6 P.M.: $40 or $48 with rental; includes all-day lift ticket and coaching/activities • **Base Lodge Facilities:** Food court, lounge, lockers, free ski check, accessory shop, rental center, repair shop, ski/snowboard school, guest services • **Day Care:** For children 18 months to 8 years of age, available 9 A.M.–6 P.M., $5/child, additional $5 for lunch • **Racing** NASTAR held on Switch trail weekends 10 A.M.–3 P.M. and Tuesday nights.

Room & Board

The closest lodging is one mile from the mountain, and there's no shortage of beds nearby. Over 30 hotels, motels, and inns are all close by, as well as shopping malls, movie theaters, and restaurants. The resort's cafeteria and pub run until 10 P.M. nightly, with more selective dinners and aprés-ski nearby in Scranton and Wilkes-Barre.

Lodging

Nearby

Woodlands Inn & Resort, Wilkes-Barre, 179 rooms, indoor pool, Jacuzzi, health club, restaurant, lounges with band and DJ, call for rates; 1–800–897–8991, (570) 824–9831 • **Hampton Inn/Marvelous Muggs Restaurant & Pub**, on Montage Mountain, 129 rooms, indoor pool, hot tub, excercise room, free breakfast, rates $75–$80/night; 1–800–HAMPTON; (570) 342–7002 • **Ponda-Rowland Inn** (B&B) at Rowland Farm, Dallas, PA, with two fireplace suites & rooms for families, rates $75–$95/room; 1–800–854–3286 • **Victoria Inns/Jad's Place dining, JP's Lounge**, Pittston (one mile from Montage); 1–800–937–INN5, (570) 655–1234 • **Big Bass Lake**, Gouldsboro; 1–800–762–6669, (570) 842–7600 • **Holiday Inn**, Scranton; 1–800–HOLIDAY, (570) 654–3300 • **Econo Lodge**, Scranton; 1–800–424–4777 • **Knights Inn**, Scranton; 1–800–662–4084 • **Kelley's Inn**, Gouldsboro; 1–800–432–5253.

Dining/Aprés-Ski

On-site

Cafeteria and pub open until 10 P.M.

Nearby

Arcaro & Genell's, Old Forge; (570) 457–5555 • **The Dough Company**, Wilkes-Barre; (570) 824–1003 • **The Lobster Trap**, Wilkes-Barre; (570) 825–6909 • **Tom & Jerry's**, Scranton; (570) 344–1771 • **Smith's Restaurant**, Scranton; (570) 961–9192 • **Gabello's Pizza** • Variety of bars in nearby Scranton area, notably **Tinks** and **Whistlers**; **Rascals** in Dickson City; and **Jim Dandy's** in Chinchilla.

New at Montage

A new children's snowtubing lane with three to four easy lanes will operate next door to the current tubing facility. Both areas will operate nightly under lights, and the larger, five-lane tubing area will soon be expanded to accommodate growing numbers of tubers.

Seven Springs

Seven Spring Mountain Resort
Road 1
Champion, PA 15622

Ski Report: 1–800–523–7777
Info: 1–800–452–2223, (814) 352–7777
TTY Reservations: #18143527313
Internet: *www.7Springs.com*
E-mail: skitrips@7springs.com

Credit Cards: MC, VISA, Discover

Operating Hours
9 A.M.–10 P.M. Sunday–Thursday
9 A.M.–11 P.M. Friday–Saturday

Season: December to April

Backdrop

Seven Springs started out in 1932 as a series of private vacation cabins owned by Pittsburgh merchant Adolph Dupre. An avid skier, he would capitalize on the Laurel Highland's snow-filled bounty a few years later by introducing the area's first skiing rope tow and alpine slope. Today the resort is still Dupre-owned, despite recent legal battles that divide the family over stock ownership and proposed resort expansion and development.

Nonetheless, Seven Springs continues to rank among the east coast's top ski destinations, racking up annual skier visits at nearly the same clip as West Virginia's Snowshoe. The Seven Springs lodge is a sprawling high-rise that's easily navigable in the likeness of a shopping mall, with every amenity under the sun. There's a great atmosphere here, with friendly staff, good food, and a festive nightlife. The ski-and-stay experience is definitely worth the trip. Expect wide-open slopes during the week and some congestion and lift lines on peak weekends.

Mountain Stats

Base Elevation: 2,240 feet
Summit Elevation: 2,990 feet
Vertical Drop: 750 feet
Primary Slope Direction: North- and east-facing sides
Average Annual Snowfall: 105 inches
Skiable Terrain: 275 acres
Slopes and Trails: 15 beginner, 10 intermediate, 5 advanced
Longest Run: 1.25 miles
Lifts: 3 quads, 7 triples, 2 rope tows, 2 handle tows
Uphill Capacity: 24,600 skiers per hour
Night Skiing: 75% of area, Friday–Saturday until 11 P.M., 10 P.M. midweek
Snowmaking: 95% of area

Getting There

- **From Pittsburgh:** Take the Pennsylvania Turnpike (70/76) east to Exit 9 and Route 31 east. Follow Route 31 east to Route 711 and turn right. Turn left onto County Line Road, traveling seven miles to Seven Springs entrance.
- **From Philadelphia and eastern points:** Take the Pennsylvania Turnpike (70/76) west to Exit 10 and Route 31 west. Turn left at Pioneer Park campground. Go four miles to the stop sign, turning right onto County Line Road. Five miles to the resort.
- **From Washington, DC/Baltimore:** Take I-695 (from Baltimore) to I-70, into Pennsylvania. Get on the Pennsylvania Turnpike (70/76) traveling west. Follow the directions above.

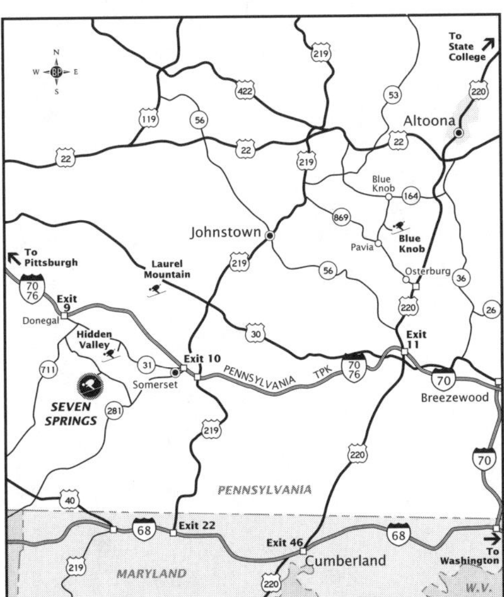

Breaking News: Big Bucks Unleashed at Seven Springs

The resort has unveiled a $230 million, four-year master plan that includes a new Bavarian village, hotel, additional terrain, a high-speed six-pack lift to replace lift #4, a high-speed quad to replace lift #7, three housing communities, an enhanced snowtubing area, and a water park. Under the plan, about $80 million will go toward the new lifts and the realigning of current ones, as well as the rebuilding of Lost Boy, Little North Face, *and* Turtleneck *trails. Additionally, on-site lodging capacity will double, while hundreds of new homes will be built in the area. It was just a year ago that the resort pumped in $6.5 million for a new Skier Services building, the new/reconfigured* Giant Boulder *trail on the North Face (see Trail Profiles), and a new electronic ski ticket system.*

Trail Profile

Seven Springs is a two-face mountain with 750 vertical feet on its more advanced North Face and 300 to 600 vertical on its short front face. The mountain lacks length but more than makes up for it in width and wide-open, big-carving terrain and some great beginner terrain. Aside from its narrow, gradual, and easily identifiable green trails, the front face is essentially an extra-broad expanse of terrain with a consistent intermediate pitch. The wide-open turf on both faces makes snowmaking and grooming a snap of the finger for the snowmaking crew. Get out on the slopes early to find the good snow with some elbow room. Also, check out weather conditions ahead of time and come prepared—the North Face can get windy and cold.

Jonesing for bumps? Find them on the front face's *Avalanche* and *Goosebumps*, but knock these out early (unless there's fresh powder) before the ice and ruts set in. Otherwise, make a beeline for the North Face and the mountain's full 750 vertical feet. There are good steeps right off the bat on 600-foot-wide *North Face Slope*, as well as *Giant Steps* and *Gunnar*, both 250 feet wide. The entire North Face runs a quick descent to a mid-shelf, followed by more steeps and a runout toward the bottom. Make fast, giant-slalom turns and let your skis or board run freeform over the terraced terrain. And when there's good snow, take a run through the trees on new glade sections like *North Face Glades* and the two glades off the #10 chair: *Turtleneck* and *Turtle Claw*. There aren't a ton of jumps on the mountain, but you can find some quick thrills off some of the cat tracks and intersecting runs between the two faces.

Without a whole lot of vertical on the front face, many of the blue runs are short but all completely wide open. From the base lodge, the face seems as broad as it is tall. The blue

Did You Know?

Seven Springs is right there at the top of the list when it comes to making and grooming snow. Way back when, the resort relied on the area's dependable natural snow, mixed in with some sparse snowmaking. Today the snowmaking system can pump more than 30,000 gallons of water per minute through 856 on-site towers that blanket 95% of its 275 skiable acres. Source water comes from the summit's Lake Tahoe, holding 100 million gallons of water. When the snowmaking system is firing—and it often is—source water gets replenished with water pumped from 64 on-site collecting ponds and lakes. In the right conditions, the resort's fleet of portable snow cannons and towers can knock out up to 54 acres of snow in just 5 hours. Snowmaking here continues to outdo itself, and you can usually count on most of the terrain open even in the midst of winter thaws.

The mountain collected a record 234 inches of natural snow during the 1995–96 ski season.

Try racing on a new NASTAR course located on intermediate Tyrol. It's $6 for two runs and just a buck more for each additional.

Yeah, it snows a lot here, so the resort paved the plaza walkways with new heated brick to free the surface of snow and ice. Also, a new skier arrival plaza allows easy dropoff and pickup. And get one-stop service at the ticket windows for tix, rentals, lessons, and kids programs.

Snowboarding Highlights

Snowboarders have it pretty good at Seven Springs: a 500-foot big-air terrain park, long connecting halfpipe, and widespread terrain. In the park are a handful of jumps with lots of runout, a tabletop, rail slide, and quarterpipe. The 400- by 50-foot halfpipe also gets high marks. It's not a deep pipe, but there's ample vertical drop and plenty of length to pull off some trickery. The pipe is groomed by a new Bombardier HPG halfpipe groomer and an attachment to help cut the pipe. There's a rope tow for the pipe, and a sound system cranks music in the park all day.

There's also wide-open turf all over the mountain to cut sweeping GS turns. Find good pitches and football-field widths on the North Face. And, look for annual snowboard events like the Mid-Atlantic Snowboard Series and the FatAir Snowboard Contest.

Snowboard Rentals: Day $29, night $19, weekend $55: **Snowboard School:** 15 instructors: Private $44/hour; Group $18/1.5 hours • **Beginner Snowboard Program:** $65 adult, $55 child.

runs on the front face have a consistent intermediate pitch but the runs don't last very long. *Sunset* is one of the longer ones, at over a half-mile and about 650 feet of vertical drop. The big news for intermediates is the excavation and reconfiguration of *Giant Steps* slope into a new run called *Giant Boulder* on the more advanced *North Face*. It's a 4,000-foot run, framed by evergreen trees, on a grade ranging from 12–25 percent. Find this new terrain between *North Face* trail and *Giant Steps*. And check out the fun, narrow cut on *Little North Face* trail.

There's plenty of gentle real estate, with easy runs on the far side of the front face and some narrow intersecting novice trails between the two faces. Kids can get initiated on a secluded ski school learning area with its own rope tow and another small section at the bottom of *Fawn Lane*, with a handle tow lift. Ride a long, easy path on 1.25-mile *Lost Boy*. It's lightly graded with some slow turning areas, and is a fantastic night run under lights and the quiet of the thick forest. *Turtleneck* also meanders leisurely through the mountain's hardwoods, with two connecting slopes to provide a longer run. The resort offers top-notch instruction and a variety of programs and activities for kids.

More Fun in the Flakes

On-site

Snowtubing, located near the end of the Main Lodge parking lot. Open daily for two-hour sessions, with 10 chutes and four handle tow bars. $12/adult, $9/ages 4–11. **Tubing** hour run from 11 A.M.–10 P.M. weekdays and 9 A.M.–10 P.M. Saturday (8 P.M. Sunday) • **Horse-drawn backcountry sleigh rides** offered daily from 10 A.M.–8 P.M.; rates: $10/person • Sledding hill.

Nearby

Cross-country skiing, weather permitting, at Hidden Valley Ski Area *(see page 55)*, Laurel Ridge State Park *(see page 222)*, and Kooser State Park *(see page 236)* • **Ice skating** and **ice fishing** 12 miles away in Somerset.

Skier Services

To its credit, the resort hasn't jacked up its rates in some time. But they are adept at finding your wallet. The resort's giant lodge houses everything from indoor pools and specialty shopping to a bowling alley and mini-golf. An efficient, spacious rental shop is on the ski lodge's lower level. You can get your skis tuned in the main level of the ski lodge, or find the ski school in the new Skier Services building on the plaza level. Child care is available here, as long as your kids are old enough to walk.

Lift Tickets

9 A.M.–7 P.M.: weekday $32, weekend $40; ages 11 and under: $25, $32 • 1 P.M.–10 P.M.: Monday–Thursday and 1 P.M.–11 P.M. Fri.–Sat.: $32, Sunday $40; ages 11 and under $25, $32 • 4:30 P.M.–10 P.M.: Sunday–Thursday $24 • 4:30 P.M.–11 P.M.: Friday–Saturday $25, ages 11 and under $18 • Friday night to Sunday special: $75; kids $55 • Children under 5 and adults 70+ ski free.

Ski Rentals

Day and twilight: adult $20, child $15 • Night: adult $16, child $12 • Full weekend: $38, $28.

Services

Ski School: Private $44/hour; Group $18/1.5 hours; Junior Ski/Ride Program (ages 7–18) offered daily, 10 A.M.–3 P.M., $75 includes ticket/instruction; Tiny Tot Ski School (ages 4–7), offered daily; $75 full day, $66 half-day; Beginner program, offered daily: $55 adult/$45 child, includes rental, group lesson, and lift ticket • **Base Lodge Facilities:** Indoor swimming and hot tubs open to overnight guests, two game rooms, miniature golf, bowling, exercise room, roller skating/rollerblading, Swedish massage, specialty and gift shops, rental and equipment shops • **Day Care:** Walking age and older; offered daily from 8:30 A.M.–4:30 P.M. and weekends, by appointment, from 6 P.M.–10 P.M.; rates: full day $45, half day $35, $25/two hours. Call x 7488.

Room & Board

No question, Seven Springs is a premiere destination ski resort. *Snow Country* and *Ski* magazines rated it one of their top 50 U.S. ski resorts for two consecutive years. On-site digs are extensive and sometimes pricey. Keep an eye out for discount packages like midweek ski-and-stay. You can stay right by the slopes in the hotel lodge, suites, chalets, and dorms, or bunk up on resort property in condos and cabins. If you want to stay off-site and save some cash, bargain lodging can be found off the turnpike in Somerset, 12 miles from Seven Springs. Between town and the resort are at least 15 B&Bs, 12 hotels/motels, and some restaurants and pubs.

There's not much just beyond the resort for aprés-ski activity, but then again there's no need to leave. The lodge's restaurants and eateries have varied menus and price ranges. The **Foggy Goggle** slopeside lounge is a favorite watering hole, and the **Tahoe Lodge** serves up sweet summit views.

Lodging

On-site

Slopeside lodging: 385 hotel rooms, 12 suites, 10 chalets, six Tyrol chalets, 10 dorms. Also, five cabins and 238 family condos on resort property, with shuttle to Main Lodge. Call 1–800–452–2223 for info • **Midweek Ski Packages**: One–five nights includes hotel lodging, lift tickets, one ski/snowboard group lesson or breakfast buffet. From $100 to $128/person, or $160–$404/person for two- to five-day packages. All rates further discounted in March • **Two-night midweek package** Sunday–Wednesday for $410, includes breakfast/dinner, taxes, resort activities • **Weekend ski package** Friday–Saturday nights includes hotel lodging, unlimited skiing, two breakfasts, free ski check and swimming. Rates from $205–$280/person, depending on month. Children under 5 stay free, ages 6–11 half price.

Condos: $450–$1,180 per two nights (up to four guests max.); cabins house six–20 people, with two-night minimum (rates from $640–$1,060).

Nearby

See Hidden Valley—Lodging, (page 55)

Aprés-ski at Seven Springs

Take it to the slopeside, newly expanded Foggy Goggle to find the post-ski crowd. Then get yourself a bite to eat and follow the sound of live tunes to the Alpine Room, on the third level of the Center Lobby. (If you're there Monday night, check out the Comedy Club.) Nightcap it at the Matterhorn in the third-floor Center Lobby, or at the Bavarian Lounge above it, where there's a happy hour from 5–7 P.M. midweek. Both shut down around 2 A.M. all week.

Dining/Aprés-Ski

On-site

Dining

Helen's Restaurant (gourmet, reservations required) • **Oak Room** and **Slopeside Grill** (buffets/traditional/seafood menu and family dining) • **Lift Line Café** (breakfast, lunch, light dinner) • **Lake Tahoe Lodge** (top of North Face trail, light meals served all day) • **Emo's Pit** (in front of lodge, serving kielbasa/hot dogs and brew) • **Rathskellar** (inside ski lodge, serving pizza, sandwiches) • **Mr. Potato** (upstairs ski lodge, cafeteria menu) • **Pizza 'n Pastry Place.**

Lounges *(see Aprés-ski sidebar)*

The Foggy Goggle • Matterhorn Lounge • Bavarian Lounge • Alpine Room.

Shawnee Mountain

12

Shawnee Mountain
P.O. Box 339
Hollow Road
Shawnee-on-Delaware, PA 18356

Ski Report: 1–800–233–4218
Information: (570) 421–7231
Internet: *www.shawneemt.com*
E-mail: ski@shawneemt.com

Credit Cards: AE, MC, VISA, Discover

Operating Hours
9 A.M.–10 P.M. Monday–Friday
8 A.M.–10 P.M. Saturday–Sunday

Season: Late November to late March

Backdrop

Since 1975 Shawnee has been a major player in the busy Pocono Mountain alpine ski scene. Situated just off the Delaware River and the New Jersey border, the ski area was originally developed as an amenity for the historic, recently renovated Shawnee Inn. With several large urban markets in under two hours' drive, Shawnee Development Co. began constructing time shares, cutting new trails, and adding more chair lifts during the 1980s. The resort's original inverted summit lodge was also replaced with a larger base-area lodge to accommodate growing numbers of day skiers. Acquired by Watershed Realty Company, Shawnee's operation was rescued through debt restructuring in 1992 by a group of local investors and longstanding Shawnee employees.

Shawnee is a good beginner and intermediate mountain, with solid SKIwee and adaptive skier programs. It also hosts the *SKI* magazine-sponsored MINIriders program, which teaches snowboarding to children ages 7–15. The resort has added snowtubing to its base area, and hosts ski events nearly each weekend. Parents have the option of dropping off their children at the base lodge's child care, offered from 9 A.M. to 5 P.M. daily. And visitors will find one of the country's largest rental shops at Shawnee, with over 4,000 sets of every kind of ski and snowboard.

Trail Profiles

The mountain is beginner to intermediate level. Trails are cut extra wide for the most part, with intersecting cat tracks off the main summit trails. Many of the runs are named for noted Native Americans who once populated the Delaware River area.

Shawnee is not the place to be for advanced snow riding. That is, unless you're a jumper. If so, head out to the challenging terrain park. The mountain is neither steep nor long, but does have one short sweet beauty in *Renegade* trail. Ride the headwall off the summit and make some turns before the runout. The rest of Shawnee's black diamonds are extensions of upper intermediate terrain and are only slightly more challenging, with the exception of *Tecumseh*. Here you can hop some bumps right underneath the double chair.

If you're a blue-level skier, get the early snow on *Delaware*. It's the longest and most varied of the intermediates, with a winding course and dog-leg finish. On the other side of the mountain is long, wide, and straight cruising on *Upper* and *Lower Bushkill*. *Kittatinny* is a baby-blue off the summit that presents a slight challenge for novices before running out past beginner *Minisink* and *Lower Pennsylvania*. If you can ride the intermediates here at Shawnee, there's a good chance you can handle the black diamonds, other than bumpy *Tecumseh*.

Shawnee's strength is its cluster of bunny terrain adjacent to the base lodge. Three secluded hills are devoted to the uninitiated skier—*Little Chief*, *Little Brave*, and the wide-open *Snowdance* slopes, with three double lifts among them. Beginners can build confidence on the wide, gentle track of *Upper* and *Lower Pennsylvania*. Remaining green runs like *Pocahontas Indian Queen*, *Meadows*, and *Minisink* are nice and wide but run through the middle of the mountain, intersecting the summit blue runs.

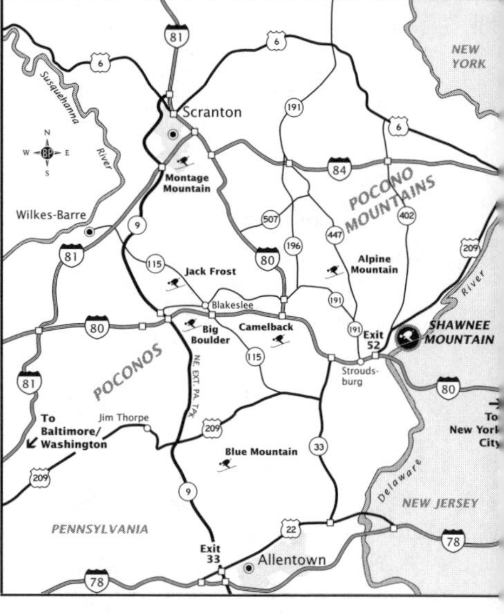

Getting There

- **From New York City and northern New Jersey**: Take I-80 west to PA Exit 52/Route 209 north. Follow signs to Shawnee.
- **From Philadelphia/Delaware**: Take the northeast extension of the PA Turnpike to Route 22 east. Exit in Allentown to Route 33 north onto I-80 east, then take PA Exit 52/Route 209 north. Follow signs to Shawnee.
- **From Washington/Baltimore**: Take I-95 north to I-695 west to I-83 to Harrisburg. Then take I-81 north to I-78 east to Route 22 east past Allentown. Exit in Allentown to Route 33 north onto I-80 east. Follow I-80 east to PA Exit 52/Route 209 north. Follow signs to Shawnee.

Mountain Stats

Base Elevation: 650 feet
Summit Elevation: 1,350 feet
Vertical Drop: 700 feet
Primary Slope Direction: North to northwest
Average Annual Snowfall: 50 inches
Skiable Terrain: 125 acres
Slopes and Trails: 7 beginner, 10 intermediate, 6 advanced
Longest Run: 5,100 feet
Lifts: 1 quad, 1 triple, 7 doubles
Uphill Capacity: 12,600 skiers per hour
Night Skiing: 95% of area, nightly until 10 P.M.
Snowmaking: 100% of area

Snowboarding Highlights

One thing Shawnee has in its favor is a good terrain park and halfpipe. It was the first Pocono resort to build a halfpipe, almost 15 years back. Located off the west summit's intermediate *Country Club* trail, the 400-foot pipe is plenty long, deep, and wide, and taken care of by a new Pipe Dragon groomer. Once the pipe opens, it's usually golden the entire season. Take a turn in the 900-foot terrain park and its variety of big hits like spines, quarter pipes, fun boxes, and table tops. There's some good air here if you want it.

The park and pipe are both lit for night boarding and are accessible directly off the Country Club double chair. The resort hosts several halfpipe and freestyle competitions. Affordable season passes are available to boarders and skiers, with additional discounts through Shawnee's Loyal Skier's Club.

Snowboard Rentals: daily $29, nightly $24 • **Snowboard School:** First-time snowboard package $60, with 1.5-hour lesson, rental, and beginner-areas lift ticket; Young Riders four-hour snowboarding program for ages 7–15: daily $45, $18 additional for rental.

More Fun in the Flakes

On-site

Snowtubing off base lodge, with six 800-foot-long chutes and two lifts. Rates: midweek $14/two hours, $22/four hours; weekend $18/two hours, $25/four hours. Sessions run from 9 A.M.–9 P.M. (5 P.M. on weekends) • **Telemark skiing** permitted on all trails.

Nearby

Cross-country skiing, sledding, and ice skating at nearby Mountain Manor Inn, (570) 223–8098, 1–800–228–4897. Weather permitting, cross-country skiing is offered on the golf course, with three trails from beginner to intermediate; $6 trail fee, $10 with rental.

Skier Services

Lift ticket rates are consistent with Pocono standards, while food and concession rates have been known to be a little high. Kids and students have discounted tickets and rentals. Other budget options include group rates, multiday and book discount tickets, Sunday night family discounts, and midweek daily specials.

Lift Tickets

Open–10 P.M.: weekday $36, weekend $41 • Under age 15: $26/all times; students ages 16–21: $32 open–close • 5 P.M.–10 P.M.: $26/all nights • Multi-day discounts available • Group rates (20–35% off) for 15 or more skiers.

Ski Rentals

Daily $24; Night $18; Ski Boards: daily $30, nightly $24.

Services

Ski School: Private $45/hour, Group $22/1.5 hours; First-time ski package, w/group lesson, rental, beginner-slopes lift ticket: $55; SKIwee (ages 6–12), Pre-SKIwee (ages 4–5), and Mountain Cruiser programs (ages 10–15): $60/daily, $45/half day ($14 additional fee for rental) • **Base and Summit Lodge Facilities:** Separate ski and snowboard shops, day care, cafeteria, food courts, pizza bar, cocktail lounges and bars • **Day Care:** 8 A.M.–5 P.M. daily: $4/hour or $22 daily • **Adaptive Ski School:** By appointment; over 500 lessons taught per season, on average.

Did You Know?

With an altitude of only 1,350 feet, winter doesn't always treat Shawnee too well. The snowmaking system is relentless though. And it's among the first Pocono ski areas to open each season, typically around the Thanksgiving holiday, when snow guns fire over the mountain early and often.

The resort is extremely active when it comes to racing and events, offering weekend NASTAR (National Standardized Racing) programs on intermediate Bushkill *trail. Both juniors and adults can also sign up for weekend training programs.*

Expect lines and long rides on the chairs as well as congestion on some weekends, since it's among the closest areas to New York and northern New Jersey. A quad has been added to help traffic on Tomahawk *trail, bringing the resort's lift capacity to 12,600 skiers per hour, and a new computerized ticket system was installed to ease the flow of incoming guests.*

Shawnee's reputable adaptive ski school, partially funded by grants and donations, has taught skiers with disabilities since 1987.

Room & Board

The Easy Bumps Saloon serves as the resort's central watering hole and post-ski site. When the nearby private chateaus, town homes, and Shawnee Inn fill to capacity, skiers can base themselves in the Stroudsburgs, Marshalls Creek, or Delaware Water Gap, which also offer numerous restaurants, pubs, and activities. Local attractions include the scenic Delaware

Water Gap National Recreation Area, 10 miles to the north, and Bushkill Falls nearby.

Lodging

On-site

65-bed ski dormitory in summit lodge, for groups only (call for rates).

Nearby

Shawnee Inn, restaurant/pub, indoor pool; call for package rates; 1–800–SHAWNEE, extension 1413 • **Shawnee Valley**, two- to three-bedroom homes/chateaus just off Shawnee Mountain, with fireplace, kitchen, whirlpool (call for rates); 1–800–SHAWNEE, extension 8970 • **Shawnee Village & Valley View**, villas, townhomes up to six and eight persons, shuttle bus service; 1–800–SHAWNEE, extension 8970 • **Budget Motel/JR's Greenscene Restaurant**; 1–800–233–8144 • **Mountain Manor Inn**, five minutes from Shawnee, country inn with two restaurants; 1–800–228–4897 • **Ramada Inn**, Delaware Water Gap, restaurant/sports bar with live weekend entertainment, indoor pool, game room, ski packages; 1–800–228–4897 • **Shannon Inn**, East Stroudsburg, restaurant/live Irish music on weekends, indoor pool; 1–800–424–8052 • **Hillside Lodge**, family lodging, dining, with fireplace/Jacuzzi rooms available; 1–800–666–4455.

Dining/Aprés-Ski

On-site

Hickory Lick's Restaurant and Bar, with lunch and light-dinner menu • **Easy Bumps Saloon**, three cocktail bars.

Nearby

Mimi's Streamside Café; (570) 424–6455 • *See Nearby Lodging above for other dining establishments.*

Ski Denton

Ski Denton
P.O. Box 367
Coudersport, Pennsylvania 16915

Ski Report/Information: (814) 435–2115
E-mail: skidenton@penn.com
Internet: *www.skidenton.com*
Credit Cards: MC, VISA, Discover

Operating Hours
10 A.M.–9 P.M. Monday, Friday
1 P.M.–9 P.M. Tuesday to Thursday
9 A.M.–9 P.M. weekends

Season: Early December to late March

Backdrop

Ski Denton resides in a remote mountain stretch of north-central Pennsylvania's snow country. Commercial skiing began here after a state study in the 1950s determined the property was a natural fit for alpine and Nordic skiing with its heavy snowfall and north-facing mountain. Beginning with just a few trails, a poma tow lift, and no snowmaking, Pennsylvania's park service ran the operation for 20 years. The state then decided the venture wasn't worth running in the red, selling off the property to a few small interest groups. After twice closing shop with no one to take the lease, locals Mike and Joyce Kneffley turned the fledgling business around and have run the mountain ever since as a private concession within Denton Hill State Park.

Trail Profiles

Make the trip here and you just might discover you've got the trails practically all to yourself. Lift lines are non-existent, even during holidays and peak weekend hours. Be sure to watch the charts because Denton gets some good snow. Powder stashes are an easy find

Mountain Stats

Base Elevation: 1,750 feet
Summit Elevation: 2,400 feet
Vertical Drop: 650 feet
Primary Slope Direction: North
Average Annual Snowfall: 100 inches
Skiable Terrain: 75 acres
Slopes and Trails: 7 beginner, 6 intermediate, 7 advanced
Longest Run: 1 mile
Lifts: 1 triple, 1 double, 2 poma lifts, 1 handle tow for tubing
Uphill Capacity: 4,200 skiers per hour
Night Skiing: 85% of area, nightly until 9 P.M.
Snowmaking: 95% of area

Getting There

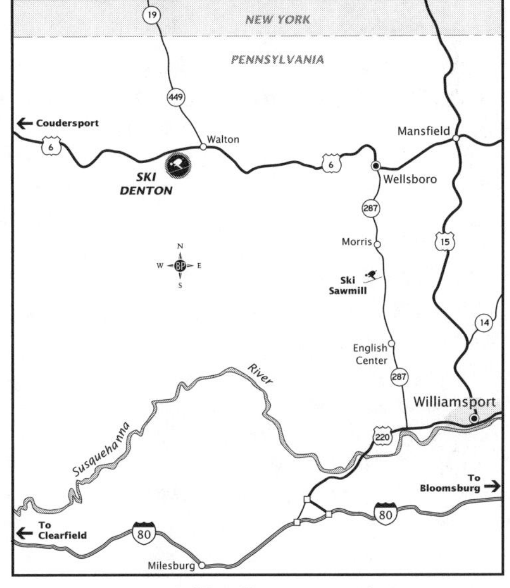

- **From points north (New York State):** Take Route 16 south to Olean, New York, then Route 417 south to Route 44 south to Route 6 east. Follow signs to Ski Denton.
- **From Cleveland and Erie:** Take U.S. 90 east to U.S. 17 east to Olean, New York. Then take Route 417 south to Route 44 south to Route 6 east. Follow signs to Ski Denton.
- **From Pittsburgh**: Take I-79 north to I-80 east to Route 66 north to Route 6 east to Coudersport. Follow signs to Ski Denton.
- **From Harrisburg**: Take U.S. 15 north to Route 6 west at Mansfield. Follow signs to Ski Denton.
- **From Washington/Baltimore**: Take I-95 north to I-695 west, then I-83 north to Harrisburg. Follow U.S. 15 north to Route 6 west at Mansfield. Follow signs to Ski Denton.

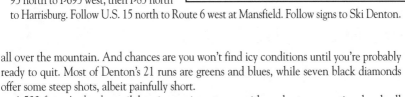

all over the mountain. And chances are you won't find icy conditions until you're probably ready to quit. Most of Denton's 21 runs are greens and blues, while seven black diamonds offer some steep shots, albeit painfully short.

1,500-foot *Avalanche* trail has impressive steeps, with a short connecting headwall known as *The Wall*. Avalanche's double fall line breaks not only straight down, but left toward the trees, which is where skiers head when they lose it. The top section of *Avalanche* is most difficult, and often quite slick, so dig in your edges and hang tight. The trail is often bumped out late in the season, and the lower two-thirds is always well groomed for fast cruising. Look next door and hop some more turns on *The Extreme*—a steep, narrow chute through the trees. Denton gets a lot of natural snow to help keep the advanced slopes running. And don't miss an opportunity to break out beyond ski boundaries to catch some air.

The Link is an advanced intermediate trail that the resort sometimes leaves ungroomed for mogul busters. When it is maintained, the trail is a comfortable, easy cruising run. Denton more consistently bumps up *Buck Run* underneath the triple chair.

Gentle slopes serving beginners and novices make up most of the mountain. Most intermediate runs can be handled by beginner skiers, who also have the option of shooting down the summit without touching the more advanced terrain, or connecting with less challenging sections of Avalanche from two locations. Two secluded green trails over one mile long wind lazily on both sides of the mountain, including the popular Sidwinder trail, which is wide enough for developing skiers to practice turning. Denton's patient ski school works out of the Snowflake bunny slope—a large, open space off the base lodge with its own poma lift.

Did You Know?

Northcentral Pennsylvania's Potter County is home to more deer than people, and Mid-Atlantic skiers are usually surprised to hear that there's a pretty good ski area here in this remote section of Allegheny wilderness. Ski Denton is tucked away amidst towering stands of maple trees in one of the state's biggest snow belts, averaging over 100 inches annually. It's a small mountain with 650 feet of vertical and 75 acres of terrain, attracting just enough of a yearly skier base to earn its keep. Visitors are comprise a mix of families, groups, and some skilled skiers who come to slide down Denton's steeper drops on fresh powder. Along with 20 runs, there's a snowboard park, tubing lanes, and virtually endless off-trail and cross-country terrain. Denton is also one of the Mid-Atlantic's friendliest ski areas, and a nice change of pace from busier east coast resorts. Look for bargain rates across the board.

While cross-country skiing isn't permitted on most trails, you can access over 100 miles of pristine state park backcountry off the summit or two miles away from the state forestry department. A $4 chair lift ride to the summit connects with a series of ridges that extends over 20 miles before circling back to the resort, where Nordic skiers can run down the beginner trail. Cross-country trails are marked with colored signs, and maps are available from the forestry department.

More Fun in the Flakes

Snowtubing: Five lanes of varying speeds, offered Saturday 2 P.M.–9 P.M. and Sunday 2 P.M.–6 P.M. (call for weekday hours); rates $5/hour; helmets required for kids under 10, with rentals available • **Cross-country skiing** throughout 100 miles of marked, ungroomed track, with trails accessible from the summit lift or two miles away at the forestry department, (814) 274–8474; no trail fee; rentals available from Denton for $13.50/day • **Sled Dog snow skate** rentals available, by the hour or two hours: $3.50–$6; resortwide access, except on Avalanche trail • **Snowblade** and **Sled Dog** rentals available.

Snowboarding Highlights

Freestylers can build their own hits in the snowboard park, where there are some sizable jumps. The park now has lights for night boarding. Beyond the park, take a tour of the whole mountain to find jumps and cat tracks just about anywhere. Also, check out Spirit of '76 and Elm Hollow trails, with natural banks on both sides.

Snowboard Rentals: $25/day; $9/two hours • **Snowboard School:** Private $30, group $12; learn-to-board package: $35 (includes four-hour lift ticket, rental, group lesson; reservations required).

Skier Services

Skiers will find all rates cheap, and downright generous, for Mid-Atlantic standards. Denton even went as far as giving lift tickets away one Christmas Eve, drawing a record crowd of 1,400 skiers. And despite its isolated location, night skiing is offered on 17 trails seven nights a week, come hell or high water, until 9 P.M. This is also a great place to pick up the sport and get personalized instruction. Staff is helpful and people are friendly. Currently, no day care is available.

Lift Tickets

Friday–Sunday: 9 A.M.–5 P.M.: adult $30, ages 6–11 $20 • 1 P.M.–5 P.M.: $24, $16 • 1 P.M.–9 P.M.: $30, $20 • 5 P.M.–9 P.M.: $24, $16 • 9 A.M.–9 P.M.: $32, $22 • Monday 10 A.M.–9 P.M. and Tuesday–Thursday 1 P.M.–9P.M • 10 A.M.–5 P.M.: adult $20, ages 6–11 $2014 • 1 P.M.–5 P.M.: $15, $12 • 1 P.M.–9 P.M.: $20, $14 • 5 P.M.–9 P.M.: $15, $12 • 10 A.M.–9 P.M.: $22, $17 • Two-day lift ticket $55, 3-day $75 • Ages 5 and under: $3.

Ski Rentals

Adult $16/day, $10/night, ages 6–11 $13.50/day, $10/night • parabolic skis $20 • Snowblades $9/hour, $25/eight hours • Sled Dogs $3.75/hour, $6.50/two hours.

Services

Ski School: Private $30/hour; Group $12/hour; SKIwee $28/three hours; Learn-to-ski program $35 (includes eight-hour lift ticket, rental, group lesson; reservations required) • **Base Lodge Facilities:** Cafeteria, ski school, rental shop, ski shop, bunkhouse lodging • **Day Care:** None • **Adaptive Ski School:** By appointment only.

New at Denton

A new snowtubing facility, dubbed the Tubeslide, offers five lanes ranging from a slow beginner to fast, bumpy chutes. Tubing hours begin at 2 P.M. on weekends, with weekday hours by reservation. Lighting has been added to the snowboard park.

Room & Board

Five cabin chalets are available on Denton's grounds, as well as group bunk lodging on the third floor of the small base lodge. Guests can also plan an economical and comfortable overnight stay in a number of bed and breakfasts or motels within 20 miles, with modest rates ranging from $25 to $45 per night.

Lodging

On-site

Five fully equipped two-bedroom **cabin chalets** (up to six persons) at the foot of the mountain, with ski-in, ski-out access, living/dining rooms, kitchen • **Bunkhouse** quarters in third floor of base lodge for large groups (up to 70 persons); weekend package: $75/person, includes two breakfasts, one dinner, weekend lodging and skiing.

Nearby

Bed & Breakfasts:

Handwerk House B&B, (814) 435–8827 • **The Poet's Walk B&B**, Port Allegheny, with/four doubles, one single; 1–800–646–5731/1068 • **Kaltenbach's B&B**, Wellsboro, with hot tub and Jacuzzis; 1–800–722–4954 • **Blackberry Inn B&B**, Smethport, 45 minutes from Denton; (814) 887–7777.

Motels/inns/Rental homes:

Pine Log Motel & Cabin Run, Galeton, one mile from Denton; (814) 435–6400 • **Potato City Motor Inn**, near Denton, fine dining restaurant/pub; 1–800–867–7133 • **Antlers' Inn**, restaurant, ski packages; (814) 435–6300 • **Evergreen Lodge** (cabin rentals), Coudersport, two miles from Denton; (814) 435–6395 • **Westgate Inn**, Coudersport, restaurant; (814) 274–0400 • **Coach Stop Inn**, Wellsboro, fine dining restaurant/lounge; 1–800–829–4130 • **Penn Wells Hotel**, Wellsboro, restaurant, indoor pool; 1–800–545–2446 • **Comfort Inn**, Mansfield, restaurant/lounge, Jacuzzi rooms, ski packages; 1–800–822–5470 • **Susque Homestead & Chalet**, Ulysses, PA, fireplaces; (814) 435–2966.

Dining/Aprés-Ski

On-site

Cafeteria

Nearby (Coudersport)

Mosch's Tavern & Country Inn; (814) 274–9932 • **Laurelwood Inn**; (814) 274–9220 • **Sweden Valley Inn**; (814) 274–7057 • **The Original Italian Pizza**; (814) 274–0455 • *See Lodging above for more dining establishments.*

Ski Liberty

14

Ski Liberty
P.O. Box SKI
Carroll Valley, PA 17320-0703

Ski Report: (717) 642–9000
Information: (717) 642–8282
Internet: *www.skiliberty.com*
E-mail: skiliberty@skiliberty.com
Credit Cards: VISA, MC, Discover

Operating Hours
9 A.M.–10 P.M. weekdays
8 A.M.–10 P.M. weekends

Season: Late November to mid-March

Backdrop

Just north of the Maryland border in Caroll Valley lies Pennsylvania's Ski Liberty—one of Baltimore and Washington, DC's closest alpine destinations. The resort was acquired in 1972 when it was known as Charnita Ski Area, re-opening in 1974 as Ski Liberty. The same conglomerate that claims nearby Ski Roundtop and New York's Ski Windham also owns Liberty.

New at Liberty

A new quad chair will replace the two painfully slow doubles on the front side. It's not a high-speed quad but will get you uphill a little faster. Ten new snow cannons were installed and a new line of rental equipment will be available. All the rooms in Liberty's slopeside hotel are refurbished.

It's a mountain of limited terrain, with just 17 slopes and trails and a little over 600 feet of vertical. Liberty's strength is its two mountain faces, which effectively separate skier traffic by ability. The back side holds some extremely steep pitches directly off the summit, while good novice terrain makes up the majority of the busier front face. Liberty is one of the few remaining Mid-Atlantic mountains not to offer snowtubing, probably because sister area Roundtop has that option covered.

Getting There

- **From Baltimore:** Take I-695 to I-795 north to Route 140 west (Route 140 west becomes Route 16 west at the Pennsylvania line). Follow Route 16 west and turn right on Route 116 east for three miles. Liberty is on the right.
- **From Washington, DC and Northern Virginia:** Take I-495 north to I-270 north to Frederick, MD. Then follow Route 15 north to Emmitsburg, PA. Exit onto South Seton Avenue, following South Seton to the traffic light. Turn left onto Route 140 west (becoming Route 16 west at the Pennsylvania line). Take Route 16 west to Route 116 east and turn right. Follow this for three miles to Liberty on the right.
- **From York, Pennsylvania:** Follow Route 30 west to the square in Gettysburg. Take the three-quarter turn on Baltimore Street. Travel one block and turn right at the stop light onto Route 116 west (Middle Street). Follow this for 10 miles to Liberty on the left side.

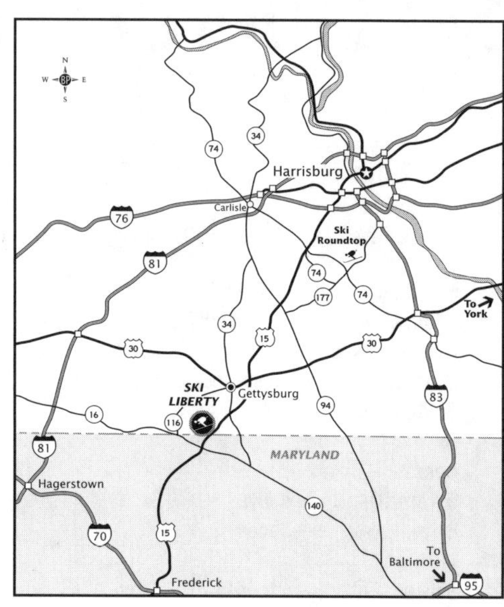

Trail Profiles

Skiers offer many different opinions of Liberty's trail system, but there's no question that the back side is quite steep—and painfully short lived. Black diamonds *Ultra*, *Eastwind*, and *Strata* each drop sharply off the summit before flowing into more intermediate track at the trails' midway points. Liberty's most challenging trail is the big bumps of *Eastwind*. Look for moguls on the steeps, a groomed transition area, then more bumps on the follow-through. More bumps can be found in a new chiseled mogul park, next to the terrain park and half-pipe. *Upper Ultra* is super steep off its headwall. Check it out to see if it's bumped or groomed. Knock out the back side early before the ice comes.

Good snow can be found on less-traveled front-side runs like *White Lightning* and *Blue Streak*. Both are better-kept secrets, especially when the mountain gets clogged. *White Lightning* starts easy, then elbows into a 90-degree elbow turn to the left before running out into the flats.

Mountain Stats

Base Elevation: 580 feet
Summit Elevation: 1,186 feet
Vertical Drop: 606 feet
Primary Slope Direction: Northeast-northwest
Average Annual Snowfall: 28 inches
Skiable Terrain: 100 acres
Slopes and Trails: 6 beginner, 6 intermediate,4 advanced
Longest Run: 5,200 feet
Lifts: 3 quads, 3 doubles, 1 J-bar, 1 handle tow
Uphill Capacity: 10,920 skiers per hour
Night Skiing: 100% of area, nightly until 10 P.M.
Snowmaking: 100% of area

Liberty's best intermediate is the *Heavenly*. It has a steep drop that breaks into a fast-carving turn before barreling out into extra-wide groomed cruising track. *Whitney's Way* is a great blue trail to find your speed and turns. Not quite ready to test the back-side black diamonds? Hop on baby-blue *Sidewinder*, next to *Upper Strata*, to get a feel for this part of the mountain and an easier route down the back side.

There's a good flow of runs for beginner skiers and boarders at Liberty, with a substantial learning zone called *First Class Area*. Liberty facilitated the area by stringing up two lifts: a quad chair lift and mid-station handle tow. Next stop—*Sneaky Pete/Nova*. There's just a little more grade here on a more narrow course. Then ride to the summit and hop on *Dipsy Doodle*. This is a good longer beginner run with just a couple of drops to practice your turns and stops. Or branch off on *Don't Worry* for slow riding.

Snowboarding Highlights

Liberty sports both a snowboard-only park and halfpipe on the far-right end of the mountain's main lodge side. In years past, you could crank on tabeltops, spines, a quarterpipe, and some other hits, but recently the resort hasn't done much with the park. Last season, there were just one big gap jump and two small kickers that were easily overshot if you had some speed going. It might be that the resort would rather keep it more of a beginner's park, and let fellow areas Roundtop and Whitetail hold the bulk of the big jumps. Liberty does expect to shape up the park this season, and in the meantime there's a specially formed mogul field right next to the park and pipe that busts out the bumps.

Adjacent to the park is Liberty's halfpipe. It's also a bit on the small side at just about 200 feet, but serves as a good foundation for getting the feel and practicing maneuvers. Availability is also a question mark. Get out to Roundtop if you want better action in the pipe. Liberty does have a good Scorpion machine to groom the walls and transitions, and a convenient J-bar lift serving both areas. There's also a good sound system and lights that run till 10 P.M. nightly. Look for halfpipe and Boardercross competitive series throughout the coming season. If you're trying boarding for the first time or just want to test a new one, take a look at Liberty's Boarderline Snowboard Shop and its huge rental fleet. Capable instructional programs are available at the ski school.

Snowboard Rentals: All week: $29/four hours, $34/eight hours • **Snowboard School:** (call for rates or check *www.skiliberty.com*)

Skier Services

Tickets and equipment rentals don't come cheap here. If you think you'll wind up packing your gear for Liberty more than six or seven times a season, consider purchasing the Ski Advantage Card. The $69 season-long pass allows 40 percent off all lift tickets and 25 percent off NASTAR racing at Liberty, Roundtop, and New York's Ski Windham. Skiers and snowboarders can also return their lift tickets within one hour of purchase if not completely satisfied, with a guaranteed return-trip voucher.

Liberty's flex ticket system offers four- and eight-hour blocks from time of purchase, which helps reduce lift lines and bottlenecks at peak hours. The flex system is a necessary function on weekends. Lift ticket sales are limited, though, to curb lengthy lift lines and overburdened slopes.

The resort is constantly upgrading both its terrain and services, and it must do so to accommodate the constant flow of its guests. The remodeled base lodge area is now a sprawling series of connected buildings, with several food venues to choose from, a restaurant/tavern, separate children's learning center and rental shop, and the adjoining 40-room hotel.

Lift Tickets

Weekend: $39/four hours, $43/eight hours, $28/night (5 P.M.–10 P.M.); Weekday: $31, $36, $28 • $4 discount for ages 6–10 • 50% off for ages 65+ midweek only • 40% ticket discounts with Ski Advantage Card ($69/person).

Ski Rentals

Weekday and weekend: $25/four hours, $29/eight hours, $26/night.

Services

Ski School: Call for current rates (Lessons held daily at 10 A.M., noon, 2 P.M., 7 P.M.); Childrens' Learning Center; Ski Camp offered daily for ages 4–10, reservations required (call for rates); Limited and all-mountain ski or snowboard learning packages • **Base Lodge Facilities:** lockers/basket check, lost and found, snowboard shop, rental/repair shops, cafeteria/restaurant/tavern/food courts, hotel, day care • **Day Care**: Ages 1–10; $5/hour; Offered Monday–Thursday 9 A.M.–5 P.M., Friday 9 A.M.–9:30 P.M., weekends/holidays 8 A.M.–9:30 P.M • **Adaptive Ski School**: By appointment only.

Room & Board

Most Liberty guests are in and out the same day. Otherwise, there's a 40-room base-side hotel and the nearby private Carroll Valley Resort Hotel. Check out the town of Emmitsburg and Mount Saint Mary's College, or stay overnight in Gettysburg. It's an easy 10-mile drive from Liberty, with a selection of B&Bs in the heart of its downtown area, several motels, restaurants/taverns, and Civil War museums and guides.

Lodging

On-site

40-room **slopeside hotel**, $79–$89/night, $139/luxury suite; (717) 642–8282 • **Carroll Valley Resort Hotel**; 1–800–548–8504.

Nearby

Bed & Breakfasts

Maplewood Inn B&B, Fairfield, three miles from Liberty; (717) 642–6290 • **The Windborne Farm B&B**, Fairfield; (717) 642–5436 • **Old Appleford Inn**, downtown Gettysburg, 10 miles from Liberty; 1–800–275–3373 • **The Tannery B&B**, downtown Gettysburg; (717) 334–2454 • **The Herr Tavern B&B/Restaurant**, Gettysburg; 1–800–362–9849 • **The Brickhouse Inn B&B**, downtown Gettysburg; 1–800–864–3464 • **Farnsworth House B&B/Restaurant**, Gettysburg; (717) 334–8838.

Gettysburg motels

Holiday Inn; 1–800–HOLIDAY • **Days Inn**; 1–800–325–2525 • **Hampton Inn**; 1–800–426–7866 • **Larson's Quality Inn**; 1–800–228–5151.

Dining/Aprés-Ski

On-site

Food court, pizza/pasta shop, deck with barbecue/entertainment • **Ski Liberty Tavern/Restaurant**, 11 A.M.–1 A.M. weekends, occasional live entertainment.

Nearby (Emmitsburg)

The Ott House

Gettysburg

Gettysburg Hotel/Restaurant, historic mansion, circa 1797, fine dining; (717) 337–2000 • **Dobbin House**, historic restaurant/bar, downtown; (717) 334–2100 • **The Pub**, popular Gettysburg tavern; (717) 334–7100 • **Cashtown Inn**, Cashtown; (717) 334–9722.

Did You Know?

An efficient Flex Ticket system gives you the flexibility to pick up four- or eight-hour tickets at your own time. It also helps filter skier traffic throughout the day.

On weekends, the front-side lifts are slow and busy, and routinely stop mid-transport. You can get a lot of runs for your money on the back side, though, and there's a long green trail in addition to the diamonds and blues.

Everything lights up at night, which makes for a good midweek late workout. Expect no more than a few hundred others out on the slopes during the week (excluding holidays).

Be prepared for lines and a lengthy rental process if you need equipment. Pay for your lift ticket and rentals in one area, then head to the rental building to pick them up.

Look for the free ski check right in front of the lodge when you need to step indoors. Lines can be a nightmare, though, so use your best judgement.

Liberty's base lodge facilities are pretty spacious and well laid out for the most part. There's good food upstairs in the cafeteria, separate pizza room, and a restaurant and lounge downstairs. Take a break or eat your lunch on the slopeside outdoor deck and grill if it's a nice day.

Snow blowers often have to work around the clock to keep the trails open, so it's a good idea to pack away the goggles just in case. You never know when you'll be subject to virtual manmade blizzards.

Lean winters, low altitude, and sun exposure force Liberty into running a top-notch snowmaking and grooming operation. Trails are smoothly packed and groomed, but often succumb to icy conditions come afternoon. Like other areas, Liberty's snowmakers have to dig and groom the snow into a hard, granular, blended pack—courtesy of the late-night freeze and resulting ice.

White Lightning and neighboring Blue Streak trails are coined after the mountain's once-densely wooded summit, which served as the site of a lucrative moonshine distillery.

Ski Roundtop

Ski Roundtop
925 Roundtop Road
Lewisberry, PA 17339

Ski Report: (717) 432-7000
Information: (717) 432-9631
Internet: *www.skiroundtop.com*
E-mail: skiroundtop@skiroundtop.com

Credit Cards: VISA, MC, Discover

Operating Hours
Weekdays 9 A.M.–10 P.M.
Weekends 8 A.M.–10 P.M.

Season: Late November to late March

Backdrop

Roundtop was originally the brainchild of a group of ski-minded businessmen from the nearby town of York. For years they would make the long trek to carve Vermont's formidable mountains. Hoping to establish a resort on one of the small plateaus in their own neck of the woods, the group knew they'd have to overcome the area's often-mild winters. The resort could only operate with an advanced snowmaking system and a north-facing mountain. What they had going for them was demographics, with Baltimore just 75 miles away and Harrisburg, Lancaster, and York all within spitting distance. Since opening in 1964 with just two slopes and a single chair lift, Roundtop has expanded to 15 runs and employs a powerful snowmaking system, and now has a family snowtubing area and a snowboard halfpipe. The same group that opened Roundtop's slopes now claim Whitetail, New York's Ski Windham, and nearby Ski Liberty, all under the name Snow Time, Inc.

Trail Profiles

No, 600 feet of vertical is not going to wet the appetite of advanced snow riders. But you can get a half- or full-day's good runs in with some degree of challenge. The top part of *Lafayette's Leap* is a lot of fun, and *Barret's Trail* is a blast when the resort can open it up. *Ramrod* and *Gunbarrel* are both plenty steep, and bumps can usually be found on *Gunbarrel's* lower stretch. Be sure to check out the ominous cliff rock next to it as you ride the chair up.

Minuteman is by far the most heavily traveled of the intermediates. It's extra wide and textbook groomed, and great for perfecting turns or running your skis fast and straight. *Exhibition* and *Recruit* are nice and wide cruisers, while *Susquehanna* throws in some switchback turns.

Beginner slopes are substantial at Roundtop, and four of its 10 lifts serve the cluster of green runs. The Discovery area and Izzy Bear Children's Learning Area are flat parcels off the main lodge exclusively for first-timers and instruction. *Fanny Hill* and *Powderhorn* are both easy, short green runs. But one thing Roundtop doesn't have is a long, slow cruising trail from the summit. If you're not ready to test the blue squares but are bored with the other greens, try *Fife and Drum*. It's got a bigger pitch and is a little more narrow.

Mountain Stats

Base Elevation: 755 feet
Summit Elevation: 1,355 feet
Vertical Drop: 600 feet
Primary Slope Direction: North
Average Annual Snowfall: 35 inches
Skiable Terrain: 100 acres
Slopes and Trails: 6 beginner, 5 intermediate, 4 advanced
Longest Run: 4,100 feet
Lifts: 2 quads, 1 triple, 2 doubles, 2 j-bars, 2 tow lifts, 1 carpet lift
Uphill Capacity: 11,200 skiers per hour
Night Skiing: 93% of area, nightly until 10 P.M.
Snowmaking: 100% of area

Getting There

- **From Harrisburg:** Take I-83 south to Exit 15. Turn left on Route 177 then right on Pinetown Road. Turn left on Moore's Mountain Road, then right on Roundtop Road.
- **From Baltimore:** Take I-83 North to Exit 13. Turn left on Route 177 then right on Pinetown Road. Turn left on Moore's Mountain Road, then right on Roundtop Road.
- **From Washington, DC and points south:** Take I-95 to 495 north, then I-270 to Route 15 North. Turn right at the first traffic light in Pennsylvania, then right on Old York Road. Turn left at the next light onto Route 177, left on Pinetown Road, then left on Roundtop Road.

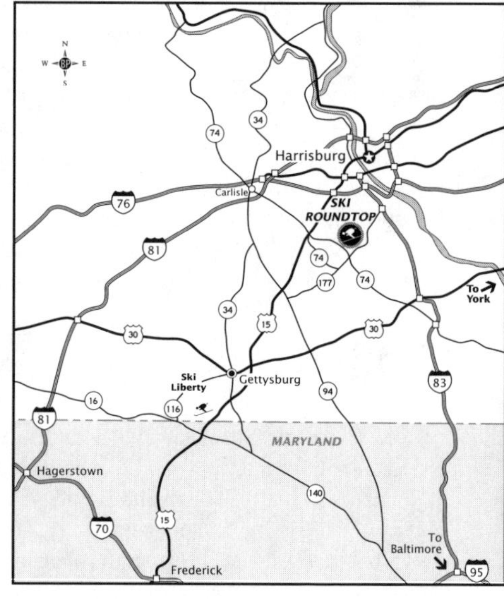

Snowboarding Highlights

Roundtop has a halfpipe that sits in its own area in front of the main lodge. It's nearly 300 x 40 feet, and also has its own J-bar lift and full lighting. The resort has a Scorpion groomer it shares with Ski Liberty, but recent seasons have found the pipe to be closed a little more than area borders would like. If maintained well, the pipe is clearly one of the better ones around.

There's not much of a snowboard park on the mountain anymore. The tabletops, gaps, and ramps that used to make up the space between *Minuteman* and *Lafayette's Leap* are all gone. Check with the resort to see what its plans are for a new terrain park.

Snowboard Rentals: All week: $29/4 hours, $34/8 hours • **Snowboard School:** call for current rates or see *www.skiroundtop.com.*

More Fun in the Flakes

Snowtubing: Five lanes, offered weekdays 4 P.M.–9 P.M., weekends 10 A.M.–9 P.M.; $7/hour.

Skier Services

While rates are on the pricey side, the resort has a friendly staff and an efficient operation. If renting, consider getting your gear off-mountain to save time on your ticket. Lifts are slow, but don't expect lines to be too long. The resort offers a supervised day care facility for children 18 months and older, and runs a limited adaptive ski school program with three-track skiing and instruction available.

Lift Tickets

Weekend: $39/four hours, $43/eight hours, $28/night (5 P.M.–10 P.M.); Weekday: $31, $36, $28 • $4 discount for ages 6–10 • 50% off for ages 65+ midweek only • 40% ticket discounts with Ski Advantage Card ($69/person).

Ski Rentals

Weekday and weekend: $25/four hours, $29/eight hours, $26/night.

Services

Ski School: Call for current rates (Lessons held daily at 10 A.M., noon, 2 P.M., 7 P.M.); Learn-to-ski/snowboard packages • **Base Lodge Facilities:** Main lodge/food court, out-

Did You Know?

Roundtop does one good job making snow, often in the face of temperate conditions. Bring your goggles in case the snow is blowing while you're there.

Roundtop's flex ticket system offers four- to eight-hour blocks from time of purchase. You still have to ante up a big chunk of change, but it provides some added flexibility.

Aprés-ski doesn't apply at Roundtop. There's no chance of sipping on a cold one after a session on the slopes. As is the case with nearby Whitetail Ski Resort, Roundtop makes its home in one of Pennsylvania's dry townships.

door barbecue, ski shop, ski school, tickets/rentals, lockers • **Day Care**: Ages 1–10; $5/hour; Offered Monday–Thursday 9 A.M.–5 P.M., Friday 9 A.M.–9:30 P.M., weekends/holidays 8 A.M.–9:30 P.M • **Racing**: NASTAR held on the intermediate Exhibition trail Fridays 6:30 P.M.–9 P.M., weekends 11 A.M.–3 P.M • **Adaptive Ski School**: By appointment only.

Room & Board

Few Roundtop guests drive very far to get here, so there's no need for lodging on the mountain. For a change of pace, a few bed and breakfasts are short drives away in the towns of Wellsville and Mechanicsburg—a large suburb of Harrisburg, which also has several chain motels.

Lodging

Nearby

Bed & Breakfasts

Warrington Farm B&B, Wellsville, five miles from Roundtop; (717) 432–9053 • **Moore's Mountain Inn B&B**, Mechanicsburg (six miles), restored brownstone tavern, circa 1798, three rooms, private bath, $75/night; (717) 766–3412.

Motels

Hampton Inn, Mechanicsburg (10 miles); 1–800–HAMPTON • **Super 8 Motel**, Etters (seven miles); (717) 938–6200 • **Fairfield Inn**, New Cumberland (14 miles); 1–800–228–2800 • **Sheraton Inn**, Harrisburg (20 miles); 1–800–644–3144.

Dining/Aprés-Ski

On-site

Food court, outdoor barbecue.

Nearby

Lewisberry

Silver Lake Inn; (717) 938–4894 • **BC's Family Restaurant**; (717) 938–9208 • **Allen's Eatery**; (717) 938–4702.

Mechanicsburg

Ale House (Ye Old); (717) 763–8929 • **Bert Brothers Family Restaurant**; (717) 697–6591.

Whitetail

16

Whitetail
13805 Blairs Valley Road
Mercersburg, PA 17236

Ski Report: (717) 328–5300
Information: (717) 328–9400
E-mail: skiwhitetail@skiwhitetail.com
Internet: *www.skiwhitetail.com*
Credit Cards: AE, MC, VISA

Operating Hours: 8:30 A.M.–10 P.M. daily

Season: December to late March

Backdrop

"Ten years in planning, ten months to build" is the phrase used by Whitetail management when referring to the resort's creation. Just a decade old, it's one of the region's sleekest operations. Situated 1,800 feet high on Two Top Mountain in south-central Pennsylvania's Tuscarora Mountain range, Whitetail has served as a necessary alternative to the busy Washington, DC, and Baltimore ski scenes. Despite the mountain's southern-exposed slopes and infrequent snowfall, the privately owned land was developed into a ski resort with two factors in its favor: 900-plus feet of vertical drop and proximity to two very profitable urban markets.

The ski area changed hands a few years back to Snow Time, which also claims nearby Ski Liberty and Roundtop. The resort has gone through some tough times financially, but Snow Time hopes to get things back on track. Plans are to develop the area into an all-seasons resort and ultimately broaden the trail network to 30 runs, occupying ample space on the mountain's outer ridges. Located just miles past the north-central Maryland state line, Whitetail is primarily a day retreat, though it now has 30 slopeside town homes for rent or purchase.

New at Whitetail

- *The terrain park has been moved from Snowpark over to Lower Angel Drop, where boarders and skiers can expect more room and a better vertical drop. The halfpipe will remain on Snowpark.*
- *Whitetail is pumping in $1 million this year in new snowmaking equipment, including new fixed guns—part of a three-year, $3 million mountain upgrade plan.*

Mountain Stats

Base Elevation: 865 feet
Summit Elevation: 1,800 feet
Vertical Drop: 935 feet
Primary Slope Direction: South
Average Annual Snowfall: 38 inches
Skiable Terrain: 108 acres
Slopes and Trails: 6 beginner, 8 intermediate, 3 advanced
Longest Run: 1 mile
Lifts: 1 high-speed quad, 2 quad, 1 double, 2 surface tows
Uphill Capacity: 11,200 skiers per hour
Snowmaking: 100% of area
Night Skiing: 70% of slopes, including snowboard park and pipe, until 10 P.M. daily (back side closed at dusk)

Getting There

- **From Pennsylvania and points north:** Take I-81 south to Exit 3 (Route 16) in Greencastle, PA. Then follow Route 16 west towards Mercersburg. Follow signs to Whitetail Ski Resort.
- **From Washington, DC, and points south:** Take I-495 north around DC toward Bethesda, Maryland. Get on I-270 north to I-70 to Exit 18 (Route 68). Go through a traffic light in Clear Spring, Maryland, and follow snowflake signs six miles to Whitetail.
- **From Baltimore:** Take I-695 to I-70, then follow the directions above.
- **From Pennsylvania points west:** Take I-76 (PA Turnpike) east to Breezewood, PA, then I-70 into Maryland to Exit 18 (Route 68). Go through the light in Clear Spring and follow signs to Whitetail.

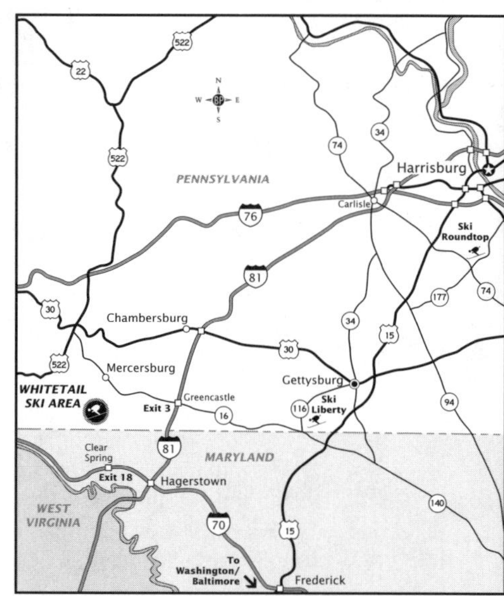

Trail Profiles

Many agree Whitetail has the best terrain of the three area Snow Time resorts. Its black and blue runs ski bigger than a lot of Mid-Atlantic areas, with longer trails, 930 feet of vertical, and a solid sustained pitch. The back side has some good steeps on its three or four black diamonds, most notably the mogul-packed *Exhibition* and *Bold Decision*. These trails are always the last to open each season, and there's no lighting here for night skiing. Get out early while the snow is still good and before lines form by mid-morning (weekends), but don't expect lines to be too long at any time. The resort's high-speed quad ensures more of your time is on the slopes.

Whitetail's intermediate terrain features good, long riding and is suitable for mid-level and advanced snow riders. *Fanciful* is the longest blue run—pretty steep and a long straightaway. *Limelite* isn't as steep but still a good ride. Check out *Angel Drop* as well. Halfway down, you can choose between its steep finish, or fork off to the long, cruising track of *Homerun*.

The resort has its own secluded section for beginners, but keep in mind that the transition from green runs to blue is not easy. There's a big difference between the lightly graded greens and the steeper track of the blues. First-time and developing skiers congregate on the beginner side's three slopes and three bunny hills. Instruction here is excellent and there's wide-open space to practice for beginners.

Did You Know?

Whitetail's mountain faces mostly due south. Snow can dissipate quickly when the sun's out, leaving snowmakers and groomers with the arduous task of keeping the mountain clean and skiable. They do a great job under the circumstances, with the help of a 100-million-gallon reservoir, but the resort has a tough time keeping its blue and black trails open when conditions suffer.

Another unique development strategy in creating Whitetail was designing a trail system that would completely separate its terrain by skier ability. The resort's three-face network features a secluded beginner area with access off four chair lifts; a five-trail intermediate section of long, wide, and smooth cruising runs; and a short but steep black diamond area. Snow Country *magazine gave Whitetail its 1992 Best Overall Resort Design Award, and the publishers of* Ski *and* Skiing *magazines awarded it their Silver Eagle Award for environmental excellence in area design.*

Whitetail's Express Quad is one of the Mid-Atlantic's fastest high-speed detachable lifts, transporting 3,000 skiers per hour with a three-minute lift time. The quad is the only chair on the heavily skied intermediate face, though, and skiers who want to reach the neighboring advanced section must take the lift and ski down before they can access the Expert's Choice quad lift.

Use Whitetail's Advance Reservation system to secure yourself a spot on the mountain, since skier limits are routinely set at 4,500 when all trails are open. Just call (717) 328–9400, extension 3517, or email the resort at sales@skiwhitetail.com to make your reservation.

Save big bucks with Whitetail's Skier Advantage Card. An $89 investment gets you 40% off each time you visit Whitetail, Liberty, and Roundtop, and every sixth visit is free. You'll also get 40% off class lessons and racing programs. An additional rental option is $39. A season pass offers access to all three area Snow Time resorts.

Don't expect to belly up to the bar after pounding the slopes. This tiny Pennsylvania township is dryer than the Sahara, and security vans roam the parking grounds to enforce the no-alcohol decree. Otherwise, the base lodge is both spacious and ultra-modern, with exceptional services and amenities and a true western-resort atmosphere.

The mountain's two summit areas provide panoramic views and photo opportunities of the hillsides and valley. From the summit, you'll likely spot the indigenous Whitetail deer that roam unencumbered throughout the resort's 1,600 acres of hunting-free property.

Snowboarding Highlights

One of the best aerial arenas around can be found at Whitetail. Boarders, skiers, and snow bladers alike are allowed in both the park and halfpipe. Its pipe is slightly longer than Liberty's and Roundtop's. It has its own transition groomer and is kept in pretty good shape. Whitetail's snowboard park has been moved from the Snowpark slope over to Lower Angel Drop, with varied hits such as big tabletops, spines, and rail slides. Creative juices may have peaked a few years ago when a Volkswagen bus was hauled into the park and filled and topped with snow, forming a sizable jump.

The resort groomed the park out to be an expert area toward the start and finish of the 1996-97 season, doubling and tripling the size of their spines and tables. Management toned down the park after one particularly nasty mid-season injury, but beefed it up again in late February with a 20-foot spine, along with a posted sign declaring the park an advanced freestyle area only.

The park's obstacles will be redesigned again this year, and a full list of competitions and events is scheduled, including the Ultimate Rider Series. Several good instructional programs are available for young and learning riders, and the Underground Snowboard Shop will tune up your board and fix your bindings or straps in little time. The pipe and park operate under strong lights nightly.

Snowboard Rentals: four-hour flex: $25 weekday, $32 weekend; eight-hour flex: $29 weekday, $35 weekend; 5 P.M.-10 P.M.: $31 all nights; Open-close: $47 all days • **Snowboard School:** Private $48/hour (reservations suggested); Group: call for current rates.

More Fun in the Flakes

Telemark skiing permitted on all slopes (telemark rentals available, lessons by appointment).

Summer Activities

When the ski season ends, **mountain biking** takes over the slopes. Whitetail's popular mountain biking center offers guests the chance to fly down the mountain and be transported back up the trails on a chair lift. The biking center runs numerous races and demo days. Also during the summer months, Whitetail hosts **scenic chairlift rides**, **hiking**, and **camping**.

Skier Services

While rates across the board are on the pricey side, the resort is extremely guest-friendly and takes care of its visitors. They'll issue free future passes for paying customers when conditions really suck. And they're pretty honest when it comes to reporting on conditions. Calling ahead and reserving lift tickets a few days before your trip also comes highly recommended on weekends.

You'll find the lodge to your liking and the food tasty. Whitetail also offers some perks uncommon for the Mid-Atlantic region, including a free ski and basket check. Sadly, the advanced back side isn't lit for night skiing, leaving just three intermediate slopes and the beginner area during later hours. Be warned that Whitetail's ski patrol will toss any skier/snowboarder it finds skiing recklessly and dangerously.

Lift Tickets

Four-hour flex: $31 weekday, $39 weekend (ages 6–12: $24, $33) • Eight-hour flex: $37 weekday, $44 weekend (ages 6–12: $29, $37) • 5 P.M.–10 P.M.: $27 (ages 6–12: $23) • Open–close: $50 daily • Kids five and under and ages 65+ ski free • Season passes; Skier Advantage card; group discounts for 25 or more skiers.

Ski Rentals

Four-hour flex: $23 weekday, $26 weekend • Eight-hour flex: $26 weekday, $29 weekend • 5 P.M.–10 P.M.: $25 all nights • Open–close: $42 all days.

Services

Ski School: Private $48/hour (reservations suggested); Group: call for current rates; Ski With Me program (for parents and their kids): $60/hour for parent and child; Kids Mountain Camp for ages 4–12; Learn-to-ski package for ages 7 and up; All-mountain packages for ages 7 and up • **Base Lodge Facilities:** Restaurant/food court, ticket/rental shops, free ski and basket checks, sports shop, snowboard shop • **Child Care:** For ages 6–12 months and ages 1–12; reservations recommended • **Racing**: NASTAR, Whitetail Race Team for ages 8–18, and an adult race team offered Wednesday nights on Home Run trail • **Adaptive Ski School:** Lessons available by appointment; 100 sets of parabolic rental skis, including Rossignol and Elan; Whitetail hosts the "Disabled Sports USA Ski Spectacular" each year in February or March.

Room & Board

Lodging

On-site

Thirty fully equipped slopeside townhomes. Call (717) 328–9400 for information.

Nearby

Bed & Breakfasts

Breezee Hill Farm, Clear Spring, MD; (301) 842–2608 • **Fox Run Inn**, Mercersburg, PA; (717) 328–3570 • **Metcalfe's B&B**, Mercersburg, PA; (717) 328–5317 • **The Mercersburg Inn** (& Restaurant); (717) 328–5231 • **The Steiger House**, Mercersburg, PA; (717) 328–5757.

Motels

Holiday Inn, Hagerstown, MD; 1–800–422–2SKI • **Econo Lodge**, Hagerstown, MD;

1–800–258–0127 • **Comfort Inn**, Greencastle, PA; (717) 597–8164 • **Howard Johnson Plaza-Hotel**, Hagerstown, MD; 1–800–732–0906.

Dining/Aprés-Ski

On-site

Windows Restaurant • **the Marketplace** (fast food) • No alcohol served at Whitetail, by township law.

Nearby (Mercersburg)

James Buchanan Pub & Restaurant; (717) 328–3008 • **Foot of the Mountain Restaurant**;(717) 328–2960 • **Mansion House**; (717) 328–5090 • **Fox's Pizza Den**; (717) 328–3699 • Several other restaurants and bars located 20 miles south of Whitetail in Hagerstown, Maryland, off I-70.

PENNSYLVANIA'S **OTHER ALPINE SKI AREAS**

Blue Marsh

Blue Marsh Winter Sports Park
P.O. Box 609
Bernville, Pennsylvania 19506

Ski Report: (610) 488–6399
Information: (610) 488–6396
Internet: *www.skibluemarsh.com*
Credit Cards: MC

Operating Hours
5 P.M.–10 P.M. weekdays
9 A.M.–10 P.M. Saturdays/holidays
9 A.M.–5 P.M. Sundays

Season: Mid-December to mid-March

Backdrop

Just 10 miles north of Reading, PA, is a learn-to-ski center called Blue Marsh. It sits at an elevation of just 590 feet on gently rolling Pennsylvania countryside. With just 300 vertical feet, the slopes serve as a great opener for beginners and children. In fact, on any given day here, you'll probably see nothing but parents and their kids. That's also a result of the ski center having turned its focus over to snowtubing—the fastest-growing winter resort activity outside of snowboarding. The Kinder Tube area has four lanes on a 75-foot vertical drop and a tow lift to transport guests uphill. A second section was constructed on the area's opposite side with five lanes, tube tow, and a 105-foot vertical for faster downhill times and bigger bumps. Plans are in the works for a half-mile tubing run with turns, bends, and banks of 50 to 65 degrees.

New at Blue Marsh

The area will be running nighttime-only hours on weekdays, from 5 P.M. to 10 P.M. The exceptions are advance-reservation large groups and school-closing days, opening at 10 A.M.

Mountain Stats

Base Elevation: 290 feet
Summit Elevation: 590 feet
Vertical Drop: 300 feet
Primary Slope Direction: North to northeast
Average Annual Snowfall: 35 inches
Skiable Terrain: 30 acres
Slopes and Trails: 1 advanced, 6 intermediate, 5 beginner
Longest Run: 2,600 feet
Lifts: 1 triple, 1 double, 1 T-bar, 4 handle tows
Uphill Capacity: 5,400 skiers per hour
Night Skiing: Saturdays until 10 P.M.
Snowmaking: 100% of area

Trail Profiles

While skiing has been overshadowed by snowtubing's rise, the area is still a natural fit for its beginner skier clientele. Blue's 12 slopes are short and easy. There's ample room on the wide-open *Jug Handle* slope to master turning techniques at the pace of your choice, and neighboring runs offer some gradual bends. *Outback Run* was added a few years ago to provide a leisurely, serpentine trek around the hill's perimeter. One advanced trail is advertised, but only relative to the other downhill runs. Realistically, *Main Street* is a straight intermediate slope that's just steep enough to move downhill at a nice speed. Novice snow riders should have a blast finding their way and gaining confidence around most of the trails.

Getting There

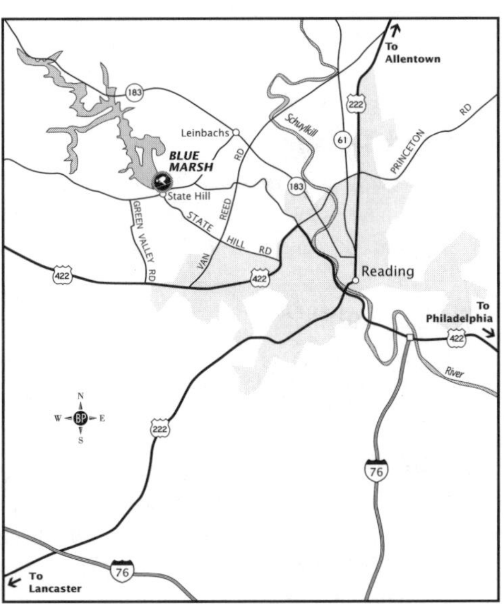

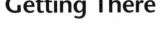

- **From Philadelphia**: Take the PA Turnpike (70/76) west to I-176 north toward Reading, then take 422 west. Pick up Route 183 and follow signs for Blue Marsh.
- **From Baltimore**: Take I-695 toward Towson, then I-83 north to Harrisburg, PA. Take I-78 east from I-83 toward Allentown, then take Route 61 south toward Reading. Pick up Route 183 and follow signs to Blue Marsh.
- **From upper Delaware**: Take Route 41 into Pennsylvania, then Route 10 north past PA Turnpike. Pick up I-176 to Reading, then follow directions above from Philadelphia.

Snowboarding Highlights

The Snowboarder's Whale Park mixes in some decent jumps with wide terrain. It's also a good area for learning snowboarders to practice their carve turns and stops.

Snowboard Rentals: Four-hour flex: $22, eight-hour flex: $26, boots only: $5

More Fun in the Flakes

Snowtubing (see Background section for description): Two separate snowtubing areas, each with five lanes; Weekday 5 P.M.–10 P.M.: $12.50; Weekends/holidays: four-hour flex: $15, eight-hour flex: $20; Kinder Tube: $12.50; Group Rates (minimum 15 persons): $10

Did You Know?

Tiny Blue Marsh was one of the early players in snowtubing's history. General Manager Joseph Aichholz, who also served as official snowmaker for the 1980 Winter Olympics in Lake Placid, designed Blue Marsh's first snowtubing runs back in the eighties. Today, you can run a tube at just about any Mid-Atlantic ski area.

midweek, $12.50 weekends • **Ice skating, ice fishing** at Blue Marsh Lake.

Skier Services

Blue Marsh is laid-back and friendly, with a lot of open space out on the slopes. You'll find most of the activity centered on the two teaching areas in front of the small base lodge. Blue Marsh runs some good programs for kids, and offers junior instructional programs and first-time-skier packages for adults and children. There's no day care, but the modest, comfortable base lodge was built with kids in mind, with a cafeteria, sun deck, and game room.

Lift Tickets

Four-hour flex: weekend $24 • Eight-hour flex: weekend $30 • 9 A.M.–10 P.M.: weekend $34 • 5 P.M.–10 P.M.: weeknight $18, weekend: $24 • Ages 10 & under: $3 off any ticket • Ages 5 & under ski free (1 child per adult) • Ages 70+ ski free.

Ski Rentals:

Four-hour flex: $18, eight-hour flex: $22 • Shaped skis: Four-hour flex $20, eight-hour flex $24 • Junior ski package (ages 10 and under): $15 • Helmets: $5/day.

Services

Ski School: Private $45/hour (offered at all times); Group $15/1.5 hours (offered at 10:30 A.M., 12:30 P.M., 2:30 P.M., 5 P.M., and 7 P.M.); Kinder Ski, for children five and under: $45 (includes rental, lesson, and lift ticket); First-time-skier/snowboarder packages (includes lesson, rental, and beginner lift ticket): weeknights: private $65, group $45; weekends: private $70, group $50 • **Base Lodge Facilities**: Cafeteria, sun deck, rental shop, lockers, game room.

Room & Board

Lodging

Nearby

Econo Lodge, Wyomissing; (610) 378–5105 • **Wilson World Hotel**, Morgantown; 1–800–342–2276.

Dining/Aprés-Ski

Nearby (Bernville) • **Old 22 Inn**; (610) 488–1458 • **Burkey's Restaurant**; (610) 488–6394 • **Jocko's Restaurant/Pizzeria**; (610) 488–0831 • **Jefferson Drive-in**; (610) 488–6166.

Mount Tone

18

Mount Tone
Wallerville Road
Lake Como, PA 18437

Information: 1–800–747–2SKI
Internet: *www.mttone.com*
Email: mail@mttone.com

Operating Hours
Friday 6 P.M.–10 P.M.
Sat.–Sun. 9 A.M.–10 P.M.

Season: Late December to mid-March

Backdrop

Mount Tone is a unique family ski area and ski camp nestled in the village of Lake Como, just five miles from the New York State border in northeastern PA. The area has operated as a quaint alpine getaway since the mid-1950s, utilizing two separate small plateau faces with 100% snowmaking. Open Friday night through Sunday, it's a ski area in the mold of a summer camp, with families and youth organizations accounting for most of its guest base. Take advantage of reasonably priced, inclusive ski-and-stay weekends. You'll get full time on the slopes, equipment rentals, unlimited lessons, special events, home-cooked meals, and lodging in bungalow-style dorms or at a nearby country inn. Weekend rates range from $100 to $146 per person. Or, come for the day and get a dirt-cheap lift ticket that's valid on both hills, with a hayride shuttle (or five-minute walk) servicing the two sections.

Trail Profiles

Mount Tone's smaller east plateau features a bunny slope with its own rope tow, three easily negotiable trails, three lifts, and all base lodge facilities, including a full-service cafeteria and ski and rental shops. It's also the site of the Beach Club snowtubing park, which holds four lanes, full snowmaking, and a T-bar lift. If you want to orient your kids to skiing or snowboarding, Mount Tone is a wise choice considering its gentle, traffic-free terrain and patient, competent teaching.

Slightly more challenging terrain can be found on the opposite north face, where a single T-bar lift serves the entire side. The terrain is lower intermediate, with nice elbow turns on Solitude and Winding Way. Skiers and snowboarders have a wide terrain park toward the end of Heaven's Gate trail, and a warming hut greets guests at the summit.

Mountain Stats

Vertical Drop: 450 feet
Primary Slope Direction: North-northeast
Average Annual Snowfall: 65 inches
Skiable Terrain: 25 acres
Slopes and Trails: 2 beginner, 5 intermediate, 3 advanced
Longest Run: 1,300 feet
Lifts: 1 triple chair, 1 rope tow, 1 handle tow, 1 T-bar
Night Skiing: Lights on the north face (right side) Friday–Saturday until 10 P.M.
Snowmaking: 90% of area

Getting There

- **From Pennsylvania and New York State:** Follow I-81 toward Pennsylvania's northeast section, and take Route 171 (a few miles from the New York State border) past Susquehanna. From there take Route 370, following signs for Mount Tone.
- **From I-84 in New York State:** Follow I-84 west to I-380 north to I-81 north, and follow directions above.
- **From I-80 in New York/New Jersey:** Follow I-80 west to I-380 north to I-81 north, and follow directions above.
- **From Baltimore and points south:** Take I-695 to I-83 north and then I-81 north to Scranton. Follow toward I-380 and take Route 6 east/Carbondale. Follow 6 miles to Exit 6/Carbondale. Pass through town, left at 7th traffic light, then left onto Route 171 north. Follow 171 for 16 miles and turn right onto Route 370 east toward Lakewood. Pass through Lakewood, pass the Preston School, and bear right on the fork onto a small state road (do not continue on 370). Follow to the village of Lake Como, cross Route 247 and look for signs for Mount Tone. Turn right on Wallerville Road and follow for two miles to Mount Tone.

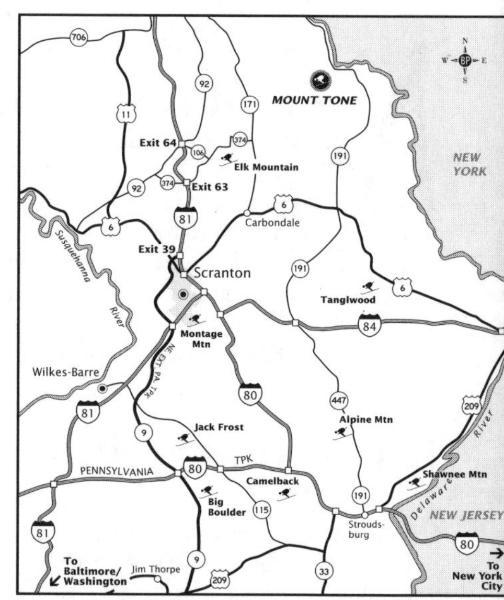

More Fun in the Flakes

A popular **snowtubing** park features four lanes over a 75-foot vertical drop, with several bumps and jumps. There are 15 kilometers available for cross-country skiers off the smaller (east) summit area on a marked, ungroomed trail network, mostly in the novice to intermediate range. Additionally, ice skating is offered on Mount Tone's base-area pond, conditions permitting.

Snowboarding Highlights

The North Face side holds the Heaven's Gate terrain park, where boarders and skiers can practice jumps of moderate sizes. A T-bar and full lighting serves the entire North Face, which also has some good cruising runs and turning opportunities on its slopes.

Snowboard Instruction: Private $26/hour, group $12/hour (lessons offered at 9:30 A.M., 10:30 A.M., 1:30 P.M.); First-time-snowboarder program: $38 (includes beginner lift ticket, rental, and group lesson) • **Snowboard Rentals:** $9.43/hour; $17.92/night session and half-day; $24.52/full day.

Other Winter Sports

Snowtubing park with four lanes and handle tow lift; $9 per session: 9:30 A.M.–12:30 P.M., 1:30 P.M.–4:30 P.M., 6:30–9:30 P.M. Open Friday night through Sunday • **Cross-country skiing** on 15 kilometers of Mount Tone's marked, ungroomed loop system; trail fee $7, rentals $7 • **Ice skating** on Mount Tone's base-side pond (no charge, no rentals).

Skier Services

Management restricts its operating hours from Friday evenings to Sunday afternoons, and a limited ticket sales policy ensures crowd-free skiing. Families and youth groups make up the primary skier base, while Mount Tone's ski camp features inclusive weekend rates that offer lift tickets, on-site lodging, and meals. Weekends are filled with events and activities like outdoor barbecues, snowshoeing expeditions, ski races, snow sculpting, and winter volleyball, while movies and music play in the base lodge's meeting room at nights.

Did You Know?

Mount Tone is home to the first installed triple chair lift east of the Mississippi River, slung up in 1972 when it was known as Snow-Hill Ski Area.

Lift Tickets

(Open Friday night through Sunday night) • Friday 6 P.M.–10 P.M.: $8/all ages • Weekend 9 A.M.–4:30 P.M.: $18 adult, $14 ages 6–10 • Weekend 12:30 P.M.–4:30 P.M.: $13 adult, $10 ages 6–10 • Weekend 12:30 P.M.–10 P.M. $18 adult, $14 ages 6–10 (trails close from 4:30–6 P.M.).

Ski Rentals

Friday 6 P.M.–10 P.M.: $8.49/all ages • Weekend 9 A.M.–4:30 P.M.: $12.26/all ages • Weekend 12:30 P.M.–4:30 P.M.: $8.49/all ages • Weekend 12:30 P.M.–10 P.M. $12.26/all ages.

Services

Ski School: Private $26/hour, group $12/hour (lessons offered at 9:30 A.M., 10:30 A.M., 1:30 P.M.); First-time-skier program: $25 (includes beginner lift ticket, rental, and group lesson) • **Base Lodge Facilities:** Cafeteria, warming hut, ski/gift shop, rental/repair shop, ski school.

Room & Board

Lodging

On-site

Near-slopeside, fully furnished ski dormitories; call for ski-and-stay weekend rates • Nearby country inn.

Dining/Aprés-Ski

Full-service cafeteria (liquor not sold on-site).

Mystic Mountain

Mystic Mountain/ Nemacolin Woodlands Resort
P.O. Box 188
Route 40 east
Farmington, PA 15437

Ski Report: 1–800–422–2736
Information: (412) 329–8555

Internet: *www.nemacolin.com/skiing.htm*
Credit Cards: MC, VISA, AE

Operating Hours
10 A.M.–10 P.M. weekdays
9 A.M.–10 P.M. Saturday
9 A.M.–6 P.M. Sunday
Season: December to mid-March

Backdrop

With the considerable snowfall that blankets southwest Pennsylvania's Laurel Highlands region, a fourth ski area was bound to emerge. Nemacolin Woodlands Resort opened its slopes in the late 90s to downhillers at Mystic Mountain. Skiing is a small piece of the posh, 1,000-acre all-seasons resort. Overshadowing it is the resort's myriad of other winter activities, luxurious base amenities, and year-round lodging in the French Renaissance-molded hotel and surrounding condominiums. *Town & Country* recently recognized Nemacolin's spa as one of its 10 Best in America, and the four-star Golden Trout restaurant has also won acclaim from *Bon Appetit* magazine.

Nemacolin resides in the small town of Farmington, 16 miles southeast of Uniontown and just a few miles from historic Fort Necessity, where George Washington's first military engagement took place in the French and Indian War.

Trail Profiles

Mystic Mountain has five gentle slopes, serving as the winter complement to all-seasons Nemacolin Woodlands Resort. There's always the option of shacking up in style at Nemacolin and making the 30-minute trip north to Seven Springs or Hidden Valley. But if you want the ski-and-stay experience, instruction, or just a few turns on the hill, Mystic may be for you. The five slopes are gradual cruising runs over just 300 feet of vertical drop, with the longest slope extending to 2,600 feet. And with sound, attentive teaching offered, you get to pick up the sport on wide-open snow with lots of elbow room and no pressure. Snowboarding is welcome on all slopes, though right now there's no terrain park or halfpipe.

Getting There

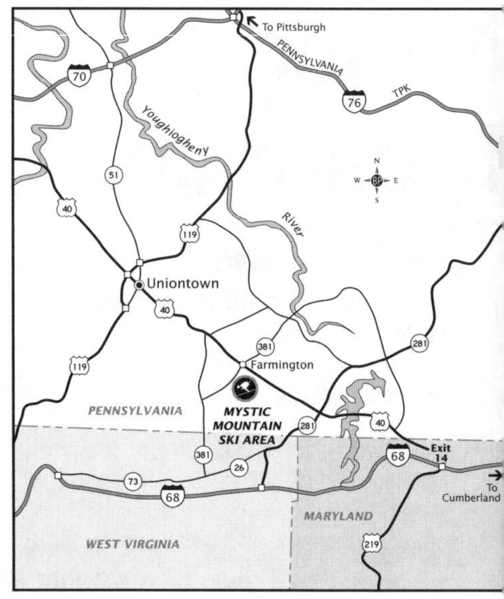

- **From Washington, DC/Baltimore**: Take I-70 west or 270 north past Hagerstown, then I-68 west past Cumberland. From Cumberland, follow Route 40 north at the Route 219 intersection. Follow this to Farmington, PA, and follow signs for Nemacolin/Mystic Mountain.
- **From eastern Pennsylvania**: Take the Pennsylvania Turnpike (76/70) west, then Route 220 south to I-68 west. Follow directions from previous page.
- **From Pittsburgh**: Take the Pennsylvania Turnpike (70/76) east, then Route 119 south to Route 40 south/east toward Farmington and follow signs for Nemacolin/Mystic Mountain.

More Fun in the Flakes

Cross-country skiing and **snowshoeing** on eight trails daily from 9 A.M. to 4 P.M.; trail fee/rentals $18, $14 ages 12 and under (includes skis, boots, poles).

Skier Services

Cross-country skiers and **snowshoers** can lay tracks on eight trails when snowfall is sufficient. Trails are fully groomed and run daily from 9 A.M. to 4 P.M., with rentals available by the day or half-day. **Horse-drawn sleigh rides** are also offered through the hardwoods and evergreens of the Allegheny Mountains' Laurel Highlands. Rounding out the all-seasons resort are two **PGA golf courses**, seven indoor and outdoor **pools**, and an **Equestrian Center**. The resort's new Adventure Center offers 30 miles of **mountain biking** and **hiking** trails, **in-line skating**, a **climbing** tower, beach **volleyball**, and a **rope course**. Childcare is offered at the Nemacolin Woodlands activities center, just below the ski area.

Lift Tickets

9 A.M.–9 P.M.: weekday $25, ages 12 and under $19 • 5 P.M.–9 P.M.: Friday–Monday $16, $12 • Friday–Sunday special: $60, $50 • Reduced rates for ages 11 and under.

Mountain Stats

Base Elevation: 1,730 feet
Summit Elevation: 2,030 feet
Vertical Drop: 300 feet
Average Annual Snowfall: 100 inches
Skiable Terrain: 25 acres
Slopes and Trails: 2 beginner, 3 intermediate
Longest Run: 2,600 feet
Lifts: 1 quad lift, 1 surface lift
Uphill Capacity: 2,000 skiers per hour
Night Skiing: 100% of area, Monday-Saturday until 10 P.M.
Snowmaking: 100% of area

Ski/Snowboard/Snowblade Rentals

Ski: Adult $20, kids $12; **Snowboard:** $25/all ages; **Snowblades:** $25/all ages • Friday–Sunday special: skis $55, snowboards $70.

Services

Ski School: Private $45/hour, $75/2 hours; Group $20/1.5 hours (offered weekdays at 10 A.M., 2 P.M.); Mystic Mountain Munchkins (ages 4–6, first-time ski/activities): 9 A.M.–4 P.M. $60, 9 A.M.–noon or 1 P.M.–4 P.M. $35; Mystic Mountain Cats (ages 7–12, full mountain): full day $75, half-day $45; Youth Ski Program (ages 7–12) • **Base Lodge and Resort Facilities:** Ski/rental shop, activities center, two indoor pools, full spa, fitness center.

Room & Board

Lodging

On-site

40 condominiums and 68 inn rooms, with 124 additional rooms under development.

Dining

On-site

Golden Trout restaurant, numerous restaurants/lounges, pizza shop.

Mountain View at Edinboro

Mountain View at Edinboro
P.O. Box 447
Edinboro, PA 16412

Ski Report/Information: (814) 734–1641
Internet: *www.skimtview.org*
E-mail: info@skimtview.org
Credit Cards: VISA, MC

Operating Hours
Monday–Thursday 3:30 P.M.–9 P.M.
Friday 3:30 P.M.–10 P.M.
Saturday 9:30 A.M.–10 P.M.
Sunday 9:30 A.M.–9 P.M.

Season: December to late March

Backdrop

Formerly known as Mount Pleasant, the small family ski area shut down in 1992 after 20 years of operation. It resurfaced again in 1992 under a group of dedicated skiers and employees that formed the Edinboro Ski Association, Inc., a nonprofit membership-owned and operated ski club. Talk of privatizing the facility to a set number of members has not materialized, and the slopes are still open to the public.

Mountain View is the only alpine ski area in remote northwestern Pennsylvania, located in the tri-state strip between Ohio and New York. It sits just 20 miles from Lake Erie, in line with the Great Lakes snow belt that dumps some of Pennsylvania's most consistent and dependable powder.

Trail Profiles

Moutain View's modest plateau offers nine slopes on a small 320-foot vertical drop, and welcomes both skiers and snowboarders. Trails are gentle with easy grades, and most of them are covered by adequate snowmaking. While just three T-bars serve uphill transport, lift lines have never been a factor. It's not surprising that a few of Pennsylvania's big resorts draw more skier visits on one peak day than Mountain View amasses in a year. With that in mind, the facility specializes in instruction, teaching lots of children in the area. The Lower Meadow section off the base lodge holds most instructional programs.

Mountain Stats

Base Elevation: 1,200 feet
Summit Elevation: 1,520 feet
Vertical Drop: 320 feet
Average Annual Snowfall: 120 inches
Skiable Terrain: 25 acres
Slopes and Trails: 4 beginner, 4 intermediate, 1 advanced
Longest Run: 2,800 feet
Lifts: 3 (all T-bars)
Uphill Capacity: 2,400 skiers per hour
Night Skiing: 100% of area: Monday–Thursday until 9 P.M.; Friday–Sunday until 10 P.M.
Snowmaking: 60% of area

Getting There

- **From Erie:** Take I-79 south to the Edinboro exit and follow Route 6N, heading east. At the traffic light in Edinboro, continue straight for four miles, then turn right on Sharp Road. Follow signs two miles to Mountain View.
- **From I-90 in Ohio and New York state:** Take I-90 into Pennsylvania to I-79 south. Follow the directions above.
- **From Pennsylvania points south:** Take I-79 north (or I-80 west to I-79), then follow the directions above.

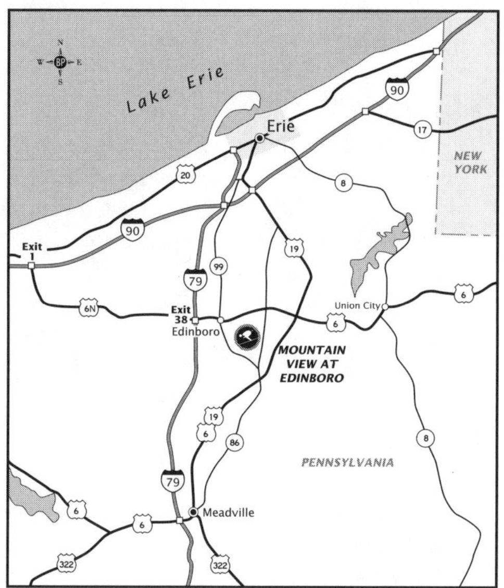

More Fun in the Flakes

Snowtubing, with four separate chutes covering 600 feet. $5/hour, $9/two hours, $12/three hours • **Snowboarding:** Rentals: Weekend $23, half-day or weekday $20.

Nearby
Snowmobiling trails in surrounding area.

Skier Services

Lift Tickets

9:30 A.M.–4 P.M. and 4 P.M.–10 P.M.: (weekend) adult $15, students $12, ages 5–8 $10 • 9:30 A.M.–10 P.M.: (weekend) adult $20, students $15, ages 5–8 $12 • 3:30 P.M.–9 P.M.: (Monday–Thursday/Friday to 10 P.M.) adult $12, students $10, ages 5–8 $8 • Beginner Lift: weekend: adult and student $10, ages 5–8 $9; weekday: adult and student $8, ages 5–8 $5.

Ski Rentals

• Weekend/all day: adult $15, student and ages 5–8 $10 • weekend/day or night: adult $13, student and ages 5–8 $8 • weekday: adult $13, student and ages 5–8 $8.

Services

Ski School: Private: $25/hour; semi-private (two–four students): $20/person; group (five–eight students): $15/hour; Beginner's Special: Monday–Friday (7 P.M.) $20, weekend (noon) $25 • **Racing Programs** (contact Mountain View for info.) • **Base Lodge Facilities:** Mountain View's two-tiered base lodge is small but comfortable, with a roaring fireplace, snack bar, and rental shop.

Room & Board

Lodging

Nearby

Ramada Inn; (814) 734–5650 • **Raspberry House B&B**; (814) 734–8997.

Dining/Aprés-Ski

Nearby (Cambridge Springs)

Riverside Inn; (814) 398–4645 • **Cambridge Family Restaurant**; (814) 398–2613 • **Betty's Restaurant**; (814) 398–8673.

Ski Sawmill

Ski Sawmill
P.O. Box 5-B
Morris, PA 16938

Ski Report/Information: 1–800–532–7669
Credit Cards: VISA, MC

Operating Hours
10 A.M.–9:45 P.M. Monday–Friday
9 A.M.–11:45 P.M. Saturday
9 A.M.–8 P.M. Sunday

Season: Mid-November to late March

Backdrop

Pennsylvania has a lot of family ski areas, but few are as affordable as north-central Pennsylvania's Ski Sawmill. Its value packages offer one of the Mid-Atlantic's cheapest lift tickets and rentals. The 32-year-old resort draws most of its visitors from Williamsport—home of the Little League World Series—and surrounding towns. It's a great place to get initiated to skiing and snowboarding, or just to make some turns, without the burden of crowded slopes and lifts. The lodge is a bit small and the services on the lean side.

Trail Profiles

The area's eight slopes are short, gradual, and easily negotiable over 515 feet of vertical drop. An attentive, PSIA-certified ski school teaches predominantly young children on *Lower Area*—its base-lodge bunny slope, with several instruction packages offered. Novices can usually ski the entire mountain with little problem. Timed racing trials are also available on weekends, and snowboarders have a park filled with a few modest jumps and obstacles.

Mountain Stats

Base Elevation: 1,700 feet
Summit Elevation: 2,215 feet
Vertical Drop: 515 feet
Average Annual Snowfall: 45 inches
Skiable Terrain: 15 acres
Slopes and Trails: 2 beginner, 3 intermediate, 3 advanced
Longest Run: 3,250 feet
Lifts: 1 double, 2 T-bars
Uphill Capacity: 3,200 skiers per hour
Night Skiing: 100% of area, weekdays until 9:45 P.M., Saturdays 11:45 P.M., and Sundays 8 P.M.
Snowmaking: 100% of area

Getting There 

- **From Williamsport**: Take Route 220 west to Route 287 north past English Center, and follow signs to Sawmill.
- **From points east**: Take I-80 west to I-180, passing Williamsport, then follow to Route 220. Pick up Route 287 north past English Center, and follow signs to Sawmill.
- **From points west**: Take I-80 east to Route 220 north toward Williamsport, then take Route 287 north, and follow signs to Sawmill.

Skier Services

Sawmill is essentially a day area, but late-night skiers have use of the slopes until 11:45 P.M. on Saturdays with a half-price lift ticket. Overnight guests can shack up in Sawmill's slopeside 32-room base lodge or fully equipped houses and cottages.

Lift Tickets

Call for current rates • $11 midweek/all times • $23.95 weekends; Ages 7–12: $11.98 • Ages 6 and under ski free.

Ski Rentals

Call for current rates • $18 weekends • $7 weekday • Ages 7–12 $12.50 .

Services

Ski School: Call for current rates; PSIA certified; Private $30/hour; Group $12/hour; Children $26.50/hour; Learn-to-Ski Package: weekend $39.95, $29.95 ages 12 and under, midweek value specials.

Room & Board

Lodging

On-site

32-room **lodge** at base, weekday $32/night, $130/weekend • Fully furnished **house and cottage rentals** • Ski & Stay Packages: $116/person includes Friday–Sunday lift tickets, Friday–Saturday slopeside lodging (children free with parents); Call 1–800–532–7669 for information/rates.

Nearby

14 hotels/motels near area (call (717) 353–7731/7521 for listing) • **Canyon Motel**, Williamsport; (717) 724–1681 • **Sherwood Motel**, Wellsboro; (717) 724–3424 • **Penn-Wells Hotel**, Wellsboro; (717) 724–2111.

Dining/Aprés-Ski

On-site

Restaurant (weekends only), lounge/cafeteria • **Inn 287**—restaurant and bar.

Nearby

Gary's Place Restaurant & Tavern, Morris; (717) 353–6641.

Spring Mountain

Spring Mountain
Box 42
Spring Mount, PA 19478

Ski Report: (610) 287–7900
Information: (610) 287–7300
Credit Cards: VISA, MC

Operating Hours
10 A.M.–10 P.M. weekdays
9 A.M.–10 P.M. Saturday
9 A.M.–9:30 P.M. Sunday

Season: Mid-December to mid-March

Backdrop

Spring Mountain has operated since 1963 as a cost-effective family ski area for the nearby Philadelphia area. The ski center sits just 528 feet above sea level on a small plateau in Western Montgomery County. It's a good place for skiers to pick up the sport, with private and group instruction for all ages. With little snowfall during most winters, Spring relies heavily on snow guns that fire around the clock. All trails are open under lights nightly, but most skiers come for the afternoon, particularly school and church groups. The ski area's selling points are its instruction, learning environment, and one-hour proximity to Philadelphia. The lodge has a cafeteria and fireplace, but no overnight accommodations aside from year-round, on-site camping.

Mountain Stats

Base Elevation: 108 feet
Summit Elevation: 528 feet
Vertical Drop: 420 feet
Average Annual Snowfall: 35 inches
Skiable Terrain: 15 acres
Slopes and Trails: 4 beginner, 3 intermediate, 1 advanced
Longest Run: 2,220 feet
Lifts: 1 triple, 3 doubles
Uphill Capacity: 8,000 skiers per hour
Snowmaking: 100% of area
Night Skiing: 100% of slopes, Monday–Saturday until 10 P.M., 9:30 P.M. Sunday

Trail Pofiles

Spring's limited terrain features two small faces: four short, contoured slopes on one side and a lightly graded hill, nearly as wide as it is long, on the other. A triple and double chair and two rope tows serve the area. You can expect very little traffic on the slopes and chairs, which is why it's the right environment to learn or just get a quick fix of turns. You can also find lots of jumps all over the mountain.

Getting There

- **From Philadelphia**: Take the Schuylkill Expressway and exit at King of Prussia, Route 202 south. Then take the 422 Expressway west to the Collegeville Exit and follow Route 29 north to Schwenksville. Follow signs to Spring Mountain.
- **From Wilmington, Delaware**: Take I-95 to Route 202 north, then take the 422 Expressway west. Follow directions above.
- **From western points**: Take the Pennsylvania Turnpike (70/76) east, then 422, and follow directions above.

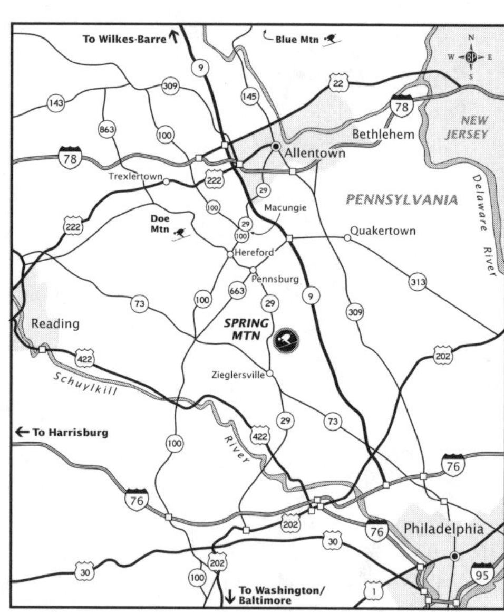

Skier Services

Lift Tickets

Call for current rates • Weekday $16; Weekend $20 • 5 P.M.–10 P.M. (9:30 P.M. Sunday) $16 • Seniors $8, ages 6 and under ski free • Group rates for 15 or more skiers.

Ski Rentals

Call for current rates • 1,500 sets: Elan, some SCX high-performance skis • Weekend $17; Weekday/evening $15.

Services

Ski School: Call (610) 287–8344 to reserve instruction; Private $35/hour (up to three persons $65/hour); Group $15/hour (five-person minimum); Learn-to-Ski and childrens' packages • **Base Lodge Facilities**: Cafeteria, ski school, rentals, lockers.

Snowboarding Highlights

A terrain garden and small halfpipe were built a few years ago on the wide track of Drifter Trail. There's not much challenging turf to offer on Spring's slopes, so boarders can make their own obstacles in the garden and pipe. They've even considered hauling in a stripped car to use as a jump. The snowboard area operates under lights after sunset, but Spring needs to set up a J-bar for its boarders. The Rocktop Ridge double chair is the current means of uphill transport.

Snowboard Rentals: Call for current rates; 40 sets: Kemper and Hammer; Weekday: $16/four hours, $20/six hours; Weekend: $20/four hours, $25/six hours • **Snowboard School**: Four instructors.

Room & Board

Lodging

Nearby

Holiday Inn; (215) 368–3800 • **Kaufman House**; (215) 234–4181 • **Bed & Breakfast of Valley Forge**; (215) 783–7838 • **Guest Quarters**; (215) 843–8300 • **Days Inn**; 1–800–329–7466.

Tanglewood

Tanglewood
P.O. Box 165
Tafton, Pennsylvania 18464

Ski Report: 1–888–226–SNOW
Information/Reservations: (717) 226–9500
Internet: *www.tanglwood.com*
E-mail: tnglwood@ptd.net
Credit Cards: VISA, MC, AE, Discover

Operating Hours
9 A.M.–10 P.M. Monday–Saturday
9 A.M.–5 P.M. Sunday

Season: Early December to mid-March

Backdrop

Overlooking Lake Wallenpaupack in the Pocono Mountains, Tanglwood Ski Area has hosted family and novice skiers each for the last 30 years. Locals may remember the resort as Paper Birch Mountain. The family-operated business turned over in 1972 to a development corporation by the name Tanglwood. The resort was sold again a handful of years ago, retaining its name.

Tanglwood's trail system features 100 percent snowmaking and full grooming, and all nine runs are well lit for night skiing, six days per week until 10 P.M. The terrain is much easier and less congested than bigger Pocono areas, and the rates more affordable. The resort issues credit for a future visit to any skier not satisfied, within one hour of ticket purchase. The resort has also added snowtubing, which runs Wednesday through Sunday.

Trail Profiles

Tanglwood is a good choice for learning skiers in the populous Scranton and Wilkes-Barre areas. It contrasts well with the intermediate to advanced terrain of Montage Resort. The resort's summit base offers a wide beginner area that covers just 70 feet of vertical drop and uses a rope tow lift. Surrounding the beginner turf are the remaining eight runs comprising novice to intermediate track, despite trail ratings advertised as more difficult. The narrow, serpentine *Weasel* trail runs on a steady grade over 2,600 feet of track. More advanced skiers have one worthy trail: *Wildcat's* wide, straight course is filled with moguls and bumps. The trail overlooks scenic Lake Wallenpaupack—one of Pennsylvania's largest manmade lakes. Tanglwood's best novice trail is *Big Bear*. It winds slowly from the summit over one mile of terrain.

Mountain Stats

Base Elevation: 1,335 feet
Summit Elevation: 1,750 feet
Vertical Drop: 415 feet
Primary Slope Direction: North
Average Annual Snowfall: 65 inches
Skiable Terrain: 35 acres
Slopes and Trails: 2 beginner, 3 intermediate, 4 advanced
Longest Run: 1 mile
Lifts: 2 doubles, 2 T-bars, 1 rope tow
Uphill Capacity: 4,300 skiers per hour
Night Skiing: 100% of area, Monday–Saturday until 10 P.M.
Snowmaking: 100% of area

Getting There

- **From New York/New Jersey**: Take I-80 west into Pennsylvania, then Route 447 north to Route 390 north. Pass I-84 on 390 and follow signs for Tanglwood. From I-84, take Exit 7, Route 390 north, and follow signs.
- **From I-81**: Follow I-81 toward Scranton, then I-380/80 to I-84 east to Route 390 north. Follow signs to Tanglwood.
- **From Philadelphia**: Take the northeast extension of the Pennsylvania Turnpike past Wilkes-Barre, then connect with I-81 north to I-380/80, then I-84 east, then Route 390 north. Follow signs for Tanglwood.

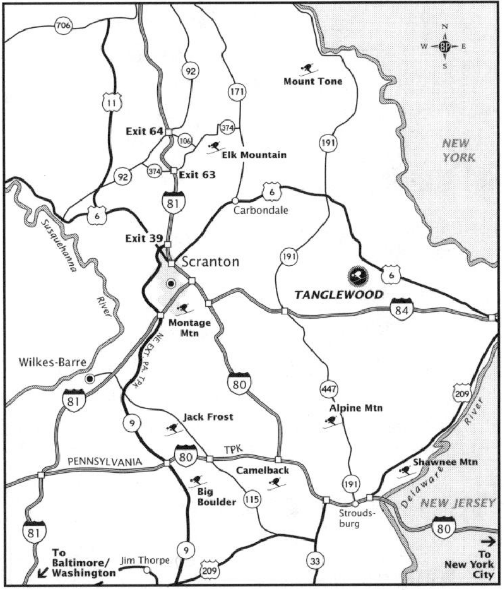

Snowboarding Highlights

A 350–foot-long, 100-foot-wide snowboard park has a series of rail slides, tickers, trick boxes, and plastic barrels. Boarders also have resort-wide access on Tanglwood's tame terrain.

Snowboard School: Private $35/hour; Group $18/hour • **Snowboard Rentals:** Day/twilight $24, night $20, extended $30

More Fun in the Flakes

While winter recreation is limited to skiing and snowboarding at Tanglwood, leisurely **cross-country ski** trails can be found nearby at both Promised Land State Park and Bruce Lake National Area (snowfall permitting). Rentals are available at both areas.

Nearby

Snowtubing: open Wednesday–Sunday: $12/three–hour session, 9 A.M.–9 P.M. Saturday, 10 A.M.–4 P.M. Sunday, and noon–9 P.M. Wednesday–Friday • **Snowmobiling, sledding, ice skating, ice fishing** at Lakeside Resort, 10 minutes from Tanglwood, 1–888–233–4130 • **Cross-country ski** trails at Promise Land State Park and Bruce lake Natural Area, within 10 minutes • **Paintball** offered year-round at Pike County AMBUSH, Inc., 1–888–2AMBUSH.

Skier Services

Lift Tickets

9 A.M.–5 P.M.: weekday $22, weekend $33 • Half day: weekday $19, weekend $26 • 1 P.M.–10 P.M.: weekday $22, weekend $33 • 5 P.M.–10 P.M.: weekday $19, weekend $26 • 9 A.M.–10 P.M.: weekday $30, weekend $41 • Reduced lift tickets for ages 6–12 • $15 lift ticket from March 6 P.M.–close.

Ski Rentals

Day/twilight $22, night $19.

Services

Ski School: Private $35/hour; Group $18/hour; Learn-to-Ski package for ages 9 and older: $44 weekday, $52 weekend (includes lift, rental, and group lesson); Childrens' programs: SKIwee (ages 5–12), weekends only: full day $60, half day $50; Junior Racing Program • **Summit Lodge Facilities:** Slopeside restaurant and lounge, ski/rental shop, lockers, game room.

Room & Board

Lodging

On-site

14 slopeside condominiums, call for rates.

Nearby

Comfort Inn, Lake Ariel, 20 minutes away, 1–800–523–4426 • **Keley's Inn The Poconos,** Gouldsboro, w/indoor pool, hot tub, English pub, 1–800–432–5253 • **Lakeside Resort,** Greentown, 1–888–233–4130.

Dining/Aprés-Ski

On-site

Restaurant, **Last Lift** slopeside lounge, with live entertainment on Saturdays.

Nearby

Ehrhardt's Lakeside Restaurant, one mile from resort, seafood, steaks, etc.; (717) 226–2124 • **AJ's Fireplace** family restaurant, Tafton; (717) 226–2701 • **Critters Restaurant**, Route 390, Tafton; (717) 226–9002.

Tussey Mountain

Tussey Mountain
Route 322
Boalsburg, PA 16827

Ski Report: 1–800–733–2754
Information: (814) 466–6810/6266
Internet: *www.tusseymountain.com*
Email: info@tusseymountain.com
Credit Cards: MC, VISA, AE, Discover

Operating Hours:
Noon to 10 P.M. weekdays
9 A.M. to 10 P.M. weekends

Season: December to late March

Backdrop

There's a little-known ski area in Boalsburg that's been serving local families and students for the last 20 years. Tussey Mountain, just a handful of miles from Penn State's campus, offers eight short runs on its 500 vertical feet. It's a great place to learn skiing and snowboarding, with personalized, friendly instruction and wide-open slopes. The area also boasts a terrain park, half-pipe, and a snowtubing area. Plus, rates are downright cheap across the board, including tickets, rentals, and lessons. There's just one main lift—a slow, antiquated quad—but lines are scarce. A comfy, spacious lodge holds everything you'll need, with good food and a festive lounge.

Trail Profiles

True, it's a small mountain, but Tussey lets its more developed clientele open it up at their own discretion. In fact, at times it can be more of a hard-core terrain park than a ski area. Build your own kickers, ledges, banks, and big-air jumps. Just leave enough groomed track for beginners. You'll more than make up for the lack of vertical and trail variety. Plus, lots of nooks and crannies can be found throughout the small trail system. *Tuscarora* might be the most challenging trail, using just about all Tussey's 500-foot vertical drop. The upper half of the run is steepest and also gets the occasional bump treatment. Racing also fits big into the Tussey culture, with recreational standard racing held on weekends.

Beginners still rule the majority of the mountain. Tussey's solid ski school teaches neophytes on a large bunny slope area. And once that's mastered, two beginner slopes offer an easy trek down a short distance. Novices should be able to handle the other wide slopes without too much difficulty.

Mountain Stats

Base Elevation: 1,310 feet
Summit Elevation: 1,810 feet
Vertical Drop: 500 feet
Primary Slope Direction: North to northeast
Average Annual Snowfall: 48 inches
Skiable Terrain: 72 acres
Slopes and Trails: 3 beginner, 3 intermediate, 2 advanced
Longest Run: 4,100 feet
Lifts: 1 quad, 1 T-bar, 1 poma lift, 2 handle tows
Uphill Capacity: **5,400 skiers per hour**
Night Skiing: 85% of area, Monday–Saturday until 10 P.M., Sunday until 9 P.M.
Snowmaking: 85% of area

Getting There

- **From State College:** Take 322 east through Boalsburg, then follow signs to Tussey Mountain.
- **From I-80:** Take Exit 24/Bellefonte, then Route 26 south to Route 322 east, and follow signs to Tussey.

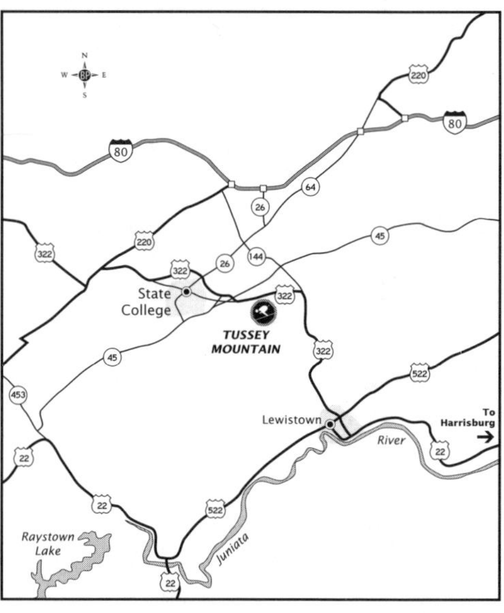

Tussey Bargains

Monday: Two for one college student lift and tubing tickets
Tuesday: Half-price night lift and tubing tickets
Wednesday: Half-price ladies night: lift, lesson, and/or rentals
Thursday: $9.70 night session lift and tube tickets, and rentals
Sunday: $20 first-time skier/snowboarder package: lesson, rental, and beginner-area lift ticket

More Fun in the Flakes

On-site

700-foot **snowtubing park** with a 200-foot vertical drop: $15/full day, $12/half day, five runs/$6. Discount group rates for parties of 10 or more; reservations required.

Nearby

Cross-country skiing, weather permitting, nearby at Stone Valley Recreation Area *(see page 227)*.

Snowboarding Highlights

A pretty good terrain park covers most of the bottom half of intermediate *Grizzly* trail. Look for a couple of spines shaped into quarterpipe-type terrain on both sides, some tabletops with multiple airs, and a few rail slides scattered throughout the course. Feel free to make up your own jumps and features here in the snowboard area. A newer halfpipe can be found on Lower Utah, but check in advance for availability. The park also welcomes skiers and is well lit nightly until 10 P.M. Tussey's snowboard school offers freestyle, freeriding, and carving lessons.

Snowboard Rentals: Original Sin, step-in boots and bindings • **Snowboard School**: 11 instructors.

Skier Services

Lift Tickets

Weekday: Noon–10 P.M. $24, noon–5 P.M. $20, 4 P.M.–10 P.M. $22, two–hour flex $15 • Weekend: 9 A.M.–10 P.M. $30, 9 A.M.–5 P.M. $28, 9 A.M.–2 P.M. $24, noon–5 P.M. and 4 P.M.–10 P.M. $24, noon–10 P.M. $28, two-hour flex $15 • Group rates for 10+ skiers: weekend $22, weeknight $18 • Reduced rates for children under 10, under 6 ski free.

Rentals

$19/full rental, $15/skis only.

Services

Ski School: Private $28/hour, junior $18; Group $14/1.5 hours; junior $11 (weekdays at 1, 3, and 7 P.M.; weekends at 11 A.M. and 1, 3, and 6 P.M.); First-time Learn to Ski program: $25/anytime (includes lesson, rental, and beginner-area lift ticket); Learn-to-ski-better program: $45 (includes group lesson, rental, and all-area lift ticket); Paw Prints program for ages 3–6: $30/two-hour lesson, bunny slope ticket, and supervised play; Mountain Lions developing child-skier program: $40/two-hour lesson, rental, and all-lift ticket; Senior Skier development program: offered Tuesday afternoon for ages 50+ • **Base Lodge Facilities:** Restaurant, cafeteria, lounge, ski shop/rentals, lockers, Skier Services building: ticket and group sales, Ski School.

Room & Board

Lodging

Nearby (call 814–466–6810 for information)

Bed & Breakfasts in historic town of Boalsburg • **Nittany Lion Inn** • **Holiday Inn State College** • **Ramada Inn** • **Days Inn**.

Dining/Aprés-Ski

On-site

Cafeteria/lounge with grill menu.

Nearby (Historic Boalsburg)

Duffy's Boalsburg Tavern, 18th-century dining; (814) 466–6241 • **The Village Eating House**; (814) 466–6865.

ALPINE RESORTS:
MARYLAND/WEST VIRGINIA

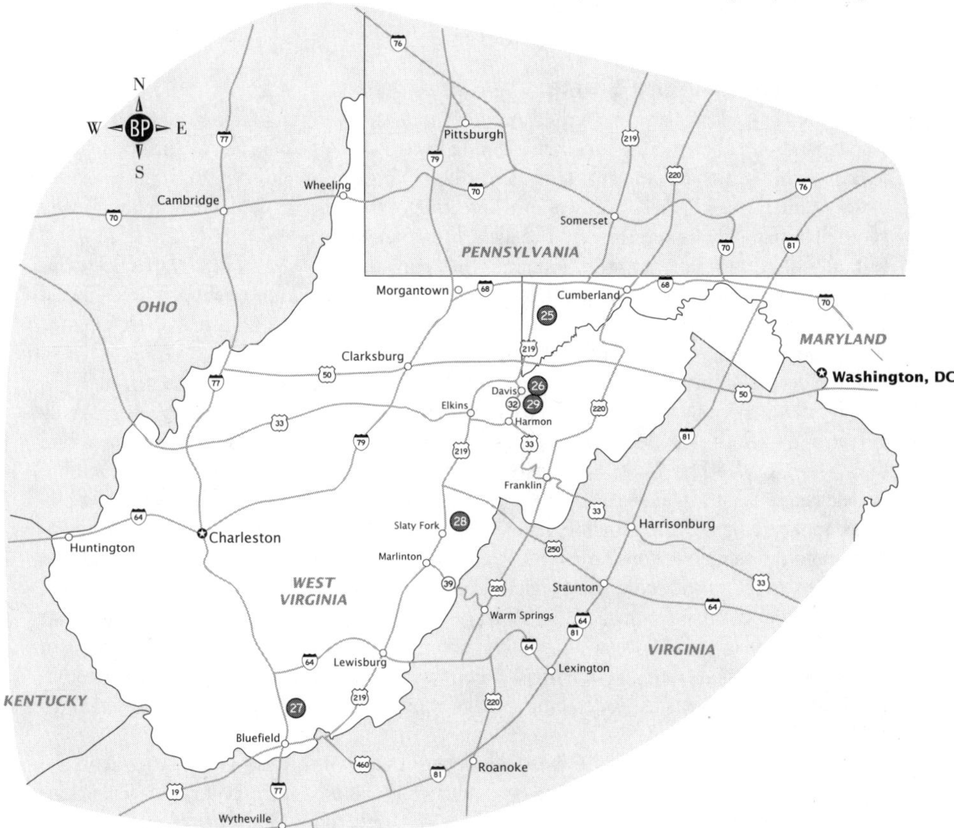

Maryland Alpine Skiing

Deep in the corner of Maryland's western Panhandle region lies Wisp—the state's only downhill ski area. This remote strip of the state sits due north of West Virginia's spacious Monongahela National Forest, with a wintry climate that's unique in Maryland. Wisp is right in-line with an Allegheny Mountain snow belt that runs southward through the Mountaineer State, picking up considerable amounts of powder at its 3,000-foot altitude.

With a limited mountainous region from which to survey, Wisp may continue as Maryland's only alpine ski destination for some time. But there has been talk, and serious planning, in recent years to introduce a second resort to the region. Near the town of Emmitsburg, which is just miles from the Pennsylvania border and Whitetail Resort, a modestly sized plateau has been considered for several years now. Since ski areas are often five to 10 years in the making, regional skiers will have to take a wait-and-see attitude.

In the meantime, cross-country skiing has never taken a back seat in Maryland. Not far from Wisp are two state parks that serve as premiere Nordic skiing spots: Herrington Manor and New Germany State Parks offer excellent trail systems that operate typically from January into late March when snowfall permits.

West Virginia Alpine Skiing

As the "East Coast's answer to the Rocky Mountains," West Virginia is an outdoor winter wonderland—an aberration in an otherwise mild lower East Coast climate. Within the massive Monongahela National Forest that borders southwest Virginia, an unusually arctic microclimate exists. Winters are long and cold here in this section of the Allegheny Mountain range. Yearly snowfall accumulations average over 150 inches, and numerous peaks exceed altitudes of 4,000 feet, allowing its ski areas to linger long into the spring seasons. Three of the state's five commercial alpine ski areas reside within the 200,000-plus acres of the Monongahela. The ski industry has served as a reliable economic source and much-needed broker of tourism in West Virginia, which has long ranked as one of the poorest states in the U.S.

Commercial skiing in the Mountaineer State began nearly 40 years ago in the rugged, high-country woodlands of Canaan Valley. Weiss Knob Ski Area, which opened in 1959, is generally known as the South's first ski area. The area surrounding the defunct resort now belongs to White Grass—one of the East Coast's premiere cross-country touring centers. It would be another decade before West Virginia's state park service took advantage of the region's substantial snowfall, stepping up in 1971 to establish Canaan Valley State Park and Ski Area. The resort complemented the warmer seasons, which began to lure Mid-Atlantic hikers, canoeists, and outdoor enthusiasts to the pristine wilderness region. Canaan's success also spurred development of what would turn out to be one of the East Coast's biggest ski resorts. Privately owned Snowshoe Resort attracts a phenomenal skier base that spans the entire eastern seaboard, offering a wealth of overnight accommodations and amenities. Adjoining, family-oriented Silver Creek was incorporated later, and the two facilities combine to make Snowshoe Mountain Resort the largest ski area in the Mid-Atlantic.

Skiing's growth spurt in the 1970s led developer David Downs to scout a new resort in the Canaan Valley region. Snowmaking had been practically mastered at this point, and would combine with the area's frequent snowstorms to provide nearly four months of skiing per season. Timberline Four Seasons Resort, just two miles from Canaan Valley State Park, opened in the early 1980s and serves up the state's most challenging and varied terrain.

New Winterplace, on the southern end of West Virginia, is the state's latest addition to commercial skiing. Though its winters don't pack the same force as its northeastern cohorts, Winterplace also posts strong yearly skier visits, operating more on aggressive snowmaking and refined grooming.

Wisp Ski Resort

Wisp Ski Resort
Deep Creek Lake
McHenry, MD 21541

Information: 1–800–462–9477
Reservations: (301) 387–4911
Internet: *www.gcnet.net/wisp*
Credit Cards: MC, VISA, AE, Discover

Operating Hours
8:30 A.M.–10 P.M. Tuesday–Saturday
8:30 A.M.–4:30 P.M. Sunday–Monday
- *Early/late season (before December 16 and March 12 to close): 8:30 A.M.-9 P.M. Tuesday-Saturday, 8:30 A.M.-4:30 P.M. Sunday-Monday*

Season: Mid-November to late-March

Backdrop

The Allegheny Mountain microclimate in Maryland's western panhandle contrasts with the state's otherwise temperate conditions. Downhill skiing does exist in Maryland, and only here at Wisp—the sole alpine beneficiary of Garrett County's strong winters. The ski area is perched 3,100 feet high atop Marsh Mountain, not far from West Virginia and Pennsylvania borders. Wisp's base lodge and East Ridge sit directly off Deep Creek Lake, the state's largest inland lake with more than 65 miles of shoreline.

Wisp is no secret to many Mid-Atlantic skiers, as it is one of the longest-running operations in the region. Skiing was crafted here in 1955 by the Helmuth Heise family to complement the development of nearby Will O'the Wisp—a woodsy retreat that has since evolved into a solid four-seasons resort. Dead on the path of Lake Erie's snow belt, Wisp is known for its cold winters and steady snow dumps. Just five years ago, an incredible 200-plus inches fell on Marsh Mountain. And with the resort's superior airless snowmaking system, you can count on November openings and over 120 skier days per year, on average. Lift chairs, though slow and somewhat dated, afford great mountain, valley, and lake views.

Getting There

- **From Washington**: Take I-495 north to I-270 north to Frederick, Maryland. Take I-70 west to Hancock, then I-68 west past Cumberland. Take Exit 14A to U.S. 219 south toward McHenry, then follow signs to Wisp.
- **From Baltimore**: Take I-695 to I-70 west to Hancock, then follow signs from Hancock above.
- **From Pittsburgh** (via Morgantown, West Virginia): Take I-79 south to I-68 east at Morgantown and follow to Exit 4 at Friendsville, Maryland. Then take Route 42 south to U.S. 219 south to McHenry, and follow signs to Wisp.

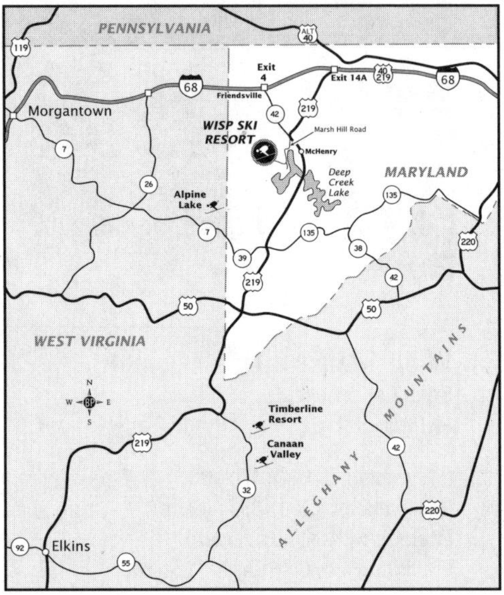

Trail Profiles

Wisp is neither the biggest nor the baddest mountain around, but a nice variety of clean terrain and striking scenery makes for high marks. Jump on the ambitiously named Chair #1 lift from base to summit, where you'll discover some interesting choices for all levels. If there's enough natural snow, drop into *Bobcat Bowl* and make some sweeping turns. Then, veer right into *Odin's Chute*—an advanced run with good steeps and technical turns that leads to intermediate cruising trails *Boulder* or *Down Under*. Or, take Chair # 1 and work your way to the right, where black diamond *Eye Opener* awaits. Chair #5 will then take you to the East Ridge's *Main Street*, where you can open it up on nearly eight acres of wide-open, steep track, usually with very little skier traffic. Sure, you need to take two chairs to reach the summit from the East Ridge, but then again, you get a lot of turns for your ticket and striking views of Deep Creek Lake on this more secluded side.

More steeps are an easy find on three short black diamonds in front of Wisp's base lodge, with a handy mid-station drop-off on Chair # 3. Moguls abound on *The Face* and its unforgiving fall line that shifts halfway down. Neighboring *Squirrel Cage* and natural snowfall *Devil's Drop* are short but plenty steep up top to guarantee lots of turning before running out to the lower flats. The resort also has an eye for racing, offering strong programs for both adults and juniors, including the national standard NASTAR and numerous annual race events.

Eleven intermediate trails are of medium-to-moderate steepness and length and offer a slew of bends and shifting widths. There's a solid intermediate pitch on *Boulder* and the East Ridge's *Down Under*, which opens swiftly and leads through Wisp's famous snow-filled tunnel. Short, negotiable blue trails are all over the resort's main side and fun for a range of abilities.

Mountain Stats

Base Elevation: 2,470 feet
Summit Elevation: 3,080 feet
Vertical Drop: 610 feet
Skiable Terrain: 80 acres
Primary Slope Direction: North to northeast
Average Annual Snowfall: 93 inches
Slopes and Trails: 4 beginner, 12 intermediate, 7 advanced
Longest Run: 1.5 miles
Lifts: 2 triples, 3 doubles, 2 surface tows
Uphill Capacity: 9,120 skiers per hour
Snowmaking: 90% of area
Night Skiing: 90% of area, Tuesday to Saturday until 10 P.M.

Two long beginner practice trails run side by side on the front face, offering over two miles of leisurely terrain between them. *Possum* skirts the plateau's scenic woodlands and the resort's golf course. The trail runs out into the wide-open *Chipmunk* slope extension, combining for a 1.5-mile run of easy grade. It's a good run for beginners to practice on after mastering the bunny slope. Parallel to *Possum* lies *Wisp Trail* for a second mile-long trek on a slightly more challenging grade. The *Belly Flop* bunny slope and rope tow are set in the midst of the base lodge, while the SKIwee and MINIrider children's programs are first-rate.

Snowboarding Highlights

Wisp's trail system gets points for diverse terrain, but it's the halfpipe and terrain park that bring out some of the region's best riders. Located underneath Chair #1, Wisp's monster halfpipe is 400 feet long by 35 feet wide, with 10-foot sidewalls. Easiest access is to hop on the bunny slope rope tow or make the short trek by foot. The pipe requires a lot of carving, cutting, and shaping from the snowboard crew and their tillers, but manages to stay open with some regularity. Look for more events and competitions this season.

Devil's Arena is the name of Wisp's terrain park, which now makes its home by the handle tow area on *The Face*. The resort relocated *Devil's Arena* so it could be serviced by its own lift. Spines, tabletops, log slides, and gap jumps are some of the park's changing features. Territorial boarders, however, must relent to skiers: The terrain park is open to anyone who dares enter. Both the park and pipe are well lit during normal night-skiing hours.

Snowboard Rentals: Rossignol, some K2: $29/day • **Snowboard School:** 14 instructors; Private $40/hour; Group $15/hour

More Fun in the Flakes

Garrett County is a virtual winter playground. Opportunities abound for cross-country skiers and snowmobilers in surrounding state parks and forests, while ice fishing and sleigh riding are offered at nearby Deep Creek Lake. And when the snow melts, the four-seasons resort schedules mountain biking and hiking on marked trails, scenic chairlift rides, and whitewater rafting trips on the Youghiogheny River. It also offers an 18-hole golf course that ranks among Maryland's best. Water sports are another big draw on the expansive Deep Creek Lake. Rentals are available for nearly every type of boat at several local marinas, and fly fishing and water skiing programs are run on-site at the lake. Brown, rainbow, and brook trout fishing can also be found in nearby Garrett County streams. One of the region's popular fall festivals is the annual McHenry Highland Festival, featuring bagpipe bands, Scottish country and highland dancers, and Scottish foods, shops, and athletic events. For information on any of the following, call the Deep Creek Lake/Garrett County Promotion Council at (301) 334–1948.

On-site

- **Sled Dog** snow runner rentals, permitted on all trails.

Nearby

Cross-country skiing at New Germany State Park *(see page 253)* and Herrington Manor State Park *(see page 254)* • **Snowmobiling** permitted on 35 miles of marked state forest trails (call Garrett County's Promotion Office, (301) 334–1948 for information/maps) and in state parks with valid snowmobile permits; additional snowmobile trails at Deep Creek Lake: (301) 387–5563; • **Ice fishing** and **sleigh riding** at Deep Creek Lake.

The Latest at Wisp

The biggest news to hit Wisp since skiers first made tracks here 46 years ago is now official. The resort was recently turned over by founder Helmuth Heise to a local development group for a price tag of just under $12 million. The sale is part of a deal between DC Development and not-for-profit Adventure Sports Center, whose mission is the development of an international sports center in western Maryland. The group hopes final development will allow for a run at the 2012 Summer Olympics, while it also works to increase tourism to Maryland's western panhandle in the meantime.

Plans for the sale include a new lodge at Wisp, snowtubing lanes, and more intermediate terrain off the summit. Proposals are also in the works for a retail village, indoor performing arts center, and an adventure sports park. DC Development has donated 550 acres of adjacent land for mountain biking, hiking, and rock climbing. The group's long-term vision includes 25 sports from ice skating to kayacking on a quarter-mile recirculating whitewater course.

(Info. provided by Ski Area Management Magazine *and* www.DCski.com.*)*

Skier Services

Wisp is a fun, low-key resort that won't keep tugging at your wallet. Prices are manageable, and keep your eyes and ears open for bargains like early and late-season rates and two-for-one-ticket Mondays. Wisp is bound to wear the commercial stamp now that the resort's ownership has changed hands, but that should only enhance what is already widely considered a first-rate ski area.

Lift Tickets

8:30 A.M.–4:30 P.M. or 1 P.M.–10 P.M.: weekend $42, weekday $35 • 1 P.M.–4:30 P.M. or 4:30 P.M.–10 P.M.: weekend $25, weekday $21 • 25%–35% discounts for ages 6–11 • Half-price tickets for ages 65–69; 70+ ski free all times; children under 6 ski free • Two-for-one lift ticket specials on Mondays • Early and late season ticket: $20/adult or child (season's open to December 15 and March 12 to season's close).

Rentals

1,200 sets: traditional skis $20/day, Rossignol shaped skis $29/day ($15, $23 early and late seasons) • New Rossignol Winter Adventure Center: rentals and instruction in parabolic skis, snowboards, and snow runners.

Services

Ski School: Private $40/hour; Group $15/hour; Beginner ski package: Weekend Junior Ski and Guide Program; SKIwee and MINIrider programs (reservations required): $62/day, $47/half-day, $89/all-day private; Adventure Center coaching/special instruction: $65 midweek, $95/weekends • **Base Lodge Facilities**: Rental/ski shops, lockers/basket check, information office, ski school, two restaurants, two lounges, pastry and pizzeria shops • **Adaptive Ski School**: Handicapped skiers accommodated, but no specific program; free midweek lift passes for handicapped, blind, and deaf skiers, half price on weekends/holidays • **Racing**: NASTAR offered weekends and some weekdays on advanced Squirrel Cage trail • **Day Care:** Children's Center, run daily at the base lodge: $62/full day; $47/half-day.

Room & Board

Wisp's base lodge isn't full of flash but is comfortable, low-key, and well equipped in a small European resort likeness. Both families and aprés-skiers have options, with two restaurants, two pubs, and several eateries. The resort's slopeside hotel offers several different ski packages covering lift tickets and meals. Also in great supply in the surrounding Deep Creek area are scenic rental houses and condos, motels and inns, and bed and breakfasts. Guests who want to break away from the slopes can hit some of the area's many shops and stores, including the Christmas Chalet in McHenry, Inglenook Gift & Craft Shop, and eight specialty shops at Oakland's Grand Central Station.

Lodging

On-site

168-unit **slopeside hotel** at base area, with restaurants/pub, indoor pool/Jacuzzi, fitness center and racquetball courts (call 1-800-462-9477 or 301-387-4911 for rates) • **Camping facility** two miles away.

Nearby

Will O'The Wisp condominium suites and rooms (call 301-387-4911 for information) • **Alpine Village**, Oakland, lakeside chalets and efficiency rooms with fireplaces, dining and shopping within walking distance; 1-800-343-5253/(301) 387-5534 • **A&A Realty**, Vacation rentals, McHenry, 1-800-336-7303 • **Timberlake Rentals**, Oakland; (301) 387-0336 • **Comfort Inn–Deep Creek Lake**; 1-800-228-5150 • **Lake Breeze Motel**; (301) 387-5503 • **Lakeside Motor Court**; (301) 387-5566.

Bed and Breakfasts:

The Country Inn Bed and Breakfast, McHenry, (301) 387-6694 • **Carmel Cove Inn B&B**, Deep Creek Lake, (301) 387-0067 • **Lake Point Inn B&B**, Deep Creek Lake, walking distance to Wisp; 1-800-523-LAKE • **Red Run Lodge B&B**, Deep Creek Lake, 1-800-898-7786 • **Harley Farm B&B**, Deep Creek Lake, (301) 387-9050.

Dining

On-site

The Bavarian Room restaurant, Pizzazz Pizzeria, The Gathering sandwich shop, cafeteria • **Shenanigans Lounge**, 23 Below Lounge, with live weekend entertainment.

Nearby (McHenry)

The Four Seasons Dining Room, five miles away at Will O'the Wisp • **The Silver Tree Inn**, Route 219/Glendale Bridge Road; (301) 387-5524 • **Pizzeria Uno** restaurant/pub; (301) 387-4866 • **JG's Pub**, Route 219; (301) 387-6369 • **Cornish Manor Victorian restaurant**, circa 1868, fine dining, live piano music • **Country Kitchen Restaurant**, Route 42; (301) 746-5583 • **Dominick's New York Style Italian Pizzeria**, Deep Creek Drive; (301) 387-6800 • **Le French Cafe**, Route 219; (301) 387-5900 • **McClive's Lakeside Restaurant & Lounge**, Deep Creek Drive; (301) 387-6172.

Canaan Valley

Canaan Valley
Route 1, Canaan Valley State Park
Davis, WV 26260

Info: 1–800–622–4121/(304) 866–4121
Internet: *www.canaanresort.com*
Credit Cards: VISA, MC, AE, Discover

Operating Hours
9 A.M.–4:30 P.M. Monday–Thursday
9 A.M.–9 P.M. Friday–Sunday

Season: December to late March

Backdrop

Following the widespread timber operations that finally dried up in the 1940s, backcountry skiing got going in Canaan Valley after pilots reported abundant amounts of snow that held strong long into April. Some 30 years ago, 3,000 acres of the wilderness area was donated privately to West Virginia, with the stipulation that the state would pick up the tab and match the acreage, turning the area into a state park. A nine-hole golf course was erected first, and the resort's first ski trails and chair lifts were open for business shortly after in 1971 here in the highest valley east of the Mississippi.

The ski area is part of a 6,000-acre state park that features the country's second largest inland wetland—home to white-tail deer, black bear, fox, wild turkey, beaver, and waterfowl. And, a handful of years ago, the nation's 500th wildlife preserve was established just minutes from the resort.

Trail Profiles

In a natural bowl recessed between two mountains, Canaan's trails run against a backdrop of inspiring vistas and scenery. Canaan is a model novice and intermediate skier's mountain, with boulevard-width slopes and diverse terrain running down 850 vertical feet. While the trail system is a scarce 80 acres, guests will be pleased with the variety of terrain and typically strong snow conditions. The mountain's real gem is the intermediate *Weiss*

Mountain Stats

Base Elevation: 3,430 feet
Summit Elevation: 4,280 feet
Vertical Drop: 850 feet
Longest Run: 1.25 miles
Primary Slope Direction: Northwest
Skiable Terrain: 80 acres
Average Annual Snowfall: 155 inches
Slopes and Trails: 10 beginner, 14 intermediate, 10 advanced
Snowmaking: 85% of area
Lifts: 1 quad, 2 triples
Uphill Capacity: 6,100 skiers per hour
Night Skiing: 30% of area, Friday-Sunday until 9 P.M.

Meadows section and its sampling of glade skiing on wide-open, tree-lined terrain. *Weiss Meadows 3* trail is a large expanse of slalom-turning terrain, as wide as it is long, with a narrow, contoured chute through the trees on Weiss Road. *Meadows 3* opens only as natural conditions permit, but tends to retain snow pretty well on this side of the mountain. *Meadows 2*, unlike the other runs, is equipped with snowmaking, but it's always the last trail on the mountain to receive it.

Advanced skiers might get bored with the paucity of steeps here at Canaan. The same consistently moderate pitch can be found practically everywhere on the trail network. Make sure, though, to check out *Gravity* when the freshies come dropping from the sky. It's the resort's steepest and most challenging trail, with a headwall off the summit, sustained pitches over 3,300 feet, and good bumps by mid-afternoon. Snowmakers blow extra snow on the trail, then groom it out and carve it to make the pitch even steeper, allowing moguls to form toward the top for bump skiers.

The Latest at Canaan Valley

A new snowboard terrain park can be found on the Weiss Meadows I section, and several slopes have been widened, including Upper Canaan Curve, Cutback, and Lower Timber Run. The resort has also increased snowmaking in needed spots throughout the mountain, while the snowtubing park has been extended some 200 feet, giving each of the five tubing lanes 850 feet in length.

On blue trail *Valley Vista*, skiers can carve under a chair-lift audience before dropping onto steeper track on *The Face*. *Green Circle* and *Blue Square* trails are also bountiful slopes. The beginner area is set in its own area, with two broad hills served by a triple lift, and the adjacent *Bunny Buster* trail caters to small children at its base lodge location.

Occasional warm snaps have been known to shut some of the more advanced trails down. The resort could definitely benefit from some investors willing to help purchase the goods necessary to lay down snow on the entire mountain. Some classic novice runs that do feature snowmaking include *Timber Trail*—a 6,000-foot meander off the northwest summit that eases developing skiers into slow-moving turns and gradual, confidence-building gliding.

Getting There

- **From Baltimore, Washington, DC and points north:** Take I-495 to I-66 west to I-81 south. Near Strasburg, VA, exit onto Route 55 west through Petersburg, West Virginia, heading to Harman. At Harman take Route 32 north to Canaan Valley. Follow signs to Canaan Valley Ski Area.
- **From Richmond, VA:** Take I-64 west to I-81 north to Harrisonburg. At Harrisonburg take Route 33 west to Harman, West Virginia, then follow 32 north to Canaan Valley Ski Area.
- **From Pittsburgh and points north:** Take I-79 south to Morgantown, West Virginia, then pick up I-68 east to Route 42 south at Friendsville, Maryland. From there follow Route 219 south at McHenry to Thomas, West Virginia, then take Route 32 south to Canaan Valley Ski Area.

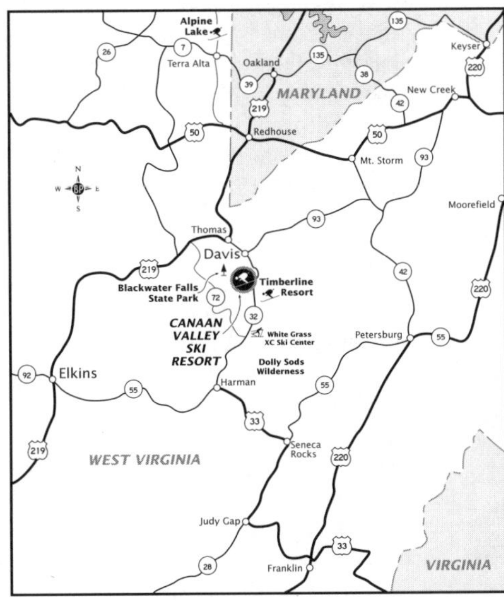

- **From Columbus, Ohio:** Take I-70 east into Pennsylvania, then take I-79 south to Morgantown, West Virginia, and follow directions above.
- **From Charleston:** Take I-79 north to Weston. Exit onto Route 33 east to Harman. At Harman pick up Route 32 north to Canaan Valley Ski Area.

Snowboarding Highlights

Canaan finally broke through the bureaucratic red tape of the state-park system a few years back and ushered in a new snowboard and skier terrain park on *Weiss Meadows I*. Boarders can also carve it out on the resort's diverse trail network. Riding Canaan's frequent natural powder is somewhat of a rare treasure in the Mid-Atlantic, so snowboarders are starting to make Canaan Valley and Timberline a change-of-pace stop.

Snowboard Rentals: Adult $26; ages 12 and under $21; Alter Ego Sports (off-mountain), specializing in snowboards/rentals, (304) 259–2219/866–4698 • **Snowboard School:** Six instructors, ski rates apply: Ride Ranger instruction program for boarders ages 10 and older

More Fun in the Flakes

Cross-country and **Telemark** skiing is a hot activity at Canaan, where consistent snowfall ensures plentiful opportunities during most seasons. The resort's Nordic ski center sits one mile from the ski lodge, with a connector trail that accesses an ungroomed, 18-mile trail system of wide-open meadows and backcountry wilderness. "Skinny skiers" can also traverse the eight-mile *Blackwater/Canaan* trail and the Dolly Sods Wilderness Area from the resort's summit, while both Blackwater Falls State Park and the acclaimed White Grass Touring Center are just a few miles away • A new **snowtubing** park features five lanes over 850 feet and a handle-tow lift.

On-site

Cross-country skiing at Canaan's touring center *(see page 262)* • **Snowtubing**: Five lanes serviced by a handle tow; adult $10, junior $8.50; two-hour sessions begin at 11:30 A.M. and 2 P.M. • Lighted, outdoor **ice-skating** rink, with rentals, overlooking the Allegheny Mountains.

Nearby

Cross-country skiing at White Grass Touring Center, one mile from Canaan *(see page 260)* and Blackwater Falls State Park, also with tobogganing/sled run (*see page 265*) • Additional Nordic skiing trails in the rugged, ungroomed Dolly Sods Wilderness Area • **Ice fishing** on the Blackwater River.

Skier Services

Night skiing isn't much factored into the equation, as just 11 slopes and trails currently have lights. The resort has tinkered with transitioning to a daytime-only operation because of dwindling night ticket sales and competition with nearby Timberline. With just a small lounge and eatery at the ski base lodge, there's not much nightlife here at Canaan. On the other hand, Canaan's overnight lodge (based two miles from the ski area) is clean and affordable, with two restaurants, pool and spa, ice skating, and an arcade.

Lift Tickets

Prime season (January/February): 9 A.M.–9 P.M.: weekday $32, weekend $43 • 9 A.M.–4:30 P.M.: $29, $39 • 12:30 P.M.–4:30 P.M.: weekday $24, $29 • 12:30 P.M.–9 P.M.: $29, $39; 4:30 P.M.–9 P.M.: Friday $19, weekend $25 • Discount rates for ages 12 and under • Multi-day discounts available and reduced rates offered during value ski seasons (before Christmas and after February).

Ski Rentals

$19/all adult rentals; $16/ages 12 and under; Off-mountain Rental Shops • The Ski Barn/demo ski center, full fleet of shaped and regular skis, snowboards, tuning service, (304) 866–4444.

Services

Ski School: 30 instructors: PSIA certified; Private: $42/hour; Group: $16/1.5 hours; Ski & Play programs for ages 4–6 and 7–12; half-day or full-day sessions; call for current rates • **Base Lodge Facilities:** Lodge 1: ticket office, information, ski and rental shops, lockers, ski school; Lodge 2: day care, lockers, cafeteria, and pub • **Day Care**: Available at base lodge, reservations suggested • **Racing:** NASTAR held weekends and some midweek days on intermediate *Ramble* trail.

Calendar of Events

Races, events, and demo days held periodically throughout ski season • **January**: Special Olympics Winter Games • **March**: Annual Governor's Cup ski race (slalom and giant slalom) on *Ramble* trail; Annual Spring Thing weekend—events, races, festivities.

Room & Board

While there's no on-site lodging at Canaan, guests can base themselves at Canaan's 250-room lodge two miles from the slopes, or at a selection of mountain cabins and year-round campsites. Weekend and vacation skiers also have over 500 private home and condominium properties rented and sold by local realtors and development companies, as well as numerous bed and breakfasts, inns, and motels in Canaan Valley and the nearby towns of Davis and Thomas.

Davis is the highest elevated incorporated town east of the Mississippi, and combines with the nearby borough of Thomas to offer a host of historic restaurants, saloons, art and photography stores, and antique and specialty shops. Thomas, two miles north of Davis, is home of the landmark **Christmas Shop and Eagles Nest stores**, open year-round. Also within driving distance is the picturesque **Seneca Rocks-Spruce Knob National Recreation Area**, the natural formations of Smoke Hole and Seneca Caverns (open year-round with constant 56-degree temperatures), and **Harper's Old Country Store**. Built in 1902, Harper's is one of the state's oldest continuously operated businesses, situated in front of scenic Seneca Rocks and Spruce Knob—West Virginia's highest point (4,861 feet).

Did You Know?

Vacationers can get a lot of bang for their buck in Canaan Valley. Considering the area's usually-bountiful snowfall, there's a good shot at most terrain being open when you pick your vacation time. Rates across-the-board are already a good bit cheaper than most Mid-Atlantic resorts, and guests have both Canaan Valley and Timberline areas at their disposal. And big bargains can be found at a wide selection of beautiful rental homes during early season and in March, which historically has been a heavy-snow producing month here in the Valley.

Summer seasons at the resort bring out thousands of vacationing urban dwellers seeking refuge from the east coast's muggy heat. Canaan's cool mountain air combines with an average summer temperature of 75 degrees to make the resort's numerous outdoor activities even more appealing. Some of Canaan's offerings include a 72-par golf course, tennis courts,

Olympic-size swimming pool, chair lift rides overlooking scenic mountain vistas, and 18 miles of hiking trails that wind through Canaan's network and rise to the towering peak of Bald Knob.

Lodging

On-site/State Park Area

Canaan Valley Resort State Park, two miles from ski area: 250-room lodge (one to four bedroom units, efficiencies, suites from $61–$82/night during value season; $79 to $113/night during January/February); indoor pool, hot tub, saunas, fitness center, table tennis/game rooms • **23 mountain cabins** (one to four bedrooms) with fireplaces, full kitchens; rates $125–$194/night • **34 year-round campsites** with electrical hookups (no running water during winter).

On-site and Nearby

Canaan Realty, 104 chalets and five condo properties slopeside or nearby, with fireplaces, hot tubs, large decks; personal checks only for rentals; 1–800–448–0074 • **Northpoint**, Canaan Valley, popular cross-country ski lodging, bordering Monongahela National Forest with 30-mile Nordic/hiking/biking trail system; 46 large, modern fireplace units include chalets and cabins with hot tubs, and townhomes and log cabins; views of Timberline and Canaan slopes; all units (sleeping four to 14 persons) fully furnished with full kitchens; rates $285–$700 per four nights; 1–800–542–8355 • **Black Bear Resort/Condos**, Davis, 44 cottages and six condos with full kitchen, living/dining room, fireplace, Jacuzzi; 12 inn rooms with Jacuzzi; indoor pool; restaurant/lounge; rates $110–$200 nightly per unit; 1–800–553–2327 • **Deerfield Village Resort and Restaurant**, Canaan Valley, 125 villas with full kitchen, fireplace (most with Jacuzzis); restaurant; shops/groceries/ski rentals; rates (two-night minimum) $125–$180/night, up to 10 persons $250/night; 1–800–342–3217 • **Mountain Top Rentals**, Canaan Valley, 90 units: condos, cabins, chalets, and large homes at Timberline and close to Canaan ski areas; most with fireplaces, some with hot tubs/Jacuzzis; all units with full kitchens; also 20 efficiency condos in Davis, with kitchenettes, at Pendletonheim; rates at Mountain Top $240–$900/3 nights for two to 16 people; 1–800–624–4341 • **Yokum's Vacationland**, Seneca Rocks, 30 miles from Canaan, 45–50 units, including fireplace/Jacuzzi cabins, motel units with kitchenettes, efficiency apartments, and home trailers, all with private baths; winter campground with showers and electrical hook-ups; restaurant and deli on-site; rates from $30–$95/night; 1–800–772–8342.

Nearby Bed and Breakfasts

Meyer House B&B (the Green Gables of Davis), large five-room country house, circa 1885, popular lodging for cross-country skiers, one mile from Blackwater Falls State Park trails, also skiing out the back door along Blackwater River leading to the canyon; four restaurants close by; rates $65–$85/two persons nightly; (304) 259–5451 • **Bright Morning B&B**, Davis, 10 miles from Canaan, eight rooms with private bath; dining room with breakfast/lunch (also open to non-guests); rates $60 nightly/two persons; (304) 259–5119 • **Pour**

Victoria B&B, circa 1883 Queen Anne Victorian inn, with antique furnishings, 20 minutes from Canaan in Parsons; (304) 478–1103 • **Hill House B&B**, Davis, circa 1890 Victorian house, three rooms with shared bath, kitchen and living room privileges; full country breakfast; rates $75 nightly/two persons; (304) 259–5883 • **White Oak B&B**, Parsons, 25 miles from Canaan Valley, four single rooms and one suite with three rooms, kitchenette, fireplace; breakfast extra; restaurants nearby; rates $45/double, $35/single; (304) 478–4705.

Other Nearby Lodging

Mountain Aire Lodge, Davis, at entrance to Blackwater Falls State Park, 11 standard, affordable rooms, restaurant next door; 1–800–553–0724 • **Best Western Alpine Lodge**, Davis; (304) 259–5245 • **Montwood Motor Inn**; (304) 463–4114 • **Tucker Country Inn**; (304) 478–2100 • **Windwood-Fly Inn**; 1–888–359–4667 • **Village Inn**; (304) 866–4166.

Dining/Aprés-Ski

On-site

Cafeteria, pub, pizza cellar • Nearby **Canaan Lodge** offers fine dining at the Aspen Dining Room and Laurel Lounge.

Nearby

White Grass Natural Foods Cafe, Canaan Valley; (304) 866–4114 • **Body and Soul Cafe**, Thomas, coffee bar/light menu, art/gift/book shop, live jazz/blues/folk music, poetry, and storytelling; (304) 463–4458 • **Golden Anchor & Portside Pub**, Canaan Valley, acclaimed seafood menu; (304) 866–2722 • **Tucker Country Inn**, Parsons, homestyle meals and baked breads, desserts; (304) 478–2100 • **Amelia's Restaurant/Yeager's Bar** at the Windwood-Fly Inn, Canaan Valley; 1–888–359–4667 • **Oriskany Inn Restaurant/Lounge**, fine dining at the entrance to Timberline Resort; (304) 866–4514 • **Sirianni's Cafe**, Davis, well-known family restaurant with Italian menu; (304) 259–5454 • **The Sawmill Restaurant at Best Western**, Davis, country cooking with affordable menu; (304) 259–5245 • **Blackwater Lodge Restaurant/Lounge**, Davis; (304) 259–5216 • **Joe's Italian Supper Club & Lounge**, Davis, breakfast-dinner; (304) 463–4291 • **The Front Porch**, Seneca Rocks, gourmet casual dining and clear views of Seneca Rocks and surrounding Allegheny Mountains; (304) 567–2555.

New Winterplace

New Winterplace
P.O. Box 1
Flat Top, West Virginia 25841

Ski Report/Info/Res.: 1–800–607–7669
Express Ski: 1–800–977–3754
Local: (304) 787–3221
Internet: *www.winterplace.com*
Email: winterplace@winterplace.com
Credit Cards: MC, VISA, AE, Discover

Operating Hours
9 A.M.–10 P.M. weekdays
8 A.M.–10 P.M. weekends, holidays

Season: Early December to late March

Backdrop

Flat Top Mountain is home to New Winterplace—West Virginia's southernmost and only ski area outside the expansive Monongahela National Forest. The 25-year-old resort is located between the towns of Beckley and Princeton, in the state's southeastern region.

Though far removed from large metropolitan areas, Winterplace still has demographics in its favor. It's one of the South's favorite ski destinations, luring guests from Charlotte, Raleigh/Durham, Columbia, South Carolina, southern Virginia, and more locally based skiers from Charleston and Huntington. The resort's 27-trail network far surpasses North Carolina's biggest ski areas, and offers slopeside condominiums and a long list of nearby facilities. Skiing Winterplace also means easy access, just two miles off I-77. It's a distinction that's heavily marketed by the resort since the region averages 100 inches of snow per year. Southern skiers especially cherish the opportunity to carve through natural powder, but are generally less inclined than northerners to drive on it, which is why the resort's convenient highway access helps draw a strong yearly skier base.

Years ago, jammed slopes and interminable lift lines were the scourge of skiing at Winterplace. Ownership has since responded by increasing uphill capacity and adding new terrain. A much-needed quad lift was strung up next to the triple chair on the advanced section, and another new quad reaches the often-congested mid-summit area. Four new trails introduced years ago have also helped distribute the flow of traffic. The resort also continues to excel at snowmaking, pumping out mega-gallons of water fed from its 27-million-gallon reservoir.

Otherwise, for a resort on the smaller side, the staff is exceptionally cordial and the SKIwee program is outstanding. Keep in mind that crowds can get a bit heavy on weekends, so those renting equipment might save some on the slopes by getting their equipment from the shop near the resort entrance, with cheaper rates and newer equipment.

Mountain Stats

Base Elevation: 2,997 feet
Summit Elevation: 3,600 feet
Vertical Drop: 603 feet
Longest Run: 1.25 miles
Primary Slope Direction: North
Skiable Terrain: 90 acres
Annual Snowfall: 100 inches
Snowmaking: 100% of area
Slopes and Trails: 11 beginner, 12 intermediate, 4 advanced
Night Skiing: 90% of area, nightly until 10 P.M.
Lifts: 2 quads, 3 triples, 2 doubles, 2 surface lifts
Uphill Capacity: 13,000 skiers per hour

Getting There

- **From Charleston**: Take I-77 south to Exit 28, Flat Top, and follow signs two miles to New Winterplace.
- **From Huntington**: Take I-64 east to I-77/I-64 south. Follow directions above.
- **From Washington, DC**: Take I-66 west to I-81 south to I-64 south/west into West Virginia. Then follow I-64 west to Beckley, picking up I-77 south. Take Exit 28, Flat Top, and follow signs two miles to New Winterplace.
- **From Charlotte, North Carolina and Columbia, South Carolina**: Take I-77 north through Virginia, then take Exit 28, Flat Top, West Virginia, and follow signs two miles to New Winterplace.
- **From Raleigh/Durham and Greensboro, North Carolina**: Take I-40 northwest to I-77 north, then follow directions above.

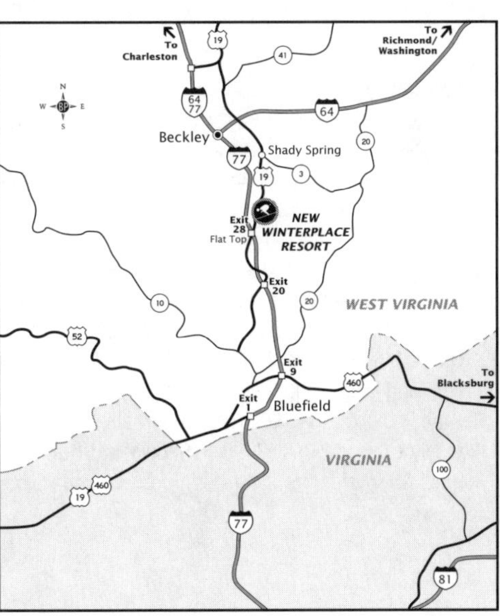

Trail Profiles

The mountain's two-face system separates the limited advanced terrain from the more prevalent beginner track. One major drawback at Winterplace, however, is the resort's awkward trail design: Two chair lifts are required to reach the summit. Most of the resort's trails are on the short side, but beginners have over one mile of continuous cruising on the summit's *Ridgerunner* trail—an easy jaunt leading down to the base. There's also considerable bunny turf and slow-skiing terrain off the base lodge. *Wood's Run* is a notable beginner run—a long, narrow run off the summit that zig zags along the outskirts of the trail network down to the new quad lift.

New at Winterplace

The resort is constantly looking for ways to improve the guest experience. One such idea is free night skiing with an all-day lift ticket. Or, call the resort one day in advance, and the new Express Ski Service will have your lift ticket and/or rental ready as you pull into the lot. Snowtubing has also taken off at Winterplace, now with 10 lanes and three lifts. In fact, tubing has gotten big enough that lift lines can be longer here than on the trails.

Don't expect too many hair-raising, extreme drops from Winterplace's 600 feet of vertical drop. The resort's four black diamond trails are somewhat steep, but short-lived and rarely bumped out with moguls. The steepest drops can be found on the wide-open summit bowl, which flows into more narrow, tree-lined terrain on the advanced *Plunge* and *Nosedive*. *Turkey Chute* and *Drop Off* are blue runs disguised as black diamonds on satisfyingly pitched cruising terrain. Winterplace hosts the popular NASTAR time-trial racing program on the intermediate *Look At Me* trail.

Snowboarding Highlights

Winterplace has an exclusive snowboard park, halfpipe, and surface lift in a centrally located, tree-lined cul-de-sac area. The 1.5-acre park boasts tabletops, hips, rails, gaps, and a few other hits periodically thrown in for good measure. Strong lights keep the park open nightly, and boarders have the entire mountain at their disposal. The resort has a strong variety of new boards for rental, and offers an affordable learn-to-board package that includes beginner ticket, board and boots, and a lesson.

Learn-To-Snowboard: Beginner lift ticket (valid for lifts 1, 4, 5, and 6), snowboard rental with boots, and a lesson; Weekdays: $37.95; Weekends/Holidays: $59.95 • **Lift, Lesson, and Rental:** Package: Includes a full mountain lift ticket and equipment rental; Weekdays: $78.95; Weekends/Holidays: $92.95 • **Snowboard Rentals**: $23–$30 (includes boots) • **Snowboard School:** 45 instructors, ski rates apply; Beginner snowboard package: $30–$50.

Skier Services

Lift Tickets

Call 1–800–977–3754 for current rates; 9 A.M.–10 P.M.: weekend $41, weekday $27; 3 P.M.–10 P.M.: $28, $25; Reduced rates for ages 6–12; 5 & under ski free; Multiday discounts on lift tickets and rentals.

Ski Rentals

Over 2,000 sets: Rossignol, Elan; Adult $14–$18, junior $11–$14; New: Salomon Snowblades; Parabolic (shaped) skis $23–$28.

Services

Ski School: 200 instructors: PSIA certified; Private $40; Group $16/$11 per additional person; SKIwee program for ages 4–11, with half-day and full-day sessions; call for rates 1–800–607–SNOW); Learn-to-ski or snowboard package, weekday $20–$30, weekend $40–$50, includes beginner lift ticket, rental, lesson; full-mountain beginner package also available; Shaped ski instruction and rental package $30 • **Adaptive ski program:** No formal program, but skiers are accommodated, with adaptive ski rentals available • **Base Lodge Facilities:** Ski/rental shop, Ski School/SKIwee program, group rental area, ski accessory shops, ski and boot lockers, day care, restaurants/lounges • **Day care**: Offered daily at base lodge, half or full day, 24-hour reservations required (call 1–800–607–SNOW) • **Racing**: NASTAR held daily on Look at Me trail.

Calendar of Events

Mountain Bike Slalom Snow Races held each weekend • Family Fun Day Saturdays, with events and giveaways • **January:** Annual Winter Carnival; Annual West Virginia Shovel Race Championship.

Other Winter Sports

On-site

10-lane **snowtubing** park with three surface lifts. Weekday, four hours: $15, eight hours: $20. Weekends: $15–$23. Group tubing prices available • **Telemark** skiing allowed on all slopes.

Nearby

Cross-country skiing 35 miles away at Pipestem Resort State Park *(see page 267)*.

Room & Board

Nighttime is the right time at Winterplace, where most of the day-ticket crowds are long gone but the revelry continues under lights. Over 90 percent of the trails and a snowboarding terrain park are equipped with lights. The **Snowdrift Lounge** runs until midnight with live music and entertainment on weekends, and the **Mountain House** is a mid-mountain restaurant/lounge that also hosts live bands. In all, the resort has five eateries and three lounges.

Beyond the limited slopeside lodging at the **Winterhaven Condos**, numerous bedding options are available just off the mountain and in both Princeton and Beckley (10 miles). Overnight guests have the choice of basing themselves at luxury inns, affordable motels, or century-old bed & breakfasts. Winterplace's sister resort, **Glade Springs**, is a 10-minute drive from the mountain, offering free shuttle service between the two.

Lodging

On-site

Winterhaven Condos—36 slopeside rooms with kitchenettes, hot tubs/spas, and fireplaces; rates $160–$300/night (up to six persons); (304) 787–3202.

Nearby (10 minutes)

Appalachian Resort Inn, with restaurant, one-half mile from resort; rates $45–$80/night; 1–800–231–0054 • **Glade Springs Resort** (New Winterplace's sister resort), eight miles away—shuttle service available, with kitchenettes, hot tubs, fireplaces, indoor tennis, exercise room; rates $60–$325/night (up to eight persons); 1–800–634–5233 • **Econolodge**, one mile from resort; rates $45–$78/night; (304) 787–3250 • **Country Cabins**, 14 miles from resort, with kitchenettes, fireplaces; rates $80–$250/night (up to 10 persons); (304) 466–3930 • **Sleep Inn,** Beckley; rates $41–$59/night; (304) 255–4222 • **Best Western Motor Lodge**, Beckley; rates $41–$62; 1–800–528–1234 • **Comfort Inn**, Beckley, with exercise room; rates $41–$61/night; (304) 255–2161 • **Days Inn**, Princeton, with kitchenettes, hot tubs, indoor pool; rates $45–$67; 1–800–222–0511 • **Hampton Inn**, Beckley; rates $64–$76; 1–800–465–4329 • **Super 8 Motel**, Beckley; rates $40–$57; 1–800–848–8888.

Bed and Breakfasts:

Historic Hinton Manor B&B, 22 miles from resort; rates $60–$150/night; (304) 466–3930 • **Dogwood Ridge B&B**, 47 miles from resort, with hot tub; rates $65–$120/night; 1–800–816–1255.

Dining/Aprés-Ski

On-site

Mickey's Mountain Café, American cuisine • **The Mountain House**, food court • **Snowdrift Lounge**, open from 11 A.M. to midnight, with live music/videos • **Almost Heaven**, The Deck at Winterplace • **Mountain Mama's** Food Court.

Nearby

Holiday Inn, Beckley, restaurant/lounge, 17 miles from resort; 1–800–465–4329 • **Ramada Inn**, Beckley, restaurant/lounge, 15 miles from resort; 1–800–341–6455.

Snowshoe Silver Creek

Snowshoe/Silver Creek
1 Snowshoe Drive
Snowshoe, WV 26209

Ski Report: (304) 572–4636
Information: (304) 572–1000
Lodging Reservations: 1–877–441–4386
Internet: *www.snowshoemtn.com*
Credit Cards: VISA, MC, AE

Operating Hours
Snowshoe: 8:30 A.M.–4:30 P.M. daily
Silver Creek: 8:30 A.M.–10 P.M. daily

Season: Mid-November to late March

Backdrop

Decades after the last logging outfits left behind the highlands of Pocahontas County's Cheat Mountain, Snowshoe was conceived when Dr. Thomas Brigham and his crew examined these snow-filled mountaintops of maple, cherry, and red spruce hardwoods. They broke ground in 1973 by cutting nine trails and slinging up three chair lifts on the 4,800-foot-high summit of Cheat Mountain.

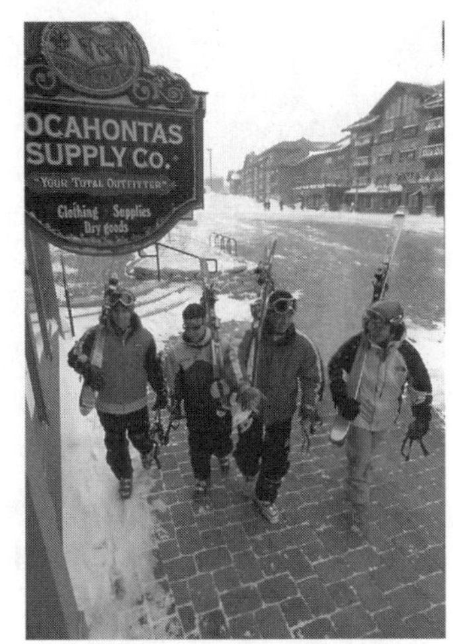

Today, with an annual visitor count that ranks in the top five percent of North American ski areas, Snowshoe Mountain Resort is the Mid-Atlantic's premiere ski destination. The virtual ski town comprises two ski areas: Snowshoe and Silver Creek, with a combined 57 runs, same-day reciprocal lift ticket, and shuttle buses servicing both facilities. Snowshoe is the bigger of the two and owns the Mid-Atlantic's biggest vertical drop of 1,500 feet. Just across the mountain is Silver Creek, which caters primarily to families and developing skiers but also is home to an outstanding snowboard terrain park and snowtubing lanes.

The entire resort was acquired in 1995 by Vancouver, British Columbia's Intrawest Corporation—the leading real estate developer and mountain resort operator in North America. Intrawest also owns such alpine giants as Vermont's Stratton; California's Mammoth; British Columbia's Blackcomb, Whistler, and Panorama; Colorado's Copper; and Quebec's Mont Tremblant. With Intrawest on board, no resort in the Mid-Atlantic has come close to investing in the kind of capital improvements that Snowshoe has. To the tune of over $82 million in the last four years, the laundry list includes new advanced and beginner terrain, a high-speed detachable quad, increased snowmaking, snowtubing, snowboard halfpipe, improved night skiing at Silver Creek, and a host of swank new restaurants and lodges. It's a strong bet you'll have a great time at Snowshoe, and don't forget to bring the camera gear to capture Snowshoe's snow-capped treeline and valleys.

Getting There

- **From Baltimore and points north**: Take I-695 in Baltimore to I-70, drive past Frederick, and take 340 west to Harper's Ferry, WV. Take the 340 south exit, then 7 west towards Winchester, VA. Exit onto I-81 south and take 55 west into West Virginia to 28 south through Greenbank, then Route 66 west to Snowshoe. Alternately, take I-695 to I-70 west to I-81 south to 55 west and follow directions above.
- **From Washington, DC**: Take I-495 to I-66 west to I-81 south and follow first directions above. Alternately, take 66 west to I-81 south to Staunton, VA. Then take Route 250 west to 42 south to Goshen. From Goshen, follow 39 west to Marlinton, West Virginia, and travel 26 miles north on Route 219 to Snowshoe.

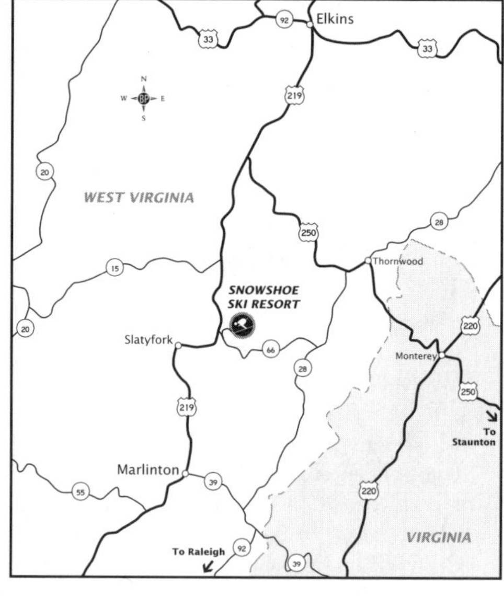

- **From Richmond:** Take I-64 west to I-81 north to Staunton. Then take Route 250 west to 42 south to Goshen. From Goshen, follow 39 west to Marlinton, West Virginia, and travel 26 miles north on Route 219 to Snowshoe.
- **From Pittsburgh:** Take I-79 south to Weston, West Virginia, then travel east on Route 33 to Elkins. From Elkins, follow 219 south for 48 miles to Snowshoe.
- **From Cleveland**: Take I-77 south to Parkersburg, West Virginia, then Route 50 east to Clarksburg and I-79 south to Weston. Follow Route 33 east to Elkins, and travel 48 miles south on Route 219 to Snowshoe.

- **From Raleigh/Durham and Greensboro, North Carolina**: Take Route 220 north to Clifton Forge, Virginia, then take I-64 west to White Sulphur Springs. From White Sulphur Springs, follow Route 92 north to West Virginia Route 39 , heading west to Marlinton. Follow Route 219 north 26 miles to Snowshoe.
- **From Atlanta; Columbia, South Carolina; and Charlotte, North Carolina:** Take I-77 north to Beckley, West Virginia, then take I-64 east to White Sulphur Springs. From White Sulphur Springs, follow Route 92 north to West Virginia Route 39 , heading west to Marlinton. Follow Route 219 north 26 miles to Snowshoe.

Mountain Stats

Base Elevation: Snowshoe: 3,250 feet; Silver Creek: 4,155 feet
Summit Elevation: Snowshoe: 4,848 feet; Silver Creek: 4,818 feet
Vertical Drop: Snowshoe: 1,500 feet; Silver Creek: 670 feet
Skiable Terrain: Snowshoe: 132 acres; Silver Creek: 92 acres
Primary Slope Direction: North to northeast
Average Annual Snowfall: 180 inches
Slopes and Trails: Snowshoe area: 21 beginner, 10 intermediate, 8 advanced; Silver Creek area: 6 beginner, 10 intermediate, 2 advanced
Longest Run
Snowshoe: 1.5 miles
Silver Creek: 1 mile
Lifts: 2 fixed quads, 2 high-speed detachable quads, 7 triples, 3 surface lifts
Uphill Capacity: Snowshoe/Silver Creek: 22,900 skiers per hour
Snowmaking: 100% of both areas
Night Skiing: Snowshoe: lifts close at 4:30 P.M.; Silver Creek: over 70% of area nightly until 10 P.M.

Trail Profiles

Snowshoe

Snowshoe's north-facing mountain is somewhat of an elliptical bowl, with nearly 900 vertical feet covering the main side and 1,500 feet of vert on the ridge's other side, the Western Territory. The main face's 36 runs are mostly of the beginner to intermediate variety on short, narrow and well-groomed terrain. Don't expect anything too tremendously steep at Snowshoe. The sharpest pitch is most likely on *Widowmaker* on the ridge's far side and highest tip. It's a steep, straight shot down, and usually clear of skiers. Otherwise, the Western Territory is the place for upper-intermediate and advanced skiers. (Simply put, nowhere else in the Mid-Atlantic can you ride and slide this fast and for this long on such varied terrain.)

To reach the Northern Territory, just walk across the road from the Powder Monkey lift and pick one of two 1.5-mile long, 1,500-foot vertical runs: classic *Cupp Run* or newer *Shay's*

What's New at the Shoe

Seems there's always something brewing at Snowshoe, and this season is no exception. The resort will usher in a new family aqua center as part of the Village at Snowshoe, and is also widening and improving many of its intermediate trails. Another recent terrain addition is a good beginner run called Yew Pines in the expanded Northern Tract. Upscale, slopeside Rimfire Lodge and Highland House have joined the community-plaza atmosphere in the Village at Snowshoe, while Allegheny Springs Lodge nears completion. And, as part of its Outdoor Adventure Program, Snowshoe now offers several guided snowmobile tours, horse-drawn sleigh rides, dogsled tours, cross-country skiing, and snowshoeing.

Revenge. *Shay's* is quick off the top, throws in some curves and continues fast and wide-open, then flattens on a shelf that overlooks the long, sustained steeps of *Lower Shay's*, dotted with big bad bumps. No worries: a cat track prior to the shelf cuts across to the second half of *Cupp Run* to spare riders from *Shay's* moguls. On neighboring *Cupp*, enjoy changing pitches, widths, and contours, and look for the gulley on *Lower Cupp*, where you can hop in and catch air on the way out. If conditions are right on, *Cupp* and *Shay's* are exquisite. If not, they're best served by early-morning runs before the track gets packed too hard or icy by afternoon. Another clutch piece of the Western Territory is the five short minutes it takes to get back top on the new high-speed detachable quad. Lift lines here are scarce, and you can get a lot of quality runs in a short span. Plus, when you ride back down, you can stop in for a bite or a nip at the new Arbuckle's Cabin.

Intermediates will have fun on *Ballhooter* and its wide terrain, with the Boathouse Grill serving as a nice respite at the bottom. Here, the high-speed Ballhooter quad makes quick uphill work of what appears to be long lift lines on some weekends. Another good blue run is *J Hook*—a serpentine trail unencumbered by intersecting trails, next to *Widowmaker*. Novice skiers have a new, expertly designed run called *Yew Pines* in the recently widened beginner area called the Northern Tract. It's wide, long, and leisurely, and affords some good turning opportunities. Other good options for beginners are the longer *Upper* and *Lower Hootenanny* and *Upper* and *Mid Flume*. Directly in front of Shavers Center and Spruce (main) Lodge are the Skidder and Crosscut first-time-skier areas and site of the resort's polished ski school.

Silver Creek

Thirty feet lower in altitude and cross-mountain lies Silver Creek. It's a natural fit for beginner skiers with its wide-open terrain and a smallish 670 vertical feet. The *Tenderfoot* bunny hill is great for small kids and has its own chair lift. Surrounding beginner slopes are plenty wide and easily negotiable, including slow-skiing *Cub Run*, which has an exclusive bunny chair.

And here's the secret that Silver Creek diehards would rather you didn't know—it's more fun than you'd expect, without tons of skier traffic. And, you can ski under lights on most of the runs until 10 P.M. Pitches on the intermediate and advanced runs are decent, especially the headwalls of *Flying Eagle* and *Bear Claw*.

The Mountaineer Terrain/Snowboard Park is in the middle of Silver Creek, but the location is actually key for all. The park and halfpipe occupy an entire (former) green/blue trail with its own lift, and there's little interference between boarders and skiers.

Silver Creek's snowtubing park, opposite the base, is part of the resort's Family Snow Adventure Area. The park features six tubing lanes and a handle tow lift. Both resorts offer numerous ski and snowboard instruction and training programs for children and adults, in addition to child care centers that are open daily.

(More) Things To Know

- *Most likely, wherever you live, bank on it taking a while to get here. It is, however, well worth the haul. A new highway is being constructed that will knock off a half-hour or so for guests traveling from the east.*
- *Just when you think you've arrived, there's still a five-mile ride up the access road to the summit. Snowshoe is an upside-down resort, with all the base facilities along a ridge at the top of the mountain.*
- *Save you and your group some time by getting your lift tickets in advance at Snowshoe's base (valley) welcome center. You'll need to stop by here as well if you're staying on the mountain.*
- *A reciprocal lift ticket affords guests access to both ski areas on one lift ticket, with Snowshoe's trails closing at 4:30 (4:15 Western Territory) and Silver Creek's (and snowboard terrain park) at 10 P.M.*
- *A free shuttle bus runs between the ski areas every half-hour. Keep in mind it can be crowded and/or a bit of a wait between 2 and 5 P.M. on weekends, taking up valuable time on your ticket.*
- *Things don't always come cheap at Snowshoe, though food and nightlife are more reasonably priced for the most part. Keep an eye out for bargain lodging packages in March, and pray for lots of snow. Recent years have found good snow late in the season and the resort makes plenty when called on.*
- *Renting equipment at Snowshoe? On a busy day, you can shake the long lines at Shaver's Center by getting in your ride and heading just up the road to the Top of the World center. Fewer lines, easy lift-ticket access, and quick service.*
- *Snowshoe routinely yields the most number of skier days per year in the Mid-Atlantic—some years as many as 130 or so. Along with an annual average snowfall of 180 inches, the resort can pump out 2,300 tons of snow per hour.*

Snowboarding Highlights

Look no further than Snowshoe to find the best all-around snowboarding experience in the Mid-Atlantic. The Silver Creek area plays home to the long and spacious Mountaineer Terrain Park and its show-stopper—a 400-plus-foot competition-size halfpipe. It has banks over 10 feet and the vertical needed for good speed. The pipe is also maintained by a Scorpion pipe groomer, so guests can count on the pipe being open most days and in solid shape. Covering the entire length of a former Silver Creek green/blue trail, the terrain park breaks out hits like tabletops, rails, kickers, gaps, berms, and other changing features made by Snowshoe's dedicated terrain park team. The area is serviced by its own lift, and there are lights for night boarding, tunes kicking on the sound system, a lounge area, and lots of competitions and events.

Boarders also have good terrain at their disposal, including 1,500 vertical feet of speed and curves on the Western Territory's *Cupp Run* and *Shay's Revenge*. Novices have a large mix of mostly green and blue terrain on Snowshoe's front side.

Snowboard Rentals: Over 500 Rossignol boards; $35/day, $20/night (includes boots) • **Snowboard School:** Call for current rates

More Fun in the Flakes

On-site

Six-lane, 600-foot **snowtubing** park at Silver Creek, serviced by handle tow lift. $12/two-hour session or $15/all-day, open from 1 P.M.–10 P.M. • Daily, one-hour guided **snowmobile tours**; $50/person, $15 each additional • Daily, two-hour **backcountry snowmobile tours** to Cheat Mountain. Fire Tower: $89/person, $20 each additional; evening 2.5 hour tour $99/person, $30/each additional • **Horse-drawn sleigh rides** on Skidder Slope, Tuesday, Thursday and Saturday nights. $5/rider. One-hour longer rides available with enough natural cover; $60/two riders in sleigh • **Nordic skiing** and **snowshoeing**: $10/trail pass, $15/half-day rental, $20/full day, $25/rental, lesson and trail pass • **Dog sled tours**, weather permitting: $49/two people • **Telemark skiing** allowed on all slopes at both Snowshoe and Silver Creek (no rentals available).

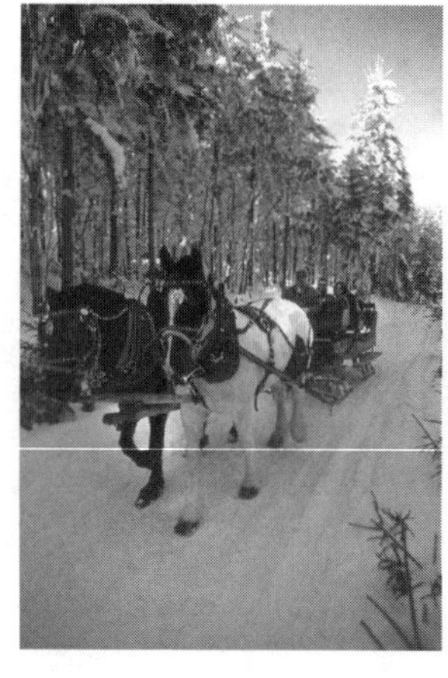

Nearby

Abundant **cross-country skiing** available at nearby Elk River Touring Center *(see page 258)*, Watoga State Park *(see page 269)*, and Monongahela National Forest; Local outfitters/guides include Appalachian Sport in Marlinton (304) 799–4050 and Cheat Mountain Outfitting & Guide in Durbin (304) 456–4023.

Summer Activities

The resort also makes a smooth transition into spring and summer with an incredible **mountain biking** and **hiking** trail system and the scenic, highly rated Hawthorne Valley **golf** course. The resort also features **horseback riding**, **fly fishing**, and **boating** on Shaver's Lake. Whitewater sports are a two-hour drive from Snowshoe on the New and Gauley Rivers, and Seneca Rocks (1.5 hours away) affords **rock climbing** and sight seeing. Closer by is the historical **Cass Scenic Railroad State Park**, where guests can catch a ride to the near-mile-high summit of Bald Knob on authentic Shay steam locomotives—some of the few left in the world.

Skier Services

Lift Tickets

Tickets are available from Snowshoe's Shaver's Centre and Top of the World; and from Silver Creek area): 8:30 A.M.–4:30 P.M.: Monday–Thursday $45, Friday–Sunday $52 • Half-day: Monday–Thursday $34, Friday–Sunday $39 • 4:30 P.M.–10 P.M. (Silver Creek only): $27 • 12:30 P.M.–10 P.M.: Monday–Thursday $57, Friday–Sunday $62 • Ages 7–12: Monday–Thursday $30/day, $23/half-day; Friday–Sunday $34/day, $26/half-day • 10%–20% ticket discounts before December 21 and after March 12 • Slight discounts for multi-day passes • Ages 5 and under ski free, discounts for seniors.

Ski Rentals

Over 5,000 sets of shaped Rossignol skis • Adult $26/day, ages 7–12 $18 • Night: $16, ages 7–12 $10 • Multi-day: $23/day, ages 7–12 $15 • Ski helmets and high-performance demos available.

Services

Ski School: Over 100 instructors: PSIA certified; call for current rates; Mogul Busters, Brr Rabbit Ski Schools for young children; Beginner skier/snowboarder package • **Adaptive Ski School:** Adaptive program offered at Silver Creek • **Summit Lodge Facilities:** *Snowshoe*: Village at Snowshoe: lodges, restaurants, pubs, shops; Shaver's Centre: ticket sales, customer services/information, Discovery Center, lockers, lost & found, ski training center, eateries, pub, specialty shops, medical clinic/ski patrol; Equipment rentals in neighboring Spruce Lodge and Top of the World; day care, rentals/repair, children's ski school, and ski shop in Edelweiss Building • *Silver Creek:* ticket sales, ski and rental shops, lockers, day care, The Cave Entertainment Center, The Deli, Micro-Grocery Mart, Red Oak Lounge, Ski Barn Gift Shop, spa/pool • **Child Care:** *Snowshoe:* Available daily for ages two and older from 8 A.M.–5 P.M.; *Silver Creek:* Daily for ages 12 weeks and older, 8 A.M.–5 P.M. • **Shops**: There are more shops, game rooms, and places to spend your money at Snowshoe/Silvercreek than you could shake a ski pole at. If you want a day off from skiing, don't worry about what to do with your time. Just start wandering.

Did You Know?

- *The resort is named after the locally revered Snowshoe Hare, whose survival is a testament to the area's long winters. The white-coated hare is rarely found south of Canada's mountain ranges but manages to make a home here, relying on heavy snow coverage and lasting conditions in order to elude predators.*
- *Snowshoe has the most vertical drop among all Mid-Atlantic ski areas, serving up 1,500 feet from summit elevation to base.*
- *Black-diamond, 1.5-mile* Cupp Run *was designed in 1973 by Olympic Gold Medallist Jean-Claude Killy,*

Room & Board

Few towns in West Virginia can match Snowshoe's population during winter, and certainly none this close to the sky. The sprawling resort offers over 1,500 condominiums, 285 lodge and inn rooms, and numerous rental homes and chalets. Just about all accommodations are ski-in/ski-out, or just a short walk to one of the summit slopes. Accommodations range from luxurious and modern to cheaper, no-frills lodging to the new rustic, snowmobile-accessed **Sunrise Backcountry Cabin**, with meals prepared by your own Snowshoe cook. And Snowshoe doesn't miss a beat when it's time to lay down the skis and boards for the night. There's a good restaurant for every appetite and budget, plus some newer treats like the tasty southern fare at **The Junction** and **Foxfire Grille**, both in the Village at Snowshoe. You'll also find eight other eateries; many specialty shops, cafes and stores; and a variety of watering holes, including a full-time **Comedy Club** and a nightclub with live bands. Wind down in one of the resort's heated pools, saunas, and Jacuzzis, or take a turn in a spa, exercise room, or massage-therapy session. Other options include miniature golf, three arcades, and an entertainment center, as well as special club nights for the under-21 crowd.

Granted, you don't have to stay at Snowshoe to ski here, but why wouldn't you? Most guests agree the ski-and-stay experience is well worth their buck. The resort is pretty remote—roughly 20 miles either way to any semblance of a town. And aside from Snowshoe's general store and **The Grocery Store** at Silver Creek, the only places around are the convenience shop and gas station near the base of the mountain at Big Spring Station. But don't feel that your lodging options are confined to Snowshoe. In the absence of nearby hotels and motels, a growing list of bed and breakfasts, inns, cabins, and chalets are available within 30 miles.

Lodging

On-site *(call (304) 572–5252 for rates and more info)*

Inn Rooms, Lodges, Condos & Townhomes:

Rimfire Lodge and Highland House (new, upscale lodging at the Village at Snowshoe) • **Timberline Lodge**, located off *Skidder* slope and near commercial areas: 50 rooms with restaurant and lounge in building, access to pool • **Spruce Lodge**, centrally located/slopeside lodging: 100 less-expensive rooms • **Whistlepunk Inn**, located off *Whistlepunk* trail and adjacent to Red Fox Restaurant and Whistlepunk Spa: 13 rooms/suites, some with lofts and sun decks • **The Inn at Snowshoe**, at the valley base: 150 rooms, with restaurant/lounge, indoor pool, Jacuzzis, sauna/spa, exercise room • **Camp 4 Condominiums**: 17 units, near Powderidge Lift • **Powderidge**, slopeside lodging: one- and two-bedroom condos/townhouses • **Shamrock**, near-slopeside lodging: one- to four-bedroom townhouses • **Powder Monkey**, adjacent to basin slopes and near Cupp Run: two- to three-bedroom condos, also near Shavers Centre, restaurants, and shops • **Stemwinder**, near slopes, restaurants, Shavers Centre: two- to four-bedroom deluxe townhouse units, some with whirlpools • **Snowcrest Village**, near-slopeside lodging, close to Widowmaker trail: one- to two-bedroom units with indoor spas/Jacuzzis/hot tubs • **Sundown Hutches**, across from Whistlepunk Village, ski-in, ski-out access to Cupp Run: one-, three-, or five-bedroom condos • **Treetop**, centrally located, near-slopeside lodging: two- to three-bedroom townhouses • **Wabasso**, near-slopeside lodging: two-bedroom units with loft, fireplace, and deck • **Whistlepunk Condominiums**, slopeside: one- to four-bedroom units with private Jacuzzi tubs; restaurant and pub, spa/massage area, outdoor hot tub and Jacuzzi, free use of pool, nautilus center, sauna • **Silver Creek Lodge Condominiums**: 240 fully furnished units with heated pool, shops, ski school/rentals, restaurant, pub, Jacuzzi • **Summit Condominiums**, short walk to slopes, restaurants, Shavers Centre: three-bedroom units with fireplaces • **Top of the World**, slopeside by *Widowmaker* trail and above Top of the World Commercial Centre: affordable one-bedroom units, with hot tubs, miniature golf, family game room, restaurant/lounge, shops.

Nearby
Bed and Breakfasts:

Slatyfork Farm B&B and cabin rentals, Slatyfork, two miles from Snowshoe, four rooms (one with private bath, hot tub), surrounded by cross-country ski trails; (304) 572–3900 • **Elk River Inn B&B**, four miles from Snowshoe; (304) 572–3771 • Buffalo Run B&B, shared bath, 20 miles from Snowshoe; (304) 456–3036 • **Jerico B&B**, 22 miles; (304) 799–6241 • **Carriage House B&B**, 28 miles; (304) 799–6706 • **Richard's Country Inn**, Huttonsville (pre-Civil War mansion, circa 1835); 1–800–636–7434.

Condominiums/Inns/Cabins:

Old Spruce Realty, fully equipped slopeside and nearby condos, with fireplaces, 1–888–5–SPRUCE/(304) 572–2946 • **Overlook Village**, Cass, 36 condo/efficiency units, hot tub; rates $45–$99/night; (304) 572–2290 • **Comfy Camping Cabins**, Cass, two fully equipped three- to four-person cabins; (304) 456–3017/456–4410 • **Erehwon Cabins**, six miles from Snowshoe, fully equipped cabin rentals; (304) 572–5140 • **Seneca State Forest**, Route 28, seven rustic cabins; 1–800–CALL–WVA/(304) 799–6231 • **Nakiska Chalets**, six miles from Snowshoe; (304) 339–6309 • **Seneca Trail Inn**, four miles from Snowshoe; (304) 572–2800 • **Cass Inn**, 10 miles from Snowshoe; (304) 456–3464.

Dining/Aprés-Ski

On-site

Nine full-service restaurants, nine express-service eateries, four pubs/lounges • **The Junction** (great Southern fare and apres-ski scene) • **Foxfire Grill** ("views, blues & barbecue") • **The Red Fox** (fine dining) • **Auntie Pasta's Ristorante** (reasonably priced Italian dishes, next to Spruce Lodge) • **Brandi's** (American cuisine at the Inn at Snowshoe)
Goodtime Bobby's (steakhouse) • **Cheat Pizza** (in Highland House/Village at Snowshoe) • **Stellar Coffee** (pastries/sandwiches).

Eateries, Pubs & Clubs:

Snowshoe Area

Arbuckle's Cabin (stews & brews at Western Territory base) • **The Boathouse Grill** (at the base of Ballhooter lift) • **Beaver Tails** (pastries & bakery items, at Rimfire Lodge) Cheat Mountain Pizza • **Pizzazz Pizza** (at Shavers Center, open late, deliveries available) • **Shaver Center Food Court** (central base lodge at Snowshoe) • **The Comedy Cellar** (Tuesday–Saturday, at Mountain Lodge) • **Hole in the Wall Pub** (Shavers Center) • **The Connection Nightclub** (live bands, happy hours, at Shavers Center) • **Goodtime Bobby's Sports Bar** (billiards, foosball, TV sports) • **Yodeler's Pub** (ski-express lunch and selection of brews & fine cigars, at Powder Monkey lift) • **Brandi's** (valley-area sports bar at The Inn at Snowshoe).

Silver Creek Area

Black Run Sugar House (express lunch, at Silver Creek Cascade lift) • **The Bear's Den** (food court at Silver Creek's lodge) • **The Red Oak Pub** (at Silver Creek; chili, hoagies, billiards & darts).

Nearby

Elk River Restaurant, Slatyfork; (304) 572–3771 • **Paradise Cafe** (Route 219 and Route 66); (304) 572–2210 • **Papa Joe's Raw Bar & Grill**, Big Spring Station, just off Snowshoe Mountain • **Suzie's Chic Inn Restaurant**, Route 219, Marlinton; (304) 799–0892 • **French's Diner**, Marlinton; (304) 799–9910 • **Godfather's Pizza**, Marlinton; (304) 799–4700.

Timberline Resort

Timberline Resort
HC 70 Box 488
Davis, WV 26260

Ski Report: 1–800–SNOWING
Information: (304) 866–4801
Lodging Information: 1–800–633–6682
Internet: *www.timberlineresort.com*
Credit Cards: VISA, MC, AMEX, Discover

Operating Hours:
9 A.M.–4:30 P.M. Monday–Wednesday
9 A.M.–9 P.M. Thursday–Friday
8 A.M.–9 P.M. Saturday
8 A.M.–4:30 P.M. Sunday

Season: December to mid-April

Backdrop

Based just two miles from Canaan Valley Ski Resort, Timberline surfaced about 20 years ago on old logging industry grounds with little more than a T-bar surface lift and limited snowmaking. At that time, most skiers had just half of the mountain's available terrain. The more challenging upper mountain relied solely on natural snowfall, accessible only by a slow trek on the resort's Piston Bully snow grooming machine. Timberline took a turn for the better in the mid-1980s when a group of Philadelphia investors purchased the resort and equipped it with a modern lift service and an airless snowmaking system from base to summit.

Surrounded by thousands of acres of state and federally owned wilderness areas, Timberline can resemble classic northeastern ski areas when conditions are on. Its north-facing mountain retains snow pretty well, and you also get the experience of real ski country with Timberline's high elevation and mountain scenery. While death-defying steeps aren't in abundance, there's a consistent fall line on 1,000-plus feet of vertical, very few flat spots, and varied terrain good for all abilities.

As for the lift system, just two chairs slowly make their way to the summit and a double serves the beginner area. The resort could use some new lifts in a big way, but fortunately overcrowding isn't a common occurrence. Look out for Timberline's antiquated black double chair, which encloses skiers inside a helmeted top that resembles a Volkswagen Bug. It's a long, slow ride to the summit, but the unique chair was designed for shelter from strong winds.

Did You Know?

When the area is blanketed with enough natural snow, you might catch Telemark (an early Scandanavian-based form of skiing) and cross-country skiers hopping the chair lift to the summit and venturing out into the adjacent Dolly Sods wilderness for some off-piste skiing. With 150-plus inches of average annual snowfall, the Canaan Valley region affords Mid-Atlantic skiers some outstanding conditions and a true mountain experience.

Timberline's 4,286-foot elevation and 150 inches average annual snowfall account for ski seasons that normally extend well into March or mid-April. Snowfall here in Canaan Valley is some of the strongest and most consistent in the Mid-Atlantic. But it's not guaranteed, and when the sky is running dry, Timberline's snowmaking operation sometimes lacks the punch to cover the whole mountain during leaner times. Some of the advanced trails close in the absence of snowmaking, while the two-mile *Salamander* trail has been known to stay open when it's barely skiable. Nonetheless, the resort will typically manage over 120 days of skiing per year and is working harder to make more snow.

Guests will appreciate good food at Timberline's lodge, and the spacious upstairs pub has nice views of the slopes and a roaring fireplace. It's a good place to wind down after a long day, and the pub kicks into high gear when the historic "Shot Ski" comes off the wall. There's not a lot happening on the mountain other than Timber's Pub, so plan ahead for your aprés-ski agenda if staying here. A selection of reasonably priced rental chalets and condos are available throughout the mountain, many offering immediate access to the trails.

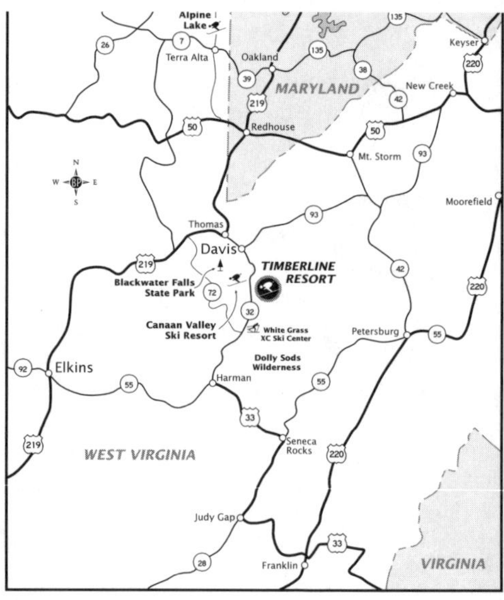

Getting There

Timberline is located two miles from Canaan Valley Ski Area on Route 32 in Davis; see directions for Canaan Valley Ski Resort on *page 137*.

Mountain Stats

Base Elevation: 3,268 feet
Summit Elevation: 4,268 feet
Vertical Drop: 1,000 feet
Skiable Terrain: 91 acres
Longest Run: 2 miles
Primary Slope Direction: North
Average Annual Snowfall: 150 inches
Slopes and Trails: 16 beginner, 10 intermediate, 9 advanced
Uphill Capacity: 4,000 skiers per hour
Snowmaking: 94% of area
Lifts: 1 triple, 2 doubles
Night Skiing: 30% of terrain, Thursday-Saturday & holiday Sundays until 9 P.M.

Trail Profiles

The resort undertook a sweeping terrain expansion eight years ago by adding eight new trails, including two black-diamond glade runs that wind through Timberline's hardwoods. The resort now advertises 35 runs over 91 acres, with about 10 trails stemming from the summit and lots of shorter runs and cat tracks mixed in. Advanced skiers won't be disappointed, though, especially when conditions are ripe. Lots of dips and rolls are built into the mountain and its 1,000-foot vertical. Three double-black-diamond trails are short-lived but steep traverses, most notably the headwall off the top of *The Drop* and the near-equal pitches of neighboring *Off the Wall*. And *Thunderdraft's* mogul fields are a true challenge for bump enthusiasts.

A rare find in the Mid-Atlantic region are gladed trails, and Timberline offers two of them for fast-turning, giant-slalom skiers and snowboarders. Double-diamond *Cherry Bowl Glades* is a satisfyingly steep, wide run and thrilling change of pace through Allegheny high-country hardwoods. On the other end of the mountain is *Pearly Glades*. The trail has more of an intermediate pitch but is a great change of pace to blaze around its trees. In recent years, both glades and some of the more advanced trails have opened only with enough natural snow.

New at Timberline

Snowboarders and skiers can tear it up on a new terrain park being constructed on existing black-diamond trail Lower Dew Drop. The park will get the full brunt of increased snowmaking on this side of the trail network. Guests can also expect minor renovations to the base lodge and a new Demo Center.

Possibly the mountain's best intermediate trail, *Upper* and *Lower Almost Heaven* is a long, continuous run with serpentine terrain that's surprisingly steep on its upper half. The top section of *Upper Dew Drop* is nearly identical in design before dropping into wide and smooth cruising track at its mid-section.

Timberline also lends itself to beginners quite capably, though neighboring resort Canaan Valley probably holds a stronger reputation for novices. Three small bunny hills facing the base lodge accommodate kids and first-time skiers, with two separate childrens' learning programs available at the base. The resort also has one of the Mid-Atlantic's longest trails in *Salamander*—a two-mile-long, trench-width run with a slow and gradual pitch. It has several slow-turning areas to help novices craft their technique. *Winterset* is another recent addition to Timberline, following a long, pleasant, rolling course around the perimeter of the trail system. Most of the remaining green runs are easy cat tracks that intersect the longer summit trails.

Snowboarding Highlights

Snowoarders have a lot more to look forward to at Timberline, now that *Lower Dew Drop* trail is being converted into a terrain park. Available to both boarders and skiers, the park will benefit from expanded snowmaking and the spacious room it occupies on the black-diamond run. Boarders can also shred on a 200-foot halfpipe near the base of *Lower Thunderstruck* and *Plywood Parkway* trails. It's a decent pipe with strong pitch, but availability can be a big question mark. It mostly banks on natural snow to stay open, and the resort is still hoping to get the right grooming equipment to better maintain the pipe. Nonetheless, Timberline has proved itself boarder-friendly over the years, hosting several boardercross and other events each season.

Still, there's a lot more than the park and pipe for boarders. Prepare for long speed runs and a good mix of bumps, curves, and rolls on its intermediate and advanced terrain, plus two long cruising runs for beginners. Advanced riders will like carving tree-lined track on *Cherry Bowl Glades* and *Pearly Glades*, and hitting jumps on *Lower Thunderstruck*.

Snowboard Rentals: 130 sets: Morrow, Generic; $17–$24; boots $8–$12 • **Snowboard School**: 10 snowboard instructors: Ski school rates apply

More Fun in the Flakes

Cross-country and **Telemark** skiing are also hot tickets at Timberline. **Nordic** skiing is allowed on all slopes and trails, and a 10-mile, marked, ungroomed backcountry trail system was recently cut off of the downhill area. It meanders through resort property and links with an expansive network in the Monongahela National Forest (Dolly Sods Wilderness Area), at the White Grass Touring Center, and the Canaan Valley State Park system.

Backcountry skiers can use a one-way lift pass to the Herz Mountain summit and head off the mountain to Blackwater Falls State Park at the north end of the valley, Canaan Valley to the south, and Dolly Sods Wilderness Area to the east. Backcountry, Telemark, and cross-country ski equipment is now available for rent from the base lodge. The resort also hosts Nordic events, races, and workshops nearly every weekend of the season. Its wide-ranging calendar of events includes several slalom and giant-slalom Telemark races, the **Timberline Nordic Festival**, and part of the West Virginia **Telemark Race Series**. Racing and carving clinics are offered periodically for all abilities; and a new introductory Telemark program teaches the art of the Norwegian-based turning technique. And rounding out the complete Nordic experience, Timberline runs guided backcountry tours, provided there's sufficient snowfall and demand.

On-site

Cross-country skiing on Timberline's 10-mile (17k) Nordic trail system off the summit area, connecting with **Canaan Valley's cross-country trail network** *(see page 262)*, **White Grass Touring Center** *(see page 260)*, **Blackwater Falls State Park** *(see page 265)*, and **Dolly Sods National Forest Area**; full instruction and rentals available at Timberline • **Telemark skiing permitted** on all trails, with instruction and rentals available.

Nearby

Sled run with rope tow at Blackwater Falls State Park • **Ice skating** facility at Canaan Valley Resort.

Summer Activities

Mountain biking takes charge at the four-seasons resort when the weather turns warm. Twenty miles of mapped and marked trails are available down Timberline's ski trails, on connecting track throughout Monongahela National Forest trails, and in valley locations. Chair-lift rides accommodate bikers, hikers, and sight-seeing spectators for single or all-day passes, from Memorial Day Weekend to October, 9 A.M. to 6 P.M. A long list of other spring to fall activities includes nearby white water rafting and canoeing, swimming, golf, tennis, hunting, fishing, horseback riding, and camping.

The History of Canaan Valley

Local legend holds that a fur trader by the name of George Casey Harness stood perched atop Cabin Mountain in 1748 and gazed at this great valley, exclaiming, "Behold, the land of Canaan," a reference to the biblical "Promised Land of Milk and Honey."

At that time, the Valley was pure wilderness, swept with huge thickets of Laurel, Spruce and hardwoods. In 1884, the first road was built, connecting Canaan Valley with the town of Davis. The railroad opened a year later, opening up widespread timber acreage. Millions of board feet of Red Spruce and wild Cherry were skidded by horse to the Blackwater River, where they were floated to Davis' mills.

Timbering was done by the early 40s and 50s, and it was about this time that pilots flying the DC-Pittsburgh route began noticing snow in the Valley well into spring. "Driftland" was organized in the mid-50s by the Ski Club of Washington, DC, and the first rope tow was erected on Cabin Mountain in 1953. A few years later, Weiss Knob premiered as the South's first commercial ski area on what is now the hallowed cross country network of White Grass Ski Touring Center. In 1971, Canaan Valley Resort State Park opened for ski business, with Timberline following suit in 1981.

To preserve the beauty of Canaan Valley, sections have been designated as a National Natural Landmark, and in 1994 the Canaan Valley National Wildlife Refuge became the nation's 500th refuge.

Skier Services

Timberline's lift tickets are reasonable considering the solid terrain. The resort hasn't jacked up its prices much in the last decade, and now offers early- and late-season discount rates that apply from December 1 to 15 and March 25 to closing date. On weekdays, the slopes are clean and free of crowds; skied mostly by smaller packs of vacation skiers. A limited number of trails are equipped for night skiing, Fridays through Sundays. The resort also offers child-care daily during operating hours.

Lift Tickets

8 A.M.–4:30 P.M.: weekday $29, weekend $39 • 8 A.M.–12:30 P.M./12:30 P.M.–4:30 P.M.: $16, $25 • 4:30 P.M.–9 P.M.: Thursday–Friday $16, weekend $20 • 12:30 P.M.–9 P.M.: Thursday–Friday $25, weekend $33 • 8 A.M.–9 P.M.: Thursday–Friday $30, weekend $40 • Ages 6–12: $13–$30; ages 5 and under ski free • Early and late season reduced rates.

Ski Rentals

400 sets: Elan; $12–$21.

Services

Ski School: Over 100 instructors: PSIA certified; Private $45/hour; Group $20/1.5 hours; Introductory ski, snowboard, or Telemark package $39; TAK program (ages 4–7) $68/day; Mountain Safari (ages 8–12) $78/day • **Adaptive Ski School**: By appointment only • **Base Lodge Facilities:** Cafeteria, pub, rental shop, ski apparel shop, lockers • **Child Care**: Offered daily at base lodge, $7/hour or $45/day • **Racing**: NASTAR held on the *Lower Thunderstruck* trail, Thursday–Monday from 1 P.M. until 3 P.M.

Calendar Of Events

January: Open Telemark Workshops; USSA Junior Giant Slalom • **February:** Nordic slalom races and clinics; USASA Boardercross Series I; Norpine Festival • **March:** Governor's Cup Giant Slalom; Telemark Spring Series Workshop; Boardercross Series.

Room & Board

Vacation skiers can base themselves either slopeside or nearby on the mountain in over 50 fully equipped private rental homes, condominiums, chalets, and cottages brokered by **Timberline Realty**. The slopeside **Herzwoods** condominiums have ski-and-stay packages and complementary equipment rentals with a minimum three-night stay. The most affordable times to vacation are during early December and late March when lodging rates drop by up to 27 percent, though you'll be taking your chances with natural conditions and full-slope availability. The towns of Davis and Elkins also offer several bed and breakfasts and lodging opportunities. For a break from the slopes, Timberline guests can go antiquing in numerous shops in Davis and Elkins, or take scenic drives throughout the region's wilderness landscape.

Lodging

On-site *(call 1–800–633–6682 for on-site lodging information and rates)*

Herzwoods and Northwoods slopeside condominiums • **Slopeside homes** along Salamander, Winterset, and Lower Dew Drop trails • **Resort homes, cabins, villas, and chalets** on the mountain and close-by • For complete lodging information in the area, *see Canaan Valley Ski Resort, Nearby Lodging, page 142.*

Dining/Aprés-ski

On-site

Timberhaus Cafeteria, with outdoor deck barbecue • **Timbers Pub** (upstairs): slopeside fireplace lounge with slope views and live weekend entertainment.

Nearby

See Canaan Valley, Nearby Dining/Aprés-ski, page 143.

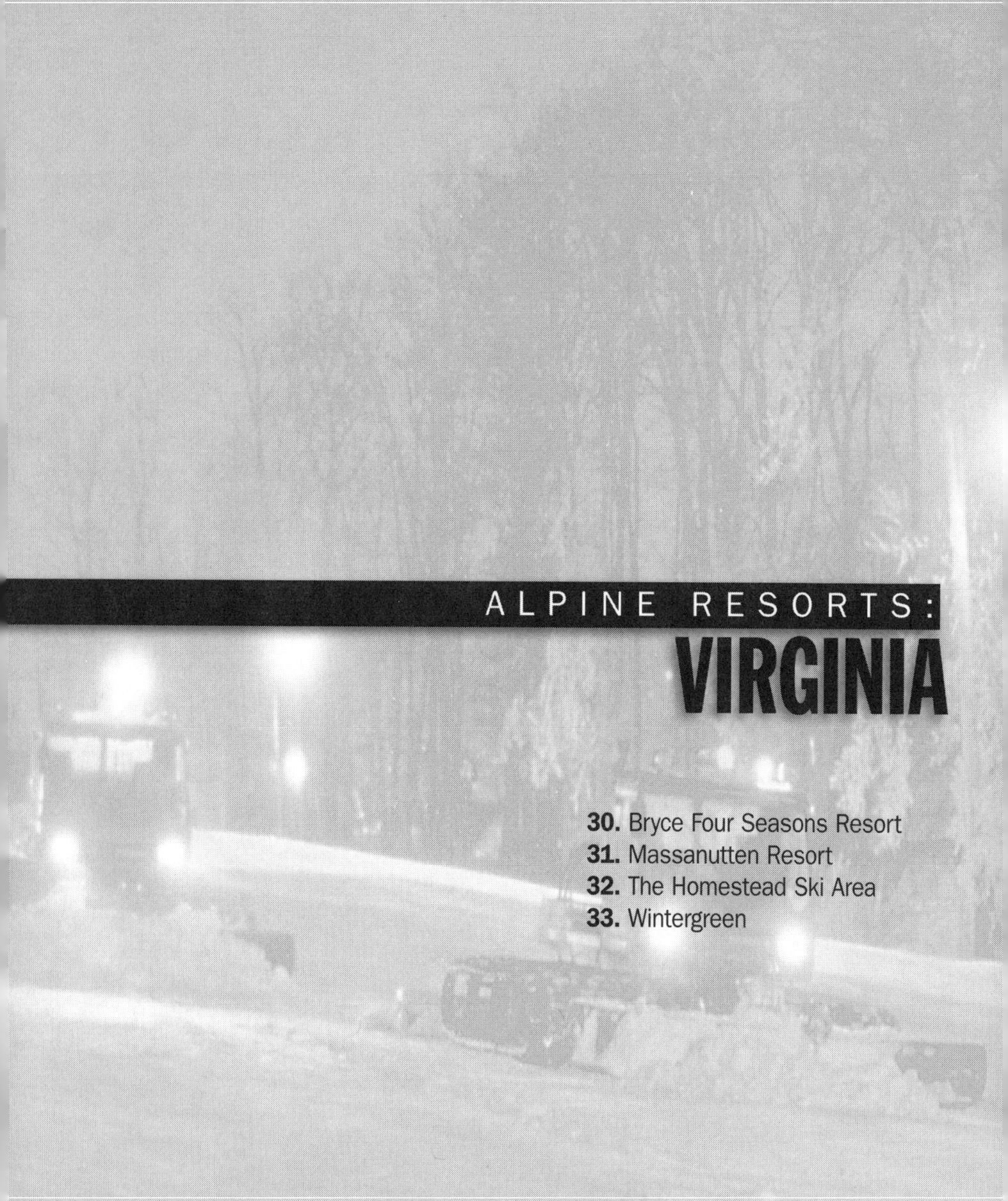

ALPINE RESORTS:

VIRGINIA

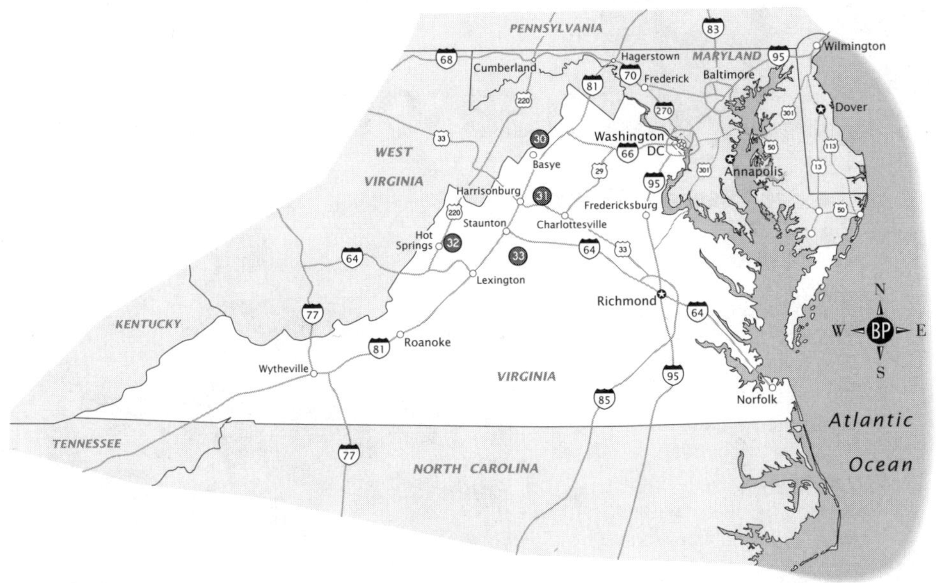

Virginia, for the most part, lacks the wintry climate that neighboring West Virginia's higher-elevation resorts are afforded. Despite this, four alpine resorts feature superlative snowmaking systems. Wintergreen, Massanutten, Bryce, and The Homestead each operate as a four-seasons resort, hosting lots of outdoor activities and comfortable lodging year-round.

Massanutten and Wintergreen both feature respectable 1,000-foot vertical drops, the latter serving up more challenging steeps off its 3,800-foot-high Blue Ridge Mountain summit. In addition to providing plentiful beginner turf, its more advanced runs are the longest and steepest around. Shenandoah Valley's Massanutten Resort, near Harrisonburg, is a bit smaller than Wintergreen and more suited to beginners and intermediates. Massanutten is also a quick two-hour jaunt from the Washington, DC area.

A little north of Massanutten is Bryce—a resort truly committed to families, children, and developing skiers. Its modest trail system aside, the nine slopes at Bryce are expertly designed for learning skiers. The Homestead, located a few miles from the West Virginia border, is another area known for solid instruction and programs. Skiing tends to get trivialized by The Homestead's grandiose resort character, but efforts are underway to bring snow riding to a new level here.

Bryce Four Seasons Resort

Bryce Four Seasons Resort
P.O. Box 3
Basye, VA 22810

Ski Report: 1–800–821–1444
Information: (540) 856–2121
Internet: *www.bryceresort.com*
E-mail: bryce@bryceresort.com
Credit Cards: VISA, MC, AE

Operating Hours
9 A.M.–9:30 P.M. Tuesday–Saturday
9 A.M.–4:30 P.M. Sunday–Monday

Season: December to mid-March

Backdrop

In the heart of Virginia's Shenandoah Valley lies all-seasons Bryce Resort, tucked on a low-lying ridge between the Blue Ridge and Allegheny Mountains and near the West Virginia border. National Masters slalom finalist (1987) Horst Locher and brother Manfred opened up shop here in 1965, bringing with them an Austrian flavor to the Shenandoah Valley. A small mountain with limited terrain, Bryce's strengths are its small crowds, beautiful scenery, and a friendly environment that serves as a welcome contrast to the bustling atmosphere of bigger Mid-Atlantic resorts. It's also one of the closest ski areas to Washington, DC and Northern Virginia, just 90 miles of scenic highway away. Skiers who prefer the skyward route have a 2,500-foot paved landing airstrip adjacent to the resort.

Trail Profiles

Unlike many resorts, Bryce doesn't unnecessarily advertise black diamonds that don't exist or facilitate its trail count by naming every turn and cat track as a separate run. It focuses instead on providing a solid learning experience and recreational skiing. Six main trails and two beginner areas are wide, smooth, and well manicured. *White Lightning* and *Bootlegger* trails, coined after the area's once-flourishing moonshine business, are the most popular

Mountain Stats

Base Elevation: 1,250 feet
Summit Elevation: 1,750 feet
Vertical Drop: 500 feet
Longest Run: 3,550 feet
Primary Slope Direction: North
Skiable Terrain: 25 acres
Average Annual Snowfall: 30 inches
Snowmaking: 100% of area
Slopes and Trails: 3 beginner, 4 intermediate, 1 advanced
Lifts: 2 doubles, 3 rope tows
Uphill Capacity: 2,500 skiers per hour
Night Skiing: 90% of area, Tuesday–Saturday until 9:30 P.M.

cruising slopes, offering sustained intermediate pitches. The resort's lone black diamond trail—*Hangover*—is a short, narrow chute connecting to *Revenuer's Run*, which has a fun switchback and a few small gladed sections. *Hangover* was recently widened and now sports additional snowmaking coverage. The wide-open *Locher Bowl* was added off the summit area a few years ago for skiers and snowboarders to cut sweeping, slalom turns. It has a surface lift for those who wish to stick to the upper-third tier of the mountain.

Redeye was expertly designed for beginner skiers to master the art of turning. From the scenic summit, its narrow, steady track becomes increasingly wider and more undulating as it winds down toward the base, providing the perfect arena for novices to negotiate its two switchbacks. Two bunny hills on opposite sides of the base lodge serve as ideal introductory slopes, each with its own rope tow lift and separated from the flow of skier traffic. The patient and highly rated Horst Locher Ski School comes highly recommended for parents who want to introduce the sport to their children in a quiet, peaceful setting. Bryce also has a firm commitment to racing, hosting one of the strongest recreational programs in the South that features clinics and competitions each weekend.

Getting There

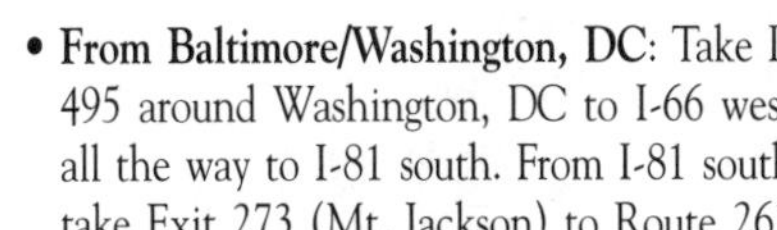

- **From Baltimore/Washington, DC**: Take I-495 around Washington, DC to I-66 west all the way to I-81 south. From I-81 south take Exit 273 (Mt. Jackson) to Route 263 west to Basye/Bryce Resort.
- **From Virginia points south and east**: Take I-64 to I-81 north, and follow directions above.

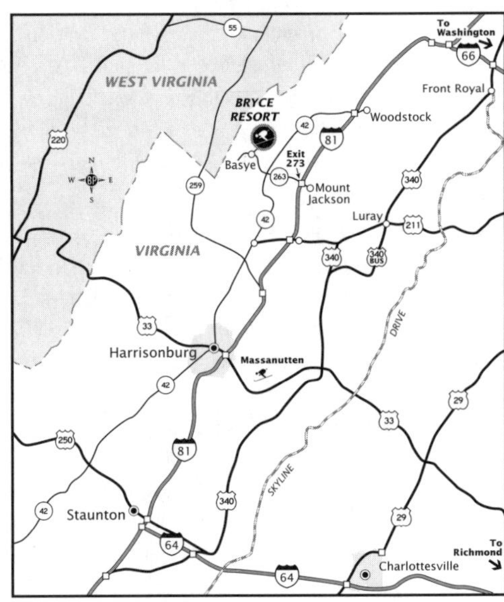

Snowboarding Highlights

Bryce permits snowboarding on all eight slopes and trails, but tight space has kept the resort from building a snowboard park or halfpipe.

Snowboard School: Five instructors; Private $45; Group $18 • **Snowboard Rentals:** 140 sets:Rossignol, Burton; Weekday $25, weekends $23

Skier Services

Lift Tickets

9 A.M.–4:30 P.M.: weekday $28, weekend $38 • 9 A.M.–12:30 P.M. or 12:30 P.M.–4:30 P.M.: weekday $18, weekend $30 • Noon–9:30 P.M.: $28, $38 • 5:30 P.M.–9:30 P.M. (Tuesday–Saturday): $18 • Weekend rates reduced for ages 12 and under and ages 65–69 (over 70 ski free) • $20 weekend/$15 weekday rope tow lift tickets available for beginner area only • Group discount rates for 20 or more skiers.

Ski Rentals

Over 700 sets: Head, Kaestle, Rossignol, and Elan skis; Salomon and Tyrolia bindings; and Salomon boots • Weekday $17, weekend $20.

Services

Ski School: 50 instructors: PSIA certified; Private $45/hour; Group $18/hour; First-time Skier Package (includes ticket, rental, lesson) $38/weekdays, $48/weekends; SKIwee childrens' program for ages 4–8 (reservations required); Half day $30, with rentals $40; Full day $50, with rentals $60 • **Racing:** NASTAR racing held on *Bootlegger* trail on weekends and holidays at 3:30 P.M., $5/session; Competitive Ski Racing Program: weekend training sessions aimed toward USSA-sanctioned races • **Base Lodge Facilities:** Rental/repair shop, ski boutique, ski school, SKIwee center, first aid center, cafeteria, restaurant, second-floor lounge.

Calander Of Events

December: Southern NASTAR Pacesetting; Shenandoah USSA Slalom/Giant Slalom • **January:** Collegiate USSA Slalom and Giant Slalom Race; Bryce Resort USSA Slalom Race; Southeastern Race Association Pro-Am Giant Slalom • **February:** Washington Ski International Race.

Summer Activities

The skiing doesn't end when the winters do: **Grass skiing** and **mountain boarding** is now being offered down its trails from late June to late October, with lift passes and rentals for $26. A first-time package includes lift ticket, rental, elbow and knee pads, and instruction.

The all-seasons resort also features an 18-hole golf course, tennis, an outdoor pool, mountain biking trails, sight-seeing lift rides, horseback riding, and boating/windsurfing on its man-made 45-acre lake.

Room & Board

Lodging

On-site

200 privately owned studio condominiums, townhouses, and chalets; Call 1–800–296–2121 for information and rates.

Nearby

Stony Court at Bryce Resort (townhouses); 1–800–296–0947 • **The Hill at Bryce** (condominiums); 1–800–307–3938 • **CMG Properties/Rentals** (condos, townhouses, chalets); 1–800–296–2149 • **Creekside Realty**; 1–800–376–3325 • **Motels/hotels** 11 miles from Bryce off I-81, Exit 273, at Mt. Jackson.

Dining/Aprés-ski

On-site

The Restaurant and **Black Bear Lounge**, with entertainment/live music on weekends. • **Skiers' Cafeteria**.

Nearby (Basye)

Coleman's Basye Bistro; (540) 856–8187 • **The 263 Diner**; (540) 856–8088.

The Latest at Bryce

The Locher brothers have pumped $1.2 million worth of capital improvements into the resort. The main lodge has been reconstructed to accommodate a visitor welcome center, retail shop, restaurant, lounge, banquet room, and offices. They've also made some key enhancements to the trail network, such as widening and adding snowmaking to the expert Hangover *trail and adding 10 new tower snow guns. Finally, a unique outdoor option opens up at Bryce when the snow of winter fades: look out for grass skiing and mountain boarding on the trails, starting in June.*

Massanutten Resort

Massanutten Resort
P.O. Box 1227
Harrisonburg, VA 22801

Ski Report/Info: 1–800–207–MASS
Local: (540) 289–9441/4954
Internet: *www.massresort.com*
E-mail: skimass@shentel.net
Credit Cards: AE, MC, VISA

Operating Hours: 9 A.M.–10 P.M. daily

Season: Mid-December to mid-March

Backdrop

Located 2,880 feet high on the windy tip of Massanutten Mountain, Massanutten is a popular, well-run ski area serving guests from Virginia's Shenandoah Valley and the Washington, DC area. The resort was initially developed by Del Webb, co-owner of the New York Yankees during the early 1970s. Massanutten is unique in that it's the only Mid-Atlantic ski area to exist inside and in conjunction with a residential community. With over 1,000 single-family lots, Massanutten Village sits along the valley below the mountain's ski area, and even has its own police department and road maintenance crew. The resort is considered a "metropolitan" ski area because of its proximity to the growing city of Harrisonburg—home to James Madison University.

Guests don't often get the chance to carve down fresh powder here—the area only averages 30 inches per year with conditions at the mercy of the Mid-Atlantic's chaotic, fluctuating winters. Nonetheless, the resort makes snow on all runs and miraculously manages to open around Thanksgiving and end in March just about every season. Skiers and boarders into spring slush skiing can get major breaks on lift tickets in March.

The mountain's smallish trail network lies in a natural recessed bowl, with 13 runs primarily catering to beginner to intermediate guests. Massanutten holds the distinction of Virginia's highest vertical drop, though the mountain skis a bit smaller than its 1,110 vertical feet. This is due in part to the resort's trail layout, which funnels a lot of its skier traffic to a busy runout, cre-

Did You Know?

The high-elevation, virtually inaccessible ridges of what is now Massanutten Resort once were the site of several moonshine operations.

ating logjams at the base lifts on busy weekends. Otherwise, Massanutten is an ideal learning mountain with some solid intermediate runs. The trail network is broken up by a mid-section, requiring two lifts to reach the summit.

Massanutten has committed its resources to developing both a model family-ski setting and a wild snowboarding haven at the same time. The secluded snowboard park is one of the Mid-Atlantic's outstanding aerial arenas: An array of jumps and obstacles offer big-time air to a growing number of boarders from Virginia and Washington, DC.

Mountain Stats

Base Elevation: 1,170 feet
Summit Elevation: 2,880 feet
Vertical Drop: 1,110 feet
Longest Run: 4,100 feet
Primary Slope Direction: North
Skiable Terrain: 68 acres
Average Annual Snowfall: 30 inches
Snowmaking: 100% of area
Slopes and Trails: 4 beginner, 6 intermediate, 3 advanced
Lifts: 1 quad, 3 doubles, 1 J-bar
Uphill Capacity: 6,350 skiers per hour
Night Skiing: 100% of slopes, nightly until 10 P.M.

Getting There

- **From Washington, DC and northeastern points**: Take I-495 around Washington, DC to I-66 west, then take I-81 south at the end of I-66, pick up Exit 247A in Harrisonburg and follow Route 33 east 10 miles to 644; entrance to Massanutten is on the left.

* *Alternate route:* Take I-66 west to Route 29 south past Madison, then turn right onto Route 230 until it ends at Route 33, turning right (west), and follow signs for 30 minutes to the resort.

- **From Richmond:** Take I-64 west (taking the 295 bypass around Richmond), then take Exit 136 (Route 15 north), follow 15 to Gordonsville, and pick up Route 33 toward Massanutten.
- **From Raleigh/Greensboro/Winston-Salem, North Carolina**: Take Route 29 north from Danville, Virginia to Route 250 west, then pick up Route 340 north in Waynesboro, turn left onto Route 649 (Island Fort Road); Turn right at the stoplight onto Route 33 east, following signs for Massanutten.

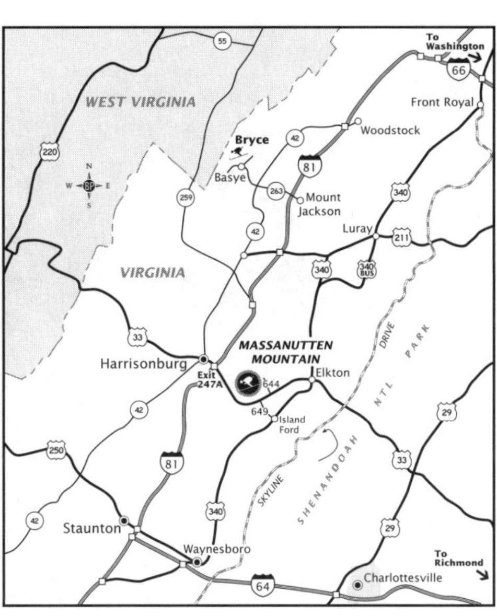

Snowboarding Highlights

Area boarders know Massanutten is the place to go for serious freestyling. It's one of the Mid-Atlantic's premiere parks, and has now opened its gates to skiers as well. The isolated terrain park is set on a former beginner trail in front of the ski lodge, hosting a relentless series of big-air obstacles to challenge the area's best riders. Look for five to seven changing hits, including a quarterpipe, some wales and spines, and a monstrous culminating gap jump, on which boarders have been known to catch over 25 feet of air. The resort formerly held rail slides and tabletops, but now constructs its hits entirely of snow and employs a crew dedicated entirely to the park. A convenient J-bar services the area, and strong lights keep the park open nightly until 10 P.M. Several instructional snowboard programs are offered, including a Skills Improvement Package for novice to intermediate boarders.

The snowboard-friendly resort hosts the Massanutten Intergalactic Race of Champions (MIROC)—a competitive Boardercross series with different age groups held seven weekends from December to March. Freestyle events are also held during the Mid-Atlantic Snowboard Series and the Edge of the World Snowboard Series.

Snowboard School: 20 instructors; Private $35/hour; Group $18/1.5 hours; First-time and Skills Improvement Package $45/weekday, $65 weekend, $35/half day, night; MINIriders (ages 7–14): weekday $50, weekend $55; includes lift ticket, rental, instruction, lunch (reservations suggested) • **Snowboard Rentals:** 300 sets: Mistral, Burton (step-in bindings); Ski rental rates apply.

Trail Profiles

The mountain's lower 500 feet of vertical constitutes primarily beginner track. The wide beginner bowl on *Geronimo* is a learning paradise, and has its own double chair, while *Southern Comfort* is a designated slow-skiing area. PSIA-certified instructors expertly teach Massanutten's SKIwee and MINIrider programs. MINIrider is a derivative of the national SKIwee childrens' program, focusing on the fundamentals of snowboarding for ages 7 to 14.

Massanutten cut black diamond trails *ParaDice* and *Diamond Jim* a few years back off of the summit, adding another 300 feet of vertical for skiers. Both trails have decent pitches on fairly long cruising terrain. Neither is truly steep enough to test experts throughout its 800 vertical feet, but the lift and terrain here is always free of big crowds. Like the resort's other lifts, the quad reaching these trails is slow, if not without its perks. Keep your eyes open for striking ridge lines and valley views. If scenery is your thing, check out great views of the Shenandoah Valley by making the short climb above the main double chair on *Rebel Yell*.

Skiers will likely find Massanutten's most challenging turf on *Dixie Dare*—a short, narrow trail that throws in a tight elbow turn before flowing into wide-open terrain on *Pacesetter*. The resort often leaves *Dixie Dare* ungroomed for mogul-busting guests.

The resort's mid-level runs are all short but somewhat satisfying. *Rebel Yell* is by far the mountain's most popular blue trail, featuring wide and nicely pitched track that's ideal for turning and carving. *Pacesetter* is the designated racing trail, where NASTAR time-trial runs are held on weekends.

More Fun in the Flakes

Massanutten's popular snowtubing park features an expanded 7 lanes and a tow lift, and operates under strong lights after sundown. Sessions are available in two-hour increments from 9 A.M. to 7 P.M. at a rate of $12/per person, all ages. Tubing tickets are known to go fast, so be sure to call one day in advance to secure a spot (1–800–207–MASS).

Summer Activities

Massanutten's mountainous fresh air and multitude of outdoor activities lure thousands of Washington, DC, vacationers every summer. Golf, tennis, hiking, swimming, and a reputable mountain bike trail system are available during summer months. And in July, 1997, Massanutten hosted one of the events within the UCI/Grundig Mountain Bike Downhill World Cup Circuit—the world's most prestigious professional mountain bike downhill race series.

Skier Services

Lift Tickets

9 A.M.–4:30 P.M./12:30 P.M.–10 P.M.: weekday $30, weekend $44 • 9 A.M.–10 P.M.: $36, $48 • 9 A.M.–12:30 P.M./12:30 P.M.–4:30 P.M.: $20 (Monday–Friday only) • 5 P.M.–10 P.M.: $20 (all week) • Reduced rates for children under 12 and adults ages 62–69 • Early and late season lift ticket discounts • Group rates available for 15 or more skiers.

Ski Rentals

Half-day (weekdays) $15 • Night $13 • Day and twilight $20–$24.

Services

Ski School: Over 80 instructors: PSIA certified; Private $35/hour; Group $18/1.5 hours; First-time Skier Package or Skills Improvement Package (ski/snowboard): $45/weekday, $65/weekend, $35/half day or night; Race lessons: weekends at noon, $18/1.5 hours; Childrens' Programs: SKIwee (ages 4–6), Mountain Explorers (ages 7–12): registration 8:30 A.M.–9:30 A.M., class 9:30 A.M.–2 P.M. Weekdays $50/child, weekends/holidays $55 (includes lift ticket, rental, instruction, activities, lunch); Call 1–800–207–MASS for reservations (24 hours in advance); Multiday session discounts available Monday through Friday • **Racing:**

NASTAR held Saturdays and Sundays on Pacesetter trail, 1 P.M.–3 P.M.; $5/two runs, $1 each additional run; registration at summit of Pacesetter; Junior race team (up to 18 years of age): Wednesdays, Saturdays, and Sundays; $350 fee includes all-season pass and coaching • **Adaptive Ski School:** Massanutten Adaptive Ski School: a nonprofit educational organization promoting ski instruction for physically handicapped individuals; Program follows the PSIA Adaptive Teaching Model as defined by National Handicapped Sports; Call 1–800–207–MASS or (540) 289–4954 for more information • **Base Lodge Facilities:** Cafeteria, restaurant/lounges, ski and snowboard shops, ski school, lockers, basket room.

Calander Of Events

Snowboard demo days held several weekends throughout the season • **December:** Massanutten Intergalactic Race of Champions (MIROC): Boardercross Series held on six weekends from December–March • **January:** Mid-Atlantic Snowboard Series (freestyle events) • **February:** Edge of the World Snowboard Series (freestyle events); Massanutten Challenge; Giant Slalom race on Diamond Jim trail.

Room & Board

Lodging options include Massanutten's **on-site hotel**, which typically finishes booking its weekend rooms early in the season. Otherwise, guests will find privately owned condominiums and townhomes scattered about the mountain. **Rental Services**, (540) 289–4952, will take care of all lodging needs, either on the mountain or nearby. All area motels and hotels offer ski-and-stay packages.

When visiting Massanutten, be sure to take a drive to the mountain's summit, where miles of hiking trails are available and clear days afford spectacular views of the surrounding hilltops and valleys. Nearby Harrisonburg has a growing downtown, and skiers may want to take some time to check out some of its many antique and specialty shops. Antique stores are also plentiful in nearby New Market, and Luray Caverns, open year-round, is only a half-hour drive from the ski area.

Lodging

On-site

Hotel at Massanutten: $90/night, per room; call (540) 289–4914 • **Massanutten Resort**: private timeshare vacation resorts/condominiums; call Rental Services at (540) 289–4952 for information • **800 timeshare units**; call (540) 289–9441.

Nearby (Harrisonburg)

The Village Inn, with optional deck/whirlpool baths; rates from $37–$53/night; 1–800–736–7355/(540) 434–7355 • **Shoney's Inn**; (540) 433–6089 • **Days Inn**; (540) 433–9353.

Dining/Aprés-ski

On-site

Base lodge cafeteria and **Encounter's Lounge**, with live music most weekends • **Fareways Restaurant & Lounge**, open year-round at the golf course area.

Nearby (Harrisonburg)

Log Cabin Barbecue, just outside the resort on Route 33; (540) 289–9400 • **Blue Stone Inn & Restaurant**; (540) 434–0535 • **Boston Beanery Restaurant & Tavern**; (540) 433–1870 • **Giuseppe's Italian Restaurant**; (540) 432–0200.

The Homestead Ski Area

The Homestead Ski Area
State Route 220
Hot Springs, VA 24445

Ski Report/Information: 1–800–838–1766
Lodging: (540) 839–7721
Credit Cards: VISA, MC, AE, Discover

Operating Hours
9 A.M.–5 P.M. Monday–Friday
8 A.M.–10 P.M. Wednesday–Saturday
8 A.M.–5 P.M. Sunday

Season: Mid-December to mid-March

Backdrop

In 1959, former Austrian national team skier Sepp Kober unleashed the South's first ski resort here at The Homestead. Located off of Interstate 81 and Route 64, just miles from the West Virginia border, the ski area today is a small slice of this historic resort better known for its posh accommodations and soothing European-style spas. The ski area entertains a main clientele of family skiers on its small trail network.

The resort offers over 15,000 acres of year-round recreation from valley to summit, where its alpine ski resort sits 3,200 feet atop a small mountain nestled in the Allegheny Mountain range. Terrain is limited, but skiers who want to get their money's worth of runs have the trails nearly always free of large crowds. A shuttle bus conveniently transports guests from the main parking directly to the base lodge. Lift tickets are generously affordable and controlled by the resort to ease traffic flow. The resort holds 10 slopes and trails throughout its 45 acres, with some additional cat tracks off the summit leading into the mountain's two main runs. Snowmaking, however, is not The Homestead's hallmark. Make plans to call ahead and get an accurate picture of the day's base and trail openings.

Homestead Thinks Big

No longer will skiing at The Homestead be just another resort activity. Today there is a commitment to both improving the existing ski area and enhancing its outdoor options. There's a new focus on maintaining the halfpipe; jumps to be built around the pipe and throughout the terrain; and snowmobiling, cross-country skiing and snowshoeing are on the plans. The resort hopes to use existing ski trails for snowmobiling, and plans to blow some snow on surrounding mountain bike trails for XC and snowshoeing enthusiasts. Call the resort at 1–800–838–1766 or check their Web site for current offerings.

Mountain Stats

Base Elevation: 2,500 feet
Summit Elevation: 3,200 feet
Vertical Drop: 700 feet
Longest Run: 4,200 feet
Primary Slope Direction: Northwest
Skiable Terrain: 45 acres
Average Annual Snowfall: 50 inches
Snowmaking: 100% of area
Slopes and Trails: 3 beginner, 3 intermediate, 4 advanced
Lifts: 1 double, 2 tow lifts, 1 J-bar, 1 T-bar
Uphill Capacity: 3,000 skiers per hour
Night Skiing: No longer offered

Getting There

- **From Baltimore/Washington, DC:** Take I-495 around Washington, DC to I-66 west, then take I-81 south to I-64 west. Pick up Route 220 north, and follow signs to The Homestead.
- **From Richmond:** Take I-64 west to I-81 south, then pick up I-64 west again to Route 220 north, and follow signs to The Homestead.
- **From Beckley, West Virginia:** Take I-64 east into Virginia to Route 220 north, and follow signs.

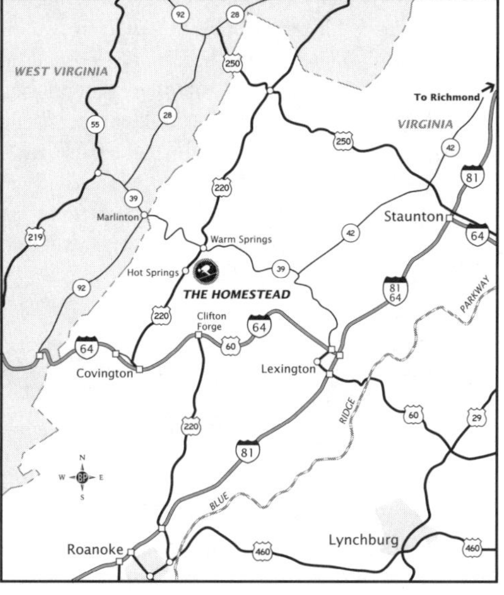

Trail Profiles

The mountain's 700 feet of vertical drop includes some advanced track found off the summit and the resort's double lift, notably the steep pitch of *The Glades*, which hosts the resort's NASTAR racing program. A tight switchback onto *Goat Trail* extends to wrap-around terrain on *Goat Farm* and *Down Draft*—three black diamonds forming one continuous run. Summit trails close occasionally because of poor conditions and grooming difficulty, so skiers looking to knock out the upper half should call ahead first for updated conditions.

Main Slope is a confidence-building trail for novice skiers, who have a mid-station drop-off option from the double lift that accesses wider track on the trail's lower half. Beginner terrain is found on the mountain's lower tier, which has four lifts. Two extremely wide novice areas punctuate the recreational atmosphere of the resort, and a tiny bunny slope with its own 170-foot tow lift accommodates absolute first-timers. The highly regarded Sepp Kober Ski School offers patient, professional instruction for skiers and snowboarders of all ages.

Snowboarding Highlights

There's a new team dedicated to enhancing the snowboarding experience at The Homestead. An existing in-ground halfpipe, served by a T-bar lift, is 260 feet long and 20 feet wide, with six foot-high walls. The resort doesn't have a Pipe Dragon to properly groom the pipe, but they're working harder to make snow and groom it out with available machines. Expect new hits and features around the pipe and scattered throughout the mountain.

Snowboard School: Same rates as ski school, with additional racing and freestyle instruction available • **Snowboard Rentals:** Boards: $20/day, boots $7/day • Night session rental: $12.

More Fun in the Flakes

As for the resort's amenities and activities, they're nothing short of extensive: The list includes an Olympic-size skating rink, cross-country skiing (weather permitting), horseback and carriage rides, naturally heated indoor pool fed by 104-degree natural hot springs, fitness center, board and table games, aroma and massage therapy in the Homestead Spa, and deluxe accommodations at The Homestead's four-star hotel. And the resort's spring to fall agenda features a championship golf course, fly fishing, shooting facilities, tennis, and bowling • **Cross-country skiing**, with rentals and repair services, available with enough natural snow on the golf course below ski area; rental rates: weekend $11, weekday $9; boots $5/all times • **Slopeside ice-skating rink**, with rentals and instruction; rates: private $20/half-hour, group $10/half-hour.

Skier Services

Lift Tickets

9 A.M.–5 P.M.: weekday $22, weekend $25 • Half-day: $13, $21 • 1 P.M.–5 P.M./6 P.M.–10 P.M.: $22, $32 • 6 P.M.–10 P.M.: $15 (Wednesday–Saturday) • Reduced rates for Homestead guests and children 12 and under.

Ski Rentals

200 sets: Elan skis, Solomon bindings • Full rental: $16/weekend, $11/weekday • Individual: $6/skis, $4/poles,$7/boots • Night rental: $10/all times • Reduced rates for ages 12 and under • Shaped skis to be introduced for 1997–98 season.

Services

Ski School: Sepp Kober Ski School: PSIA certified; Private $40/1.25 hours; Group $15/1.25 hours; Kids Club Bunny School (ages 5–11), includes ticket, rental, lesson, activities; Full day, with lunch: $60; Half day: $40 • **Racing:** NASTAR held on The Glades trail on Wednesday and weekend afternoons • **Base Lodge Facilities:** Ski/rental shops, cafeteria/restaurant/lounge, elevated sun deck, ski school, lockers.

Calendar of Events

January: Winterfest Weekends held during second half of January: ski, snowboard, and skating exhibitions; live music; fireworks; and family events.

Did You Know?

The Homestead's story is bound by chapters of early-American history, the earliest written accounts dating back to 1750. Dr. Thomas Walker, a medical missionary, told of Native Americans and European settlers who would flock to the area's natural hot spring waters for their reputed therapeutic benefits. The original Homestead Inn was erected in 1766 near Fort Dinwiddie—a frontier defense fort that George Washington built. The inn survived the Revolutionary and Civil Wars, during which time it was acquired by Dr. Thomas Goode, who promoted healing and rejuvenating powers of the mountain's spring waters. In 1890, The Homestead was transformed into a full-fledged vacation retreat. It was established by M.E. Ingalls, president of C&O and chairman of the Big Four Railroad, whose family ran the resort through four generations until 1993. The Homestead succumbed to fire in 1901, destroying all but the spa, casino, and Cottage Row. A new hotel was erected soon after, though, joined later by several elegant wings.

Room & Board

Lodging

On-site

The Homestead Hotel, with over 1,000 beds; rates include weekend and weekday specials from $218/night per couple, with lift tickets and meals provided; Call (540) 839–7721 for rates and information.

Dining/Aprés-ski

On-site

The Homestead Dining Room • **Sneads Tavern** • **The Ski Lodge** (restaurant/cafeteria) • Dining service and sports bar in The Homestead's hotel.

Nearby (Hot Springs)

Squires Table Restaurant; (540) 965–5577 • **Country Café**; (540) 839–2111 • **Albert Café**; (540) 839–7777.

Wintergreen Resort

Wintergreen Resort
P.O. Box 706
Wintergreen, VA 22958

Ski Report: 1–800–325–2100
Information: (804) 325–2200
Lodging Reservations: 1–800–266–2444
Internet: *www.wintergreenresort.com*
Email: info@wintergreenresort.com
Credit Cards: VISA, MC, AE

Operating Hours
9 A.M.–10 P.M. Sunday–Thursday
9 A.M.–11 P.M. Friday–Saturday

Season: Early December to late March

Backdrop

Considering Virginia's limited scope of alpine skiing, Wintergreen is indisputably the state's most varied ski resort. Situated within 11,000 acres of pristine woodlands and the expansive George Washington National Forest, the luxurious four-seasons resort offers a good mix of terrain for first-time to advanced skiers. Wintergreen's high-country land, formerly known as the "Big Survey," was purchased in 1952 by North Carolina's William Mattox. Twenty years later, Wintergreen Resort would be developed by Cabot, Cabot & Forbes—the same company involved in the creation of Hilton Head's Sea Pines Resort—and celebrated its first ski season in 1975.

At the resort's summit lodge, guests get the experience of big-mountain scenery, much like the high-elevation ridges of West Virginia. Wintergreen's 3,800-foot plateau reveals picturesque settings of the surrounding Blue Ridge Mountains, and the resort is bordered by scenic Blue Ridge Parkway, just one-half mile from the entrance to the ski area at Reed's Gap milepost. Nearly 4,000 acres of surrounding property is privately maintained in its natural splendor, and Wintergreen's own commitment to preservation was honored in 1987 by the American Hotel/Motel Association's National Environmental Achievement Award. The Appalachian Trail runs through the resort's property along the crest of the Blue Ridge Mountains, and a 30-mile hiking trail system connects at certain points with it. Hiking

> **Did You Know?**
>
> *A 3,000-foot elevation difference between summit and valley accounts for 10- to 15-degree temperature variations, allowing guests to take advantage of same-day ski and golf packages, weather permitting, on its nationally ranked Stoney Creek golf course.*

enthusiasts can check out waterfalls on the Shamokin trail and scenic overlooks on the Highlands Leisure trail.

With an average annual snowfall of just 40 inches, the resort depends on an aggressive snowmaking operation that works wonders even in the sloppiest of natural conditions. Like Virginia's three other resorts, Wintergreen guests sometimes have to ride notorious eastern ice or slush, but the resort does a commanding job of keeping its terrain open. As for crowds, there's no question that weekends can be extremely busy, though a quad lift has been added recently to help sift some of this heavy traffic. Parking can also be issue, made worse by a long walk from lot to lodge. Another word to the wise: a slow rental system can eat away at your time on the slopes, so consider off-mountain shops if renting equipment.

Getting There

- **From Richmond:** Take I-64 west to Exit 107 (Crozet/Route 250). Head west on Route 250, then turn left on Route 151 south. Follow Route 151 for 14 miles and turn right on Route 664. Travel four miles to Wintergreen.
- **From Baltimore/Washington, DC:** Take I-495 around Washington, DC to I-66 west, then pick up Route 29 south to Charlottesville. From Charlottesville, take I-64 west to Exit 107 (Crozet/Route 250), and follow the directions above to Wintergreen.

* *Alternate Route from Baltimore/Washington, DC:* Take I-66 all the way to I-81 south, then pick up I-64 east to Exit 99 (Afton/Route 250). Follow 250 east to Route 151 south. Follow 151 south for 14 miles, then turn right on Route 664. Travel four miles to Wintergreen.

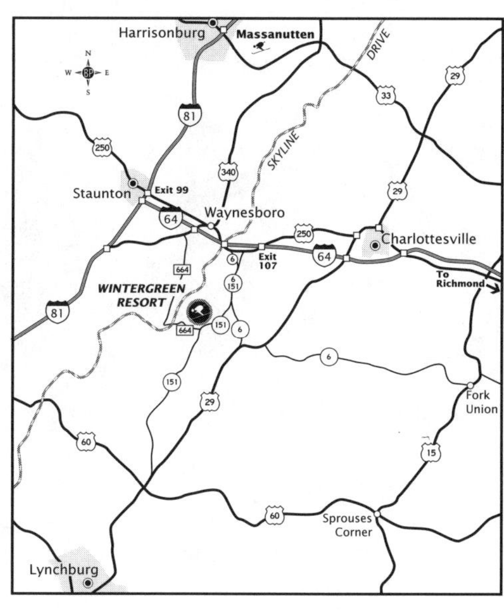

- **From West Virginia:** Take I-64 east into Virginia, then pick up I-81/I-64 north to I-64 east, and follow the Alternate Route from Washington, DC above.
- **From North Carolina:** Follow Route 29 north from Danville, Virginia, to Route 151 north. Travel 21 miles on Route 151, then turn left on Route 664, and follow four miles to Wintergreen.

Mountain Stats

Base Elevation: 2,512 feet
Summit Elevation: 3,515 feet
Vertical Drop: 1,003 feet
Longest Run: 1.4 miles
Skiable Terrain: 90 acres
Average Annual Snowfall: 40 inches
Snowmaking: 100% of area
Slopes and Trails: 8 beginner, 7 intermediate, 5 advanced
Lifts: 1 quad, 3 triples, 1 double
Uphill Capacity: 8,400 skiers per hour
Night skiing: 70% of area, 10 P.M. Sunday–Friday, 11 P.M. Sunday

Trail Profiles

The Highlands section holds some quality advanced terrain on its black diamond trails. The resort blew away long-time bashers of Virginia skiing when its *Upper Wild Turkey* trail was recognized by *Skiing* magazine in a February 1997 feature on east-coast resorts. The trail boasts several steep drops and a beastly mogul area, and *Lower Cliffhanger* serves up some nice steeps as well. Both *Wild Turkey* and *Cliffhanger* are nearly one mile long with over 1,000 feet of vertical drop; Regrettably, neither is equipped for night skiing. On the bright side, increased snowmaking should provide much better coverage in the Highlands than in recent years. On the western face, 3,000-foot *Big Acorn* is a black diamond trail more deserving of intermediate status but does offer a strong pitch off the summit and boulevard terrain for wide-arcing turns. *Tyro* is one of just three intermediate runs on the mountain, but is fairly aggressive: Its narrow course drops into a switchback that precedes wide-open terrain before a long, ensuing runout.

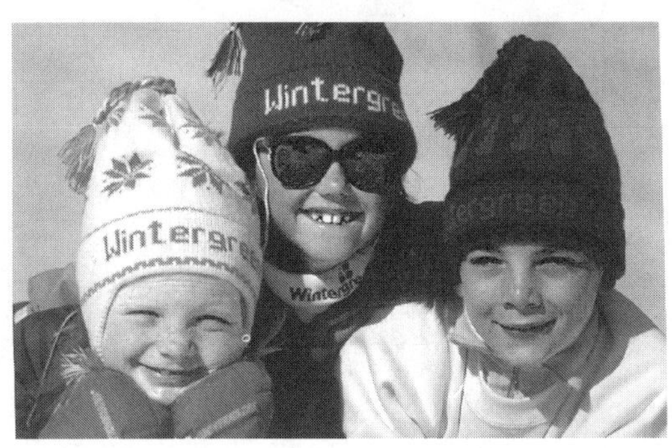

Though a long, beginner cruising run would be a welcome addition to the network of 20 slopes and trails, there are three wide learning areas off the summit lodge that accommodate novice skiers well. *Lower Dobie* and the *X Trail Loop* serve as the remaining green runs. Multitudes of childrens' instructional programs are offered for different age groups, and the resort's day care welcomes small children, with 48-hour advanced reservations.

More Fun in the Flakes

On-site

Hiking throughout the resort's 30-mile trail network (Cross-country skiing permitted but not recommended on the trails' narrow, rocky terrain).

Nearby

Cross-country skiing on the Blue Ridge Parkway, (which shuts down to auto traffic at the hint of snowfall), and on numerous adjoining side trails (see page 250 for more information).

Other Seasonal Activities

Wintergreen is one of the Mid-Atlantic's most reputable all-season destination resorts, offering two championship golf courses and a full tennis center, complete with clay and hard courts. Guests also have an extensive hiking trail system, horseback riding, indoor and outdoor pools, boating in 20-acre Lake Monohan, mountain biking throughout the valley, and fishing in creeks and lakes. The Wintergarden Spa features indoor/outdoor pools, hot tubs, an exercise room, saunas, and massage therapy. Wintergreen's summer to fall agenda has special events each weekend, including backpacking excursions, kids' camps, numerous festivals, wine and beer tastings, and fall foliage sight-seeing packages.

Snowboarding Highlights

Wintergreen has upgraded its 450-foot terrain park and now boasts Virginia's only halfpipe (now groomed masterfully by a new Pipe Dragon) on the far-right side of the beginner *Diamond Hill* trail. If you can catch enough speed in the park, its jumps can afford some decent air time on hits like gaps, tabletops, fun boxes and other changing features. A triple chair lift serves the snowboard park exclusively, and lights keep it well lit until 10 P.M. or 11 P.M. nightly. Look out for the Blue Ridge Boardercross series, hosted by Wintergreen once per month from January through March.

Snowboard School: Six instructors; Ski rates apply • **Snowboard Rentals:** Over 350 sets: Rossignol, Original Sin boards, boots, and bindings; Ski rental rates apply.

Skier Services

Wintergreen's inverted summit lodge offers a long list of amenities, as well as instant downhill access to the slopes. Though lift tickets and instruction are a bit on the expensive end, the resort does offer a free group lesson with any ski or snowboard rental, occupying a well-staffed ski school on most weekends.

$ Lift Tickets

9 A.M.–4:30 P.M.: Saturday $45, Sunday $38, weekday $34 • 9 A.M.–1 P.M./12:30 P.M.–4:30 P.M.: weekday $24 • 12:30 P.M.–11 P.M.: Saturday $45, Sunday $34, midweek $34 • 5 P.M.–10 P.M.: Sunday–Thursday $20, Friday–Saturday (11 P.M.) $24 • Reduced rates for ages 6–12 and 60–69; Children under 5 ski free • Value-season discount rates before Christmas and after March 2 • Group rate discounts for 20 or more skiers.

Ski Rentals

2,400 sets: K2, Head, and Elan SCX (all step-in bindings) • Midweek day/twilight: adult $21, youth/senior $15 • Weekend day: $26, $20 • Weekday night or half-day: $15, $12 • Free beginner lesson with rental.

Services

Ski School: 100 instructors: PSIA certified; Private $48/hour, $25/half hour; Group—call (804) 325–8065 for new rates; Childrens' Programs: Ski Cats (ages 4–12): indoor/outdoor instruction, activities, lunch, rental, beginner lift ticket; rates from $39–$89; Mountain Explorers (ages 7–14): offered weekends/holidays 10 A.M.–3 P.M., with five hours instruction, practice, lunch; rates $69–$80/day; Ski Buddy (ages 4 & up): Two hours skiing supervision; rates $36–$41 • **Adaptive Ski School:** Wintergreen Adaptive Skiing program, run by volunteers, by appointment only; Call (804) 325–2007. • **Racing:** NASTAR program on Upper Diamond Hill beginner trail; Call (804) 325–2100 for scheduled times • **Summit Lodge Facilities:** Four restaurants, Mountain Inn Conference Center/shopping gallery, Blackrock Village Center, ski center (ticket office, ski school, rentals, lockers and basket storage, child care, Cooper's Vantage restaurant/pub) • **Child Care:** Available for overnight guests and—by reservation—day skiers; rates $8/hour.

New at Wintergreen

Great news for advanced skiers! Wintergreen has increased snowmaking capacity on the 1,000-vertical-feet black-diamond Highlands area by 50%. Guests can also expect improved grooming with the resort's investment in a new Pisten Bully 2000. There's also a new mini snowtubing area on lower Potato Patch, and guests can get a free beginner ski/snowboard lesson when renting ski or snowboards from the resort.

Calendar of Events

Ski Appreciation Days offered regularly throughout season • **January–March:** Blue Ridge Boardercross series; Virginia Special Olympics Winter Games • **March:** Adaptive Ski Sno-A-Thon; Mardi Gras.

Room & Board

The resort's slopeside and on-mountain lodging can accommodate up to 1,300 guests in condominiums and houses. There are thousands of privately owned properties around Wintergreen, but only 400 are on the rental market. Dining and aprés-ski options are also incredibly varied here, with five restaurants, several pubs hosting live entertainment, and a cafeteria. Waynesboro is the nearest town with lodging, roughly 20 minutes away, offering bed and breakfasts, cabins, and motels.

Lodging

On-site

Studio to seven-bedroom condominium units and two- to seven-bedroom houses (mostly slopeside units and fully equipped); Call 1–800–325–2200 for rates and information.

Nearby

Bed and Breakfasts

The Nature Foundation at Trillium, Wintergreen; 1–800–325–9126 • **Belle Hearth B&B**, Waynesboro; (540) 943–1910 • **The Iris Inn B&B**, Waynesboro; (540) 943–1991 • **Redwood Lodge B&B**, Waynesboro; (540) 943–8765.

Cabins

Cabin Creekwood, Lyndhurst; (540) 943–8552 • **Hibernia**, Waynesboro; (540) 943–0070 • **Royal Oaks**, Lyndhurst; (540) 943–6151.

Hotels/Motels

The Inn at Afton, Waynesboro; (540) 942–5201 • **Holiday Inn Express**, Waynesboro; (540) 932–7170 • **Best Western Inn**, Waynesboro; (540) 932–3060 • **Days Inn**, Waynesboro; (540) 943–1101.

Dining/Aprés-ski

On-site

Five restaurants, one cafeteria: **The Copper Mine**: continental restaurant/lounge, with breakfast & dinner • **Cooper's Vantage Restaurant & Pub:** casual dining and live music six days per week, including blue grass and classic rock • **Blue Ridge Terrace:** outside bar & grill, weekend lunch hours only • **The Gristmill:** lounge and cappuccino bar • **Pryor's Cafeteria:** lunch and dinner • **Checkerberry Cabin:** mid-mountain lunch/snack facility.

Nearby

Broad Street Inn, Waynesboro; (540) 942–1280 • **Dulaney's Steak & Seafood**, Waynesboro; (540) 943–7167 • **Mulligan's Pub**, Staunton; (540) 248–6020 • **Scotto's Italian Restaurant**, Waynesboro; (540) 942–8715 • **Ciro's Pizza**, Waynesboro; (540) 942–5169 • **Suzanne & Company**, Waynesboro; (540) 943–5933.

ALPINE RESORTS:
NORTH CAROLINA

Major Alpine Resorts
- **34.** Beech Mountain
- **35.** Sugar Mountain

Other Alpine Ski Areas
- **36.** Appalachian Ski Mountain
- **37.** Cataloochee
- **38.** Sapphire Valley
- **39.** Wolf Laurel

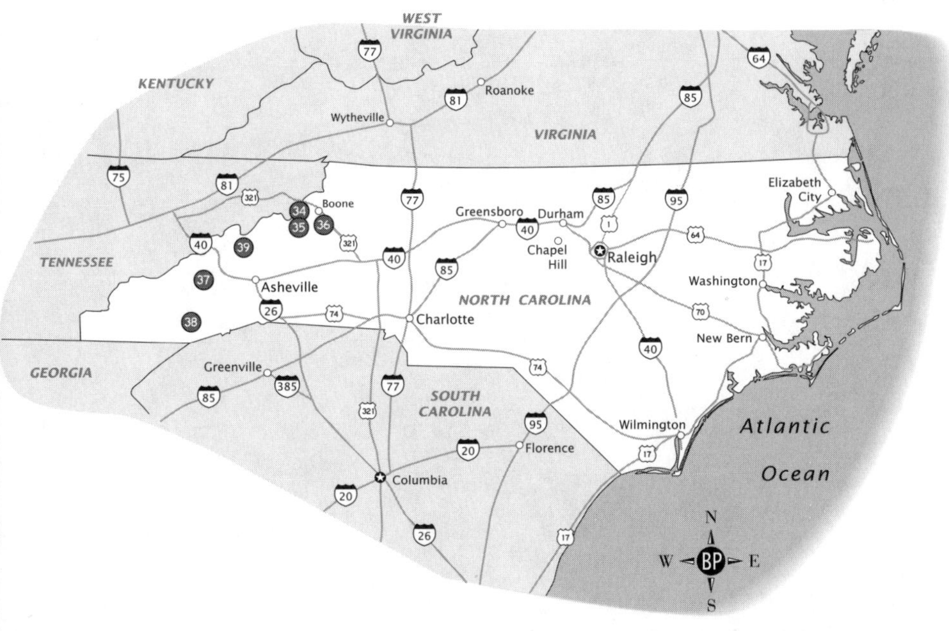

Skiing in North Carolina? Absolutely. The state holds more ski areas than Virginia and Maryland combined. How? The Tar Heel state is able to maintain skiable conditions with a combination of natural and manmade snow on its eight ski areas. All are clustered along the higher elevations of the Great Smoky Mountains of the Appalachian range, with several perched at mile-high altitudes. Granted, the considerable snowfall dumps off the Great Lakes don't travel as far south as skiers and resort owners would like, but many Carolina resorts average 60 to 80 inches of powder per year. And the higher elevations help retain both the natural powder and the manmade snow that is gunned virtually non-stop throughout the season. Unfortunately, warmer southern conditions from the Gulf Coast serve to whisk away the effects of winter at the same time.

The state isn't blessed with terribly steep mountains and plateaus, but its ski areas do well with the terrain available. Neighboring Beech and Sugar Mountains are unquestionably the largest and most popular of Carolina's resorts, with lots of overnight lodging, aprés-ski options, and amenities. Hawksnest and Wolf Laurel are slightly smaller but less crowded mountains. The state's remaining areas are small, comfortable, and geared toward families. Cataloochee, Appalachian, Sapphire Valley, and Scaly Mountain are choice destinations for kids and developing skiers.

MAJOR ALPINE RESORTS: NORTH CAROLINA

Beech Mountain

34

Beech Mountain
1007 Beech Mountain Parkway
Beech Mountain, NC 28604

Ski Report: (828) 387–2011
Information: 1–800–438–2093
Internet: *www.skibeech.com*
E-mail: skibeech@infoave.com
Credit Cards: VISA, AE, MC, Discover

Operating Hours
8:30 A.M.–4:30 P.M. daily
6 P.M.–10 P.M. nightly

Season: Mid-November to mid-March

Backdrop

North Carolina's biggest alpine resort sits 5,505 feet above sea level on a windy knob of the Blue Ridge Mountains in western North Carolina. Beech's towering altitude affords striking views into both Tennessee and Virginia, and reveals the surrounding peaks and valleys, including the 6,300-foot summit of nearby Grandfather Mountain. Beech was also the state's first ski area to incorporate an alpine village resort setting when it opened for the 1968–69 season.

Roughly two hours from Asheville and 10 minutes from Banner Elk, Beech remains one of the South's biggest ski draws and is exceptionally accommodating to families and developing snow riders. Ski resorts are rare commodities in these southern regions, and Beech is a huge attraction for surrounding states, including South Carolina, Tennessee, Georgia, and Florida.

The mountain's mile-high elevation affords one of the coldest climates in the South, and a surprisingly high 60-plus inches of snow is recorded per year on average. The resort is slightly more exposed to the elements than nearby Sugar Mountain—the state's other major downhill ski resort. Despite high elevation and respectable snowfall numbers, wintry conditions tend to be short lived: The mountain gets bursts of warm air from the Gulf Coast, while northern cold snaps often don't

extend this far south. In general, North Carolina skiing is fueled by snow guns and persistent grooming, and Beech's expert snowmaking staff reliably maintains its trail network.

A word to the wise—Bring goggles, face masks, and hats to combat common round-the-clock snow blowing and swirling winds. And during storm periods, the road leading to Beech can prove somewhat perilous as it winds steeply upward to the summit, then drops back down to the lodge. Under such conditions, many skiers, particularly families, head off to Sugar Mountain, which is slightly smaller, more accessible, and generally less crowded.

Beech has built a reputation as North Carolina's premiere ski area by marketing the complete family package. The 100-acre resort serves mostly beginners to intermediates on a fairly small system of 15 slopes and trails. A handful of sections are considered challenging for advanced skiers, but the resort has added a few twists recently to appeal to a broader base. A 475-foot tubing park off the Lower Sunny Hall slope includes three 12-foot-wide flumes and its own chair lift. Night skiing has also been instituted, with strong lights covering the entire mountain. The transition from day to night is plagued, though, by a 90-minute interruption: Trails close at 4:30 P.M. daily so snowmakers can pump the mountain full of man-made snow (when it needs it) before the night session begins at 6 P.M.

Getting There

- **From Boone, NC**: Take Route 105 south to Route 184 north through Banner Elk, and follow signs for four miles to Beech Mountain.
- **From Asheville:** Take I-40 east to Route 221 north to Linville, then pick up 184 toward Banner Elk and follow signs to Beech Mountain.
- **From Charlotte**: Take I-85 or I-77 north to Highway 321 at Gastonia. Follow 321 north toward Boone, then take Route 105 south to Route 184 north through Banner Elk, and follow signs for four miles to Beech Mountain.
- **From Virginia:** Take I-81 south into Tennessee, then take Route 23 south to Route 19 and follow signs for Beech Mountain.
- **From Atlanta, GA:** Take I-85 north to Greenville/Spartanburg, then take Route 221 north to 184 and follow signs to Beech Mountain.
- **From Knoxville, Tennessee:** Take I-81 to Johnson City, then take Route 19 into North Carolina, and follow signs to Beech Mountain.

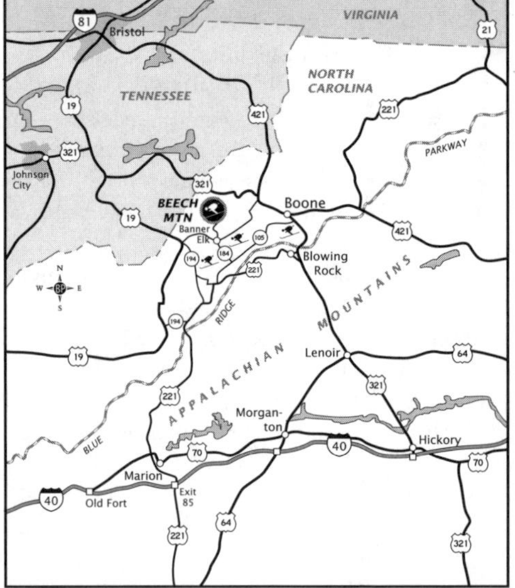

Mountain Stats

Base Elevation: 4,675 feet
Summit Elevation: 5,505 feet
Vertical Drop: 830 feet
Longest Run: 5,000 feet
Primary Slope Direction: North
Skiable Terrain: 100 acres
Average Annual Snowfall: 70 inches
Snowmaking: 100% of area
Slopes and Trails: 3 beginner, 8 intermediate, 4 advanced
Night Skiing: 100% of trails, nightly until 10 P.M.
Lifts: 1 high-speed detachable quad, 6 doubles, 1 J-bar, 1 rope tow, 1 handle pull
Uphill Capacity: 8,400 skiers per hour

Trail Profiles

Novice and intermediate skiers have the run of the mountain on primarily smooth cruising track. A tiny, secluded, introductory-level area with its own rope tow can be found on *College Park*, while neighboring *Play Yard* has similarly easy turf and utilizes a J-bar lift. Next on the beginner depth charts are *Freestyle* slope and *Powder Bowl*. One of the resort's blemishes is that most trails funnel into a narrow bottleneck at the mid-station before accessing these beginner areas. And on high-traffic weekends, many Beech guests opt for the more efficient quad chair, though doing so requires poking through the *Powder Bowl* and navigating around slower skiers. Nonetheless, there is a good variety of beginner terrain, and the resort offers a wide selection of good instructional programs for children, including PEEwee, SKIwee, and Mountain Mashers.

Did You Know?

Beech is the highest-elevated commercial ski area in eastern North America at 5,505 feet.

As a rule, there's not a lot of mogul action in North Carolina: Bumpy terrain just doesn't suit the novice to mid-level skier majority. However, sections of the black diamond trail *Southern Star* often hold some challenging bumps over its extra-wide track. *White Lightning* is the only other advanced trail offered, but it's one of the steepest runs in a state otherwise not regarded for its heavily pitched terrain. Bear in mind, though, that both black diamonds tend to pack hard and ice over very quickly.

Top sections of intermediates *Shawneehaw* and *Robbin's Run* provide some more decent vertical, with a more narrow course and an elbow turn on *Lower Shawneehaw*. *Oz Run* is a baby-blue intermediate off the summit's back side that serves to whisk away some of the traffic off the center face. The trail is easily 40 yards wide over the entire run and has a smooth, reliably packed surface over an easy downhill grade. It's also the resort's best means of separating beginners from its monster crowds. Unfortunately, it's open only with enough natural snowfall.

Beech's high-speed quad lift has been a tremendous help in reducing lift lines. The efficient chair provides a fast three- to four-minute ride to the heavily traveled summit. The resort's other lifts are somewhat slow, particularly the double on the back side.

Snowboarding Highlights

Beech's snowboard park and halfpipe can be found in the Meadows section, near the mountain's base. Snowboarders tend to drop into the pipe for a few jumps, but it's still more or less a novice arena. Boarders can also carve the resort's 14 trails with few restrictions, but advanced freestylers will find only a few scattered jumps and banks on otherwise smooth cruising terrain.

Snowboard School: 12 instructors; Private $40/hour; Group $15/hour • **Snowboard Rentals:** Weekday: $20/day or twilight session, $15/half-day, $15/night session Sunday–Thursday; Weekend: $25, $15, $12

More Fun in the Flakes

On-site

375-foot **snowtubing** run with three lanes on Lower Sunny Hall slope, accessed by #1 lift; rates: $12/two-hour session, rental included • 7,800-square-foot **ice-skating** rink at base lodge; rates: $5/session, $5/rental.

Nearby

Cross-country skiing (natural conditions permitting) at Mount Mitchell State Park (*see page 285*), Blue Ridge Parkway (*see page 282*), Great Smoky Mountains National Park (*see page 283*), and Pisgah National Forest (*see page 284*); cross-country ski rentals in Banner Elk.

Skier Services

Lift Tickets

8:30 A.M.–4:30 P.M.: weekday $28, weekend $45 • 8:30 A.M.–12:30 P.M./12:30 P.M.–4:30 P.M.: $21, $35 • 6 P.M.–10 P.M. Sunday–Thursday: $18, Friday–Saturday $22 • Reduced rates for ages 5–12 and 65+ (15%–25% discounts on tickets, rentals, & lessons) • Children under 5 ski free • Group rates for 15 or more skiers • Coupon books available with discounts on tickets, rentals, & lessons.

Ski Rentals

3,000 sets; Weekday, all ages $10–$12 • Weekend/holiday $12–$16 • Bib & coat rental $10 each, $15/both.

Services

Ski School: 125 instructors: PSIA certified; Private $40/hour, $15/each additional person; Group $15/hour, $15/each additional person; Weekday Learn-to-Ski Special: limited lift access, rental, group lesson: $45• **Childrens' Learning Center:** PEEwee snow/play program: instruction and day care for three-year olds; SKIwee program: five hours snow/indoor instruction for ages 4–8; Mountain Mashers ski program: ages 9–14 (Following rates apply to all Learning Center programs: $45/half day, $58/full day); Beech Boarders snowboard program, ages 8–14: $75 • **Adaptive Skier Program:** National Handicapped Ski Association event held one weekend each January • **Racing:** NASTAR scheduled during event weekends • **Day Care:** Available for children ages six months to three years from 8:30 A.M.–4:30 P.M., reservations suggested; rates: $7/hour, $50/day • **Base Lodge Facilities:** Beech Tree Village: outdoor ice-skating rink, three eateries and two lounges, Red Baron Snowboard Shop, Ski Beech Sports Shop: rentals and demos, specialty shops, nursery, lockers/ski lock-ups (in three locations: ski center building, sports shop, and group sales center).

Calender of Events

January: Red Baron Room Boarder Events; High Country GS; Adaptive Learn-to-ski Events • **February:** Edge of the World Snowboard Series Competition; Jimmy Heauga Toyota Ski Express: marathon fundraiser for MS, with ski/snowboard races.

Room & Board

Beech Mountain Resort has assumed the name of the small mountaintop area on which it sits. The resort was designed to keep skiers on the mountain, with extensive facilities and recreation opportunities that include several retail shops, restaurants and lounges, nursery, video game facility, outdoor ice skating, and tourist supplements. Guests can base themselves on the mountain or nearby in one of hundreds of houses, chalets, or other rental units. Reserve your lodging far in advance of your trip: Beech is a big-time destination resort, and accommodations fill quickly. Ten miles away in the college town of **Banner Elk**, plenty of aprés-ski establishments can be found, as well as one of the region's best snowboard shops at **Edge of the World**. Beech-bound skiers and snowboarders renting equipment might squeeze in some more runs on the slopes by using one of the shops in Banner Elk and foregoing long weekend rental lines at the resort. Most off-mountain shops stay open one hour past Beech's 10 P.M. closing time.

Lodging

For lodging information, call 1–800–GO–BEECH or Beech Mountain Chamber of Commerce; 1–800–468–5506.

Slopeside and Nearby

8,000 total beds include privately owned slopeside lodging and secluded nearby accommodations, including 650 chalets and townhomes, four inns, and several bed and breakfasts • **Accommodations Center & Action Realty;** 1–800–258–6198 • **Archers Mountain Inn;** (828) 898–9004 • **Beech Alpen Inn;** (828) 387–2252 • **Buchanan's Beech** • **Mountain Rentals,** 1- 800–438–2095 • **4 Seasons at Beech;** (828) 387–4421 • **Pinnacle Inn Resort;** 1–800–438–2097 • **Beechwood Realty, Inc.;** (828) 387–4251 • **Banner Elk/Beech**

Mountain Rentals; 1–800–845–6164 • **Beech Mountain Chalet Rentals**; 1–800–368–7404 • **Beech Mountain Realty and Rentals**; 1–800–845–6164 • **Beech Mountain Slopeside Chalet Rentals, Inc.**; 1–800–692–2061 • **Ridgeview Chalet Rentals**; (828) 387–2484.

Dining/Aprés-ski

On-site

Beech Tree Restaurant & Pub and **View Haus** cafeteria/lounge, open until 10 P.M., with live weekend entertainment some weekends.

Nearby

Rascals Bar-B-Que & Pub; (828) 387–2266 • **Beech Alpen Restaurant**; (828) 387–2161 • **Vasarelys Fine Dining Restaurant**; (828) 387–4900 • **O'Shaughnessey's**; (828) 387–2266 • **Ganders Restaurant & Pub**; (828) 387–2222 • **Beech Haus Restaurant**; (828) 989–4246 • **Brick Oven Pizzeria**; (828) 387–4209 • **Banner Elk Café**; (828) 898–4090.

Sugar Mountain

35

Sugar Mountain
P.O. Box 369
Banner Elk, NC 28604

Ski Report/Information: 1–800–SUGARMT
Local: (828) 898–4521
Internet: *www.skisugar.com*
Credit Cards: VISA, MC

Operating Hours
9 A.M.–4:30 P.M.
6 P.M.–10 P.M. daily

Season: Mid-November to mid-March

Backdrop

Sugar Mountain couples with nearby Beech Mountain to form the two major players in the limited scheme of downhill skiing below West Virginia. A few years after its inception in 1969 as a four-seasons resort in Blue Ridge Mountain high country, Sugar was rescued from bankruptcy as new owners looked to capitalize on the decade's national ski boom. The ski area has since operated as a separate entity from the four-seasons resort, and benefited from a skier base that stretches across numerous southern states.

Sugar's impressive 1,200 vertical feet runs second-highest in the Mid-Atlantic behind West Virginia's Snowshoe Mountain Resort. The mountain's face is somewhat narrow, but longer runs and good pitch give the resort some variety. The resort has added snowtubing near the golf course, and maintains a halfpipe for snowboarders.

Trail Profiles

The satisfying steeps and contours on black diamonds *Tom Terrific* and *Boulder Dash* are strongly pitched but short lived, and run out into longer cruising on *Sugar Slalom* and *Upper Flying Mile*. *Tom Terrific* is the staple mogul course for bump skiers; *Boulder Dash* is nearly as steep and more of a fast cruising course, occasionally getting the ungroomed bump treatment. Another option for aggressive downhillers exists off the summit on *Northridge*. The short terrain of *Northridge* features a wall on the inside of the trail that skiers and snowboarders often use for jumping.

Since many skiers seem intent on reaching the top of the mountain, Sugar's best-kept secret may be *Big Red*, off the lower summit area. It's a wide-open, secluded trail on which guests can open it up with giant slalom turns, and has its own lift to the Sugar Ski and

Getting There

- **From Virginia and points north:** Take I-81 south to Tennessee Route 91 south, then pick up Route 421 south; take Route 105 south to Route 184 west, and follow two miles to Sugar Mountain.
- **From Raleigh/Durham and points east:** Take I-40 west to Route 421 north, then pick up Route 105 south to Route 184 west and follow two miles to Sugar Mountain.

* *Alternate route:* Take I-40 west to North Carolina Route 181 north, then pick up Route 105 north to Route 184 west and follow two miles to Sugar Mountain.

- **From Columbia, South Carolina:** Take I-77 north to Route 421 north and follow directions above from Raleigh/Durham. 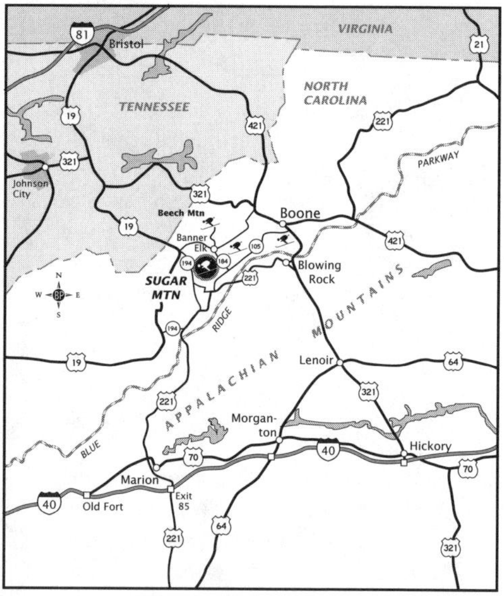
- **From Asheville:** Take I-40 east past Marion and follow Route 181 north to Sugar Mountain.
- **From Atlanta and points south:** Take I-85 north past Greenville, South Carolina, then take Route 221 north to Route 105 north, and follow Route 184 west for two miles to Sugar Mountain.
- **From Tennessee and points west:** Take I-81 north to I-181 south, then pick up Tennessee Route 67 north to Route 321 south. From Route 321, take Route 19E south to Route 194 north, then follow Route 184 east to Sugar Mountain.

Mountain Stats

Base Elevation: 4,100 feet
Summit Elevation: 5,300 feet
Vertical Drop: 1,200 feet
Skiable Terrain: 115 acres
Longest Run: 1.5 miles
Primary Slope Direction: North to northeast
Average Annual Snowfall: 78 inches
Slopes and Trails: seven beginner, nine intermediate, two advanced
Uphill Capacity: 8,800 skiers per hour
Snowmaking: 100% of area
Lifts: one triple, four doubles, one T-bar, one platter pull, one rope tow
Night Skiing: 90% of area, Sunday–Friday until 9 P.M., Saturday 10 P.M.

Country Club. The resort's active racing programs are held either on *Big Red* or *Sugar Slalom*, and include U.S. Ski Association events, NASTAR on weekends, and races throughout the season.

The resort's lower half, below the three-quarter lift station, is marked by wide, beginner track, where novice skiers have several bunny hills and broad slopes for learning. Three lifts exclusively serve the lower-half terrain, with areas set aside for instructional groups and developing skiers. The Sugar Bear Ski School is available for children ages five to 10.

Snowboarding Highlights

The Dead End Snowboard Park features some spines, gaps, table tops, and rail slides, as well as an occasional quarterpipe. The park will benefit from better grooming with the purchase of the new Winch Cat, though the terrain still suffers from its narrow course and lack of vertical drop. To its credit, Sugar installed a poma lift for the park and added lights for night boarding.

The resort hosts the Edge of the World Snowboard Series in January, and there's also a pro race with a division for boarders, usually held the same month. Guests can also rent Big Foot skis and use the snowboard park. Snowmaking can be suspect in the park, so boarders should call ahead to confirm its opening.

Snowboard School: Private $30; Group $15 • **Snowboard Rentals:** Mostly Burton boards, some with step-in bindings; $25/day, $16/night ($20 deposit required)

More Fun in the Flakes

Snowtubing: located on the Sugar's golf course; four tubing lanes over 700 feet in length, equipped with two lifts and lit for night tubing. $12/two-hour session, starting at 10 A.M. • **Cross-country skiing**, weather permitting, at nearby state parks and forests; *See the North Carolina cross-country section*.

Skier Services

Keep in mind that Sugar is North Carolina's busiest ski area. Skiers and snowboarders renting equipment might save time by using the private shop at the mountain's entrance. Although there's no chance of exchanging off-mountain rentals in the event of equipment failure, you'll get newer skis, cheaper rates, and possibly one or two more downhill runs by bypassing the resort's rental shop.

Did You Know?

Sugar has the second-highest vertical drop among all Mid-Atlantic ski areas at 1,200 feet. Only West Virginia's Snowshoe (1,500 feet) has more vertical feet of terrain.

Lift Tickets

Full day: weekday $32, weekend $49 • 12:30 P.M.–4:30 P.M.: weekday $23, weekend $38 • 12:30 P.M.–close: Monday–Thursday $32, Friday $36, Saturday $49, Sunday $41 • 6 P.M.–close: Monday–Thursday $20, Friday–Saturday $24, Sunday $20 • Reduced rates for children 11 and under (15%–25%) • Group rates available.

Ski Rentals

2,700 sets, with step-in bindings • Weekday $12 • Weekend $15 • Discounts for ages 11 and under • Big Foot ski rentals available.

Services

Ski School: 60 instructors: PSIA certified; Private $40/hour; Group $15/person; Learn-to-Ski Package $45, midweek only (includes ticket, rental, lesson); Sugar Bear Ski School at the Childrens' Learning Center for ages five–10: $55, 10A.M.–3 P.M. (includes ticket, rental, lesson, lunch, supervision) • **Racing:** NASTAR held on Sugar Slalom or Big Red trails, weekends at noon • **Base Lodge Facilities:** Ticket/rental offices, ski school, cafeterias, lounge, sports shop, repair shop, locker rooms, game room • **Other Winter Sports:** Cross-country skiing, weather permitting, at nearby state parks and forests; See the North Carolina cross-country section, *pages 281–285*.

Summer Activities

Mountain bikers can access over 10 miles of trails year-round, with some runs closed during the ski season. The annual Oktoberfest celebration is held each fall at the resort, with live bands, authentic German foods, and events and festivities. And a challenging par-64 golf course and six-court tennis facility are offered from mid-April through October.

New at Sugar

Expect 100% grooming on all three of Sugar's expert trails with the addition of Sugar's new 280 Pisten Winch Cat. The Cat will also get good use carving and refining Sugar's snowboard and tubing parks.

Calander Of Events

Slalom and giant slalom races held numerous weekends throughout the season • **December:** Sugar Race Clinics; Burton demo days; USSA Holiday Slalom and Giant Slalom Races • **January:** Edge of the World Snowboard Series, with races held in snowboard park; Septuagenarian Ski Party (ages 70 and older); Southern Region Pro Race • **February:** Stewart Smith Memorial Sugar Cup Slalom; Snowboard demo days.

Room & Board

Guests can choose from on-mountain accommodations such as condominiums, chalets, homes, and a slopeside lodge. The nearby towns of Boone and Blowing Rock offer a longer list of inns, bed and breakfasts, resorts, hotels, and motels. Guests will also find all the tourist trappings they can handle in Boone, including numerous specialty shops and attractions.

Lodging

On-site

32-room slopeside lodge, condominiums, chalets, and homes; Call 1–800–438–4555 for complete on–site lodging information and rates • **Sugar Mountain Accommodations** (condominiums and houses); 1–800–545–9475 • **Sugar Top Resort** (condominiums); (828) 898–5226.

Nearby

Era Realty & Rentals, Banner Elk; 1–800–438–4555 • **High Country Realty**, Banner Elk; 1–800–227–6521 • **Highlands at Sugar**, Banner Elk; (828) 898–9601 • *See Beach Mountain, Nearby Lodging*, for bed and breakfasts, cabins/condominiums/houses, resorts, and hotels/motels in nearby Blowing Rock and Boone, *page 195*.

Dining/Aprés-ski

On-site

Two cafeterias, deck grill (weather permitting), the Last Run Lounge (pub grub, fireplace, music, television).

Nearby

See Beech Mountain, Nearby Dining/Aprés-ski, page 196.

NORTH CAROLINA'S **OTHER ALPINE SKI AREAS**

Appalachian Ski Mountain

Appalachian Ski Mountain
P.O. Box 106
Blowing Rock, NC

Ski Report: (704) 295–7828
Info/Reservations: 1–800–322–2373
Credit Cards: VISA, MC, AE, Discover

Operating Hours
9 A.M.–4 P.M. and 6 P.M.–10 P.M. daily

Season: Late November to late March

Backdrop

Around the same time that Cataloochee Ski Area opened to mark the advent of commercial alpine skiing in North Carolina, Blowing Rock Ski Lodge followed suit in the state's western High Country region. The stockholder-owned turned family-run resort changed its name six years later in 1968 to Appalachian Ski Mountain, and has become one of the state's most highly regarded facilities for learning skiers. Guests with little or no skiing experience can expect attentive and patient instruction from the resort's acclaimed French-Swiss Ski College.

Appalachian is located a few miles from Boone and is equidistant from nearby alpine giants Beech and Sugar Mountains. The resort was designed with families and large groups in mind, and caters to all ages; it even offers complete accessory and clothing rentals for the true neophyte skier. And though there's more chance of injury by colliding with other skiers than spilling on the resort's gentle slopes, Appalachian rents junior helmets for children ages four to 12. The base lodge nursery cares for infants ages one to four daily, and the trail network is small enough that parents can spot their kids on the slopes from the balcony of the spacious Bavarian lodge. Rounding out the area is a lighted outdoor ice-skating rink that is open throughout the season and on Christmas Day from noon to 9 P.M., with rentals and instruction available.

Most of Appalachian's beginner skiers could care less about snow conditions as long as there's something to slide on, but conditions are usually kept pretty well in check. Southern downhillers love their spring skiing on oatmeal snow, so Appalachian does its best to keep its slopes open well into March.

Mountain Stats

Base Elevation: 3,635 feet
Summit Elevation: 4,000 feet
Vertical Drop: 365 feet
Longest Run: 2,700 feet
Primary Slope Direction: North
Skiable Terrain: 22 acres
Average Annual Snowfall: 60 inches
Snowmaking: 100% of area
Slopes and Trails: 2 beginner, 4 intermediate, 3 advanced
Lifts: 2 quads, 1 double, 1 rope tow, 1 handle tow
Uphill Capacity: 5,650 skiers per hour
Night Skiing: 100% of area, nightly until 10 P.M.

Getting There

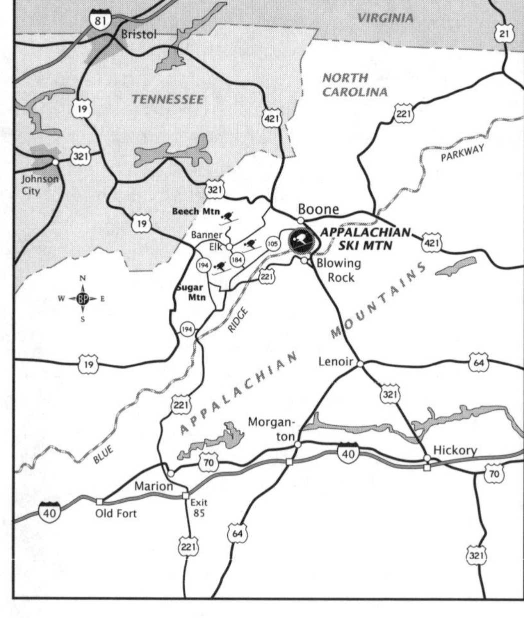

- **From Asheville:** Take I-40 east to Route 221/105 north toward Boone, then pick up Route 221/321 toward Blowing Rock and follow signs for Appalachian Ski Mountain.
- **From Atlanta, GA:** Take I-85 to I-26 north to Asheville and follow directions from here.
- **From Columbia, SC**: Take I-77 north to I-40 west toward Hickory, then take Route 321 north past Blowing Rock and follow signs to Appalachian Ski Mountain.
- **From Johnson City, TN**: Take Route 321 east to Boone, then pick up Route 221/321 toward Blowing Rock and follow signs to Appalachian Ski Mountain.
- **From western Virginia**: Take I-81 south into Tennessee and turn off onto I-81 south/Route 23 to Johnson City. Follow directions above from Johnson City.

Trail Profiles

Appalachian's terrain is solidly beginner throughout nine short, wide trails over a gradual 365-foot vertical descent. Two tiny, nearly flat bunny hill areas, each serviced by its own tow lift, help ease young children into the sport. The remaining trails offer gentle, straight courses—aside from a fun elbow turn on *Orchard Run*. A few trails are marked as advanced runs but are simply a bit steeper and narrower relative to easier blue slopes, with little variation in pitch among them.

What novice skiers can be assured of at Appalachian are affordable prices and plenty of runs, minus the lift lines of bigger Carolina resorts. Five chair lifts, including two quads, just about guarantee an active day's session on the slopes.

Snowboarding Highlights

No longer does Appalachian ban snowboarding on its trails. Riders can shred all of its trails and now have their own terrain park, filled with a nice variety of jumps.

More Fun in the Flakes

6,000-foot outdoor **ice skating rink**, with two-hour sessions from noon–9 P.M.; Rentals and lessons available • **Sled Dog** snow skates allowed on slopes; rentals available

Skier Services

A reputable ski school offers *SKI* magazine's national SKIwee program, and additional emphasis is placed on special programs for disabled skiers, including the North Carolina Winter Games of the Special Olympics which the resort hosts each January.

Lift prices are reasonable, with major markdowns for children 12 and under and senior citizens. Guests can also bypass ticket lines through a prepaid reservation system. Look for free skiing opportunities on opening day and reduced price lift tickets during early and late seasons.

$ Lift Tickets

9 A.M.–4 P.M.: weekday $22, weekend $32 • 9 A.M.–4 P.M./6 P.M.–10 P.M.: weekday $26, weekend $38 • 1 P.M.–4 P.M.: Sunday $21, weekday $14 • 1 P.M.–4 P.M./6 P.M.–10 P.M.: weekday $20, weekend $30 • 6 P.M.–10 P.M.: weekday $13, weekend $16 • 9 A.M.–1:30 P.M.: $25 (Sunday only) • Reduced rates (20%–35%) for ages 12 and under and 60+ • Early- and late-season discounts open to December 14 and from March 10 to close • Group rates for 15 or more skiers, reduced multi-day passes, and student discounts available.

Ski Rentals

1,600 sets: Rossignol, Volkl • Salomon step-in bindings, Nordica boots • Adult: Call 1–800–322–2373 for current rates. Discounted rates for ages 12 and under and 60+ • Clothing Rentals: jackets, bibs, gloves, goggles $4–$5, complete set $13.

Services

Ski School: 65 instructors: PSIA-certified; Call 1–800–322–2373 for current rates; Learn-to-Ski package $21 (includes group lesson, rental, beginner lift ticket); SKIwee program (ages 4–12): 9:30 A.M.–3:30 P.M. $43; 1 P.M.–3:30 P.M. $30 • **Adaptive Skier Program:** Lessons arranged by appointment • **Child Care:** Offered daily from 8 A.M.–4:30 P.M. for ages 1–4; rates: half day $16, full day $28 • **Base Lodge Facilities:** Cafeteria/restaurant, gift shop, ski/rental shop, childrens' facility, lockers.

Calender Of Events

January/February: New Year's Eve Celebration: late-night skiing and ice skating, fireworks; North Carolina and Southeast Region Special Olympic Games • **March:** Subaru Master the Mountain Week.

Cataloochee Ski Area

Cataloochee Ski Area
1080 Ski Lodge Road
Maggie Valley, NC 28751

Ski Report: 1–800–768–3588, (828) 926–3588
Information: 1–800–768–0285
Group Skiing: (828) 926–0285
Internet: *www.cataloochee.com*

Email: ski@cataloochee.com
Credit Cards: VISA, MC

Operating Hours
9 A.M.–4:30 P.M. daily
1 P.M.–10 P.M. Tuesday–Saturday

Season: Thanksgiving to mid-March

Backdrop

North Carolina's oldest ski area began operating in 1961 when Cataloochee Ranch owner Tom Alexander converted his isolated, mile-high pasture-land peak into a small alpine facility on Moody Top Mountain. Alexander developed the mountain into a ski area to further the region's tourism trade and to keep his ranch hands employed through the winter months. Cataloochee sits in western Carolina's

Maggie Valley, 35 miles west of Asheville, with part of the resort property bordering the Great Smoky Mountains National Park.

Mountain Stats

Base Elevation: 4,600 feet
Summit Elevation: 5,400 feet
Vertical Drop: 740 feet
Longest Run: 4,000 feet
Primary Slope Direction: North
Skiable Terrain: 15 acres
Average Annual Snowfall: 55 inches
Snowmaking: 100% of area
Slopes and Trails: 3 beginner, 4 intermediate, 2 advanced
Lifts: 1 quad, 2 doubles, 1 rope tow
Uphill Capacity: 2,200 skiers per hour
Night Skiing: 100% of area, Tuesday–Saturday until 10 P.M.

Getting There

- **From Asheville, Raleigh, and Durham**: Take I-40 west to Exit 27 and follow Route 276. At the 276/19 intersection, turn right at the stoplight and follow 12 miles to Cataloochee Ski Area (look for Ghost Town in the Sky signs).
- **From Charlotte**: Take I-77 north to I-40 west and follow directions above.
- **From Columbia, SC**: Take I-26 north to Asheville and follow directions above from there.
- **From Knoxville, TN**: Take I-40 east to Exit 20 and follow Route 19 and signs for Maggie Valley and Cataloochee Ski Area.
- **From Atlanta, GA**: Take I-85 north to Route 23 north, then pick up Route 19 and follow signs for Maggie Valley and Cataloochee Ski Area.

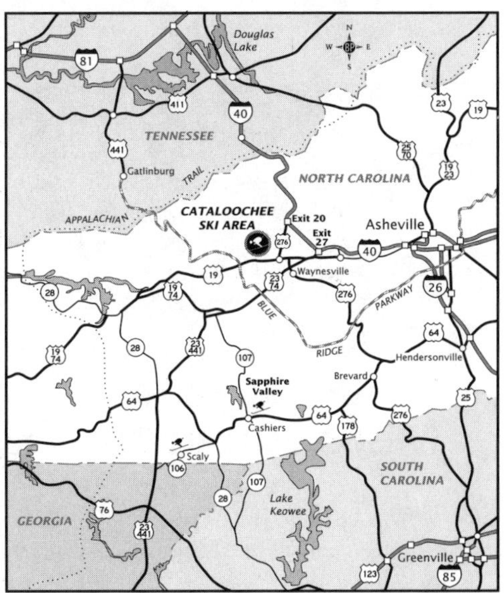

Trail Profiles

Cataloochee's small network of slopes and trails features a nice blend of tree-lined intermediate cruisers and gentle, wide novice runs. Cataloochee's headliner trail is *Omigosh*—a fast, steep run from the summit. It features an initial steep drop-off, nicknamed "The

New at Cataloochee

The Rock Island quad chairlift, serving three-quarters of the mountain. The Cat Cage—the resort's new terrain park for boarders and skiers. Increased snowmaking, including new air and water snow towers, additional airless fan guns and an air compressor, and over a mile of pipe for increased snowmaking capacity.

Headwall," which flattens out to some degree on a couple of small turns, then runs to the mid-station lift with a moderately steep pitch. Part of a $2.1 million capital campaign to improve the resort's infrastructure over the next three years is the new Rock Island quad lift. Before this new lift was erected, guests would have to negotiate the steeper section of *Upper Omigosh* to reach other slopes. Now skiers of all levels can access most of the runs immediately.

The resort's designated racing trail is *Alley Cat*—a short trail with a nice pitch and a few small turning areas. At the base of the resort lie a small bunny hill and a slow beginner slope above it.

There's wide-open bowl skiing available off the ridge in Cataloochee's *High Meadow* section, opening up another 80 acres of terrain that's suitable for all abilities when natural conditions permit. *High Meadow* is a beauty when it's open, but requires at least 14 inches of a powder base to ski. And because there's somewhat of a natural funnel on the mountain, strong winds tend to blow snow right off the meadow. A wet-consistency snowfall is typically required to keep the trail open.

Snowboarding Highlights

Cataloochee sees a lot more boarders with the inception of its new Cat Cage Terrain Park, open to skiers and snowboarders. Located near the base, the Cage serves up tabletops, spine jumps, and other hits, and is accessible from the Easy Way chairlift. Additionally, all slopes and trails are open to carving.

Snowboard School: Private $28/hour; Group $13/1.5 hours • **Snowboard Rentals:** $25 per any session

More Fun in the Flakes

When enough natural powder graces the region, cross-country skiers and winter hikers can access trails in the Great Smoky Mountains National Park or hit closed sections of the Blue Ridge Parkway. Aside from skiing, Cataloochee's other big draw is the **Cherokee Casino**, 20 miles west of Maggie Valley. The Cherokee Native Americans first established the facility in the mid-1980s, and Harrah's is currently building a new facility. Ghost Town in the Sky is a mountaintop amusement park built in the 1960s around a Wild West theme, open during the summer season only.

Cross-country skiing, natural snow permitting, is found on nearby Blue Ridge Parkway (closest access from ski area is in Maggie Valley, three miles west, on Route 19); Cross-country skiing is also available nearby in the Great Smoky Mountains National Park (see page 251 for information).

Skier Services

The ski school is excellent, which is why many families introduce their young ones to the sport at Cataloochee. Group instruction is also a popular and affordable ticket, with preregistered troops of 15 or more. Families can take advantage of special midweek offers, including free lift tickets for ages 17 and under on Wednesdays after the first week in January.

As far as Carolina resorts go, Cataloochee is one of its least crowded. Weekend lift lines rarely exceed 15 minutes on peak Saturdays. Night skiing is available Tuesday to Saturday until 10 P.M., and is used mainly by local skiers and nearby high schools and colleges through programs and races.

Lift Tickets

9 A.M.–4:30 P.M.: weekday $23, weekend $36 • 9 A.M.–12:30 P.M.: weekday $18, weekend $29 • 1 P.M.–4:30 P.M.: weekday $18, weekend $29 • 1 P.M.–10 P.M.: weekday #23, weekend $36 • 6 P.M.–10 P.M.: Tuesday–Thursday $18, Friday–Saturday $21 • Discount rates for students and ages 7–12; ages 6 and under and 65+ ski free • Group rates for 15 or more skiers.

Ski Rentals

Weekdays $10–$13, weekend $11–$15 • Discount rates for students and ages 12 and under.

Services

Ski School: 75 instructors: PSIA certified; Private $40/hour, $16/half-hour; Group $16/1.5 hours • **Childrens' Programs:** Catt Trackers (ages 4–7): half day $45,full day $65; Catt Explorers (ages 8–12): $45, $65 • **Racing:** Weekly school slalom races, normally held on Upper Omigosh or Lower Omigosh trails • **Base Lodge Facilities:** Cafeteria/lounge, rental and gift shops, ski school.

Calendar of Events

Weekly Interscholastic High School Slalom Race Series • **December:** Early season discount days • **March:** Spring Frolic: races and events.

Room & Board

Vacationing skiers have numerous resorts, inns, and motels just outside the ski area in Maggie Valley, all of which offer ski-and-stay packages. The Cataloochee Dude Ranch is one mile away, offering year-round lodging in their main ranch house and adjoining cabins.

Lodging

Nearby (Maggie Valley)

Cataloochee Ranch, one mile from the ski area, with 25 units in both cabins and the main ranch house; Call 1–800–868–1401 for information • **Maggie Valley Resort & Country Club**; 1–800–438–3861, (828) 926–1616 • **Best Western Maggie Valley**; 1–800–528–1234, (828) 926–3962 • **Four Seasons Inn**; (828) 926–8505/8501 • **Comfort Inn**; (828) 926–9106 • **Smokey Shadows Lodge**; (828) 926–0001 • **Meadowlark Motel**; (828) 926–1717 • Most lodging includes day lift ticket.

Dining/Aprés-ski

On-site

Cafeteria/lounge, open until 10 P.M.

Nearby (Maggie Valley)

Arf's Restaurant & Lounge; (828) 926–1566 • **J. Arthurs Restaurant**; (828) 926–1817 • **JB's Café & Tavern**; (828) 926–3828 • **Maggie Valley Resort & Country Club**; (828) 926–1616 • **Mountaineer Buffet Restaurant**; (828) 926–1730 • **The Copper Kettle Steak House**; (828) 926–1710.

38 Sapphire Valley

Sapphire Valley
4350 Highway 64 West
Sapphire, NC 28774

Ski Report: (828) 743–1162
Information: (828) 743–1163/1164
Lodging/Ski Packages: 1–800–722–3956, 1–800–533–8268

Operating Hours:
1 P.M.–6 P.M. Monday–Thursday
1 P.M.–10 P.M. Friday
9 A.M.–10 P.M. weekends

Season: Mid-December to early March

Backdrop

Just five miles from the South Carolina and Georgia borders lies this four-seasons' retreat situated nearly one mile high in a secluded valley wedge of the Blue Ridge Mountains. Jackson County's Sapphire Valley Ski Area is but one small component of the popular resort, offering three short slopes for its property owners, resort guests, and day skiers. It's a comfortable environment for introducing the sport to new skiers, and a patient ski school welcomes anyone from young children to senior first-timers.

Sapphire offers three short runs, including a small novice hill with an easy pitch and extra-wide shoulders. The area is conveniently serviced by a rope tow. An intermediate and advanced slope each hold 2,000-plus feet of wide cruising track over a steady 425-foot vertical drop. Snowboarding is also welcomed on the slopes.

As expected from a small ski facility, weekend guests rarely have to wait more than 10 minutes at any time for a spot on the double chair. Sapphire also offers continuous weekend skiing from 9 A.M. to 10 P.M., on the off chance that guests wish to ski the same few runs some 30 times over.

The resort is easily accessible off Highway 64, three miles east of the small town of Cashiers. Its clientele essentially comprises families looking to get away for a day, with Asheville just 50 miles away, Atlanta 135 miles away, and Athens and Chattanooga both within 90 miles. Families opting for an alternative to Christmas Day indoors can ski from 3 P.M. to 10 P.M., with 9 A.M. to 10 P.M. hours from December 23 to January 3.

Sapphire has added snowtubing lanes, and also will roll out a modified rental area and renovated ski lodge.

Mountain Stats

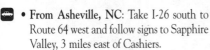

Base Elevation: 4,375 feet
Summit Elevation: 4,800 feet
Vertical Drop: 425 feet
Longest Run: 2,400 feet
Skiable Terrain: 16 acres
Slopes and Trails: 2 beginner, 1 intermediate, 1 advanced
Lifts: 1 double, 1 rope tow
Uphill Capacity: 1,800 skiers per hour
Average Annual Snowfall: 22 inches
Snowmaking: 100% of area
Night Skiing: 6 P.M.–10 P.M. Friday–Sunday

Getting There

- **From Asheville, NC**: Take I-26 south to Route 64 west and follow signs to Sapphire Valley, 3 miles east of Cashiers.
- **From Atlanta, GA:** Take I-85 north to I-985 north, then take Route 23/441 north to the Georgia/North Carolina border. Pick up Route 106 toward Cashiers and follow signs for Sapphire Valley.
- **From Athens, GA**: Take Route 441 north to Route 23/441 north and follow directions above.
- **From Greenville, SC**: Take Route 123 west to 178 north into North Carolina, then follow Route 106 and signs for Sapphire Valley.

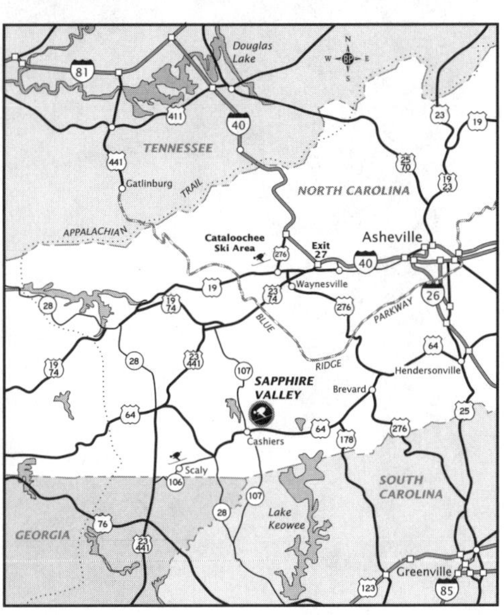

Skier Services

Sapphire bills itself as the cheapest lift ticket in North Carolina, and affordable lodging/ski packages provide full use of resort facilities. Golf, tennis, horseback riding, canoeing, fishing, swimming, and hiking round out the list of activities during the warmer seasons at the 5,700-acre resort.

Lift Tickets

Weekday: $19/adult, $10/children/students • Weekend: $27, $15 • Night Skiing: weekday: $12, $8, weekend: $12, $15 • Ages 17 and under and students with valid I.D. • 25% group rate discount for 6 or more people (tickets and rentals).

Ski Rentals

Weekday: $15/adult; $10/children, students • Weekend: $17, $12 • Night Skiing: weekday $10, $8; weekend $12, $10 • **Snowboard Rentals**: $25/three hours.

Services

Ski Instruction: Private $20/hour; Group $10/hour; Learn-to-Ski package: $50/adult, $30/child (includes lift ticket, rental, group lesson) • **Base Lodge Facilities:** Cafeteria, ski/rental shop.

Room & Board

The ski slopes are little more than an added amenity to the four-seasons' resort. Vacationing guests usually spend more time inside—the resort offers a restaurant and lounge, indoor pool, Jacuzzi, sauna, health club, and exercise and game rooms. Sapphire's cozy base lodge features a wood-burning fireplace, cafeteria, and a ski and rental shop.

Lodging

250-room Sapphire Valley Resort; Call 1–800–722–3956 or 1–800–533–8268 for information and rates.

Dining

On-site

Restaurant/lounge.

Nearby (Sapphire)

Mount Toxaway Restaurant; (828) 966–9660 • **Restaurant Vienna**; (828) 884–9727.

Wolf Laurel

Wolf Laurel
Route 3, Box 129
Mars Hill, NC 28754

Info/Reservations: 1–800–817–4111
Local: (828) 689–4111

Internet: *www.skiwolflaurel.com*
Credit Cards: VISA, MC, Discover

Operating Hours: 9 A.M.–10 P.M. daily

Season: Late November to mid-March

Backdrop

Just over the eastern tip of Tennessee and directly off the Appalachian Trail lies Wolf Laurel—a mom-and-pop ski area serving nearby Asheville; Knoxville, Tennessee; and surrounding locales. The newest of Carolina's ski resorts, "The Wolf" has a prevailing free-for-all atmosphere. There's a mix of families, snowboarders, and Telemark skiers, and in early spring you might spot some good-ol'-boys flying down the slopes in T-shirts and jeans.

A small network of 13 slopes and trails is great for families and beginning skiers, and its 700-foot vertical drop isn't altogether shabby for southern standards. But what keeps Wolf Laurel regulars coming back time and time again is the resort's unconventional grooming methods. Forget about grooming all its terrain smooth and flat! The Wolf blows its snow into wales and rollers, leaving the bumps and ruts left behind a virtual terrain park on a good portion of its 54 acres.

For all its charm, friendly staff, and affordable prices, the resort can occasionally suffer from a tight base and loading area. A quad and double chair lift run skiers efficiently to two mid-stations and summit areas, and expect slow-moving traffic on the narrow run to the base. All slopes are equipped for night skiing, with some areas dimly lit.

Trail Profiles

The Wolf isn't known for its abundance of trails. But do look out for summit-flowing *Howling* trail—a steep, longer run with a prolonged pitch and a natural headwall at the midsection, where skiers and snowboarders can catch some major air. Without an official policy on jumping, the resort only asks that skiers use extreme caution and respect others. Two black diamonds—*The Bowl* and *Flame Out*—drop into a wide bowl area for some good slalom-turning.

Mountain Stats

Base Elevation: 3,950 feet
Summit Elevation: 4,650 feet
Vertical Drop: 700 feet
Longest Run: 1 mile
Skiable Terrain: 54 acres
Primary Slope Direction: North
Average Annual Snowfall: 60 inches
Slopes and Trails: 2 beginner, 10 intermediate, 2 advanced
Uphill Capacity: 2,200 skiers per hour
Snowmaking: 100% of area
Lifts: 1 quad, 1 double, 1 surface tow
Night Skiing: 100% of slopes, nightly until 10 P.M.

Most of the remaining runs are baby blues that novice skiers should be able to negotiate with ease. Wolf recently cut a short beginner track off the quad lift midway station that opens up to the wide run-out of *Broadway*'s beginner section. There's a smallish bunny hill with its own handle tow set aside from the lodge, and the only other learning area is in *Broadway*, where on a busy day you may see a convergence of faster and slower beginners.

Did You Know?

Wolf Laurel holds the distinction of having the first nationally certified snowboard patrol in the country. A handful of years back, general manager Dave Durham assembled a group of dedicated riders and developed a snowboard demonstration project. The program is now certified through the National Ski Patrol. But that doesn't mean snowboarders can't open it up on the trails—the boarder patrol just monitors reckless behavior and helps to ensure a good, safe time for all.

Getting There

- **From Atlanta:** Take I-85 north to Greenville, South Carolina, then take Route 25 north to I-26 to Asheville. Pick up Route 23 north and follow signs to Wolf Laurel.
- **From Tennessee**: Take I-40 east to Asheville, then take Route 23 north and follow signs to Wolf Laurel.
- **From Raleigh/Durham**: Take Route 40 west to Asheville, then take Route 23 north and follow signs to Wolf Laurel.
- **From Virginia and points north:** Take I-81 south into Tennessee, then pick up Route 23 south and follow signs to Wolf Laurel.

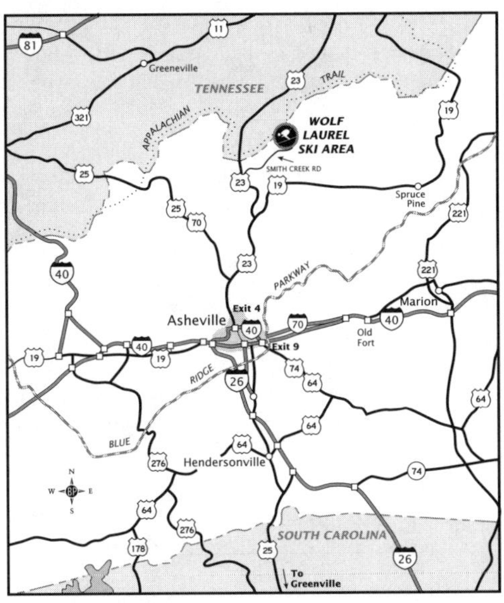

Snowboarding Highlights

Along with Hawksnest Ski Resort, Wolf Laurel is one of North Carolina's burgeoning snowboard destinations. The usual mass of boarders here is a testament to the resort's alternative style of trail grooming. When the snow guns finish firing, what's left after grooming out the track and its contours are wales, mounds, and ruts that boarders use for carving and jumping. The resort's trails are completely slopestyle, with naturally rolling terrain. Snowboarders also have some small glade sections on the trails and a mid-mountain natural bowl for big turns.

Wolf Laurel's 400-foot halfpipe sits in a slip above the Broadway area. Freestylers will find some clean obstacles incorporated into the pipe, such as rail and pipe slides, spools, and a gap jump.

Snowboard Rentals: 150 sets: Ride, Oxygen, Hooger, Fosfour (some with step-in bindings); $25/board and boots, $20/board only • **Snowboard School:** 15 instructors: Ski school rates apply.

More Fun in the Flakes

Wolf's upgraded **snowtubing** park features lights and a new rope tow. There's also a small **sled run** behind the lodge for children who don't find skiing the bunny hill to their liking.

FYI

The Wolf is rolling out its upgraded snowtubing park with lights and a new rope tow. Tubers can pick any two-hour session or grind it out on an all-day ticket.

On-site

Snowtubing park, with lights; rates: $10 per two-hour session; $30/all day • **Telemark skiing** permitted on all trails.

Nearby

Cross-country skiing, snowfall permitting, at the top of Wolf Laurel on Big Bald Mountain, with a small network of roads and trails.

Skier Services

The resort's operating hours sometimes seem as varied as the weather conditions, so don't pack your skis or snowboards before calling ahead first. Group skiing is the hot ticket at Wolf Laurel, with reservations guaranteeing slope time, and significant discounts on lift passes, rentals, lessons, and dining packages. Laid-back, personalized instruction ranges from the Wolf Cub Ski School (ages four to seven), adult and junior lessons, and racing and snowboarding clinics. Guests wishing to learn the Norwegian-based Telemark ski turn can take private lessons offered by the resort's Telemark-certified ski school.

Lift Tickets

9 A.M.–4:30 P.M.: weekday $24, weekend $34 • 1 P.M.–4:30 P.M.: weekday $17, weekend $24 • 1 P.M.–10 P.M.: weekday $24, weekend $34 • 6 P.M.–10 P.M.: weekday $17, weekend $24 • Reduced rates for ages 9–12 and under 8; ages 65 and over ski free • Group rates for 16 or more skiers.

Ski Rentals

1,600 sets: Dynamic, with Salomon bindings and boots, $10–$16.

Services

Ski School: 35 instructors: PSIA certified; Private $30/hour; Group $12/hour; Wolf Cub Ski School (ages 4–7): half day $35, full day $50; Telemark ski instruction (private lessons only): $30/hour • **Racing**: Racing clinics and events held some weekends • **Base Lodge Facilities:** Grill/cafeteria, ski/rental shop, viewing deck.

Calendar Of Events

January: Winter Carnival: snowboard races and various events • **February:** Edge of the World Snowboard Series: freestyle events; Memorial Ski Race.

Room & Board

Wolf Laurel's lodge was expanded recently, adding much-needed space on a second floor that overlooks the base of the slopes. There's a grill inside the lodge serving up good dishes but no suds—Wolf Laurel sits in a dry county. The resort's limited rooming options include The Wolf Laurel Inn, with inn/motel and dorm-style housing, while rental cabins and homes are available on and around the mountain. Other than a few establishments in Mars Hill, the closest town with full-service dining and aprés-ski options is Asheville, which has more than its share of eateries, pubs, and entertainment. The historic town—home of the renowned Biltmore House—is a wise choice for Wolf Laurel overnighters who don't mind the 45-minute haul to the slopes.

Lodging

On-site

Wolf Laurel Inn, with motel-style rooms and dorm rooms; 1–800–541–1738 • **40 rental houses and log cabins**; 1–800–541–1738.

Nearby

Comfort Inn, Asheville; 1–800–836–6732 • **Days Inn North**, Asheville; (704) 645–9191 • **Hampton Inn**, Asheville; (704) 255–9220 • **Shoney's Inn,** Arden; (704) 684–6688.

Dining/Aprés-ski

On-site

Base lodge grill.

Nearby (Asheville)

Annabelle's Restaurant & Pub; (704) 298–8082 • **Applebee's Neighborhood Bar & Grill**; (704) 251–9194 • **Barley's Brew Pub**; (704) 255–0504 • **Beaver Lake Seafood & Steak Restaurant**; (704) 252–4343 • **Cahoots Eating & Drinking Emporium**; (704) 252–2838 • **Angelo's Family Restaurant**; (704) 628–4031.

CROSS-COUNTRY SKIING

Cross-Country Ski Touring Centers

1. Laurel Ridge State Park
2. Hidden Valley
3. The Inn at Starlight Lake
4. Hanley's Happy Hill
5. Sterling Inn
6. Stone Valley Recreation Area
7. Callender's Windy Acre Farms
8. Crystal Lake Ski Center
9. Skytop Lodge
10. Camp Spears Eljabar/YMCA

CROSS-COUNTRY SKIING: PENNSYLVANIA

State Parks and Forests

Southwest Pennsylvania:
11. Blue Knob State Park
12. Forbes State Forest
13. Kooser State Park
14. Ohiopyle State Park

South-Central Pennsylvania:
15. Caledonia State Park
16. Cowans Gap State Park
17. Gifford Pinchot State Park

Southeast Pennsylvania:
18. Delaware Canal State Park

Northeast Pennsylvania:
19. Lackawanna State Forest

North-Central Pennsylvania:
20. Elk State Forest

Northwest Pennsylvania:
21. Cook Forest State Park
22. Oil Creek State Park

Allegheney National Forest:
23. Laurel Mill Cross-country Ski Center/Hiking Area
24. Brush Hollow Cross-country Ski Center/Hiking Area
25. Westline Cross-country Ski Center/Hiking Area

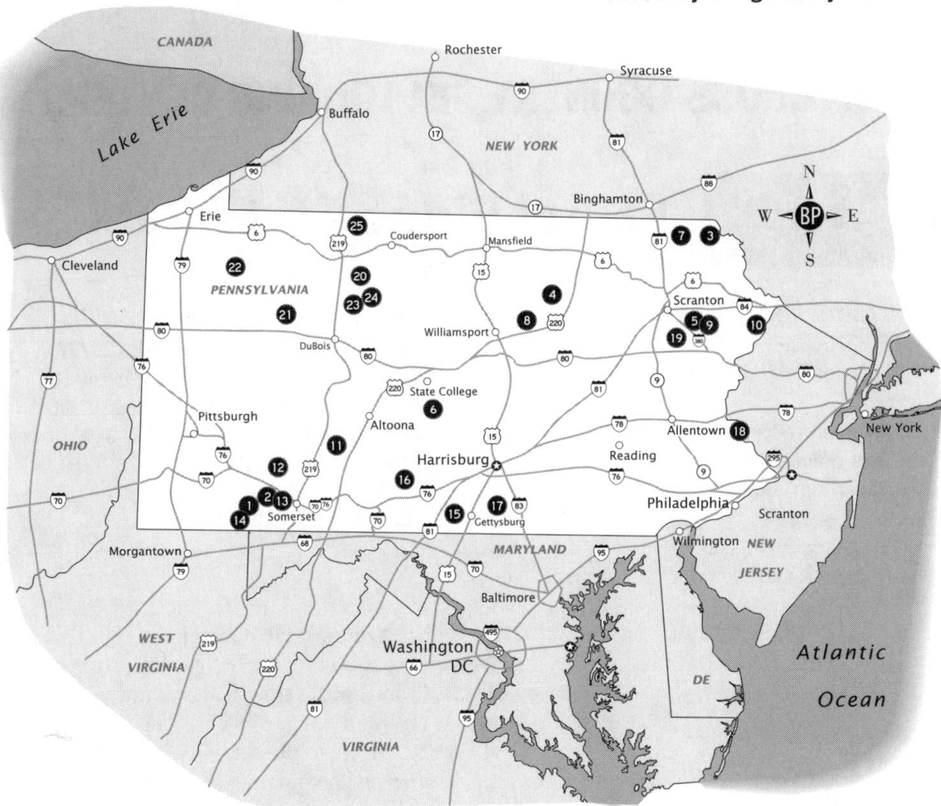

Pennsylvania's considerable size and several strong snowfall regions allow a large number of cross-country touring centers and state and national parks and forests to operate. Most Nordic touring centers are concentrated in two sections of the state: the snow-filled, high-elevation Laurel Highlands region (one hour southeast of Pittsburgh) and the Pocono and Endless Mountains in northeastern Pennsylvania, where snowfall is slightly less consistent. A few other touring facilities are scattered throughout the state, including far-western Pennsylvania's Elk Valley, near the town of Erie, and centrally located Crystal Lake and Stone Valley Recreation Area. All Pennsylvania touring centers offer equipment rentals and instruction, with the exception of Stone Valley Recreation Area, which recently closed its rental shop.

With so many state parks and forests in Pennsylvania, the areas that are most commonly used by Nordic skiers are listed herein, representing different regions in the state. Laurel Ridge State Park, which benefits from major snowfall in the region, is the only state-run facility to offer a complete touring center. A sampling of other state parks extend rental equipment on-site, including Cook Forest and Kooser State Parks.

Lodging is available at a few touring centers, some of which operate as year-round resorts, while some state parks offer fully equipped cabin rentals. Nearby lodging and dining is listed when available. (See the at-a-glance chart on the next page for an easy-to-reference listing of lodging, amenities, and winter recreation in the Pocono Mountain area).

CROSS-COUNTRY SKI TOURING CENTERS

Laurel Ridge State Park

Laurel Ridge State Park

RR 3, Box 246
Rockwood, PA 15557-8703

Ski Report/Concessionaire: (724) 455–7303
Park Office: (724) 455–3744
Operating Hours: Thursday–Sunday 10 A.M.–4:30 P.M.
Elevation: 2,700 feet
Average Annual Snowfall: 100 inches

Getting There

- **From the Pennsylvania Turnpike (70/76):** Take Exit 9 (Donegal), then follow Route 711 south to Normalville; Pick up Route 653 east for 6 miles and follow signs to Laurel Ridge State Park.

Perched high atop Laurel Mountain in southwest Pennsylvania, Laurel Ridge State Park offers excellent backcountry skiing throughout 20 miles of marked, groomed, set track on a single loop system. Laurel Ridge is Pennsylvania's only state park to operate a cross-country ski touring center, and therefore charges a nominal trail fee. The park hosts some outstanding terrain for daring Nordic skiers, with some trails actually too steep for the park service to groom. And Laurel's high elevation and north-facing mountain help hold the region's typically abundant amounts of snowfall for long periods of winter.

The terrain is tremendously varied, suitable for the neophyte skier to the expert. Three miles of novice track are even lit for night skiing. There's a small beginner loop, intermediate trails, and an expert run filled with steep ascents and descents. Sections of the 70-mile Laurel Highlands Hiking Trail, which runs from Ohiopyle State Park to Johnstown, Pennsylvania, are open to skiing without a trail fee, but should only be attempted by experts. Log erosion barriers, stone stairways, and a multitude of switchbacks make for difficult skiing on the trail's narrow singletrack.

A warming hut and snack bar are available at the touring center, in addition to a rental fleet featuring both skating and touring skis. Nordic instruction is available by appointment. Guests have ample parking at the base, and primitive winter camping is permitted on the Highlands Hiking Trail. Call the park for a free trail map and current snow conditions.

Information

Trail Fee
$4–$6; $13–$15 with ski rental (cross-country skating and touring skis) • Half price for ages 6–12

Instruction
Arranged by appointment with River Sports; (724) 395–5744

Lodging
Primitive winter camping on Laurel Highlands hiking trail by reservation, with well water available via pump; Call park office for information • For nearby lodging and dining, *see Laurel Mountain,* page 60; *Hidden Valley Ski Resort, page 55; and Seven Springs Resort, page 70.*

Hidden Valley

2

Hidden Valley

1 Craighead Drive
Hidden Valley, PA 15502

Ski Report: 1–800–443–SKII, ext. 473
Information: (814) 443–8000
Operating Hours: 9 A.M.–5 P.M.

Elevation: 2,300–2,900 feet
Average Annual Snowfall: 150 inches

Lodging/Dining/Getting There

See Hidden Valley Ski Area, page 55.

Western Pennsylvania's Laurel Highlands is the home of Hidden Valley—one of the Mid-Atlantic's premiere cross-country touring centers for the last 23 years. Eighteen trails over 33 miles are available altogether, including access to endless track on adjacent Kooser State Park and Forbes State Forest. Hidden Valley has been selected as a host site for Ski Fest '97—a national celebration of cross-country skiing at various touring centers across the nation. Events, races, and clinics will be held for cross-country skiers of all ages and abilities; Call the touring center for information and dates.

Hidden Valley's touring trails surround its popular family alpine ski area (see *page 57*): The more advanced Valley View and Gardner's Nordic trails connect with Hidden Valley Ski Resort's summit and base locations. Several trails wind over the mountaintop golf course, offering views of the Laurel Highlands, while other runs follow old logging and tram roads built in the late 1800s. Most runs can be finished in under one hour. For experts, four secluded trails combine open, rolling terrain with several steep drops. The four-mile Mountain View trail is a staple among seasoned gliders with its varying pitches, and there's a warming hut at the trail's midway point. Kooser trail is a beginner's favorite—a four-mile flat trek that winds past old rustic cabins and a scenic lake. Expansion is planned off the Greenbrier trail to provide additional terrain.

Located one hour southeast of Pittsburgh, the Laurel Highlands region is a virtual snow magnet (the touring center averages 40 to 65 skiable days per year). Hidden Valley also machine grooms most of its terrain, packing it when necessary with snowmobiles, and will also set track periodically on connecting Kooser State Park and Forbes State Forest trails when conditions permit. Hidden Valley's trails are marked by blue triangles, while red triangles indicate Kooser and Forbes trails.

Look for the cross-country center in the lower level of the Barn, near the entrance to the resort. The center offers instruction, full ski rentals, and childcare. The neighboring four-seasons resort has deluxe accommodations and amenities.

Information

Trail Fee

Adult: $14/ day • Ages 6–12: $12

Rentals

Touring skis and new Fisher Control shorter skis (147s and 167s); no skating or telemark ski rentals • Adult: $12/full day, $7/half day • Ages 6–12: $10/full day; $5/half day

Instruction (weekends only)

Private $20/hour; Group $12/hour • Beginner weekend package $25 (includes lesson, rental, trail fee)

The Inn At Starlight Lake

The Inn At Starlight Lake Touring Center

P.O. Box 27
Starlight, PA 18461

Ski Report/Reservations/Information: 1–800–248–2519

Operating Hours: 9 A.M.–dark (daily), conditions permitting

Elevation: 1,500 feet–1,800 feet

Average Annual Snowfall: 100 inches

Getting There

- **From points east in New York/New Jersey:** Take Route 17 west to Hancock, New York (at the northeastern tip of Pennsylvania and the Delaware River), then take Exit 87, Pennsylvania Route 191, to Route 370 and follow signs to Starlight.
- **From points south:** Take I-81 north to Exit 62, then take Route 107 east to Route 247 north; Follow Route 171 northeast to Route 370 east, and turn left on Route 370 at the sign for Starlight Inn.

* Shortline Bus service available from Port Authority Terminal in New York City to Hancock, New York, with Starlight shuttle (by reservation).

Located one hour northeast of Scranton and just a few miles from the New York state border sits the stately Starlight Lake—a 90-year-old, five-star country inn and Nordic touring center set in the Lake District of northeastern Pennsylvania's Appalachian Mountains. Starlight offers nine miles of marked, groomed track, six miles of which are set on abandoned logging roads, rolling hills and meadows, and through hardwood forest. Its diverse landscape includes ridges, stone quarries, fern banks, moss-covered boulders, and clear spring-water lakes.

Situated at the foothills of the Moosic range of the Appalachian Trail, Starlight is a closed-loop system of varied difficulty with several turnaround points for novice skiers. Yes-You-Can trail winds steeply uphill before opening to a wide field that's ideal for Telemark turns. The most challenging trail is Uranus, which features two difficult turns toward its finish.

Abundant amounts of light, fluffy snow grace this neck of the woods most winters: Starlight averages 35 to 50 skiable days per year. From the 1,800-foot peak, guests can catch views as far as the New York Catskills on clear days, and summit vistas are available on both sides of the trail system.

Guests can return from their backcountry excursions to the inn's wood-burning fireplace and stovepipe lounge, with homemade meals served in the turn-of-the-century lakeside dining room. Equipment rentals and instruction are available, and guided tours can be arranged by appointment. Starlight also extends free ice-skating privileges on its front-yard lake and sled rentals on its surrounding hills. Alpine enthusiasts have solid downhill skiing at Elk Mountain, 30 minutes away, and beginner terrain at Mount Tone within 15 minutes.

Information

Trail Fees
Adult: $10/day; $5/half day • Ages 12 and under ski free

Rentals
Track and Fisher touring skis • Adult: $8–$15 • Ages 12 and under: $4–$8

Instruction
Private $18/hour; Group $10/hour * *Reservations recommended*

Lodging/Dining
Inn at Starlight Lake
26-room inn, most with private baths • one suite available • Rates range from $127/night (midweek, double occupancy) to $140/night on weekends • **Restaurant and fireplace lounge**

Nearby
The Nethercott Inn/Bed & Breakfast, Starruca; (570) 727–2211

Hanley's Happy Hill

4

Hanley's Happy Hill

Route 42, Laporte and Ridge Avenue
Eaglesmere, PA 17731

Information: (570) 525–3461
Operating Hours: 9 A.M.–4:30 P.M. weekends, Friday noon–dusk, and occasional Wednesdays
Elevation: 2,100 feet
Average Annual Snowfall: 85 inches

Getting There

- **From the Northeast Extension of the Pennsylvania Turnpike:** Follow the turnpike to I-80 west, then take Exit 34 (Buckhorn), heading north on Route 42 from the Exit ramp; Follow through town 1.5 miles and look for signs to Hanley's Happy Hill.
- **From points east and west:** Take I-80 and follow signs above.
- **From points north:** Take I-81 south to I-80 west and follow signs above.

Hanley's Happy Hill began in 1957 as an alpine ski center, ceasing operations in 1986. The area's acreage was later developed throughout scenic Eaglesmere for cross-country touring terrain, opening up in 1972. The atmosphere at Hanley's Happy Hill is as pleasant as its name implies. An honor system even applies for signs-ins and trail fees.

The expansive 31-mile trail system in northeastern Pennsylvania's Endless Mountains is a series of loops beginning from the trailhead. Hanley's grooms and maintains 25 miles of its terrain, setting track on flats and hills of varying sizes, elevations, and difficulty. There's also a designated section for ski skating and an additional six miles of ungroomed, unmarked wilderness trails for more advanced skinny skiers. Because of the remoteness of its east wilderness section, Hanley's closes its advanced Big Run Trail—a three-mile backcountry run that culminates down a steep hill—at 2:30 P.M. Intermediate Rooker and Scenic Trails also offer some steep sections and access the backcountry, staying open until dusk.

Beginners can use a half-hour-long warm-up jaunt that loops or leads to several intermediate trails. Hanley's easier terrain meanders past bogs, meadows, and a beaver pond, while views of North Mountain and Eaglesmere across the valley are afforded from surrounding trails.

Heaps of snowfall blanket the region most winters, allowing 50 skiable days per year on average. Over 90 days of touring were available during the blizzard season of 1995–96. Powder sticks around a lot longer at this elevation, and it often snows here when it's dry elsewhere in the region.

Hanley's trails are marked by letters, and there's a warming hut, with microwave, at the trailhead. The lodge offers rentals, instruction, and guided tours, and a restaurant sits nearby. Other winter activities include a community-operated ice toboggan slide in town, several nearby snowmobile trails on state-run land, and two miles of easy ski touring at nearby World's End State Park, which also offers cabin rentals. Two miles away in Eaglesmere there are several beautiful but pricey Bed & Breakfasts, a few quaint country inns, and more reasonable rates at the Sonestown Hotel, eight miles out of town.

Information

Trail Fees
Weekend $10/day; $23/day with rental • Weekday $7/day • Rentals by reservation

Rentals (trail fee included)
300 sets: Karhu skis, Solomon step-in bindings (touring skis only) • Full day $21; Half day $17; Friday–Sunday $35

Instruction (with advanced notice)
Private $18; Group $10

Lodging/Dining
Nearby in Eaglesmere:
The Flora Villa Bed & Breakfast: old Victorian house; (570) 525–3245 • **Shady Lane Bed & Breakfast**; (570) 525–3394 • **The Crestmont Inn**, with lounge; (570) 525–3519 • **The Eaglesmere Inn**, with lounge; (570) 525–3273 • **Sonestown Hotel**: moderately priced, 8 miles from Eaglesmere; (570) 482–3000 • **The Lodge in Eaglesmere**: large dormitory with 9 rooms, hot tub, excellent for large groups; (570) 525–3169 • **Cottage rentals** available in Eaglesmere (call Hanley's Happy Hill)

5 Sterling Inn

Sterling Inn
South Sterling, PA 18460

Information/Reservations: 1–800–523–8200
Local: (570) 676–3311
Operating Hours: 9 A.M.–5 P.M.
Elevation: 1,900 feet
Average Annual Snowfall: 60 inches

Getting There

- **From New York/New Jersey:** Take I-84 or I-80 west. From I-84, take Exit 6 and follow Route 507 south, then take Route 191 south in Newfoundland, and follow 4 miles to the inn. From I-80, bypass Stroudsburg, then bear right on I-380 north to Route 423 north (Tobyhanna). Turn left on Route 191 and follow to Sterling Inn.
- **From points south:** Follow the Northeast Extension of the Pennsylvania Turnpike to Exit 35, then follow Routes 940 east, 423, and 191 north to the inn.

Cross-country skiing at the Sterling Inn, located in the heart of the Pocono Mountains, is just a small feature of this posh country inn and resort. The moderate, five-mile touring system offers varied landscapes and is snowmobile tracked. Unfortunately, it's available only to guests of the inn, and inconsistent snowfall limits skiable days.

Most of the skiing here is easy, punctuated by a scenic beginner trail that skirts Sterling's lake. Six connecting trails meander through open fields and woodlands. Slightly more challenging terrain can be found on upper hiking trails that lead up the ridge of the Pocono Mountains. Trails are nameless but are well marked by color blazes.

Sterling recently erected a new ski shop and purchased a new line of rental equipment after its previous building succumbed to fire. The inn also offers its guests ice-skating on its lake, snow tubing, and nearby horse-drawn sleigh rides and an ice toboggan slide. The historic lakeside town of Eaglesmere sits two miles from Sterling, where inn guests can explore the Gas Light Village specialty shops and Cheney's Gallery and Craft Shop.

More novice ski touring trails can be found at nearby Tobyhanna State Park (four miles away), and Promised Land and Gouldsboro State Parks. Additionally, four Pocono Mountain downhill ski resorts are within 20 miles of Sterling.

Information

Trail Fees
Free to inn guests

Rentals
60 sets: Alpina touring skis • $11/day, $7/half-day

Instruction
Free beginner lesson for inn guests

Lodging/Dining
54 rooms at the inn, including standard suites and a few Victorian fireplace suites • Indoor pool and Jacuzzi; fine dining in the **Hearthstone Dining Room** • Midweek discount ski packages available.

Stone Valley Rec. Area

Stone Valley Recreation Area

108 Business Services Building
University Park, PA 16802

Ski Report/Information: (814) 863–0762
Website: *www.psu.edu/Stone_Valley*
Operating Hours: sunrise to sunset
Elevation: 1,000 feet
Average Annual Snowfall: 48 inches

Getting There

- **From I-80:** Take the Boalsburg exit onto Route 45, which turns into Route 26, then follow signs from Route 26 to Stone Valley Recreation Area/Shaver's Creek Environmental Center.
- **From Baltimore/Washington, DC:** Take I-695 to I-83 north past Harrisburg, then pick up Route 15 north to I-80 west and follow directions above.

Part of and operated by Pennsylvania State University, Stone Valley's 25-mile multi-use trail network winds through a wooded backdrop of tall pine and parallels several streams. It's a big-time destination for intermediate to expert skiers, with little in the way of novice terrain. Regrettably, natural conditions vary: Skiing opportunities can be few and far between when Mother Nature doesn't cooperate. Just nine skiable days were available during the warm 1996–97 season. During normal winters, Stone Valley averages 25 days.

When conditions permit, the recreation area grooms roughly 11 miles of track, including the popular 1.25-mile circular loop Lake Trail. Twelve other trails feature mainly rolling, hilly terrain, with steeply pitched downhill runs and long uphill climbs. Iron Stone and Mid-State trails are long, difficult runs that, on occasion, are tracked by snowmobiles, though other skiers tend to pack the narrow trails down sufficiently themselves. All trails are marked by color blazes and numbered intersection markers.

The concession holds private and group Nordic instruction but gave up renting equipment last year. On-site winter lodging is available in 11 cabins, while nearby State College (15 miles) hosts several bed & breakfasts and hotels/motels. Families bringing the kids can use the sledding hills off the Civil Engineering Lodge's west entrance. Additionally, ice skating (with rentals) and ice fishing are offered on the Lawrence J. Perez Lake, near the east entrance. Stone Valley's Lake Winter Extended Fishing program runs until the end of February.

Information

Trail Fees/Rentals
None

Instruction
- Private $18/hour
- Group $12/hour

Lodging/Dining
On-site
Year-round cabins, $11/night

Nearby (State College)
Bed & Breakfasts:
- **Fairmount B&B**; (814) 237–1101
- **Ginther's B&B**; (814) 234–0772
- **Brewmeister's B&B**; (814) 238–0015
- **Cooke Tavern B&B**; (814) 422–8787
- **Windswept Farm B&B**; (814) 355–1233

Hotels/Motels:
Days Inn at Penn State; 1–800–258–DAYS • **Hampton Inn**, State College; 1–800–HAMPTON • **Ramada Inn**, State College; (814) 238–3001

Callender's Windy Acre Farms

Callender's Windy Acre Farms

RD #2, Box 174
Thompson, PA 18465

Ski Report/Information: (570) 727–2982
Operating Hours: 10 A.M.–sunset Friday–Monday; Tuesday–Thursday by appointment
Elevation: 1,989 feet
Average Annual Snowfall: 40 inches

Getting There

- **From New York/New Jersey:** Take I-80 west to I-380 north and follow to I-81 north, then take Exit 64 (Lennox). Bear left on Exit 106 south for 500 yards, then turn right on Route 92 north for 8 miles. Turn right off Route 92 at the sign in Thompson and follow for 7 miles. Turn left on Route 171 north, traveling 1 mile through Thompson, and make a right turn at the firehouse. Follow 2.5 miles and turn right into the driveway at Callender's.
- **From Philadelphia and points south:** Take the Northeast Extension of the Pennsylvania Turnpike to its end at Clarks Summit, then pick up I-81 north to Exit 64 (Lennox) and follow directions above.

Located in Pennsylvania's northeast corridor in Susquehanna County, Callender's is a dairy farm that turns into a cross-country touring center during the winter. Skiers have nearly 10 miles of marked trails through meadows, pastures, open fields, and logging and maple-sap roads, all flanked by scores of maple trees that are tapped each spring to make syrup. With the farm's overwhelmingly easy grade and snowmobile-groomed track, Callender's makes for a leisurely Nordic skiing excursion.

The novice Maple Trail is a flat trek through maple woods—an ideal first run. The longer and more intermediate Blackbear Trail winds outside the perimeter of Callender's network over steady, rolling hills. The Windy Meadows trail is aptly named: It's a wide, open jaunt through an exposed windy tip of Callender's meadow area. There's also a scenic run past an evergreen swamp area on the novice Evergreen Trail.

The farm has managed over 200 skiable days over the last three years, including 90 during 1995–96. Callender's also draws a growing number of snowshoers, and rents eight sets of snowshoes from its concession. Outstanding alpine skiing is within 20 miles at Elk Mountain, and a section of the state's northeastern Rails-to-Trails project is just a few miles away for winter hiking and ski touring.

Information

Trail Fees

$10.50/day with rentals; $7/half day • $5/day without rentals * *Reduced rates for children under 12*

Rentals

100 sets of touring skis: Fisher, Trak, Asnes, Voltenen childrens' skis • 8 sets of snowshoes

Instruction

By appointment only

Lodging/Dining

Within 5 miles

Nethercott Inn/B&B, Starrucca; (570) 727–2211 • **Jefferson Inn/B&B**, Thompson; (570) 727–2625 * *For more nearby lodging/dining information, see Elk Mountain, page 50.*

Crystal Lake Ski Center

Crystal Lake Ski Center

RR 1, Box 308
Hughesville, PA 17737

Ski Report: (570) 584–4209
Information/Reservations: (570) 584–2698
E-mail: *clcamps@aol.com*
Operating Hours: 9 A.M.–5 P.M. weekends/holidays
Elevation: 1,500 feet–2,100 feet
Average Annual Snowfall: 50 inches

Getting There

- **From I-80:** Take Exit 31 (Interstate 180), following 180 west to Route 220 north to Hughesville. Continue on Route 220 for 5 miles to Tivoli, then turn left at the sign for Crystal Lake Camp/Ski Center, and follow 7 miles to the area.
- **From Washington, DC:** Take I-495 to I-270. Follow I-270/Route 15 through Frederick, Gettysburg, and Harrisburg all the way to I-80. Turn east on I-80 for 1 mile across the Susquehanna River, then take Exit 31 (Interstate 180), and follow directions above.
- **From Philadelphia:** Take the Northeast Extension of the Pennsylvania Turnpike, then take I-80 west from the turnpike to Exit 31 (Interstate 180), and follow directions above.

Crystal Lake is one of the state's first cross-country touring centers—and arguably its best. Before opening in 1971, the area was known as Highlands Ski Center. It was moved from its former valley location to its present 2,100-foot elevation, where the cross-country operation benefited from a surge in skinny skiing's popularity during the mid-1970s. Crystal Lake is a member of the Cross-Country Ski Areas of North America, and was chosen as a host site of Ski Fest '96. The center used to hold numerous cross-country races, but ended the practice after complaints that competitions tarnished the laid-back atmosphere of the resort.

With 960 acres of mountain woodlands in a remote section of northern Pennsylvania, cross-country skiers have 24 miles of trails, 18 miles of which are machine groomed and track-set. There's an even mix of beginner to expert terrain, and an easy, two-mile stretch is equipped with snowmaking when lean natural conditions plague the area. Trails leading from the plateau's 2,100-foot summit drop 600 feet through forest-sheltered trails that hold snowfall longer than nearby valley locations. Crystal Lake doesn't lie in the state's major snow belt, but most winters allow between 30 and 60 days of skiing per year from mid-December through March.

When the snow arrives in full force, getting to the area can be a hairy task. Road conditions get very slippery during sudden temperature dips, freezing rain, or sudden snow squalls, so bring your tire chains along for the ride if you don't have a four-wheel-drive vehicle. The steep mountain doesn't get plowed regularly in snow-filled conditions, making access quite difficult.

The network is expertly maintained over a maze of short, winding, intersecting trails that roll past three lakes and several streams. Crystal Lake's Nordic terrain surrounds its small downhill ski area, which welcomes guests on any type of skis. Some of the steeper cross-country trails travel down to the alpine area, and skiers often use the lifts to get back up to their backwoods trails. Crystal Lake charges $1 per trip to reach the Mountain and Laurel trails.

Beginner-level terrain is in the slight majority, but 12 advanced trails offer numerous steeps and plenty of serpentine track. At the Grand Central Station intersection, skiers will find fast downhills and modest climbs, dips, and bumps. Hungry Bear trail is the expert's choice, featuring steep drops and tight switchbacks between Whipple Mill and YoYo trails. Bear Creek trail is a pleasant, long intermediate run with a steady pitch that breaks into sharper steeps and over a bridge toward the bottom.

There's a day lodge at the base that offers lunches in its restaurant, and Crystal Lake guests can reserve one of a limited number of partially equipped or primitive cabins accommodating up to 180 visitors. The cabins go quickly: Your best bet is to reserve them a full year in advance. Otherwise, the closest lodging to the isolated area is 30 minutes away in either Eaglesmere or Williamsport. The wealthy lakeside cabin community of Eaglesmere offers several well-appointed bed & breakfasts. Williamsport has a larger variety of accommodations, and skiers may wish to stay in the town's old lumbering community, where large frame houses built by lumber barons of yesteryear have since been converted into inns and restaurants.

Information

More Fun In The Flakes

On-site

Three-lane **snow tubing** area, with tow lift; rates: $10/day, $7/half day • **Telemark**, cross-country skiers, and snowshoers welcome on alpine slopes • **Ice skating**, with rentals, and **ice fishing** offered on the lake near the rental shop.

Cross-Country Trail Fees

$10 weekend • $7 weekdays

Cross-Country Ski School

Nordic, skating, and Telemark lessons • Private $35/hour; semi-private $20/hour; group $10/hour

Cross-Country Ski Rentals

Touring and Telemark skis and snowshoes • $7/weekday, $10/weekend; Telemark skis: $15

Lodging

On-site

12 cabins (2 with kitchens) sleeping 6–50 people • **2 primitive cabins** without electricity, running water, or bedding * *Cabins by reservation only, often a full year in advance.*

Nearby

See Hanley's Happy Hill Touring Center, page 225, for more lodging information in Eaglesmere • Williamsport area (28 miles away) • **The Reighard House Bed & Breakfast**: beautifully restored inn; (570) 326–3593 • **Snyder House Victorian Bed & Breakfast,** set in the downtown restored lumbering community; (570) 326–0411 • **Holiday Inn**; (570) 326–1981 • **Econo Lodge**; (570) 326–1501

Dining/Aprés-ski

On-site

Restaurant at base area

Nearby

Herdic House Restaurant, next-door to Snyder House Victorian B&B in Williamsport; (570) 322–0165 • *See Hanley's Happy Hill Touring Center, page 225, for more dining information in Eaglesmere.*

Skytop Lodge

Skytop Lodge
One Skytop Road
Skytop, PA 18357

Ski Report/Information: (570) 595–7401
Operating Hours: 9:30 A.M.–12:30 P.M./1:30 P.M.–4:30 P.M. Friday–Monday
Elevation: 1,700 feet
Average Annual Snowfall: 50 inches

Getting There

- **From New York/New Jersey:** Take I-80 west through the Delaware Water Gap toll booth, then turn right at Exit 52. Stay in the inner lane and bear left on Route 447 north for 25 minutes. Then travel through the village of Canadensis, turn right onto Route 390, and follow signs 3 miles to Skytop.
- **From the Northeast Extension of the Pennsylvania Turnpike:** Take Exit 35, then take Route 940 east. Follow 940 to Route 390 north and look for Skytop signs.

Skytop Lodge is a sprawling estate and lavish resort with unlimited year-round activities on its 5,500 acres. The lodge offers both cross-country and alpine skiing free to guests only, closing the trails to outsiders. The Nordic trail network covers 12 miles on sections of the lodge's golf course and, to a larger degree, through forest and wetlands surrounded by pine, birch, and oak. Skiers will find a mix of rolling and flat terrain past scenic waterfalls, trout streams, and beaver ponds, with spectacular summit vistas of Pocono valleys. Without the benefit of major snowfall in the area, the cross-country operation is open sporadically, at best, as conditions permit. But with enough natural powder, a small portion of the trail system is groomed by snowmobile track. The flat, beginner loop on the golf course offers the option of doubling back or accessing the more expansive but relatively flat backcountry.

The lodge's small downhill ski area sits next to Skytop Lake. Six trails over a 295-foot vertical drop are served by two poma lifts and 100 percent snowmaking. Skytop's alpine trails generally get more action than the Nordic trails, catering mainly to families and children. Instruction and rentals are available for downhill skiing, while instruction, but no rentals, is offered for cross-country skiing. The lodge also has an outdoor ice-skating pavilion (with rentals), snowshoe rentals for the golf course trail, guided tours of the backcountry, and a toboggan slide over the lake that's open under freezing temperatures. Inn guests often use the Pocono Mountains' Camelback (*page* 40) and Alpine Mountain (*page* 17) ski areas, both within 20 miles.

Information

Trail Fee
Included in lodging packages

Rentals
60 sets of touring skis: mostly Atomic • 100 sets of alpine skis: Head, Atomic • $15/full day, $10/half day

Instruction
Alpine ski school on weekends by appointment • Nordic lessons by appointment only • Private $35/hour; Group $12–$16/hour

Lodging/Dining
Skytop Lodge offers mini, family, and VIP suites (meals provided with rates) and several bed & breakfast rooms.

Camp Spears Eljabar/YMCA

Camp Spears Eljabar/YMCA

RD 1
Dingmans Ferry, PA

Ski Report/Information: (570) 828–2329
Operating Hours: 9 A.M.–4 P.M. weekends/holidays
Elevation: 1,800 feet
Average Annual Snowfall: 50 inches

Getting There

- **From I-84 west (New York):** Follow I-84 west to Exit 9 (Lord's Valley/Dingman's Ferry). Then turn left after Exit to Route 739 south. Follow Route 739 for approximately 8 miles, and look for Camp Spears signs on the right.
- **From I-84 east:** Take Exit 9 (Lord's Valley/Dingman's Ferry), turn right, and follow directions above.
- **From New Jersey:** Take I-80 west to Route 15 north, which turns into Route 206 north, and follow to Route 560 north. Then turn right at the blinking light, follow over Dingman's Ferry Bridge to Route 739 north, and look for Camp Spears signs.

Camp Spears is a YMCA-operated cross-country ski center set in the Pocono Mountains, with 9.5 miles of machine-groomed novice trails. Located just miles from the Delaware River and the Delaware Water Gap National Recreation Area, Camp Spears is a loop system of interconnecting trails through woodlands and meadows, and around several wetland bogs and private 42-acre lake. The center is a big draw for conference groups and families, offering a variety of near-flat, easily negotiable trails marked by signposts and arrows. Its only advanced trail is the Grand Loop, which holds moderately steep ascents and drops on slightly more narrow track, but is still suitable for beginners. Sporadic snowfall and weekend-only hours provide just 10 to 20 skiable days per season on average.

Information

Trail Fee
- Free to YMCA members
- $5/all others

Rentals
- Adult $15/day
- Ages 11 and under $10/day

Instruction
Group lesson $6

Lodging/Dining
Motels/hotels eight miles away in Milford; Call (570) 828–2329 for information.

STATE PARKS AND FORESTS

All Pennsylvania state parks and forests, excluding the full touring center at Laurel Ridge State Park (*see page 222*), offer free use of their trail systems for cross-country skiing and/or hiking. A small number of state parks offer equipment rentals and instruction. Call the park offices for trail maps (usually no charge), information, and current snow conditions. Pennsylvania state park office hours are 8 A.M. to 4 P.M., Monday through Friday. Keep in mind that some of the following addresses listed for state parks are for their park headquarters, and are not necessarily the location of their trail systems.

Southwest Pennsylvania

Blue Knob State Park

Blue Knob State Park
RR 1, Box 449
Imler, PA 16655-9407

Ski Report: (814) 239–5111
Information/State Park Office: (814) 276–3576

Operating Hours: 8 A.M.–dusk daily
Elevation: 2,100 feet–2,500 feet
Average Annual Snowfall: over 100 inches

Getting There

See Blue Knob Ski Resort, pages 27

Highly regarded as Pennsylvania's most challenging alpine ski area, Blue Knob's surrounding state park land also has an enormous expanse of terrain for cross-country skiing. With an elevation that ranks among the highest in the state, the extensive, forested Nordic network provides excellent scenery on the foothills of the Appalachian plateau and beautiful vistas of the topography below. Bountiful snowfall graces Blue Knob's mountaintops, providing over three months of ski touring during strong winters. Its north-facing mountain and high altitude help keep powder stashes around long after the last snowfall.

Most visitors are of the beginner variety, and want nothing more than a field to try the sport. Others wish to explore some of the unmarked, rugged trails available throughout the mountain. Skiers have 5,600-plus acres of ungroomed, blaze-marked, terrain, with a huge trail system inside park boundaries that has numerous loop trails. Some trails are marked for Nordic skiing, while others are designated for hiking. Skiers are permitted on hiking trails, which are extremely narrow, more rugged, and quite challenging—even by expert standards. Skiers should use extreme caution on all park trails: Expect some incredibly steep drops, arduous climbs, varying trail widths, and a multitude of natural obstacles.

A popular touring run is offered on a designated seven-mile loop trail that makes use of four hiking trails. It has several steep grades, most of which are on roadways closed off to vehicles. The trail takes skiers from the start at the campground down the mountain toward the park office, then back across the Chappels Field unloading area. One of the problems, though, with skiing the terrain down to the state park office is that it's difficult to get back to your car from there. Trails are also marked somewhat poorly here with small red tags. The Chappels Field area near the campground (closed during winter) is good beginner turf, with several open areas for skiing. Most skiers, though, tend to stick near Blue Knob's summit golf course area, where they can traverse easy, open fields and not steer far from their vehicles.

Blue Knob's downhill ski area (*page 27*), which lies primarily on state property, rents cross-country ski equipment at its summit lodge, and also features a cafeteria and lounge. Cross-country and Telemark skiers are welcome on its alpine trails as well.

Information

Rentals
Call Blue Knob Ski Resort for current rates; (814) 239–5111/1–800–458–3403

Lodging/Dining
See Blue Knob Ski Resort, pages 27

Forbes State Forest

12

Forbes State Forest
P.O. Box 519
Laughlintown, PA 15655

Information: (412) 238–9533
Operating Hours: Dusk to dawn
Elevation: 2,500 feet–2,900 feet
Average Annual Snowfall: 110 inches

Getting There

- **Laurel Highlands Ski Touring Area:** From Pittsburgh (heading east), follow Route 30, which parallels the Pennsylvania Turnpike (70/76), to the top of Laurel Mountain. Then turn right onto Laurel Summit Road, and follow roughly two miles to the state forest entrance. *From Route 30 heading west, follow to the top of the mountain and turn left onto Laurel Summit Road, then travel 2 miles to the state forest entrance.
- **North Woods Ski Touring Area:** From the Pennsylvania Turnpike (70/76), take Exit 9 (Donegal), then follow Route 31 east, passing Firetower Road. Drive down the road and turn left onto Tunnel Road (opposite the entrance to the stone quarry), then continue a half-mile to the small lot on the left and access trails from there.
- **Roaring Run Natural Area:** Take Exit 9 (Donegal) from the Pennsylvania Turnpike, following Route 31 east. Then turn right onto Firetower Road at the top of the mountain, which leads into Roaring Run.

High atop Pennsylvania's Laurel Highlands sits Forbes State Forest. Over 50 miles of well-marked backcountry trails is available in three separate areas: Laurel Highlands Ski Touring Area, North Woods Ski Touring Area, and Roaring Run Natural Area. Laurel Highlands is the most popular cross-country destination of the three areas, combining mostly flat track with a few rolling hills. The North Woods area features the steepest

trails and is also widely used, while Roaring Run is rarely skied, though suitable for touring. Easily negotiable Spruce Run and Summit Trails are the Laurel Highlands' signature runs.

Another way to access the state forest (either North Woods or Roaring Run) is from Hidden Valley (*page* 55). Its Nordic trail system utilizes much of Forbes' territory, though it surely doesn't advertise it. You'll have to pay a trail fee if you park at Hidden Valley, and if you park in the state forest and enter Hidden Valley's trails, they'll knock you up for a fee as well. There's plenty of parking at Forbes' three separate area lots, but little winter maintenance on the roads. When snow hits the area hard, as it's apt to do, it's wise to park at Hidden Valley and suck up its trail fee. Calling the state forest office also comes highly recommended before making the trip out here; They'll give you a snow, trail, and road report.

All state forest cross-country trails are marked by red rectangles. Hiking trails, which also accommodate skiing, are designated by blue marks. Snowmobilers have 80 miles of trail in surrounding areas, and are restricted from using any Nordic trails. Occasionally, skiers will encounter illegal snowmobilers, so keep your ears open for the sound of motors.

Information

Lodging/Dining

See Hidden Valley Ski Resort Nearby Lodging and Dining/Aprés-ski, *page 58*, and Seven Springs Resort, *page 70*.

13 Kooser State Park

Kooser State Park

RR 4, Box 256
Somerset, PA 15501-8509

Information: (814) 445–8673
Operating Hours: dusk to dawn
Elevation: 2,600 feet
Average Annual Snowfall: 130 inches

Getting There

- **From Pittsburgh:** Take the Pennsylvania Turnpike (70/76) and pick up Exit 9 (Donegal) onto Route 31, then follow signs for Kooser State Park.
- **From eastern points:** Take the Pennsylvania Turnpike (70/76) and pick up Exit 10 (Somerset). Then get on Route 31 west for roughly 12 miles, and follow signs for Kooser State Park.

Just across the highway from Forbes State Forest lies Kooser State Park—a popular cross-country skiing destination. The mountainous region receives heaps of snowfall each year, and Kooser gets a more-than-healthy portion of it at its high altitude, lingering long into spring. Located on the eastern foothills of the Laurel Mountain summit, Kooser offers a 1.5-mile groomed and marked trail that's suitable for novice skiers. The level trail crosses six bridges over Kooser Run and circles Kooser Lake, using an old railroad bed and park roads for easy skiing. The trail connects with other state park trails as well as Hidden Valley Touring Center's trails and its varied terrain. The 70-mile Laurel Ridge Hiking Trail also accommodates skiers, and can be accessed by the Kooser Tower.

Skiers can shack up in Kooser's rustic cabins, open year-round, with affordable Sunday through Thursday lodging rates. The park also rents a full line of equipment, by reservation only. Send a self-addressed, stamped envelope for maps and information of the area, or call the park office.

Information

Rentals

Ski rentals available inside the park at Winter Cabin Rentals; (814) 359–2893

Lodging/Dining

On-site

Nine cabins for 4, 6, 7, or 9 persons; rates from $100–$150/weekend

Nearby

See Hidden Valley Ski Resort, On-site and Nearby Lodging and Dining/Aprés-ski, *page 58*, and Seven Springs Resort, *page 70*.

Ohiopyle State Park

14

Ohiopyle State Park

P.O. Box 105
Ohiopyle, PA 15470-0105

Information: (724) 329–8591
Elevation: 2,600 feet
Average Annual Snowfall: 90 inches

Getting There

- **From western points along the Pennsylvania Turnpike (70/76):** Take Exit 9 (Donegal) and turn left onto Route 31. Then travel two miles and turn right onto Route 381. Follow Route 381 for 25 miles heading south into Ohiopyle State Park.
- **From eastern points (Washington, DC, Harrisburg, New York):** Take the Pennsylvania Turnpike (70/76) to Exit 10 (Somerset), and turn right into Somerset. Then take Route 281 south and follow for 25 miles to Confluence. Continue 3 miles uphill, turn right at the church onto Sugarloaf Road, and follow nine miles to Ohiopyle.

Located five miles from West Virginia and Maryland on Pennsylvania's southern tip, Ohiopyle's 30-mile, marked, ungroomed trail system holds some challenging terrain for advanced skiers. Steep drops, long climbs, and near-singletrack width mark many of its trails. There's also a bike trail alongside the river that can be used for ski touring. But it's the striking scenery that makes Ohiopyle a destination not to be passed up. Skiers can traverse pristine trails along the Youghiogheny River Gorge and spot waterfalls along Jonathan and Cucumber Runs. Other trails offer views of river rapids and connect with nearly 200 acres of open land. There is one trail available for snowmobilers, so be on the lookout. Ohiopyle's parking lot offers plenty of spaces. Get a trail map from the park office and access the trails directly from there.

Information

Nearby Lodging

Stone House Bed & Breakfast, Farmington; (724) 329–8876 • **Laurel Highlands River Tours** (guest house), Ohiopyle; 1–800–472–3846 • **The Lodge at Chalk Hill**, on Route 40; 1–800–833–4283 • **National Trails Motel**, Markleysburg; (724) 329–5531.

Pennsylvania's Laurel Highlands Region

The towering-elevation region of southwestern Pennsylvania's Laurel Highlands hosts an array of winter recreation that extends beyond its outstanding alpine and cross-country skiing. The following is a list of winter activities offered at selected state parks and forests.

- ***Blue Knob State Park****; (814) 276–3576: 8 miles of* ***snowmobile trails, ice skating***
- ***Forbes State Forest****; (412) 238–9533: 80 miles of* ***snowmobile trails***
- ***Keystone State Park****; (412) 668–2939: 5 miles of* ***snowmobile trails, ice skating, ice fishing, sledding***
- ***Laurel Hill State Park****; (814) 445–7725: 10 miles of* ***snowmobile trails, ice skating, ice fishing***
- ***Laurel Ridge State Park****; (412) 455–3744: 2 miles of* ***snowmobile trails***
- ***Ohiopyle State Park****; (412) 329–8591: 19 miles of* ***snowmobile trails, sledding***
- ***Prince Gallitzin State Park****; (814) 674–1000: 20 miles of* ***snowmobile trails, ice skating, ice fishing, ice boating, sledding***

For more information on recreation and lodging/dining in the Laurel Highlands, contact: Laurel Highlands Visitors Bureau, 120 E. Main Street, Ligonier, PA 15658; (412) 238–5661

South-Central Pennsylvania

Caledonia State Park

Caledonia State Park

40 Rocky Mountain Road
Fayetteville, PA 17222-9610

Information: (717) 352–2161
Elevation: 1,000 feet to 1,200 feet
Average Annual Snowfall: 38 inches

Getting There

- **From Washington, DC:** Take I-495 to I-270 and follow to Route 15 north to Gettysburg. Then take Route 30 west and follow signs for Caledonia.
- **From the Pennsylvania Turnpike (70/76):** Take the Carlisle Exit (near Harrisburg) and get on I-81 south. Then take Exit 8 (Scotland) and turn south on Route 997. Follow 6–8 miles and take Route 30 east, then travel 2 miles to the intersection of Routes 30 and 233. Turn left here, take the first road to the left, and follow to the park office.

Caledonia doesn't get the snowfall numbers necessary for consistent skiing opportunities, but when the powder falls in excess it can be a worthwhile venture. Ten miles of marked track over seven trails is available, including two difficult miles of the rugged Appalachian Trail. Remaining runs are mainly flat, intersecting with several streams. Visitors can use any skiing/hiking trails that are suitable for them, though many aren't recommended, including Charcoal Harth, Ramble, and Whispering Pine trails. Charcoal Harth is quite steep, traveling up one side to the mountain's summit and back down on a difficult loop trail. Ramble is set partially near a swampy area and also has steep areas that are too difficult to negotiate on skis.

The most appropriate skiing trail is Thaddeus Stevens—a fairly flat meander that's about a mile long. Guest will also find Midland trail to their liking. It's a nice, level jaunt that runs roughly three-quarters of one mile. Most beginners who use Ohiopyle take advantage of its baseball field, which opens up 20 acres of wide-open skiing.

None of the terrain is groomed or maintained for skiers, and bridges are a particular problem because they're designed for flood planes. Skiers have to step up to some of the bridges rather than glide over them.

Located 10 miles east of Interstate 81, near Chambersburg and Gettysburg, Caledonia offers two large, modern cabins that stay open during winter months.

Information

Lodging/Dining

On-site

Two modern cabins, up to 10 persons each; Call the state park office for information.

Nearby

See Ski Liberty, *page 87*

16 Cowans Gap State Park

Cowans Gap State Park

HC 17266
Fort Loudon, PA 17224-9801

Information: (717) 485–3948
Elevation: 2,000 feet
Average Annual Snowfall: 80 inches

Getting There

- **From Pittsburgh:** Take Route 30 and follow to the top of Tuscarora Mountain. Turn left at the signs for Cowans Gap State Park onto Augwick Road and follow roughly 5 miles into the park.
- **From Route 30 heading west:** Follow Route 30 onto Route 75 north at Fort Loudon. Then travel approximately 4 miles, turn left on Richmond Furnace Road, and follow 3 miles to Cowans Gap State Park.

Located smack in the middle of Buchanan State Forest, Cowans Gap has a wide variety of terrain throughout its 10 miles for cross-country skiers. Ski Trail is only a half-mile long, but it's not necessarily for beginners. The terrain is rather rocky and generally unsuitable for skiing. Plenty of other trails are available, including the Lakeside Trail—a novice, 1.25-mile run that circles the lake over primarily level track. Overlook Trail climbs 1.5 miles on steady terrain to a mountain summit vista. From there skiers can access state forest game land trails. This section is tricky and rather steep, though, and should be reserved for strong intermediates and experts. The trail also features a fire road off to the left, which leads back to the valley over eight or nine miles of track. Unfortunately, it dead ends on an unskiable road, so skiers have to turn around.

Advanced skiers can also access part of the 220-mile Tuscarora Trail that cuts through parts of Cowans Gap on a considerably steep area. Its narrow singletrack has many rocky sections, and closes down when strong storms force tree limbs and debris onto its course. The Tuscarora Trail winds through a large section of central Pennsylvania, and dead ends on the Appalachian Trail.

Most guests prefer to roam unplowed parking lots, the campground area, and park roads, in addition to logging and fire roads that run throughout the mountain. All roads are skiable: The park plows one lane for car access.

Information

Lodging

10 rustic cabins for up to four persons, with adjacent showers/toilets.

Gifford Pinchot State Park

Gifford Pinchot State Park

2200 Rosstown Road
Lewisberry, PA 17339-9787

Information: (717) 432–5011
Elevation: 470 feet
Average Annual Snowfall: 35 inches

Getting There

- **From Baltimore/Washington, DC:** Take I-95 north to I-695 west to I-83 north. Then pick up Exit 13, heading west on Route 382. Take Route 177 west from there and follow signs to the state park office.
- **From I-83 south:** Take Exit 15, pick up Route 177 west, and follow signs to the park office.
- **From the Pennsylvania Turnpike (70/76):** Take Exit 18 onto I-83 south and follow directions above.

Located a few miles from Ski Roundtop—a popular alpine ski area for Baltimore and southern Pennsylvania residents (*page* 93)—Gifford Pinchot affords eight miles of marked, ungroomed cross-country/hiking trails through pine and evergreen countryside. Its 12 trails form a series of interconnecting loops. Skiers can choose from short trips under one mile or longer, more undulating loop trails. Most runs are plenty wide for beginner skiers, with just a few small downhill sections on the network's 150-foot vertical drop. Two general areas are most served by skiers: state park trails, which join some flat beach and grassy turf areas, and the campground, which provides level, open skiing.

As Ski Roundtop downhillers can attest, the area isn't subject to great amounts of snowfall, so Nordic skiers have to be opportunists. The park plows the parking lots during snow storms, but only a limited number of spaces are available. There are, however, portable bathrooms open during winter months.

Information

Lodging/Dining

On-site

10 year-round modern cabins, sleeping 6–8 persons; Call park office for fees.

Nearby

See Ski Roundtop, Nearby Lodging and Dining/Aprés-ski, *page 96*.

Delaware Canal State Park

Delaware Canal State Park

RR 1, Box 615 A
Upper Black Eddy, PA 18972-9540

Information: (610) 982–5560
Elevation: 700 feet
Average Annual Snowfall: 35 inches

Getting There

- **From Philadelphia and Allentown:** Follow Route 32/611, which parallels the 60-mile course and the Delaware River. Park anywhere in public areas, including county parks and public roads. Park-and-ski access can be found in the city of Easton; the towns of Robbsville, Rieglesville, and New Hope; Tinicum County Park; and the Virginia Forrest Recreation Area.
- **From eastern and western points:** Take I-80 or I-78 toward the Delaware River, exit onto Route 32/611, and follow directions above.

This Philadelphia and Allentown Nordic-skier attraction is a 60-mile-long tow path that runs parallel to old Delaware Canal. Over a century ago, mules would pull canal boats along the tow path. The trail starts in Easton and runs south to Bristol, just north of Philadelphia. Hundreds of roads intersect the path, including eight public recreation areas along the way. Many skiers prefer to park along River Road, north of Washington's Crossing. Route 32/611, which parallels the 60-mile course and the Delaware River that separates Pennsylvania and New Jersey, covers 40 miles of the path.

Its level terrain crosses some roads and other light obstructions, and is open to hiking, biking, horseback, and cross-country skiing. No side trails exist off the towpath, but there are several bridges connecting with points in New Jersey.

The area doesn't get enough snow to allow many skiable days per year, so waste no time getting out on the trails after a good snowfall—it's often gone in a few days. And the trail is so close to the Delaware River that its water effect often turns the snow into ice crystals quickly.

Northeast Pennsylvania

Lackawanna State Forest 19

Lackawanna State Forest

401 Samters Bldg., 101 Penn Ave.
Scranton, PA 18503

Information: (570) 963–4561
Elevation: 1,000 feet
Average Annual Snowfall: 52 inches

Getting There

- **From the Northeast Extension of the Pennsylvania Turnpike:** Take Exit 35 (White Haven) onto Route 940 east, then turn left onto Route 115 toward Wilkes-Barre, crossing the Lehigh River. Then follow 1.25 miles to LR40042, turn right toward Thornhurst, then turn left onto LR 2016. Follow 4 miles to the trailhead on the right.
- **From I-81:** Take Exit 49 to Route 315 one mile to Dupont. At the second light in Dupont, turn left onto Suscon Road (southeast), which follows to Lackawanna State Forest after 10 miles. The trailhead is on the left, one mile east of the Luzerne/Lackawanna county line.

Near most major Pocono ski areas, Lackawanna State Forest offers 24 miles of cross-country touring on a multi-use and snowmobile trail system. There's a mix of flat and rolling terrain through woodlands and around small streams. Trails are marked by signposts and machine groomed by the park whenever possible. The winding, level terrain suits mostly novice skiers. The northern section's Pinehill Vista area is the major intersection, with several connecting trails.

Lackawanna sits in the village of Thornhurst, and skiers can access the forest from two parking lots along SR 2016, northwest of Thornhurst. The closest Pocono alpine ski area is Montage. Lodging isn't available at the state park, but winter camping is allowed anywhere within the park. Lackawanna keeps a map box and trail register a short distance from the trailhead.

Information

Lodging/Dining

See Montage Mountain Ski Area, Nearby Lodging and Dining/Aprés-ski, *page* 69.

North-Central Pennsylvania

Elk State Forest

Elk State Forest

RR 1, Route 155, Box 327
Emporium, PA 15834

Information: (814) 486–3354
Elevation: 1,500 feet
Average Annual Snowfall: 90 inches

Getting There

- **From eastern points off I-80:** Take Exit 22 heading north (Snowshoe) and take Route 144 to Moshannon. Then take Route 879 to Karthaus, and follow the Quehanna Highway to the trail system. There are several parking points here with access to the trail system.
- **From western points off I-80:** Take Exit 17 (Route 255 north) to Penfield and turn right at Penfield. Then travel south on Route 153 for roughly 4 miles, and turn left onto the state forest road to Parker Dam State Park.

The Quehanna Wild Area of Cameron County is the site of Elk State Forest, and its 25 miles of trails marked by blue paint blazes. Its remote location and snow-filled, extreme winters offer diverse topography and wildlife, including white-tailed deer and turkeys. Abandoned logging roads and railroad grades make up most of the system, with a host of switchbacks, steeps, and climbs to satisfy advanced skiers. The forest is so isolated and primitive, with occasionally brutal weather, that skiing is recommended only for experienced intermediates and experts. Local volunteer groups partially maintain the network of hiking and ski touring trails, though the terrain is mostly ungroomed.

There's no park office here, so call ahead to receive your trail map, available by calling (814) 486–3354. The forest is located about 30 miles southwest of Ski Denton (alpine skiing on *page XXX*), where ample lodging and dining facilities are available.

Skiers can also use Sizerville State Park, which lies north of Emporium, and has a rental shop (closed last season, but likely re-opening). The park offers additional ski touring on snowmobile trails and blocked roads. Parking is available at the Sizerville State Park trailhead.

Information

Lodging/Dining

See Ski Denton, Nearby Lodging and Dining/Aprés-ski, *page 86*.

Northwest Pennsylvania

Cook Forest State Park

Cook Forest State Park

Address: P.O. Box 120
Cooksburg, PA 16217-0120

Information: (814) 744–8407
Operating Hours: 8 A.M. to dusk
Elevation: 1,520 feet
Average Annual Snowfall: 100 inches

Getting There

- **From eastern points:** Take I-80 to Exit 13, then follow Route 36 north to the state park.
- **From western points:** Take I-80 to Exit 8, then take Route 66 north to Leeper. Follow Route 36 south for 7 miles to the state park.

This 6,668-acre state park sits just outside the southern tip of the expansive Allegheny National Forest in one of Pennsylvania's heaviest snow belts. Skiers are afforded numerous winter days to wander through Cook's nine miles of marked trails. Virgin white pine and hemlock timber form the backdrop of the state park, designated by the National Park Service as a registered National Natural Landmark. The trail leading from the park concession drops off to an abandoned fire tower: Its stairs can be climbed to provide glimpses of surrounding vistas. Nearby Seneca Point Overlook also provides scenic photo opportunities of the Clarion River Valley.

Most skiers use the two beginner/intermediate trails, which consist mostly of steady terrain with a few sizable hills. Several side trails are available, as well as three dirt roads open in the winter months for ski touring and snowmobiling. Cook's trails, closed to snowmobilers, are sign-marked and machine groomed. The state park runs a rental concession at the entrance to Ridge Campground off Route 36, open mainly on weekends during agreeable weather and weekdays by appointment. For skiers who can do without amenities, there are 24 rustic cabins open year-round and 12 additional river cabins. Nearby deluxe accommodations can be found at Gateway Lodge—the four-seasons resort at the foothills of Cook Forest State Park on Route 36 in Cooksburg. The lodge has a fine-dining restaurant and offers ski rentals.

The North Country National Scenic Trail (NST) flows through part of Cook's network. The NST is one of the country's emerging trail systems, estimated to be 4,400 miles long, with over 1,400 miles open to the public in seven northern states.

Information

Rentals
50 sets of touring skis; $8.50/day

Nearby Lodging
Gateway Lodge; (814) 744–8017

Oil Creek State Park

Oil Creek State Park

RD 1, Box 207
Oil City, PA 16301

Information: (814) 676–5915
Elevation: 1,200–1,300 feet
Average Annual Snowfall: 85 inches

Getting There

- **From I-80:** Take Exit 3 (Route 8 north), then turn right on Route 227 in Rouseville. Travel 2.8 miles and follow signs for Oil Creek State Park and directional arrows to cross-country skiing parking area. Numerous access points for skiing can be found along Route 8, with directional signs posted.

Western Pennsylvania's snow belt provides enough powder in this region that it often lasts well into spring, and Oil Creek State Park provides the turf on which to cross-country ski. One of five state parks created through the Western Pennsylvania Conservancy, Oil Creek's 7,000-plus acres includes a 10-mile Nordic trail system (three marked trails) with groomed track on the plateau of its historic gorge's east rim. There's a one-mile connector road—and a 500-foot elevation difference—between the flood plain and the higher-lying rim of the gorge. The park also features a level, 9.7-mile bike path, which also serves winter ski tourists and hikers. It occupies an old railroad grade with a general width of about eight feet.

Experts also have access to a 36-mile hiking trail that features lots of steeps and turns on narrow terrain, but it's considered too rugged for good skiing.

A warming hut is available, open weekends from 9 A.M. to 5 P.M., in which skiers can pick up trail maps and information and rest before a wood-burning fire. A reasonable number of parking spaces can be found at the beginner/intermediate trailhead near Plumer, as well as at the trail junction at the Drake Well Park and Oil Creek Park office. Maps are also offered at the park office, which lies about one mile from the ski trails, and a few shops rent equipment in nearby Oil City.

Information

Nearby Lodging

The Lamberton House Bed & Breakfast, Franklin; (814) 432–7908 • **McMullen House Bed & Breakfast**, Titusville; (814) 827–1592 • **Oil Creek Lodge Bed & Breakfast**, Titusville; (814) 677–4684 • **The Inn at Franklin**; 1–800–535–4052 • **Corbett Inn**, Oil City; (814) 676–0803 • **Holiday Inn**, Oil City; (814) 677–1221

Nearby Dining

Hoss's Steak & Sea House, Oil City; (814) 677–3002 • **Famoore's Family Restaurant**, Oil City; (814) 676–4789 • **Badland's Barbecue**, Franklin; (814) 437–7427

Allegheny National Forest

The national forest encompasses 500,000 acres of woodlands, and several districts have trails equipped for cross-country skiing. Lodging is few and far between in the region, with a few inns and bed & breakfasts available, but winter camping is allowed anywhere within the forest.

Laurel Mill Cross-Country

Laurel Mill Cross-Country Ski/ Hiking Area

Ridgway Ranger Station, Box 28A
Ridgway, PA 15853

Information: (814) 776–6172
TTY: (814) 726–2710
Elevation: 1,200 feet to 1,800 feet
Average Annual Snowfall: 80 inches

Getting There

- **From I-80:** Take Route 219 north at DuBois, then take Township Road 307 (Spring Creek Road) and follow signs for Laurel Mill Cross-Country Ski Area (located 3 miles west of Ridgway).

Laurel Mill is the most popular Nordic skiing site among national forest trail networks in Pennsylvania. The forest service grooms most trails, and cross-country ski races are held yearly. Roughly 10 miles of terrain includes seven trails ranging from under one mile to 3.2 miles. The terrain is mostly level, and not extremely difficult to negotiate, though a few steep downhill sections do exist.

Parking is plentiful, and there's a warming hut available at the trailhead. The area receives a fair shake of snow, allowing many ski opportunities each winter.

Information

Nearby Lodging

Faircroft Bed & Breakfast, Ridgway; (814) 776–2539 • **The Post House Bed & Breakfast**, Ridgway

Brush Hollow Cross-Country

Brush Hollow Cross-Country

Ridgway Ranger District, Box 28A
Ridgway, PA 15853

Information: (814) 776–6172
TTY: (814) 726–2710
Elevation: 1,200 feet–1,800 feet
Average Annual Snowfall: 80 inches

Getting There

- **From I-80:** Take Route 219 north at DuBois to Ridgway, then take Route 948 north for roughly 10 miles. Follow signs for Brush Hollow Cross-Country Ski Area.

Brush Hollow is another widely used cross-country ski area, but unlike Laurel Mill, its trails get no grooming. The terrain is much steeper, though, and attracts many expert Nordic skiers, particularly Telemarkers. Three major loop trails are available, two of which have solid vertical drops and climbs. Challenger Loop is suitable only for the advanced skier. The trail requires a bit more snow than other runs, considering its many changes in elevation and numerous nooks and crannies that get frequent sun exposure.

An overlook on Brush Hollow is breathtaking, and wildlife is abundant. Skiers will likely meet up with white-tailed deer and turkey, and may spot a black bear on rare occurrences. Adequate parking is available for 20 to 25 cars.

Information

Nearby Lodging

The Kane Manor Country Inn/Bed & Breakfast; (814) 837–6522 • **Kane Motel**, Kane; (814) 837–6161 • **Kane View Motel**, Kane; (814) 837–8600 • **Reazley Hotel**; (814) 837–9111

Westline Cross-Country

Westline Cross-Country

Bradford Ranger District
Bradford, PA 16701

Information: (814) 362–4613
Elevation: 1,464 feet to 2,611 feet
Average Annual Snowfall: 85 inches

Getting There

- **From I-80:** Take Route 219 north at DuBois and follow roughly 45 minutes past Ridgway. Then take Route 59 west and follow signs for Westline Cross-Country Ski Area.

When adequate snowfall permits, Westline is an ideal setting for cross-country skiing. Nearly 10 miles of track is available over five trails. Four trails are under 1.5 miles, while Thundershower provides four miles of steeper, more rugged terrain. The trail also holds a splendid view of Thundershower River, which flows into the old milling village of Westline. Parking is abundant off Route 59. Overnight accomodations and restaurants are in short supply in the area. Call the national forest office for further information.

Information

Nearby Lodging

Westline Inn, 4 miles to the south

Pennsylvania's Northern Alleghenies

There's a winter wonderland in the Northern Allegheny mountain range that offers an assortment of outdoor activities. ***Snowmobilers*** *can explore over 300 miles of designated groomed trails throughout Allegheny wilderness. Many of the trails have taverns, restaurants, and services directly on their paths. For* ***cross-country skiers****, numerous groomed trail networks are available in prime snow country in the Allegheny National Forest, with warming huts on many of them.* *(See page 247 for Allegheny National Forest cross-country skiing information.)* *The Allegheny River Reservoir and surrounding lakes—stocked with walleye, perch, and bass—provide outstanding* ***ice fishing*** *opportunities. Call the Allegheny Fishing Hotline (814–726–0164) for updated information. And* ***dog sled racing*** *is another popular pastime in the Northern Alleghenies. The Bell Atlantic Classic is held each January at the national forest's Westline area and the Pennsylvania Dog Sled Classic runs each February at Chapman Dam State Park.*

For more information on any of the following, call the Northern Alleghenies Vacation Region at 1–800–624–7802 or (814) 726–1222. Inquirers can also write to P.O. Box 608, Tionesta, Pennsylvania 16353, or E-mail: TNA@PENN.COM

Maryland:

26. New Germany State Park

27. Herrington Manor State Park

Other State Parks and Forests

28. Cunningham Falls State Park

29. Patapsco Valley State Park

30. Greenbrier State Park

31. Gunpowder Falls State Park

CROSS-COUNTRY SKIING: MARYLAND/WEST VIRGINIA

West Virginia:

Cross-Country Ski Touring Centers

32. Alpine Lake Resort Nordic Center

33. Elk River Touring Center

34. White Grass Ski Touring Center

35. Canaan Valley Resort State Park

State Parks and Forests

36. Cathedral State Park

37. Blackwater Falls State Park

38. Babcock State Park

39. Pipestem Resort State Park

40. Watoga State Park

41. Coopers Rock State Forest

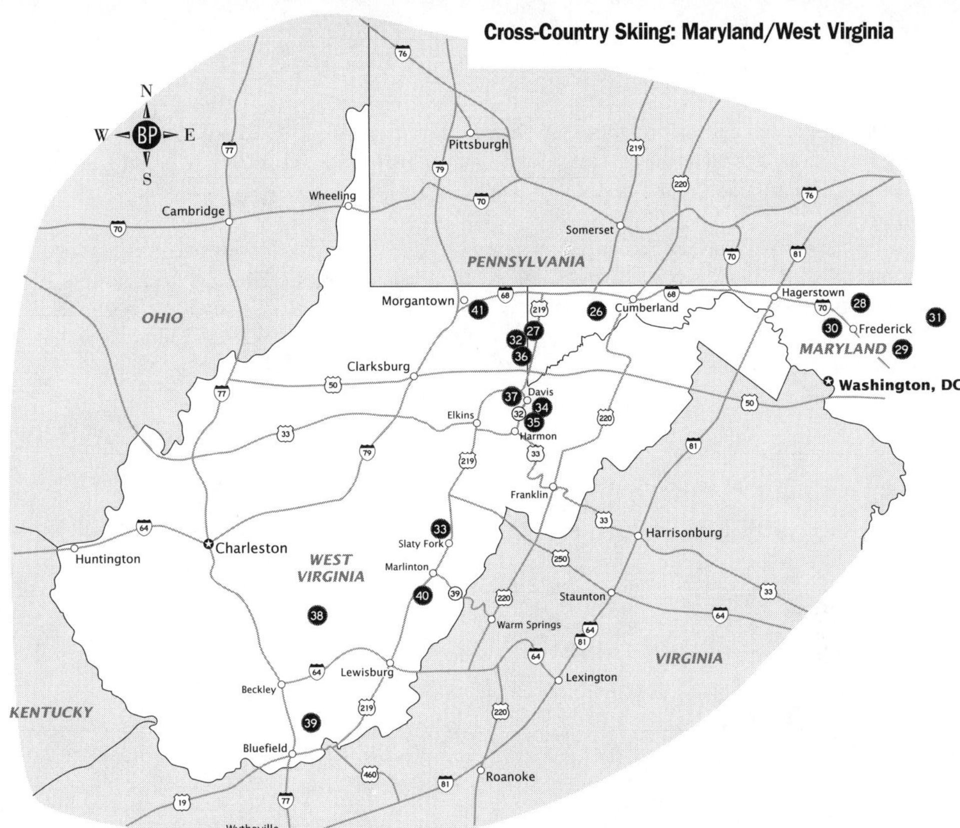

MARYLAND

Like its alpine ski scene, Maryland's cross-country terrain is limited, but nonetheless quite exceptional. New Germany and Herrington Manor State Parks form the backbone of Nordic skiing in Maryland, both of which benefit from Garrett County's strong, powder-packed winters and offer designated, groomed ski trails. Cabin rentals are available year-round at both parks, while ample accommodations can be found nearby. In January of 1997, the state incorporated a 1–800 reservation system for cabin rentals (1–800–432–CAMP). It's recommended that reservations be made one year in advance, since cabins go quickly.

WEST VIRGINIA

With the Mid-Atlantic's most abundant snowfall, it's no surprise that West Virginia hosts some of its best cross-country trail networks. White Grass and Elk River make up two of the state's three privately run Nordic touring centers. Each offers groomed, on-site trails and access to surrounding backcountry terrain. Several state parks hold touring centers or rental facilities on their trail networks, including Canaan Valley, Blackwater Falls, and Pipestem. Remaining state and national parks and forests offer ungroomed hiking/cross-country skiing systems—many of which provide more difficult, rugged terrain, without trail fees. Trail maps are available free of charge from park and forest headquarters, by mail or in person.

To facilitate cross-country skiing in the state, the West Virginia Department of Tourism offers a toll-free telephone number for many state parks and forests (1–800–CALL–WVA), from which guests can get free ski reports and information and reserve lodging at various state parks. The line is available weekdays from 8:30 A.M. to 4:30 P.M., and is listed herein at state parks/forests that it services.

Skiers will find on-site accommodations at many of West Virginia's touring centers and state parks, including lodges, houses, condominiums, chalets, townhomes, cabins, and campsites. State park cabins are equipped with electricity, modern kitchens and appliances, and bathrooms with showers, and can be rented by the day, for weekends, or for the week. Reservations here are strongly recommended, as these cabins—like the ones in Maryland—are very popular.

New Germany State Park 26

New Germany State Park

349 Headquarters Lane
Grantsville, MD 21536

Information: (301) 895–5453
TTY: (410) 974–3683
Elevation: 2,400–2,700 feet
Average Annual Snowfall: 110 inches

Getting There

- **From Washington/Baltimore:** Take I-70 west through Maryland to I-68 west. Follow I-68 to Exit 22, and turn left on Chestnut Ridge Road. Travel roughly 3.5 miles and turn left on New Germany Road, then follow 2 miles to New Germany State Park.
- **From Pittsburgh/Morgantown:** Take I-79 to I-68 east, then take Exit 22. Turn right on Chestnut Ridge Road and follow directions above.

Savage River State Forest's 52,812 acres includes New Germany State Park—a popular cross-country trail network in Garrett County. Heavy snowfall provides the perfect setting for ski touring on 12 miles of marked, groomed track on New Germany's nine-trail system. Some advanced terrain is available, but the trail system more realistically suits novice to intermediate skiers. Most runs are in the half-mile to 1.5-mile range, winding past streams, over bridges, and through Western Maryland forestland. Snowmobiles are prohibited from the cross-country trail system.

The park is located on the site of a flourishing sawmilling and gristmilling center that operated during the 1800s. New Germany's 13-acre lake was formed when Swauger's Mill Dam was constructed on Poplar Lick Run to operate the mills. The gristmill ran until 1859. The sawmill closed after the advent of the circular saw in the late 1800s. The dam was later repaired and reconstructed in the 1930s by the Civilian Conservation Corps.

Surrounding New Germany are miles and miles of state forest hiking trails on which advanced skiers can test their mettle. The six-mile Poplar Lick trail begins at New Germany, crossing four streams before ending at Savage River. Five other trails ranging from 1.5 miles to 24 miles are extremely narrow and rough. The state doesn't advertise Nordic skiing on these hiking trails because of their rugged nature: Skiers will encounter log barriers, steps, and other obstacles along the difficult terrain.

Visitors are charged a $2 park entrance fee on weekends and holidays, but have the parking lots completely plowed. Skiers can also wind down in the park's recreation hall and its fireplace and wood stove. Hot drinks and snacks can be found at New Germany's weekend-running concession, and nearby Meadow Mountain Ski Rental (301–689–8515) offers Nordic rentals, instruction, and backcountry tours.

Eleven year-round cabins offering two- to eight-person occupancy come fully equipped, including fireplaces, heat, electric stoves, water heaters, refrigerators, shower/bathrooms, cooking utensils, and full bedding.

Information

Lodging/Dining
On-site

11 log cabins (sleeping 2–8) from $65–$95/night to $325–$475/week; call (301) 895–5453 for more information • **Winter camping**, with bathhouse; rates $10/night

Nearby

Carmel Cove Inn, Deep Creek; (301) 387–0067 • **Savage River Inn Bed & Breakfast**, McHenry; (301) 245–4440 • **Country Inn Bed & Breakfast**, McHenry; (301) 387–6694 • **Lake Point Inn Bed & Breakfast**, McHenry; 1–800–523–LAKE, (301) 387–0111 • **Oak & Apple Bed & Breakfast**, Oakland; (301) 334–9265 • **Deer Park Inn/Bed & Breakfast**, Oakland; (301) 334–2308 • **Board Room Motel**, with restaurant, Oakland; (301) 334–2126 **See Wisp Resort, Nearby Lodging and Dining, page 136, for further lodging and dining information.*

Herrington Manor State Park

Herrington Manor State Park

Address: 222 Herrington Lane
Oakland, Maryland 21550

Information: (301) 334–9180
TTY: (301) 974–3683
Elevation: 2,400–2,700 feet
Average Annual Snowfall: 110 inches

Getting There

- **From Washington/Baltimore:** Follow I-70 west to I-68 west, passing Cumberland. Then exit off I-68 onto 14A south (Route 219 south), and travel roughly 19 miles before turning right on Mayhew Inn Road. Follow 4.5 miles, and turn left at the stop sign onto Oakland Sang Run Road. Then turn right on Swallow Falls Road and follow 5 miles to Herrington Manor State Park.
- **From Pittsburgh/Morgantown:** Take I-79 to I-68 east and follow directions above.

The 365-acre state park was originally part of a 2,000-acre tract donated to the state in 1906 by the Garrett brothers—of B&O Railroad fame—with the stipulation that the land be used for the protection of wildlife and advancement of forestry. Herrington Manor's name derives from Sgt. Abijah Herrington, who patrolled the surrounding forestland during the Revolutionary War.

Plentiful snowfall graces this picturesque section of the Alleghenies, with over 200 inches posted during the 1995–96 season. The park's loop trail system includes six miles of essentially flat, easily negotiable terrain around Herrington Lake. Its four wooded trails range from one to 2.5 miles, and are well marked by color names and blazes. Herrington Manor track sets the trail system when conditions permit, and another six miles of primitive trails are available for more experienced cross-country enthusiasts. Each January, Herrington Manor hosts a cross-country ski race on its groomed course.

In addition, there's a 5.5-mile trail that extends from the parking lot into Swallow Falls State Park, which also holds hiking trails suitable for Nordic skiing. The trail leading to Swallow Falls boasts several stream crossings before finishing with some scenic overlooks.

Skiers can base themselves in one of the park's 20 fully equipped log cabins situated in a pine-hemlock setting. The park also rents cross-country skis at its concession on weekends.

Information

Ski Rentals

$13/day, $11/half day • $22/two days

Lodging/Dining

On-site

20 fully furnished log cabins (with fireplaces), sleeping 2–6 persons; call (301) 334–9180 for rates and information *

Snack bar open on weekends at the concession.

Nearby

See New Germany State Park, *page 253*, and Wisp Resort, *page 131*, for more lodging and dining information.

Other Maryland State Parks and Forests

Several of Maryland's 50 state parks and forests feature ungroomed hiking trails and open tracts of land that Nordic skiers are welcome to use. Outside of Garrett County, though, snowfall is much less prevalent, so skiers have to be opportunity-driven. Hiking trails are narrow enough to demand some experience on the part of skiers, but many novices use the parks' lots and any campgrounds and open fields available. The following is an abbreviated listing of state parks offering trail systems and/or available land for ski touring. Call the park offices for updated weather and trail conditions before departing.

28. Cunningham Falls State Park

14039 Catoctin Hollow Road
Thurmont, MD 21788
(301) 271–7574

This Frederick County park in the scenic Catoctin Mountains features a winding trail system that meanders past mountain streams and a 43-acre lake. Cunningham Falls is a 78-foot cascading waterfall inside a rocky gorge.

29. Patapsco Valley State Park

8020 Baltimore National Pike
Ellicott City, MD 21043
(410) 461–5005

Patapsco's 12,699 acres spans Baltimore, Howard, Carroll and Anne Arundel Counties, with five separate recreation areas.

30. Greenbrier State Park

21843 National Pike
Boonsboro, MD 21713
(301) 791–4767

Just 10 miles east of Hagerstown, Greenbrier's multi-use park permits cross-country skiing on its campground area and around its 42-acre manmade lake.

31. Gunpowder Falls State Park

10815 Harford Road
P.O. Box 5032
Glen Arm, MD 21057
(410) 592–2897

With 13,000 acres in Baltimore and Harford Counties, over 100 miles of hiking trails are available for Nordic skiers in the Gunpowder River Valley, including the gently pitched Northern Central Rail Trail.

Maryland's Ice Fishing

The state's best ice fishing can be found at Western Maryland's Deep Creek Lake and Savage River Reservoir, typically during January and February. The most abundant species are yellow perch and walleye, with smaller numbers of northern pike, trout, pickerel, crappie, and bass. The following rules should be observed for ice fishing.

- *Only emergency vehicles are permitted on the ice of Deep Creek Lake.*
- *Fishermen should exercise extreme caution when ice conditions are unsafe from weather conditions or lake level fluctuations.*
- *Swimming and diving are restricted on any area of Deep Creek Lake where waters are covered by ice.*

WEST VIRGINIA
Cross-Country Ski Touring Centers

Alpine Lake Resort Nordic Center

Alpine Lake Resort Nordic Center
Route 2, Box 99-D2
Terra Alta, WV 26764

Info: 1–800–752–7179, (304) 789–2481
Operating Hours: 9 A.M.–4:30 P.M. weekends
Elevation: 3,000 feet
Average Annual Snowfall: 150 inches

Surrounding Alpine Lake's small downhill ski area is a 15-mile cross-country trail network, also known as the Terra Alta Touring Center, that rambles through open rolling meadows, lakeside track, and backcountry woodlands. The full Nordic center lies in a prime snow area, with an extraordinary 300 inches having dropped during the stormy season of 1995–96 and over 150 inches last year. Its 3,000-foot elevation and north-facing tip of the Alleghenies doesn't hurt either. Ski seasons generally begin in December and extend into early April.

There's a nice mix of easy to difficult terrain over four trails that range from 2.8 miles to seven miles, and about two-thirds of the track is machine groomed by the resort. The Seven Bridges/Lakeside Loop trail is the designated beginner loop that winds nearly three miles around Alpine Lake on extra-wide terrain. Six miles of ungroomed backcountry pine-woodland trails are available for more adventurous skinny skiers—most notably Camp Rock trail. It's a side run off the Castle Rock trail that leads to a West Virginia/Maryland historical boundary marker, and features several steep drops and natural barriers such as rocky outcroppings.

The Alpine Lake touring center offers cross-country rentals, instruction, guided tours, and a warming hut. Overnight guests can base themselves in one of 42 units and suites at the resort, which features an indoor heated pool, hot tub, sauna, and fitness center. And Maryland's Wisp Ski Resort is a short drive from Alpine Lake, with numerous on-site and nearby lodging options.

Information

Trail Fees
$6.50/full day, $4.50/half day (combination alpine, Nordic, and sledding passes available).

Rentals
$16/day, $11/half day • **Junior rates**: $13/day, $9/half day • **Snowshoe rentals** available (call resort for rates).

Instruction
(both classical and skating techniques) • **Private** $20/hour • **Group** $10/hour • **Free beginner lesson** available with rental.

Elk River Touring Center

Elk River Touring Center

Highway 219
Slatyfork, WV 26291

Information/Ski Report: (304) 572–3771
Internet: *www.ertc.com*
Operating Hours: 8:30 A.M.–4:30 P.M. daily
Elevation: 2,700 feet to 4,400 feet
Average Annual Snowfall: 180 inches

Getting There

- **From I-81 in Virginia:** Take the 250 exit to Route 254 west through Stanton to Buffalo Gap, then take Route 42 south to Goshen. Follow Route 39 west to Marlinton, West Virginia, then take Route 219 north 15.5 miles to the sign for Elk River and turn left.
- **From northern West Virginia:** Take Route 219 south, travel 4 miles south of Snowshoe Road, and turn right at the sign for Elk River (1 mile past Slatyfork Post Office).

Elk River, along with nearby White Grass, make up two of the most prominent cross-country touring centers in the Mid-Atlantic. Situated on a 100-year-old sheep farm on the headwaters of the Elk River—10 miles from Snowshoe Resort—the center's extensive and varied terrain includes nine miles on-site and another 31 miles in the adjoining Monongahela National Forest, off Scenic Highway. Skiers can plow through a mixed backdrop of fields and meadows, dense hardwood forest, logging roads, and railroad grades. A nominal trail fee is charged for use of Elk's trails, while stronger skiers can explore trails in the Monongahela with free access. Elk River's Nordic Specialty Shop offers full rentals and instruction, and full-moon tours are available during agreeable conditions.

The Blizzard of 1995–96 overwhelmed Elk, dumping an incredible 300 inches of snow on the mountain and providing 85 days of skiing, despite somewhat difficult access by car. Typical ski seasons run from mid-December to mid-March. The touring center is increasing its terrain for the 1996–97 season with a few new trails, including a two-mile upper loop for experts only. Snowshoeing is another big part of the equation at Elk River, with four designated trails that total six miles in length.

All six of the touring center's base trails are machine-groomed and marked by triangle blazes and ability. There's an even mix of beginner, intermediate, and advanced trails, which generally run at car's width. Novice skiers tend to occupy the flat meadow sections—the site of Elk's Nordic ski school—while considerably steeper trails are available for the true expert. Minnie's Loop Trail, named after the woman who previously ran the farm, has been expanded to include longer terrain and a few small climbs. Gay Sharp Knob is another well traveled run, located across from Scenic Highway, offering excellent ski touring and scenic vistas from its windy tip.

The 10 backcountry trails off Scenic Highway are fully marked by cross-country poles. Like Elk's base runs, these trails are evenly distributed between ability levels, but include a wider variety of terrain, including difficult singletrack sections, relatively flat jeep roads with picturesque views, and some challenging downhill runs. Many skiers park at Elk and warm up on its trails before roaming into the national forest area. Another option is to park at the beginning of Scenic Highway (Route 150) and hit the side trails that feed from that point. Forest trails, some of which are extremely long, are routinely groomed by Elk River when conditions permit. The forest service closes Scenic Highway at the hint of snowfall and usually doesn't plow the road, which leaves wide track available on the highway itself. Access without four-wheel-drive can be quite tricky, so exercise caution under such conditions.

At the end of Scenic Highway—about 23 miles from its starting point—lies the Cranberry Glades, which provides additional ski trails for the more advanced skier. Strong winters practically negate any vehicle's ability to get here, but those who dare can take Route 219 south to Highway 39 west, following to the Cranberry Glades.

Regrettably, those who like to mix up the alpine and Nordic style can't access Snowshoe Resort from any of these trails. For children, though, there's a sledding hill five minutes from Elk's lodge on a forest service road. No rentals are available, so just bring your sled and they'll show you the way.

Visitors to the Restaurant at Elk River will dine in a charming but casual atmosphere, with a selection of dishes such as fresh Elk River trout, swordfish specialties, and hearty steaks. Choose from locally brewed beers and fine wine to drink, and don't miss out on their delicious apple cranberry dessert, granola, and chocolate dressing—all of which is homemade.

Information

Trail Fees

Weekdays $5 • Weekends $7 * *Free backcountry access*

Guided Tours

All-day or half-day tours available for intermediate to advanced skiers; $40–$90 fee includes transportation, equipment, and lunch (reservations required) • **Moonlight Madness Tours** offered during full-moon periods with proper conditions ($25/person, includes rentals)

Instruction

Private (cross-country/Telemark) $30/hour • **Group** $15/person

Rentals

60 sets of **touring skis**: mostly Karhu and Trak • 10 **snowshoe rentals** • Adult $15/day • Children $8/day • 20 sets **Telemark/backcountry rentals**: $25–$30/day

Lodging/Dining

On-site

Five-room farmhouse ($40/single, $45/double, $55/triple), **3 two-bedroom cabins**, and a five-room inn, with private baths; outdoor hut tub available for guests, and full breakfast included at farmhouse and inn (rates from $40–$95) • **Restaurant at Elk River** serves dinner from 5–9 P.M. nightly except Wednesdays; lunches on weekends when weather permits

Nearby

Slatyfork Farm Bed & Breakfast, 2 miles north of Elk River, with 5 rooms, outdoor hot tub; (304) 572-3900 • **Seneca Trail Inn & Restaurant**, 6 miles from Elk River, with 12 rooms; (304) 572-2800 * *See Snowshoe Mountain Resort, page 126, for on-site lodging and nearby bed & breakfasts, cabins, chalets, and motels.*

White Grass Ski Touring Center

White Grass Ski Touring Center

Route 1, Box 299
Davis, WV 26260

Information/Ski Report: (304) 866–4114
Local Lodging Information: 1–800–782–2775
Trail Conditions: 1–800–CALL–WVA
Operating Hours: 9 A.M.–dark daily
Elevation: 3,240–4,436 feet
Average Annual Snowfall: 150 inches

Getting There

- **From points north:** Take Route 79 south to Route 33 west. In Harman, take Route 32 north to Canaan Valley. White Grass is located off Freeland Road (2 miles north of Canaan Valley State Park).
- **From points south:** Take I-77 north to Charleston and I-79 north to Weston. Then take Route 33 east to Harman and Route 32 to Canaan Valley, following signs for White Grass.
- **From Washington, DC:** Take I-495 to Route 66 west to Strasburg, following Route 55 west. In Harman, take Route 32 north to Canaan Valley, and follow signs to White Grass.
- **From Pittsburgh:** Take I-79 south past Clarksburg, then pick up Route 33/55 east past Elkins. Go north on Route 32 to Canaan Valley and follow signs for White Grass.

White Grass is one of the Mid-Atlantic's favorite cross-country destinations, and the hub of Nordic skiing in West Virginia. Located just a few miles from Timberline and Canaan Valley Ski Resorts, it lies on 1,800 acres of private land within the Cabin Mountain range of the Alleghenies. The touring center occupies the old lodge of the defunct Weiss Knob Ski Area—the South's first ski resort—whose heyday was during the 1960s. White Grass retains the same classic skiing flare of that genre, and was featured by The Washington Post as one of its Top Ten Nordic Ski Areas in the nation in 1994.

When strong northwesterly winds drop out of Canada over the Great Lakes, West Virginia's arctic Canaan Valley region benefits from large dumps of snowfall that stick around in its high elevations. The touring center is afforded ideal skiable conditions, with an average annual snowfall of 150 inches. The best skiing is typically offered from January to early March.

A complete Nordic skier's haven, White Grass offers a full fleet of cross-country and Telemark rental equipment, expert PSIA-certified instruction, guided daytime and moonlight tours, special events and races, sleigh rides, a unique natural foods cafe, inn-to-inn skiing, and even a 1.3-mile beginner trail that's lit for night skiing and equipped with snow farming. Over 30 miles of well-marked terrain is available, half of which is machine groomed by White Grass. And unlike most Mid-Atlantic cross-country areas, trails are maintained entirely for Nordic skiing.

Guests can choose from 41 trails, most of which are under three miles, including nine beginner, 18 intermediate, and 14 advanced runs. Novice skiers occupy White Grass's on-site trails, but what attracts many advanced skinny skiers is the Nordic center's access to unlimited backcountry terrain in Monongahela National Forest land, Canaan and Blackwater Falls State Parks, and Dolly Sods Wilderness Areas. Guests can ski back and forth to Canaan Valley's downhill ski area and their Nordic trails via the Springer Orchard trail, as well as Timberline Resort, where skiers can traverse its alpine trails, via the Timberline trail. Access to rugged backcountry trails include the Dolly Sods Wilderness Area—part of the Monongahela National Forest.

Telemark skiing is also a staple here at White Grass, which provides designated glades. The touring center cleans out the glades, nipping trees and bushes to open the woods and to facilitate Telemarking.

White Grass trails feature a mix of wide and narrow track, depending on ability rating, with an alpine-like 1,196-foot vertical drop that begins at its 4,436-foot summit. Double Trouble trail will thrill the experts. It's a fast run offering over 600 feet of vertical on several steep drops and curves. The trail was cut on one of the access roads used by the former Weiss Knob Ski Area. The heavily traveled Three Mile trail is a novice's dream, with level, serpentine terrain that also winds to the 4,308-foot elevation of Bald Knob, offering scenic vistas of the surrounding valleys. It serves as the determination point for looping back or accessing more difficult trails.

Another White Grass specialty includes backcountry and Telemark adventures and lessons, with reduced group rates. Guided backcountry tours extend to the deeper snow and cooler conditions of its highest north-facing mountains, the lunar landscape of the Dolly Sods Wilderness, and Weiss Knob. Call the center for can't-miss full-moon tours, offered on select nights each season.

Counterculture is revisited at the funky Natural Foods Cafe, punctuated by its potbellied stove and earthy atmosphere. Even when the area is without snow, the cafe and lodge remain open for meals, videos, and reading. The menu features home-cooked lunches, baked goods, gourmet soups, and a selection of organic and fish cuisine. Dinners are by reservation only, accompanied by live acoustic music on weekends. An abundance of lodging can be found within miles of White Grass as well, including lodges, chalets, cabins, and houses at Timberline and Canaan Valley resorts, and numerous surrounding rental units and bed & breakfasts.

Information

Trail Fee
Adult $7, junior $3

Rentals
Weekday: adult $10, child $5 • Weekend/holiday: $15, $5 • Telemark rentals: $18 (adult only)

Instruction
Group $10 • Mini-lesson $5 • Telemark $15

Dining
White Grass Natural Foods Café serves lunches and Friday and Saturday night dinners (by reservation). Natural foods café complete with a unique coffeehouse atmosphere. Hearty homemade soups, chili, and baked goods complimented by herbal teas, spiced cider, and micro-brewery ales and lagers. Saturday evenings enjoy a specialty in international fare. • **Lunch:** 11:30 A.M. – 4:00 P.M. daily • **Dinner:** Saturday night: 6:00 P.M. – 8:00 P.M. reservations. (Groups of 10 or more may request dinners on other nights of the week.)

Nearby Lodging/Dining
See Canaan Valley Ski Resort, *page 137*, and Timberline Resort, *page 159*.

35 Canaan Valley Resort State Park

Canaan Valley Resort State Park and Cross-Country Touring Center
Route 1, Box 330
Davis, WV 26260

Ski Report: 1–800–CALL–WVA

Information: 1–800–622–4121
Operating Hours: 9 A.M.–4 P.M. daily
Average Annual Snowfall: 150 inches

Getting There

See Canaan Valley Ski Resort, *page 137*.

This Allegheny Mountain state park lies in one of the highest valleys east of the Mississippi, in the heart of West Virginia snow country. Located just off the Canaan Valley Ski Area and a few miles from White Grass Touring Center, the 6,000-acre park has 18 miles of marked, generally ungroomed terrain, along with access to several trails surrounding the area. Skiing and snowshoeing are permitted on nine trails, ranging from one to three miles, while three narrow runs are reserved for hiking.

With some challenging climbs and descents and a long vertical drop, the 2.5-mile Bald Knob run offers access to the trail system at White Grass, and the 4,308 elevation at the Bald Knob summit reveals a 360-degree panoramic view of the valley. Skiers can enter the Knob, marked by green circles, from the downhill ski area summit chair lift or the parking lot. Canaan's remaining eight trails represent beginner to intermediate ability, including the Loop trail's gentle, one-mile trek through a meadow section that starts from the Nature Center/parking lot. The intermediate Railroad Grade trail, on an abandoned logging rail bed, winds along the base of Canaan Mountain on mixed terrain with several elevation changes. Northern hardwoods, including American beech trees, form the backdrop of the trail. Don't be surprised to catch a distant glimpse of bobcat, black bear, and other unique wildlife. Another option for the more experienced can be found on the Canaan/Blackwater trail, joining Canaan Valley and Blackwater Falls State Parks to form an eight-mile traverse across Canaan Mountain.

The park is well maintained by the state to preserve its natural resources. Its diverse landscape features northern bog, heath barren plants, and the country's second-largest inland wetland. Canaan doesn't charge a trail fee or groom its trail system, though the terrain is used often enough by skiers that snow is self-packed. Rentals, lessons, and a retail ski store are offered at the Ski Touring Center, inside the Nature Center Building near the park headquarters. Guided tours are also available.

Information

Rentals
$13/day, $11/half day

Instruction
Private $30/hour • Group $12/hour

Lodging/Dining
See Canaan Valley Ski Resort, *page 137*

Canaan Valley—Winter Paradise of the Allegheny

In skiing terms, a "face plant" is any unplanned contact between your kisser and the snow below you. It is an effective technique in stopping especially when zipping along on cross-country skis. "There are better ways to do that, but that way will cool you down," says Matt Marcus as he swishes to a halt beside me.

I have arrived in Canaan Valley, much like discovering the last glacier of the Ice Age, alive and well in a high plateau near Davis, WV. This is snow country, "a bit of Canada gone astray," as it is promoted. If you like evergreen mountains, rivers that float through postcard-pretty valleys, and lots of snow, a visit here can overheat a body.

For the growing numbers of cross-country fans, Canaan Valley has provided a bastion of sport during winter months when nature is exceedingly stingy elsewhere. Lake effect snows spill into the lofty Allegheny plateau here, yielding over ten feet annually, more akin to Vermont-like weather.

Steep, winding roads separate Canaan from much of the world, and as a result, the valley has remained largely undeveloped. For cross-country skiers, the reward for this long, winding drive is a small, cozy resort called White Grass, nestled in an area of stunning wilderness. This is what New England must have been 30 years ago.

Cross-country is attracting a variety of people; Those interested in fitness sports, extending the hiking season, those who have become disillusioned with lift skiing, and those who simply enjoy the beauty and solitude of a snowscape.

In Canaan there are many miles of prepared ski trails criss-crossing through its four neighboring Nordic centers. Many tours begin atop either of the two downhill slopes, where the deeper snows hug the wind-shaped spruce. Cross-country showcases the wide, remote plains of the Dolly Sods after Jack Frost has done his painting here. Snow covers frozen bogs and stacks high on cranberry bushes, an untracked world seldom seen by others on the outside.

This canoe-shaped valley, highest east of the Dakotas at 3,200 feet, has more to recommend than skiing alone. The trout fishing is said to be spectacular. The cross-country trails become paths for hiking, horseback riding, mountain biking, and access to legendary whitewater runs in the warmer months of the year. Snow typically starts melting in April, but returns again in late November, to the delight of all those eager Mid-Atlantic skiers.

— Chip Chase

Cathedral State Park

Cathedral State Park

Route 1, Box 370
Aurora, West Virginia 26705

Ski Report: 1–800–CALL–WVA
Information: (304) 735–3771
Elevation: 2,460–2,620 feet
Average Annual Snowfall: 100 inches

Getting There

- **From Baltimore/Washington:** Follow I-70 or I-270 to I-68 west, then take Route 220 south at Cumberland. Take Route 50 west to Aurora, and follow signs to Cathedral State Park.
- **From Pittsburgh:** Take I-79 south to Route 50 east to Aurora, and follow signs to the state park.
- **From West Virginia points south:** Take I-79 north to Route 50 east to Aurora, and follow signs to the state park.

Northeastern West Virginia's Cathedral State Park is a good option for novice Nordic skiers, but is better known for its pristine landscape. Registered by the Society of American Foresters, the 133-acre state park is a natural community unhindered by ax or saw. It's the only stand of mixed virgin timber left in West Virginia, and one of the last of the Appalachian Highlands region. The woods were preserved by local ownership until the state purchased the area, maintaining its mix of cherry, maple, beech, and birch hardwoods, as well as mountain laurel evergreens that are beautiful in winter. Ninety-foot-tall trees form cloisters in the park, with hemlock as the climax species.

An abundance of touring centers and state parks lie to its north and south, so Cathedral sees relatively few skiers. Five miles of terrain on six well-marked, ungroomed trails are available, providing opportune beginner skiing with easy road access from Route 50 in Preston County. All trails stem from the park entrance and lower parking lot, conveniently looping back to the same area. There aren't any steeps or climbs to suit advanced skiers, and the only degree of difficulty lies in some sections where the trails become narrow. Guests will encounter several rustic bridges crossing Rhine Creek, which winds through the park's property. Cathedral Trail follows the creek on both sides.

The area normally gets a lot of snow cover—enough to ski until the first of March most winters. Cathedral's primitive nature also means few amenities: no lodging, winter bathrooms, or even ice fishing, for that matter. There is, however, plenty of lodging and dining within a short drive, including accommodations and restaurants in nearby Oakland, Maryland, and West Virginia's Alpine Lake Resort and Blackwater Falls State Park.

Information

Lodging/Dining

Oakland, MD (12 miles away):

Oak & Apple Bed & Breakfast; (301) 334–9265 • **Deer Park Inn Bed & Breakfast**; (301) 334–2308 • **Board Room Motel**, with restaurant; (301) 334–2126 * *For more nearby lodging and dining information, see Maryland's Wisp Ski Resort, page 131.*

Blackwater Falls State Park

Blackwater Falls State Park

Drawer 490
Davis, WV 26260

Ski Report: 1–800–CALL–WVA
Information: (304) 259–5216
Concession/Touring Center: (304) 259–5117
Elevation: 3,100–3,300 feet
Average Annual Snowfall: 150 inches

Getting There

- **From Baltimore/Washington:** Take I-270/I-70 to I-68 heading west, then follow Route 219 south to Route 32 south toward Davis. Follow signs for Blackwater Falls State Park onto Route 29 and the park entrance.
- **From Pittsburgh:** Take I-79 south into West Virginia, then pick up Route 50 east to Route 219 south and follow directions above.
- **From Charlottesville, Richmond, and Virginia Beach:** Take I-64 west into West Virginia, then pick up Route 219 north past Elkins, and follow signs to the state park.

Two miles north of the old logging town of Davis sits one of the state's most reliably maintained state-run ski touring centers at Blackwater Falls State Park. Its name derives from the river's 65-foot-high waterfalls that run out through an eight-mile gorge. The water's amber color is caused by leached tannic acids from hemlock, rhododendron, red spruce needles, and peat bogs. The canyon's south rim is home to the Blackwater Lodge, where views of the massive gorge combine with the waterfalls to provide ideal photo opportunities. As part of West Virginia's strongest snow region, favorable conditions allow continuous skiing that often lasts into March.

Blackwater offers 21 miles of marked hiking/skiing trails, nine miles of which are groomed, and connects with nearby Canaan Valley State Park on eight miles of the Blackwater/ Canaan Trail (B/C). To access the popular B/C from the state park, skiers can pick up the Davis trail, which follows into the dense woodlands of the Monongahela National Forest before becoming the B/C. It's a fairly long trek to Canaan, and part of the trip is fairly difficult. The first section is flat, then drops over a gradual 200 feet of vertical, with one steep downhill on the way to Canaan. Technically speaking, the B/C Trail is part of the 248-mile Allegheny Trail, which stretches from the southern end of the state all the way to Pennsylvania. A good bet for skiing the B/C trail is to check in at the park office around 10 A.M., which allows an average return time of 2–3 P.M. for the 16-mile round trip.

The small differences in elevation on the state park trails seem less than threatening, but advanced skiers should find enough to challenge them. Some of the terrain tumbles over old railroad tracks and skirts past canyons. Experts will enjoy the changing widths and pitches of Elakayla Trail, as well as views of a waterfall and the Blackwater Canyon. Beginners tend to stick to either the wide-open picnic area or the Red Spruce Trail—a wide, two-mile horse trail ideal for skiers practicing gliding and turning.

Blackwater is a year-round vacation retreat, keeping its Blackwater Lodge/Restaurant and numerous cabins open during winter. Nearby Bright Morning Bed & Breakfast—a restored boarding house fashioned in a Victorian mold—is another popular overnight destination for Blackwater visitors. Families can use the sledding and tobogganing hills adjacent to Blackwater's ski center, with a rope tow operating on weekends. The concession offers rentals, solid instruction, and free trail use.

Information

Rentals

Classical touring skis: weekend: $18/day • weekday: $15/day • Ages 12 and under: $7.50/all times * **Snowshoe** rentals available (call touring center for rates)

Instruction

Private $25/hour • Group $10/hour

Lodging/Dining

On-site

54-room Blackwater Lodge, with private baths, reservations required • **25 cabin units**, one mile from lodge, with baths and fireplaces • **Restaurant overlooking the canyon**, serving regional dishes, open year-round

Nearby

Bright Morning B&B, Davis; (304) 259–5119 * *For a complete list of nearby lodging and dining information, see Canaan Valley State Park, page 137.*

Babcock State Park

Babcock State Park

HC 35, Box 150
Clifftop, WV 25831

Information: (304) 438–3004
Cabin Reservations: (304) 438–3003
Elevation: 3,000 feet
Average Annual Snowfall: 85 inches

Getting There

- **From Pittsburgh and northern West Virginia:** Take I-79 south to Route 19 south, then pick up Route 41 south and follow signs to Babcock State Park.
- **From points east in Virginia:** take I-81 south to I-64 west into West Virginia, then follow Route 60 north/west to Route 41 south to the park entrance.
- **From North Carolina:** Take I-77 north into West Virginia to Beckley, then pick up Route 41 north and follow signs to Babcock.

Babcock State Park in south central West Virginia has 4,127 acres replete with open meadows, mountain woodlands, waterfalls, trout streams, and boulder-strewn canyons. Located near the New River Gorge National River, where whitewater rafting rules the warm seasons, Babcock is less of a cross-country destination than the Monongahela National Forest's numerous touring centers and state parks to the east. Most of Babcock's 20 miles of trails are equipped for hiking only, though experienced skiers sometimes test its narrow, tumbling pathways when snowy conditions prevail. Not recommended for skiing, the Island in the Sky trail makes for an excellent quarter-mile winter hike over rocky, steep terrain, offering scenic views of Manns Creek Gorge from the 3,000-foot summit.

Skiers most often use wide park roads for easy gliding when a six-inch or more powder base blankets the area. Visitors also take advantage of the trail's short distances to capture several scenic points on film, including the Glade Creek Gristmill across from the parking lot, which is especially beautiful under fresh snowfall. Skiing in this neck of the woods is opportunity-driven, since the area doesn't receive or retain the same amount of snow usually found in the state's eastern snow-belt region.

Information

Nearby Lodging/Dining

Garvey Bed & Breakfast, Winona, 9 miles from Babcock, with 5 rooms, private baths, scenic views, and a mountain pond; 1–800–767–3235 • **Historic Morris Harvey House**, 25 minutes south of Babcock in Fayettesville (Route 19) • **Queen Ann Victorian home**, circa 1902, near New River Gorge Bridge; (304) 574–1179 • **White Horse Bed & Breakfast**, Fayettesville, 18 rooms; (304) 574–1400

Pipestem Resort State Park

Pipestem Resort State Park

P.O. Box 150
Pipestem, West Virginia 25979

Ski Report: 1–800–CALL–WVA
Information: (304) 466–1800
Elevation: 1,500–3,000 feet
Average Annual Snowfall: 90 inches

Getting There

- **From I-77 in West Virginia and Ohio:** Take I-77 south to the Athens Road exit and follow signs for 14 miles to Pipestem Resort State Park.
- **From Pittsburgh and Morgantown:** Take I-79 south to Route 19 south, then pick up I-64/77 heading south. Take the Athens Road exit and follow signs to Pipestem.
- **From Washington:** Take I-66 west to I-81 south, then follow I-64 west into West Virginia. Take the Sandstone exit and follow 22 miles south on Route 20 to Pipestem.
- **From Richmond and Virginia Beach:** Take I-64 west into West Virginia and follow directions above.

Southern West Virginia's Pipestem Resort State Park has operated for 27 years as one of the state's most versatile year-round recreation areas. Its name is taken from the native pipestem bush (spirea alba). Centuries ago several Native American tribes used its hollow, woody stems to make clay and corncob pipes.

The park sits on a windswept plateau on the canyon rim of the Bluestone River Gorge, combining a diverse trail system with amazing landscapes and scenic vistas. Sixteen trails and a small fleet of Nordic rentals are available to skiers, most of whom prefer to traverse the golf course area. Just three inches of snow is needed to ski the course's primarily flat terrain, mixed in with some small dips and hills on the back side. Guests can also tour the color-blazed, ungroomed hiking/cross-country network, which features 11 trails under one mile long and five under three miles.

The majority of Pipestem's trails are ideal for novices and intermediates, most notably County Line trail—an exceptionally scenic two-mile run accessible from the Nature Center parking lot. It travels over a level-graded horseback trail before descending through a backdrop of hardwoods and hemlock. Rocky cliffs and a large waterfall can be viewed off Indian Branch, where skiers will encounter steeper and more rugged track on the way to the River trail. Another option for beginners is the Long Branch Lake area near McKeever Lodge, on Den Tree and Law Hollow trails. Pipestem also runs a sledding area near the amphitheater, offering rentals and a rope tow lift.

Two advanced trails should satisfy experts: 1.7-mile Canyon Rim boasts a 500-foot descent to Heritage Point and views of the Bluestone River Gorge. Farley Ridge trail, starting behind Mountain Creek Lodge, is considered the network's most difficult run, with tight switchback turns, rocky climbs, and several steeps over nearly one mile of terrain. Its midway point is Raven Rock Overlook—a sandstone outcropping that affords visitors a peak of the 1,000-foot-deep Bluestone Canyon. The canyon is accessible only by aerial tramway (open from April to fall) at Mountain Creek Lodge.

Most of the state park's various facilities are closed for the winter, including the Mountain Creek Lodge at the base of Bluestone Canyon. McKeever Lodge and its Bluestone Dining Room operate year-round, as do numerous cottages and camp sites. Spring and summer seasons at Pipestem feature two lodges and restaurants, mountain biking, hiking, two golf courses, swimming pools, and an arboretum.

Information

Rentals

Classical touring skis only • $15/day • $5/first hour, $2/each additional

Lodging/Dining

On-site

McKeever Lodge (main lodge): 113 rooms and suites, the Bluestone Dining Room, indoor pool, game room, snack bar; rates from $46/single to $52/double, with group rates available • **25 fully equipped cabins** with fireplaces (call state park for rates)

Nearby

See New Winterplace Ski Resort, Lodging and Dining, *page 144*.

Watoga State Park

40

Watoga State Park

Greenbrier River Trail, HC-82, Box 252
Marlinton, West Virginia 24954

Ski Report: 1–800–CALL–WVA
Information: (304) 799–4087
Elevation: 3,200–3,400 feet
Greenbrier Trail: 2,200 feet
Average Annual Snowfall: 65–75 inches

Getting There

- **From Virginia points east:** Take I-81 south to I-64 west into West Virginia, then follow Route 219 north toward Hillsboro. Turn right on Seebert Lane and follow through the town of Seebert. Parking is available after crossing the bridge at Greenbrier River in the state park.
- **From points south:** Take I-77 from North Carolina and southern Virginia to I-64 east in West Virginia, and follow directions above.

Seventeen miles south of Marlinton lies Watoga—West Virginia's first and largest state park, with over 10,000 acres of sprawling, high-altitude woodlands in Pocahontas County and the Monongahela National Forest. Watoga's name is derived from the Cherokee term "Watauga," or the "river of islands," referring to the Greenbrier River that borders the park. Cross-country skiing is available on 16 miles of marked, ungroomed hiking trails through Watoga's deep forests and around its 11-acre lake.

In addition to the trail system inside Watoga, the state maintains the 76-mile Greenbrier River Trail, with the park serving as its near-midway point. Greenbrier is an abandoned linear tract from the Chesapeake and Ohio Railroad, developed into a multi-use trail that skirts the park's boundary and extends almost as far north as Cass Scenic Railroad State Park (near Snowshoe Mountain Resort). The last three miles of the trail, following south toward Lewisburg, often close from flooding, but the remaining track is used for slow ski touring, with numerous access points along the way. The entire trail is as flat as a board, offering barely a one-percent grade. There is striking scenery on its path, though, as well as some tunnels and bridges. The trail requires a lot of snowfall, which typically falls heavier on its northward points. Skiers can access the Greenbrier River Trail by parking on either side of the river, directly before entering the state park. The trail link begins just in front of the river.

The state park doesn't offer a rental concession, but lodging is available in eight year-round, fully equipped cabins. The Greenbrier Trail is used for other recreation in warmer weather, including backpacking, bicycling, and horseback riding.

Information

Lodging/Dining

On-site

Eight deluxe cabins, with fireplaces, kitchens, and baths; Call state parks for rates * *25 standard cabins and two campgrounds closed from November to mid-April.*

Nearby

The Carriage House Bed & Breakfast, Huntersville, 8 miles from Watoga on Route 39, with five rooms/private baths; (304) 799–6706 • **The Current Bed & Breakfast**, Hillsborough, 20 minutes from Watoga, with four rooms/three baths, one suite with private bath, outdoor hot tub; (304) 653–4722 • **The River Place Restaurant**, Marlinton (15 miles); (304) 799–7233 • **The Frontier Restaurant**, Marlinton; (304) 799–4134.

Coopers Rock State Forest

Coopers Rock State Forest

Route 1, Box 270
Bruceton Mills, WVA 26525

Information: (304) 594–1561
Elevation: 1,000–2,200 feet
Average Annual Snowfall: 90 inches

Getting There

- **From Washington/Baltimore:** Take I-70/I-270 to I-68 west. Then take the Coopers Rock exit and follow three miles to the state forest.
- **From Pittsburgh:** Take I-79 south to I-68 east and follow directions above.
- **From West Virginia points south:** Take I-79 north to I-68 and follow directions above.

The largest of West Virginia's state forests with over 12,700 acres, Coopers Rock is located on the state's northern end, 15 miles from Morgantown and West Virginia University. Scenic overlooks and unique rock formations form Coopers' setting, and over 50 miles of ungroomed hiking trails and additional state forest roads are suitable for Nordic skiing. Federal dollars used to be available to maintain cross-country trails at Coopers Rock and most state parks and forests, but when the funds ended, so too did the practice of track setting terrain with snowmobiles.

Unfortunately for Nordic enthusiasts, skiing at Coopers Rock has recently taken a back seat to mountain biking. If snowfall is deep enough, skiers usually have the trails all to themselves. But with a base of under six inches, mountain bikers arrive in droves to plow through the trails, turning the track into mush. For this reason, most skiers use wide, level state roads that surround the area and are closed to motor vehicles during snowfall.

Of Coopers' 50 miles of hiking/skiing terrain, three designated loop trails and two additional runs are available. The half-mile Beginner's Loop trail winds past ore pits and sassafras trees on an easy ascent and culminates along the road back to the parking lot. Starting at the first intersection of the beginner loop is the 2.2-mile Intermediate trail—an out-and-back run featuring streams, footbridges, a 200-foot climb, and a long, steep drop. The 5.2-mile Advanced Loop trail also begins from the outer parking area, following the Intermediate trail before reaching the historic Henry Clay Iron Furnace, which was used in the early 1800s to make various iron products. From this point, the narrow path runs steadily uphill, past power lines, and over a stream, before turning back to the parking lot. The 7.2-mile Outer Ski trail offers more challenging terrain, but it's seldomly skied because of its narrow width, arduous climbs, and sharp drops.

The Young Adult Conservation Corps cut Coopers' trails in 1974, marking them with blue squares and signposts. To access the trails, skiers should park in the outer lot near I-68 or on the roadsides prior to the state forest entrance, as the state forest gate also closes during winter.

Information

Lodging/Dining

Nearby

Lakeview Resort at Cheat Lake, 5 miles from Coopers Rock off I-68, with 187 guest rooms and a restaurant; 1–800–624–8300

Morgantown (15 miles away):

Applewood Bed & Breakfast, with sauna, hot tub, fitness center; (304) 296–2607 • **Acacia House Bed & Breakfast**, with antique furnishings; (304) 367–1000 • **Comfort Inn**; 1–800–221–2222 • **Days Inn**; 1–800–325–2525 • **Ramada Inn/Lounge**; (304) 296–3431

CROSS-COUNTRY SKIING

VIRGINIA

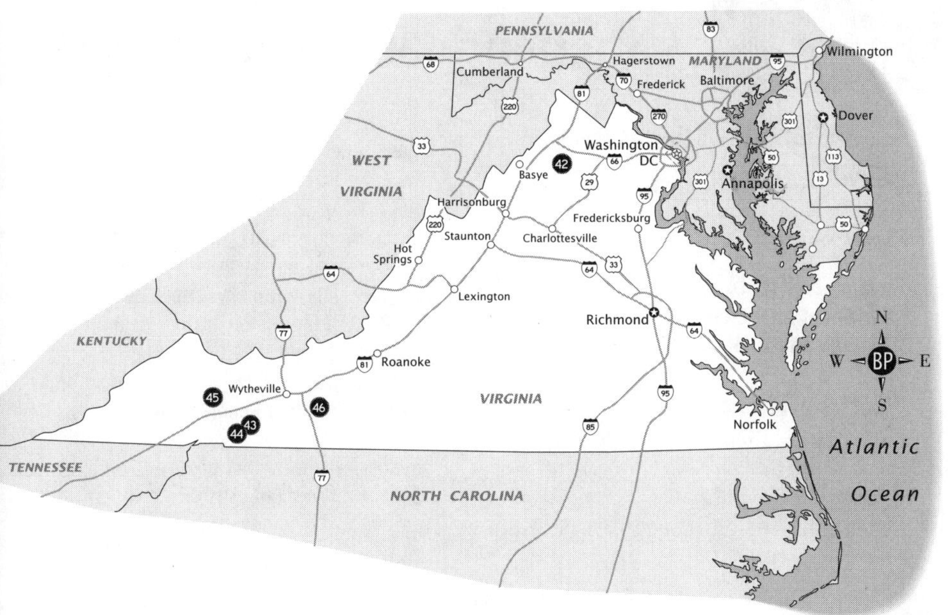

Most of Virginia's 43 state parks have hiking or multi-use trails, but just a few parks average enough snowfall to allow ski touring opportunities on a fairly consistent basis. Though remotely located for metropolitan Mid-Atlantic skiers, the southwest tip of Virginia hosts some wildly scenic and rugged backcountry terrain at its 5,000-foot Allegheny Mountain High Country elevations, including trail networks at Mount Rogers National Recreation Area and several nearby state parks. Trails are completely ungroomed and unmaintained for Nordic skiing, and snowfall is most heavily concentrated in the higher elevations, often getting a late start and extending into March. Several days of skiing are typically allotted after heavy dumps, while smaller amounts tend to blow off the crest zones. Skiers can also use all points along the Appalachian Trail—the world's second-longest footpath—which connects with several of the Nordic skiing areas listed in this section. The region is somewhat of a well-kept secret for Nordic skiers, and all trails restrict snowmobiles.

You can also strap on your skinny skis after a heavy snowfall and traverse the road shoulders of Shenandoah National Park's scenic Skyline Drive. The 105-mile stretch of Skyline Drive also has over 15 hiking trails at different mileposts—many of which are quite challenging and should be reserved for experts.

If you're looking to do some Nordic skiing in southwest Virginia's mountains, keep in mind that cabins and campsites are available only through December 2 and after March 1 each year. The town of Marion, just off Interstate 81, is within reasonable driving distance of Mount Rogers as well as each of the state parks mentioned within, and offers a few inns, motels, and restaurants.

Shenandoah National Park

Shenandoah National Park: Skyline Drive

3655 U.S. Highway 211 East
Luray, VA 22835

Information: (540) 999–3500/3283
Elevation: 1,900 feet to 3,500 feet
Average Annual Snowfall: 20–35 inches

Getting There

- Skyline Drive runs parallel to Interstate 81 in northwest Virginia, beginning at mile post 0 in Front Royal and ending at mile post 105 at Afton Mountain (Rockfish Gap), where it turns into the Blue Ridge Parkway, extending another 365 miles into North Carolina.
- Cross-country skiers can either get onto Skyline Drive after it has been plowed, or park at one of many intersections and access it from there. To park at the intersection of Route 211 and Skyline Drive near Luray, take I-81 to Route 211 east and park at either the Panorama Restaurant or at Shenandoah's entrance station. Another option—a little further south—is off Route 33 in Harrisonburg, where skiers can also park at the entrance station.

Shenandoah National Park's Skyline Drive follows the crest of the Blue Ridge Mountains for 105 miles, allowing cross-country skiers an enormous playground when Mother Nature cooperates. The low-snowfall region doesn't allow many opportunities, but Nordic skiers come out in droves after strong powder dumps. Operated by the U.S. Park Service and Department of the Interior, ski touring is available on unplowed sections of Skyline Drive and on marked, ungroomed connecting trails, most of which are suitable only for hikers and more accomplished cross-country enthusiasts.

The trick to actually skiing Skyline Drive is getting there. The park service closes sections (especially the northern half) when snowfall begins, re-opening it after it's been plowed. Skiers can park at specific mile posts if they can get onto Skyline Drive, but often have to settle for access from one of the many intersecting highways and roads. When a thick base blankets the region, most skiers use the shoulders of Skyline Drive, which carry heaps of powder stashes pushed onto the sides from the park's snow removal equipment. The road changes elevations slowly and almost unnoticeably, making for an easy excursion. Recreational skiers also tend to use the Big Meadows Area—a 12-acre flat-basin section located at milepost 50.

More daring Nordic tourists can venture off onto numerous hiking/cross-country trails in the park's North and Central Districts. All trails are marked by color blazes, including the Appalachian Trail (AT) that intersects and runs parallel to the park. Blue blazes represent hiking trails, yellow marks the park's horse trails and fire roads, and white indicates the AT. At least a foot of snowfall is required to ski the AT, which generally isn't recommended because of its narrow track and rugged terrain. A better bet is on the yellow-marked fire roads and their extra width and gentle pitches.

The North District holds largely beginner to intermediate terrain on five trails ranging from 1.5 to 5 miles, with additional track on two administrative roads and the Mount

Marshall Trail. Dickey Ridge trail is an easy and accessible 1.3-mile jaunt beginning at the north entrance to Skyline Drive at milepost 0 (Front Royal). At milepost 10.4, skiers can park at Compton Gap on the east side of Skyline Drive—or at Indian Run Overlook (mile 10.8)—to traverse the Compton Gap-Fort Windham Rocks trail. Weather permitting, the novice 1.5-mile trip also affords views of the Virginia Piedmont and ice formations from the overlook's rock ledges. If Skyline Drive is closed, enter the park from the east off Route 610.

The more challenging Central District holds a mix of terrain for all levels, including several difficult climbs and exhilarating downhills. Expert-only Whiteoak Fire Road trail begins on the sharp curve at milepost 45. An easy first mile precedes a steep, 2,500-foot downhill run that culminates at a stream. Skiers should return via the same path, but can walk a short distance from the stream to the scenic Whiteoak Canyon Falls. A few other trails offer shorter, more leisurely terrain, while others access more difficult stretches of the AT off Skyline Drive.

For free trail maps and information, call the Byrd Visitor Center at (540) 999–3283, or visit them at milepost 51, where rangers will be glad to assist with any questions.

Mount Roger National Recreation Area

43

Mount Roger National Recreation Area

Route 1, Box 303
Marion, VA 24354

Information: (540) 783–5196
Elevation: 4,450–5,729 feet
Average Annual Snowfall: 60–80 inches

Getting There

- **Virginia Highlands Horse Trail:** Take I-81 to Exit 35 (Chilhowie), then follow Route 762, which turns into Route 600. Stay on 600 until Konnarock and follow to Elk Garden parking area. Trail access is available from the parking lot, and the Appalachian Trail can also be reached within a short walk.

- **Virginia Creeper Trail:** Take I-81 to Exit 20 (the second of the three Abingdon Exits), then turn right off the ramp. Take the first road on the right and follow one-half mile to the parking area on the right. The parking area is just beyond the train tracks, with trail access available from there.

One of Virginia's best cross-country skiing circuits, Mount Rogers (Virginia's highest peak at 5,729 feet) lies in a remote region of southwest Virginia inside the expansive Jefferson National Forest. Known as the "Rooftop of Virginia," Mount Rogers National Recreation Area is run by the Forest Service of the U.S. Department of Agriculture. It has over 140,000 acres of pristine woodlands that include huge wildfire balds and red spruce and fraser fir forests. The area borders Grayson Highlands, Virginia's highest state park and another focal point in the state's limited scheme of Nordic skiing.

Mount Rogers offers the state's largest expanse of high-country wilderness skiing on its scenic, snow-filled crest zones, generally drawing a limited number of visitors. A surprising amount of snowfall is concentrated at the higher elevations and an abundant trail system. The terrain isn't terribly steep, but does have numerous skiable basin areas. The popular Virginia Highlands Horse Trail begins on a roadbed at Elk Garden Gap on Route 600, where ample parking is provided. Skiers have several choices on the trail's open meadows and woodlands, including access to the Appalachian Trail (AT). The AT is the preferred ski route to Virginia's highest peak at Mount Rogers—the 5,729-foot elevation of Lewis Fork Wilderness. The Virginia Highlands Trail is broken into six sections over 67 miles and is marked by orange blazes and plastic diamonds. Most skiers are content with the two-mile trek to Deep Gap, which features a roadbed, downhill bowl run, and a culminating wooded ascent. More determined visitors can continue past Deep Gap and climb steeply to the open meadows at Briar Ridge. (Turning around here marks a six-mile trip.) Continuing further, the trail leads to the balds of Wilbur Ridge and access to bordering Grayson Highlands State Park.

Over 400 miles of trail are available within Mount Rogers, including the 33-mile Virginia Creeper Trail—a multi-use path connecting Abingdon with the Virginia/North Carolina line. The trail began as a Native American footpath, later used by Daniel Boone and many European pioneers. The 15.9 miles of trail between Iron Bridge (mile 17.5) and the state line represents the Mount Rogers National Recreation Area of the Jefferson National Forest. Aside from a small stretch through Taylor's Valley, the property is open to the public for ski touring and hiking.

Skiers are advised to check in with the park office before hitting the trails. Track may be difficult to find in extreme wintry conditions, so bring extra copies of trail maps and a compass. The National Park Area prohibits snowmobiling on its trails.

Information

Nearby Lodging

Mount Rogers Inn, Chilhowie (off I-81 and Route 16); (540) 646–8981 • **Best Western**, Marion; (540) 783–3193 • **Fox Hill Inn Bed & Breakfast**, Troutdale; 1–800–874–3313

Nearby Dining

Mountainside Restaurant at Mount Rogers Inn, Chilhowie; (540) 646–3086 • **Happy's Restaurant**, Marion; (540) 783–5515

Grayson Highlands State Park

Grayson Highlands State Park

Route 2, Box 141
Mouth of Wilson, VA 24363

Information: (540) 579–7092
Elevation: 4,600–5,700 feet
Average Annual Snowfall: 60–80 inches

Getting There

Take I-81 to Exit 45 in Marion, then take Route 16 to Volney and follow west on Route 58. The entrance to Grayson Highlands is along Route 58. After paying the parking fee, drive to the Massie Gap parking area and obtain trail maps from the kiosk station.

Located near Virginia's highest point, Grayson Highlands State Park borders the south-central end of Mount Rogers National Recreation Area. The park's landscape includes scenic waterfalls and spectacular mile-high peaks of surrounding open balds and woodlands. During winters, considerable amounts of snow grace the high elevations of the state park, providing many opportunities for cross-country skiing on eight marked, ungroomed trails that range in length from a half-mile to two miles. As is the case with nearby Mount Rogers, wind tends to blow a lot of the snow away, so expect a combination of skiing and walking in some areas. For this reason, snowshoes are a good bet for your backpack.

Novice and intermediate skiers have the benefit of short trail lengths and relatively moderate terrain over wide-open meadows and woodlands. Only a few steep sections exist on the trail system, but more advanced skiers have a few options beyond the state park. They can connect with rugged sections of the Appalachian Trail (AT) that lead to trails and roads inside Mount Rogers. The AT can be reached by following the Rhododendron Trail one-half mile from the Massie Gap parking area, though it's recommended for hiking only. Few skiers actually make their way out to this isolated neck of the woods. Access, though, is one factor in its favor. For a nominal trail fee, skiers can drive paved roads all the way to Massie Gap, where trail access is available. Because of constantly changing conditions, be sure to call ahead to the park office for trail updates and maps. It's often difficult to plan a trip here in light of the varying weather patterns, but skiers have been known to find snow stashes in the higher elevations well into late spring.

Information

Lodging/Dining

* See Mount Rogers National Recreation Area, *page 275.*

Hungry Mother State Park

45

Hungry Mother State Park

Route 5, Box 109
Marion, Virginia 24354

Information: (540) 783–3422
Elevation: 3,500 feet
Average Annual Snowfall: 35–45 inches

Getting There

Take I-81 to the town of Marion in southwest Virginia, and follow Route 16 north to Hungry Mother State Park.

The story of Hungry Mother dates back a few hundred years. After Native Americans raided and destroyed several settlements along the New River, two prisoners managed to escape their clutches—Molly Marley and her young child. Virginia legend holds that Molly collapsed in the surrounding wilderness after eating wild berries, leaving her small child wandering along a creek and muttering the words "hungry mother." A search party arrived at the foot of the mountain, only to find Molly passed away. Today the state park sits on Molly's Knob Mountain and includes the 108-acre Hungry Mother Lake, which was dammed from the storied creek when the park opened in the 1930s.

Situated between the Appalachian Trail and Mount Rogers, the 2,000-acre state park offers nine miles of marked, ungroomed woodland trails for hiking and Nordic skiing. Its trail system features a backdrop of oak, maple, pine, and hemlock trees inside the Brushy Mountain range. When conditions permit, the 2.7-mile Lake Trail serves as an easy loop for novice skiers. The trail has a level grade, as well as convenient parking at the trailhead. Beginners can also use asphalt pathways that network through the activities and recreation areas. The park's remaining six trails are short but fairly narrow, demanding a higher level of experience.

Cabins and bathhouses are available until December, but there's often not enough snowfall by that time to welcome skiers. The town of Marion is just two miles away from the park entrance, with several options for lodging and dining.

Information

Lodging/Dining
See Mount Rogers National Recreation Area, *page 275*.

46 New River Trail State Park

New River Trail State Park
Route 2, Box 126 F
Foster Falls, VA 24360

Information: (540) 699–6778
Elevation: 1,800–2,100 feet
Average Annual Snowfall: 30–50 inches

Getting There

The trail can be accessed from Ivanhoe, Fries, Galax, Draper, Pulaski, and Shot Tower State Park.

- **To reach the office headquarters and trailhead access at Foster Falls:** Take I-81 to I-77 south (or follow I-77 north from North Carolina), then take Exit 24 (Popler Camp), and follow signs to Foster Falls and New River Trail State Park.
- **To reach the northernmost entrance to the trail:** Take I-81 to Exit 94 north (Route 99) into downtown Pulaski. Then turn onto Xaloy Drive, and look for parking there.

Virginia's New River is the world's second-oldest river—surpassed in age only by the great Nile. It's also the rarest of rivers that flow from south to north. The state park gets better use out of the other seasons, but occasional strong Virginia winters allow leisurely cross-country skiing on its 54-mile linear pathway. The trail follows an abandoned railroad right-of-way and parallels the scenic New River for 39 miles. A three-mile stretch at mile 17–19 (Barren Springs at the Route 100 bridge) is closed and under development, but when the park is completed it should stretch to a total of 57 miles. The park winds through four different Southwest Virginia counties: Carroll, Grayson, Pulaski, and Wythe.

Norfolk Southern Corporation donated the 57-mile tract to the state in 1986 to be maintained as a state park. Its cinder roadbed required little grading because of the prior rail track, and the park opened just one year later with four miles of completed trail, set mostly by volunteer groups. The trail features two long tunnels, three major bridges (Hiwassee, Ivanhoe, and Fries Junction), and roughly 30 smaller bridges and trestles. With enough snowfall at its 2,000-foot elevation, the trail is actively pursued by ski tourists, who have an easy four-percent grade and a width that averages 80 feet.

The park also links with Mount Rogers National Recreation Area, two Department of Game and Inland Fisheries boat launches, and Shot Tower State Historical Park, and borders Grayson Highlands and Clayton Lake State Parks.

The park's new administrative headquarters is at Foster Falls, and bathrooms are available at five or six points along the 57-mile track. Skiers can park and access the trail from six different points between Pulaski/Xaloy and Galax.

Information

Lodging/Dining

Restaurants and motels in the town of Galax, located at the intersection of Routes 58 and 89.

CROSS-COUNTRY SKIING: NORTH CAROLINA

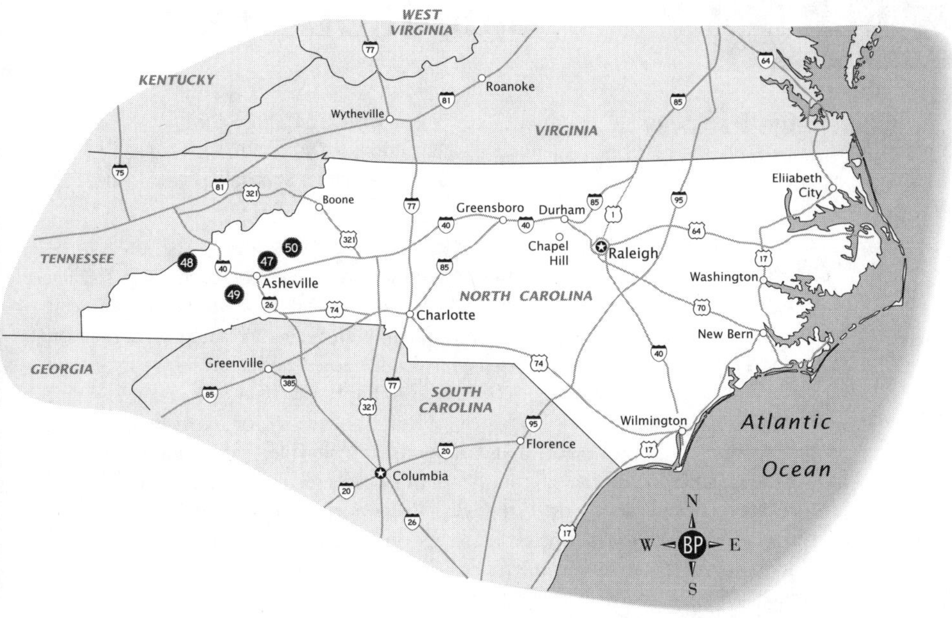

Nordic skiing opportunities do exist in North Carolina—but on an extremely limited basis. A select number of western Carolina state and national parks and forests serves cross-country ski tourists on hiking trails and roads. The region's towering, mile-high elevations afford fairly consistent snowfall, though conditions are often patchy. Wind tends to blow powder off skiers' paths, while sunlight exposure also does its damage. Skiers must therefore be opportunists. But even then, access to trails and roads can be quite difficult, as many park and forest roads either close down in winter or remain unplowed.

Like Virginia, North Carolina has no designated Nordic touring centers, and none of its downhill resorts offers on-site cross-country skiing. Most ski areas are, however, within a short commute of the parks and forests listed herein, including Roan Mountain State Park, which lies inside Pisgah National Forest. At Wolf Laurel Ski Area, a small network of roads and trails sits near it on Big Bald Mountain. And several ski shops in the town of Banner Elk, near Beech and Sugar Mountains, offer cross-country equipment rentals.

Cross-country skiers can also enjoy the wide roadways of the scenic Blue Ridge Parkway when snowfall permits. All points of the Parkway, from Carolina to Virginia, are open to skiers, but most snowfall is concentrated on the high altitudes of North Carolina's western mountainous regions. For this reason, Virginia sections of the Parkway are not listed in the book. Skyline Drive, which culminates at the northern end of the Parkway, is listed under Virginia's cross-country skiing section.

Blue Ridge Parkway

Blue Ridge Parkway
Park Headquarters: 400 BB&T Building
Asheville, NC 28801

Voice Mail: (704) 298–0398
Elevation: 2,780 feet to 6,047 feet
Average Annual Snowfall: 35–80 inches

An agency of the National Park Service and U.S. Department of the Interior, the Blue Ridge Parkway stretches 469 miles over the Southern Appalachian Mountains, from Virginia's Shenandoah National Park to North Carolina's Great Smoky Mountain National Park. The Parkway permits cross-country skiing when the road closes from strong snowfall, with several high-altitude access points on intersecting state highways, including Balsam Gap, Soco Gap, Mount Pisgah, Craggy Gardens, Mount Mitchell, and the Boone-Blowing Rock area. The most abundant snow, on average, is found on the higher elevations of Black Mountain, north of Asheville, and around the Boone-Blowing Rock and Mount Mitchell turn-offs. After a hefty snowfall, visitors can park their cars on state roads and traverse the Parkway's 20-foot-wide, easy-rolling roadway, which has an average grade of six to eight percent. For updates on road conditions during periods of snow, inquiring skiers can leave a message on Parkway headquarters voice mail and expect a returned call.

Two of the most widely used sections of the road are Balsam Gap—milepost 443.1 (40 miles west of Asheville) at the Highway 23/74 intersection, and nearby 5,200-foot Soco Gap—mile post 455.7, at Highway 19. Mile-high Mount Pisgah is accessible near the crossroads of Highways 215 and 276, Craggy Gardens and Mount Mitchell are near Highway 80, and Boone-Blowing Rock is near the Route 321 and 221 intersection. Parking isn't allowed by closed gates, so skiers have to park on state roads and walk to Parkway points they wish to ski.

Creation of the Blue Ridge Parkway stemmed from an idea brokered by President Roosevelt and members of his cabinet, who suggested that a scenic mountain route be built to connect the Shenandoah and Great Smoky Mountains National Park. Road construction began in 1935 in North Carolina, and in 1959, the National Association of Travel Organizations declared the Parkway "America's most scenic highway."

The Parkway is an extension of Virginia's Skyline Drive, beginning near Waynesboro at Rockfish Gap and the intersection of Interstate 64. The road contours the peaks of the Blue Ridge Mountains for 355 miles, skirting the southern end of the mammoth Black Mountains before winding down in the Great Smokies. More snowfall is concentrated in western North Carolina regions than in lower-lying Virginia locations. Elevations range from 649 feet at Virginia's Otter Creek to 6,047 feet at milepost 432, near North Carolina's Richland Balsam and the town of Waynesville. The Historic Appalachian Trail winds through the Parkway at several points as well.

Great Smoky Mountains National Park

48

Great Smoky Mountains National Park

107 Park Headquarters Road
Gatlinburg, Tennessee 37738

Information: (423) 436–1200
Elevation: 6,643 feet (peak altitude)
Average Annual Snowfall: 80 inches

Getting There

- **From Asheville and southern points:** Take Route 19 north into Cherokee, then follow Route 441 north toward Gatlinburg. From there, travel 17 miles to the Newfound Gap parking area.
- **From I-40:** Take I-40 to Exit 407 (Great Smoky Mountains, Gatlinburg exit), follow signs to the state park for 18 miles, then travel 15 miles from the park boundary to the Newfound Gap parking area.

Over 520,000 acres make up the massive Great Smoky Mountains National Park in North Carolina and Tennessee. The park headquarters is in Tennessee, but more than half of the park's acreage lies in North Carolina. And while Nordic skiing is allowed throughout the park, the best site is at the state border on Clingmans Dome Road, which is closed to vehicular traffic from December 1 to April 1 and remains unplowed during winter storms. Visitors can park at the intersection of the state line at Newfound Gap Overlook. In the right conditions, the road makes for excellent ski touring over gradual climbs and some steeper stretches. The altitude here is 5,400 feet, rising to 6,643 feet at the Clingmans Dome parking area and observation tower (the second-highest peak east of the Mississippi). The 1,200-foot vertical rise is spread out over seven miles, and skiers who make the gradual, uniform climb to Clingmans Dome can catch incredible views before skiing back down. Without an abundance of trees to break up views of North Carolina valleys, skiers can see the Snowbird Mountains and Fontana Lake—a 60-mile reservoir along the Tennessee River. The bordering state of Tennessee, however, isn't visible over top the ridges.

Snow conditions are tremendously varied here, but the highest elevations often get over 90 inches of powder during hardy winters. The road follows the southern edge of a ridge, with unshaded snow typically melting from exposure, then refreezing. Opportunistic skiers should therefore move quickly. Regrettably, lack of access takes away from the skiing equation. Guests need to have precise timing to ski here since Newfound Gap Road also closes in heavy snow. The environmentally conscious national park doesn't fill the roads with salt when plowing, and it's often a few days before the roads re-open. Unfortunately still, the best skiing usually exists when Route 441 is closed. The road is subject to short-term closures in heavy snow and ice, and there's no alternate route outside of Route 441.

Clingmans Dome Road sits off Newfound Gap Road—the main artery between Gatlinburg, Tennessee and Cherokee, North Carolina. The area can be reached from Highway 441, which leads to abundant parking on Newfound Gap Road at the state border intersection. Signs will direct you from there to Clingmans Dome.

Pisgah National Forest

Pisgah National Forest

Forest Headquarters:
U.S. Forest Service
P.O. Box 2750
Asheville, NC 28802

Information: (704) 257–4200/257–4202
Elevation: 6,285 feet
Average Annual Snowfall: 90 inches

Getting There

- **From I-40:** Take Route 221 north at Marion, then take Route 226 to Spruce Pine. Stay on 226 to Bakersville, then take Route 261 and follow signs for Carver's Gap and parking.
- **From Asheville:** Take Route 19 east to Spruce Pine, then follow Route 226 north to Bakersville. Turn right on Route 261 and follow signs to Carver's Gap and parking.

Like Great Smoky to the north, Pisgah National Forest permits ski touring throughout its Blue Ridge Mountain acreage. The destination of choice during optimal wintry conditions is Roan Mountain on the North Carolina/Tennessee border, roughly 20 miles southeast of Johnson City.

Closed roads off Carver's Gap make up the skiable terrain, with parking available at the gated road at the mountaintop. The towering elevation accounts for large doses of snowfall, though smaller dumps frequently blow away quickly, leaving patchy conditions. Stronger winters see blizzards that last well into March and April. When the snow falls in abundance, cross-country skiers and snowshoers head to Roan Mountain's 6,285-foot altitude to traverse park roads, trails, and open meadows and mountain balds surrounded by strands of spruce fir forest. The roads are mostly level but can get pretty steep and winding in some areas, particularly in the open mountain balds that lie immediately north of Carver's Gap, providing truly opportune Nordic skiing. One thing skiers should look out for is freezing rain and road ice, which can also make access quite difficult by car.

Experienced skiers can also head off on the Appalachian Trail's rugged hiking terrain that winds through the national forest, connecting at one point close to the parking area at Carver's Gap.

Mount Mitchell State Park

Mount Mitchell State Park

Route 5, Box 700
Burnsville, NC 28714

Information: (704) 675–4611
E-mail: *jsharpe@yancey.main.nc.us*
Elevation: 6,684 feet
Average Annual Snowfall: 90 inches

Getting There

The only road access is via the Blue Ridge Parkway. Follow the Parkway to milepost 355 and signs to Mount Mitchell State Park. Skiers can take Route 80 from Burnsville or Marion, then head south on this frequently plowed section of the Blue Ridge Parkway to Mount Mitchell. The state park is approximately one hour from Asheville, Burnsville, Marion and Spruce Pine.

Mount Mitchell's 6,684-foot summit crest lies on Black Mountain—the highest point east of the Mississippi River. Trails are available during strong snowfall for cross-country skiers, who may feel the mist of low-lying clouds at the park's lofty elevation. Mount Mitchell's altitude also affords striking, mile-high views of surrounding ridges and valleys. The park borders Pisgah National Forest, with many connecting trails. The Commissary Shelter trail is the primary ski run. It's an old railroad bed, requiring deep snow, and offers a steady grade with very little change in elevation. Surrounding park roads usually get plowed, so they're not a good option for ski touring. The observation tower at the east coast's highest peak can be reached via the Mount Mitchell, Camp Alice, or Old Mount Mitchell trails, but they're not equipped for skiing. Many points of the trails are only 18 inches wide, demanding a hike to get to the observation tower.

The area averages nearly 100 inches of snowfall per year, but is plagued by frequent rains that melt powder within days. Another problem stifling ski opportunities at Mount Mitchell is road access. The only means of getting there is on the Blue Ridge Parkway, which quickly closes—specifically from Asheville and northern points—if it's snowing badly or major ice sets in. The state does plow the Parkway from Mount Mitchell to Route 80, and drivers can usually make it there via the Parkway, which is typically accessible within two to three days of major snowfall for administrative access and ski tourists. Call the park office for updated skiable conditions and to find out which sections of the Parkway are open to driving.

Appendix

Glossary of Ski Terms

A

AASI: American Association of Snowboard Instructors.

alpine: the term used to define downhill skiing.

aprés-ski: post-ski entertainment, such as dining, drinking, or dancing.

average annual snowfall: a mountain's average per-season snowfall, based on the last 10 years.

B

backcountry skiing: a term most often used to describe cross-country, or Nordic, skiing on terrain that is often ungroomed and outside a ski area's boundaries.

base elevation: the altitude, in feet, of a ski resort's lowest-lying (base) area.

berm: a bank or wall of snow.

big air: a snowboarding term used by freestylers indicating flight/elevation off a jump or obstacle.

binding: a device used to fasten feet to skis and snowboards.

black diamond: an advanced or expert trail, relative to the ski area's other slopes.

blue-bird days: heli-ski slang for clear, blue skies

blue-level (blue square): reference made to an intermediate run. Intermediate runs are marked with a blue square.

boardercross: a head-to-head snowboard race down an obstacle course that includes banked turns and jumps. Multiple racers on course at once.

boards: skis.

bonking: slang for running out of energy.

bowl: a wide-open, basin-shaped snow field.

bump run: also known as a mogul run, bumps are formed when terrain is left ungroomed, leaving mounds of snow shaped by continuous turning made in the same spot.

bunny slope: a gentle, low-grade slope used by beginner skiers and a resort's ski school.

C

camber: tension built into the ski to facilitate turning. If you place a ski on a flat surface only the tip and tail touches the surface. The ski is flexed much like a bow.

carve: a term used to describe the correct method of making and finishing a turn.

CASI: Canadian Association of Snowboard Instructors.

cat track: a mountain's major thru-way, made by a grooming maching. Often a flat, fairly narrow connector slope (also known as a traverse) between runs. catch lines: a rope line put up by the ski patrol to mark the area boundary and prevent snowriders from skiing out of bounds.

cat-ski: snowriding from a snow cat instead of a chair lift. Often used for out-of-bounds and/or difficult terrain.

cliff bands: a band of cliffs. A cliff line.

cop air: jump.

corduroy: a term used to describe snow wales furnished by fresh grooming of trails.

cornice: an overhanging mass of snow or ice usually found near the top of a mountain ridge.

corn snow (corn flakes): granualar snow formed by alternating thawing and freezing of snow that is produced in the spring.

couloires: a steep mountainside chute or gorge.

crud: cut-up snow that may be heavy, wet, and more than a day old.

cruisers: a long, smooth trail or slope generally groomed by machine.

D

decamber: to force the ski flat or even to force the ski to bow in the opposite direction.

diagonal stride: a cross-country skiing term describing the classic kick and glide technique, in which skiers kick with one ski and pole, using the opposite pole for propulsion.

disco sticks: shape skis

double lift: an uphill transport lift that can accommodate up to two persons.

E

ego snow: soft, light snow that is generally easier to ski than heavy snow or ice, which can reveal weaknesses and can crush egos.

F

face shots: snow that splashes in your face with each turn because it is so light, dry, and deep.

fall line: the natural line of descent between two points on a slope.

freeriders: a term used to describe just going out to have fun. No racing, no competitions of any kind, just out on the hill having fun.

freeskiing: just skiing—no lessons, no racing, no teaching—just fun on the slopes.

freestyle: a term used in both skiing and snowboarding in which anything goes on the mountain.

freshies: fresh tracks in light, deep, fluffy powder.

frosted flakes: fresh snowfall.

fun box: a snowboard obstacle, sometimes known as a mailbox, made of different types of objects. Boarders can jump, stall, or slide on the object.

G

gap jump: a large snowboard obstacle, constructed of snow, with a space in the middle over which boarders can catch varying degrees of air time.

glade skiing: a trail in which skiers can wind through stands of trees, as opposed to a wide-open slope.

ghosts: trees entirely covered in snow, such that they look like "ghosts."

gladed: snowriding through strands of trees, rather than on an open slope.

gondola: an enclosed cabin suspended from an overhead cable. Gondola transports snowriders up and down a slope or over other terrain.

goofy-foot: a snowboarding term indicating a right-foot-forward stance on a snowboard.

granular snow: powder granules identified as hard (near-frozen), loose, or wet.

grooming: a ski area's practice of using equipment—usually snowcats—to smoothen trail surfaces.

GS turns: Giant Slalom turns. Derives from GS course.

H

halfpipe: a concave, cylindrical, snow-filled ditch with hard-packed walls, fashioned like skateboard ramps, that snowboarders use to perform aerial maneuvers. Halfpipes are generally several hundred feet long, over 20 feet wide, and more than 10 feet deep (depending on snowfall).

handle tow: a surface tow lift in which snowriders are transported while grabbing a handle.

heli-ski: snowriding from a helicopter.

hero snow: see "ego snow."

hit: another term for a snowboard obstacle; Any snow mound or object used by boarders to jump, slide, or grind.

hucking: the act of jumping off big cliffs; e.g., "huck yourself over the edge."

I

in-bounds: refers to the designated, marked terrain within a ski area.

kicker: a jump that propels snowriders straight up in the air rather than a steady, gradual take-off.

L

lifter: jump.

long boards: long skis. Downhill or giant slalom (GS) skis.

longest run: the longest, continuous trail on a ski area's network, measured in feet or miles.

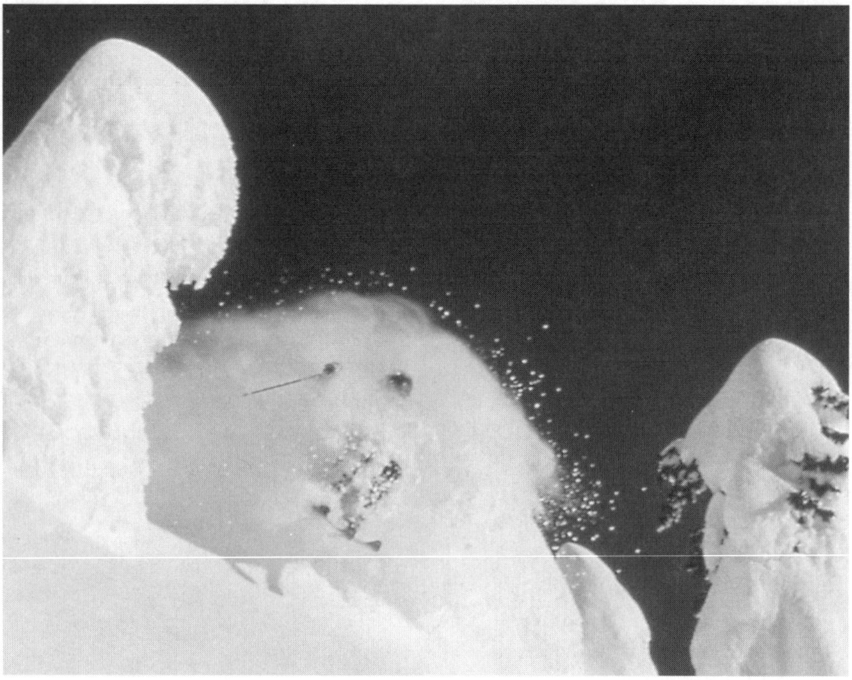

M

moguls: also known as bumps, moguls are formed when terrain is left ungroomed, leaving mounds of snow shaped by continuous turning made in the same spot.

mono-ski: a single, wide ski featuring two bindings that face forward.

N

NASTAR: short for National Standardized Racing, NASTAR is an event run at ski areas to simulate slalom racing around a series of gates. Skiers and snowboarders use NASTAR to compare their timed runs with a national standard and other downhillers during the day's events.

night skiing: the number or percentage of slopes and trails equipped with lights.

Nordic: a Scandinavian-based term for cross-country skiing or touring.

O

off-piste skiing: snowriding beyond a ski area's marked, designated boundaries on ungroomed, uncut terrain—to be performed by experts only, at their own risk.

one-plankers: snowboarders.

out-of-bounds skiing: see "off-piste skiing."

P

packed snow: loose powder compressed by grooming machines or skier traffic.

parabolic ski: see "shape ski."

Pipe Dragon: a relatively new type of grooming machine designed specifically to till and groom snowboard halfpipes.

poma lift: a surface tow lift that uses a disk attached to a cable, to transport skiers.

pow pow: slang for light, deep, fluffy powder.

primary slope direction: the bearing of a resort's mountain, facing either north, south, east, or west. North-facing slopes hold snowfall longer, while southern-facing mountains leave trails exposed to sunlight.

PSIA: Professional Ski Instructors of America.

Q

quad lift: an uphill transport lift that can accommodate up to four persons.

quarterpipe: one sidewall of a halfpipe.

R

rail slide: a snowboard tabletop with a flat, steel rail on which boarders slide. Rail slides can be found in a variety of places, including snowboard parks, halfpipes, or quarterpipes.

regular-foot: a snowboard term indicating a left-foot-forward stance on a snowboard.

rollerz: a series of small mounds lined up to create undulating terrain. Similar to a roller coaster that rolls up an down quickly.

roll-over pitches: these keep snowriders from seeing the bottom of the run until they commit to going over the top.

rope tow: the first form of uphill transport employed by ski areas, still in use today. Skiers are pulled up the mountain via a continuous loop of moving rope.

runouts: a flat spot at the bottom of a slope that allows skiers and boarders to coast to a stop.

S

serpentine: an adjective used to describe a trail that twists and undulates, shaped somewhat like a snake.

shape ski: a relatively new type of ski that is shaped somewhat like an hourglass. The shape ski is recommended for learning skiers, allowing for easier and more efficient turning.

shred: a snowboarding term equivalent to "carving."

side slip: releasing your edges and sliding downhill without turning into the fall line. You slip down the hill sideways or with your skis perpendicular to the fall line.

skate-skiing: a variation of cross-country in which skiers move by pushing off at an angle; Skating skis are usually shorter than classic Nordic skis.

skiable days: the number of days, per season, open for skiing at a resort.

skiable terrain: the acreage of land available for snowriding.

skier's left: directional reference to any object while the snowrider is looking down the hill, mountain, trail, or run.

skier's right: directional reference to any object while the snowrider is looking down the hill, mountain, trail, or run.

skier visits: the number of lift tickets sold at a ski area during a given year. Some resorts prefer not to divulge their numbers.

skinny skiers/skaters: another term for Nordic skiers, based on cross-country's thin equipment.

ski rags: ski magazines.

ski-in ski-out lodging: lodging featuring instant slope access, from door to snow.

slalom: competitive racing around a series of gates; Giant Slalom requires extreme precision around more narrowly placed gates.

sled dogs: a type of snow skate.

sleds: skis

slopes and trails: a total count of individual runs and skiable areas offered at a resort. Slopes and trails are broken down by the number of beginner, intermediate, and advanced runs available.

snow base: the depth of snow on a ski area's track, not including freshly fallen powder.

snowboard park: also known as a terrain park, a tract of downhill terrain with built-in obstacles or hits (made of either snow or objects) that snowboarders use to catch air, ride, slide, or perform maneuvers.

snowcat: a vehicle used by ski areas to spread and groom manmade snow over slopes and trails.

snow gun: equipment used by ski areas to produce man-made snow. Snow guns spray atomized water that falls and freezes on slopes and trails.

snowmaking: machine-made snow crystals produced by snow guns in the absence of natural snowfall. The percentage of slopes and trails a ski area equips with manmade snow.

snowrider: anyone who rides the snow. Includes skis, snowboard, ski blades, or other devices.

snowshoeing: an on-snow activity. A snowshoe has a webbed, racket-shaped frame that enables the wearer to walk and slide on deep snow.

spine: a terrain park obstacle in which two quarterpipe-like snow mounds meet. Snowboarders grind on the top, middle section or rail—known as the spine.

steeps: steep terrain

sticks: skis

summit elevation: a resort's highest skiable point, in elevation.

surface lift: means of uphill transport in which skiers are pulled on the snow itself. Surface lifts include poma, rope tow, or T-bar.

switchback: terrain that turns at an angle, requiring a quick carve by snowriders.

T

tabletops: a snowboard park obstacle with a launch ramp, a flat area in the middle, and a landing ramp. Boarders work the level middle section.

T-bar: a surface tow lift that uses a pole with a crossbar attached to a moving cable, for uphill transport.

Telemark skiing: an early form of skiing, the Telemark ski has a detachable heel for uphill climbing, while its sturdy frame allows skiers to carve turns downhill.

terrain park: see snowboard park.

tracked-up: snow that is cut up, as opposed to fresh snow with no tracks in it.

trackset: tracks that are groomed into the snow.

trannies: the transition between the floor of the halfpipe and the vert or wall of the halfpipe.

tree skiing: gladed skiing.

treeline: the elevation point on a particular mountain at which trees do not grow above.

triple lift: an uphill transport lift that can accommodate up to three persons.

U

un-weight: means to un-weight the skis by pulling them toward your body or by raising your body away from the snow.

uphill capacity: the number of skiers a resort's combined lifts can transport per hour.

verts: walls of a halfpipe.

vertical drop: a measure of the drop in feet from a ski area's highest point to its base; summit elevation minus base elevation.

wedge turns: executing turns while your skis are positioned in the shape of a wedge. In other words, your tips are a pole basket width apart and your tails are open just past your shoulders-like a piece of pie.

whoop de do's: undulating terrain. Up and down rollers like on a roller coaster.

yard sale: the unfortunate event of crashing and leaving equipment and clothing littered on the slopes.

Index

Index

A

B

C

E

H

L

M

N

S

T

W

Meet the Author

A native of Newark, Delaware, John Phillips is a 1992 graduate of the University of Delaware and currently works as a marketing manager in Hunt Valley, Maryland. He has been an active snowboarder since his cousin Keith sold him his first Burton board 10 years ago. John helps publish other regional guides in Beachway Press and The Globe Pequot Press's *Ski & Snowboard America*™ series, and he covers the Mid-Atlantic ski scene for several publications and web sites. He can be found riding and sliding Mid-Atlantic terrain just about every winter weekend, and is known to suspiciously disappear whenever there's mid-week snow. John lives with his wife in Owings Mills, Maryland, and welcomes emails at *juansboard@hotmail.com*.

Author